UNTYING THE TEXT

UNTYING THE TEXT:
A Post-Structuralist Reader

Edited and introduced by
Robert Young

ROUTLEDGE & KEGAN PAUL
Boston, London and Henley

First published in 1981
by Routledge & Kegan Paul Ltd
9 Park Street,
Boston, Mass. 02108, USA,
39 Store Street,
London WC1E 7DD and
Broadway House,
Newtown Road,
Henley-on-Thames,
Oxon RG9 1BN
Printed in the United States of America

British Library Cataloguing in Publication Data

Untying the text.
1. Structuralism (Literary analysis)   PN
I. Young, Robert
801'.95   PN98.S7   45

                                          .U5

ISBN 0-7100-0804-X
ISBN 0-7100-0805-8 Pbk

CONTENTS

PREFACE

In retrospect, it is clear that 'structuralism' was a much more diverse movement than its single name suggests. In fact, since the late 1960s, many of the figures associated with structuralism have produced work which is directly critical of structuralist assumptions. Whereas Todorov, Greimas or the early Barthes sought to elevate their work to the condition of a science, post-structuralist thinkers, such as Derrida, Foucault and Lacan, have questioned the status of science itself, and the possibility of the objectivity of any language of description or analysis, as well as the assumptions implicit in the Saussurian model of linguistics on which structuralism may be said to be broadly based. The effect of this work on contemporary theories of criticism has been considerable. Recently, its impact has begun to extend towards criticism generally, affecting the way we think about literature and, more specifically, the way we read.

Yet one of the problems of this sort of work for students of literature is its difficulty. 'Untying the Text' has been designed from the first to make it more accessible. Its method is to present not a selection of the theoretical (i.e., philosophical, psycho-analytical, etc.) material itself, but examples of the work of various critics who have absorbed and developed different aspects of this material to produce new theories of the text and new readings of specific texts.

To a large extent, therefore, this selection has concentrated on specific textual analyses, with the idea that if the reader at least knows the text that is being analysed, it will be much easier to recognise the extraordinary effects of this sort of work and its success in opening up literature in a new and compelling way. Each essay is also accompanied by suggestions for further reading which give references to any particular theoretical writings that have been called into play, as well as to related critical work. I hope that this will prove more digestible and more suggestive than a single bibliography.

The headnotes are provided as guides to the articles themselves. They attempt to put each article in its intellectual context, to give a short analysis of what it is doing, and to suggest interesting problems and questions which it may raise. Since the onus is on accessibility, various articles originally in French have been translated, and all references are wherever possible to translations. It is often the case that virtually a whole book has been translated, if one knows where to find different parts in different journals, and the aim here has been to provide this sort of information. In general it will become clear how much of the work in this field is produced, discussed and developed in journals.

In Chapter 1 I have tried, briefly, to indicate some of the main areas of the more specifically theoretical work in which post-structuralism is engaged. It should be stressed that my emphasis on the work of Derrida, Foucault and Lacan is not necessarily a generally recognised way of describing 'post-structuralism'. There is not a great deal of consensus about what, if anything, post-structuralism is, apart perhaps from the recognition that it involves the work of Derrida. This is the result of the peculiar nature of an activity whose most characteristic aspect is its own refusal of a definition. Nevertheless, something *has* happened since what one might term the formal structuralist period; I have attempted to describe what seem to me to be the most important, interrelated areas of work, and to suggest why they have consequences for literary criticism. The work is interrelated, but it is not homogeneous. The essays that follow are divided into various sections, but it will be clear also that there is not an absolute separation between them. In general the title of each section should be taken as the mark of difference rather than as an indication of an opposing critical position.

'Reading,' Barthes remarks in 'S/Z', 'is a form of *work*.' Although I have made every attempt to make this material accessible, this does not mean that it has become easy. It is reading itself which is difficult, not theory. There is no possibility of a 'non-theoretical' criticism. The only choice is between a criticism that is self-reflexive, that is aware of how and why it is doing what it is doing, and a criticism that is not. No criticism is without an implicit - if not explicit - theoretical position. Thus the complaint most often levelled against so-called 'theoretical' criticism - that it *imposes* its theories on to texts rather than reading the texts themselves - is in fact most applicable to so-called 'non-theoretical' criticism, whose preconceptions about how to read, and what to read for, are so fundamental that they remain unvoiced and unthought, and thus appear 'natural', 'intuitive', free of theory and 'abstract ideas'. Few people, in fact, could claim to read more carefully, more patiently, than Derrida. Or as Harold Bloom put it recently, 'deconstruction *is* reading'.

Many people have helped me in the preparation of this anthology. I would particularly like to thank Maud Ellmann, Nicholas Royle and Ann Wordsworth for advice and assistance at every stage. I would also like to thank Geoff Bennington and Ian McLeod for their careful work on the translations, and to thank too Isobel Armstrong, Derek Attridge, Cathy Crawford, Jonathan Culler, Norma Martin, Edmund Papst and Frank Stack, for suggestions about the selection, discussions about the articles and various drafts of the headnotes and introduction, and much other invaluable help.

Southampton, June 1980

ACKNOWLEDGMENTS

Etienne Balibar and Pierre Macherey, On Literature as an Ideological Form: Some Marxist Propositions, reprinted with permission from the 'Oxford Literary Review', 3:1, 1978, pp.4-12, © 'The Oxford Literary Review'.

Roland Barthes, Theory of the Text, translated from 'Encyclopaedia Universalis', vol. 15, pp.1014-17, © 'Encyclopaedia Universalis', by permission.

Roland Barthes, Textual Analysis of Poe's Valdemar, translated from 'Sémiotique narrative et textuelle', ed Claude Chabrol, pp. 29-54, © Société encyclopédique universelle, by permission.

Paul de Man, Action and Identity in Nietzsche, reprinted from 'Yale French Studies', 52, 1975, pp.16-30, by permission, © 'Yale French Studies'.

Michel Foucault, The Order of Discourse, originally published in French under the title L'Ordre du discours, Gallimard, 1971, © Gallimard, translated by permission.

J. Hillis Miller, The Stone and the Shell: The Problem of Poetic Form in Wordsworth's Dream of the Arab. Substantial portions of this essay are taken from a chapter on Wordsworth of 'The Linguistic Moment', by J. Hillis Miller, to be published by Princeton University Press, and are copyrighted © 1981 by Princeton University Press.

Barbara Johnson, The Critical Difference, reprinted from 'Diacritics', 8:2, June 1978, pp.2-9, published by Johns Hopkins University Press, by permission, © Johns Hopkins University Press.

Barbara Johnson, The Frame of Reference: Poe, Lacan, Derrida, reprinted from 'Psychoanalysis and the Question of the Text', ed Geoffrey Hartman, Baltimore, Johns Hopkins University Press, 1978, pp.149-171, by permission, © Johns Hopkins University Press.

Jeffrey Mehlman, Trimethylamin: Notes on Freud's Specimen Dream, reprinted from 'Diacritics', 6:1, 1976, pp.42-45, published by Johns Hopkins University Press, by permission

© Johns Hopkins University Press.

Richard A. Rand, Geraldine. A shorter version of this essay appeared in 'Glyph', 3, 1978, pp.74-97, Weber and Sussman, eds, published by Johns Hopkins University Press. Reprinted by permission, © Johns Hopkins University Press.

Michael Riffaterre, Interpretation and Descriptive Poetry: A Reading of Wordsworth's 'Yew-Trees', reprinted from 'New Literary History', 4:2, 1973, pp.229-57, published by Johns Hopkins University Press, by permission, © Johns Hopkins University Press.

EDITOR'S NOTE

References to editions of books vary according to availability. When the book is published in both the UK and USA, reference is to the UK edition. However, in the majority of cases, the pagination is the same for both.

1 POST-STRUCTURALISM:
An Introduction

Robert Young

Theoretical does not, of course, mean abstract. From my point
of view, it means *reflexive*, something which turns back on itself: a discourse which turns back on itself is by virtue of
this very fact theoretical (Roland Barthes).

I: HOW MYTHS DIE

We will be concerned here with the death of myths, not in time,
but in space. We know that myths transform themselves (Claude
Lévi-Strauss).

The name 'post-structuralism' is useful in so far as it is an
umbrella word, significantly defining itself only in terms of a
temporal, spatial relationship to structuralism. This need not
imply the organicist fiction of a development, for it involves,
rather, a displacement. It is more a question of an interrogation
of structuralism's methods and assumptions, of transforming
structuralist concepts by turning one against another. But the
name 'post-structuralism' is not useful if it recalls that other
spatio-temporal metaphor, the Fall. For the notion of the Fall,
and its complement (the concept of origin), is precisely what
post-structuralism denies. Structuralism as an origin never
existed in a pre-lapsarian purity or ontological fulness; post-
structuralism traces the trace of structuralism's difference from
itself.
  'Structuralism' as a proper name includes a number of diverse
practices across different disciplines in the human sciences.
What they all have in common is a use of Saussurian linguistics.[1]
The possibility of this was posited by Lévi-Strauss in 1945, in
his essay, -Structural Analysis in Linguistics and in Anthro-
pology-:

> Although they belong to *another order of reality*, kinship
> phenomena are *of the same type* as linguistic phenomena. Can
> the anthropologist, using a method analogous *in form* (if not
> content) to the method used in structural linguistics, achieve
> the same kind of progress in his own science as that which has
> taken place in linguistics?[2]

In view of their importance to structuralism and post-
structuralism it may be useful to recall briefly here the most

significant formulations of Saussurian linguistics. In the 'Cours de linguistique générale' (given between 1906 and 1911), Saussure suggested that language could only be made the object of a science if it was limited to a discernible object.[3] To study 'language' in general is an impossible enterprise, given the vagueness of the term and the diffuseness of its possible attributes. Saussure therefore proposed the following taxonomic delimitations: firstly, a distinction between synchronic analysis – that is, of language as a functioning totality at any given period, and diachronic analysis – that is, of the change of specific elements of language through historical periods. Secondly, a fundamental distinction between 'langue' – the system of any particular language (its social codes, rules, norms) which gives meaning to individual communications, and 'parole' – the act of utilisation of the system, the individual act of language as executed by a particular speaker. The object of linguistics, should be the first in each case: a synchronic analysis of 'langue'. The material of this now constituted object is the linguistic sign. The sign, according to Saussure, is 'a double entity, one formed by the associating of two terms' (p. 65). These two facets of the sign consist not of a name and a thing, but of a sound image, which Saussure called the 'signifier', and the concept to which it refers, which he called the 'signified'. These two terms are 'united in the brain by an associative bond'. The linguistic sign which they form is thus 'a two-sided psychological entity' which has no direct reference to the real (p. 66). Saussure stressed that the relation between signifier and signified is just as arbitrary as the link between word and thing, adding, 'since I mean by the sign the whole that results from the associating of the signifier with the signified, I can simply say: the linguistic sign is arbitrary'. (p. 67). The sign has no necessary, natural or substantive meaning; it only achieves meaning diacritically, through the system in which it is differentiated from all other signs. *'Language is a form and not a substance'* (p. 122), or, as Saussure put it in a now famous phrase, 'in language there are only differences *without positive terms'* (p. 120).[4] This concept of difference is Saussure's most radical insight, and one which can be seen to impinge on other aspects of his theory.

As Lévi-Strauss notes, Saussure's theories were later developed into the basis for structuralist systematizing by the linguist N.S. Troubetzkoy:

> In one programmatic statement, he reduced the structural method to four basic operations. First, structural linguistics shifts from the study of *conscious* linguistic phenomena to study of their *unconscious* infrastructure; second, it does not treat *terms* as independent entities, taking instead as its basis of analysis the *relations* between terms; third, it introduces the concept of *system* . . .; finally, structural linguistics aims at discovering general laws.[5]

It was this 'structural method' which Lévi-Strauss saw could be developed for anthropology, and which others after him developed for the other social sciences. This, in fact, fulfilled Saussure's prediction fifty years earlier that linguistics would become simply a part of a general science of signs, 'semiology'.[6] Semiology (or, in the USA, after C.S. Peirce, semiotics) is not easy to distinguish from structuralism. Strictly, semiology is a science of signs, whereas structuralism is a method of analysis.

The structuralist method, then, assumes that meaning is made possible by the existence of underlying systems of conventions which enable elements to function individually as signs. Structuralist analysis addresses itself to the system of rules and relations underlying each signifying practice: its activity more often than not consists in producing a model of this system. This is as true of Lévi-Strauss's models of kinship systems or myths as of narratologists' models of narrative grammar. Structuralism bases its methodology on Saussurian linguistics; its object can be any signifying practice, from fashion to folk stories.

In literary criticism, structuralism began by attempting to constitute itself as a science; as Todorov put it:

> the structural analysis of literature is nothing other than an attempt to transform literary studies into a scientific discipline . . . a coherent body of concepts and methods aiming at the knowledge of underlying laws.[7]

One of the first concerns of literary structuralism was with the analysis of narrative form. For Barthes, in 1966, faced with the infinite number of narratives from which he was attempting to extract a principle, it was natural to compare himself to Saussure confronted by the heterogeneity of language, and to conclude that the structural analysis of narrative should take linguistics as its founding model.

> So what of narrative analysis, faced as it is with millions of narratives? Of necessity, it is condemned to a deductive procedure, obliged first to devise *a hypothetical model of description* (what American linguists call a 'theory') and then gradually to work down from this model towards the different narrative species which at once conform to and depart from the model [my italics].[8]

But it is precisely around this notion of the model that structuralism turns. The structuralist procedure of seeking out recurrent elements and their patterns assumes that the final model will consist of an autonomous entity of interdependent parts which condition each other reciprocally. It also assumes that meaning and signification are both transparent and already in place, as well as the possibility of objective scientific verification of its findings. But the articulation of a formal structure or set of conventions cannot in itself guarantee any scientific status. This has been

clearly demonstrated in literary analyses by the absence of any
unified theory of narratives or signifying practices in literary
texts.[9]

A significant critique of the assumptions implicit in structuralist
literary criticism was made by Macherey as early as 1965. In his
essay, -Literary Analysis: the Tomb of Structures-, Macherey
as might have been expected from a contributor to Althusser's
'Reading Capital', attacks structuralism for its ahistoricism.[10]
But the essay's formulations go much further than this, particularly in their development of certain remarks made by Foucault
at the beginning of 'The Birth of the Clinic'. Macherey's critique
is made on four grounds. First, he questions the status of the
use of linguistics in literary criticism and the unproblematised
transference of knowledge from one discipline to another. This,
he argues, disallows the claim for scientific status: 'scientific
borrowing is not just a colonization, a new world founded from a
fragment of the mother country.'[11] The use of the concept of
structure as defined in linguistics may in the end enable the
resolution of critical problems, but it would have been unable to
pose them in the first place.

Second, Macherey argues that the appropriation of the idea of
structure from linguistics to literature is in fact a misappropria-
tion. It goes back, he suggests, to

> the entirely unscientific hypothesis that the work has an
> intrinsic meaning (though this doesn't imply that the meaning
> is explicit); paradoxically this enables it to be read before it
> has been written. To extricate a structure is to decipher an
> enigma, to dig up a buried meaning . . . . Criticism merely
> produces a pre-established truth; but that might be called an
> innovation, because ideally it precedes the work (p. 141).

In other words, Macherey argues that both traditional and structuralist criticism seek an interpretation from 'within' the work.
They both hold that the work will reveal its secret, its 'myth of
interiority' and its nebulous origins.

This assumption is pursued in Macherey's third criticism, that,
for structuralists, analysis is the discovery of the 'rationality',
the secret coherence of an object. He illustrates this by citing
from Barthes's programmatic text, -The Structuralist Activity-:

> The goal of all structuralist activity, whether reflexive or
> poetic, is to reconstruct *(reconstituer)* an 'object', in such a
> way as to manifest the rules of functioning (the 'functions') of
> this object. Structure is in fact a *simulacrum* of the object, but
> a controlled interested *simulacrum,* since the copy of the object
> brings out something previously invisible, or . . . unintelligible
> in the natural object.[12]

Macherey comments that this implies that analysis is a repetition,
which in turn ensures a fidelity, that we won't be told anything

that hasn't already been said in the work itself; yet it also implies that analysis somehow also produces new meaning. For the new object, the copy or simulacrum, produces something which had previously been invisible or unintelligible. It is at this point of alleged contradiction that Macherey produces his most significant objection to structuralist literary criticism. It is, he argues, only necessary to stand the terms on their feet to discern a distinct reminiscence of Plato:

> When Barthes says that analysis elaborates a copy of the work, it must be understood that the work is itself already a copy. The object analysed is considered as the simulacrum of a structure. To rediscover the structure is to construct a simulacrum of the simulacrum. This method of analysis which allows for a confusion between reading and writing actually derives from the very traditional notion of the *model* (pp. 143-4).

Macherey is here using Althusser's influential critique of essentialism, which includes 'all "epistemologies" that oppose a given subject to a given object and call knowledge the abstraction by the subject of the essence of the object.'[13] This critique of the idea of an object having an 'essence' discernible by the subject impinges on both the status of the 'model' and, as will be discussed a little later, on the status of criticism as 'metalanguage'. From this dualistic structure, Macherey argues, structuralist criticism produces an inevitably illusory object which it constitutes itself. The writer's production, the text, is merely an appearance; the object of the critic's gaze, is located behind or within it.

Lastly, developing from this, Macherey argues that structuralism presupposes the traditional and metaphysical notion of harmony and unity: a work only exists in so far as it realises a totality. Hence structuralism presupposes a 'theology of creation'. The organic structure, of interdependent parts creating a whole, is only a variant of a causal teleology. As Starobinski puts it,

> The same scheme is often activated in doctrines which rise from superstructure to infrastructure, particularly those which aspire to unite a content which is *latent* in basic assumptions of manifest expressions of psychic, social, or economic life. It is not difficult to recognize a similarity of structure between these various explanatory activities, whether they assume analytic or deductive form; the theology of emanation lies behind them as their common model.[14]

The product, the work, occurs as a device which can be explained and explained away by reference to the structure which inhabits it. The work is never related to the material conditions of its production, but to its 'principle', its ideal possibility, which is its simulacrum.

Thus criticism simply becomes commentary. Commentary (traditional or structuralist) questions a text as to what it says and what it intended to say, and by doing so reveals a deeper meaning that points to its 'essential truth'. 'In other words,' as Foucault puts it, 'in stating what has been said, one has to re-state what has never been said.' Such criticism demands and pursues 'a necessary unformulated remainder of thought that language has left in the shade – a remainder that is the very essence of that thought' – which sleeps inside, waiting for the word of the critic to bring it alive.[15] The work of literature is full, replete, imbued with a (metaphysical) presence that is the essence of its literarity; yet the critic and his criticism is necessary for this presence to become present, in order to reveal the essence, to produce the work's identity with itself.

Although there are problems involved in his own position, Macherey's exceptionally clear critique of the assumptions implicit in structuralism is useful here precisely because it is those assumptions that have been questioned by and transformed in post-structuralism. It remains the case that post-structuralism would have been impossible without this route through structuralism. And it is precisely in the form of the autocritique that post-structuralism manifests itself most characteristically. The word post-structuralism itself shifts the emphasis from any single meaning or theory towards an unbound movement through time and space, suggesting that there will never be, and can never be, any definitive 'theory of post-structuralism'. Instead it consists of a perpetual detour towards a 'truth' that has lost any status or finality. If the word itself enacts its own meaning, then the relation of post-structuralism to structuralism is also implicit in the methodology of this essay, which takes structuralism apart and watches the mutation that occurs in the interrogation of itself by itself. For it will not be a question of comparing a structuralist to a post-structuralist text, but of analysing the specificity of structuralism's difference from itself.

The first thing to be questioned is the status of theory per se, and the essentialist implications, already noted, of the opposition theory/practice, or criticism/text. For Barthes in 1963 it was fairly straightforward:

> The object of criticism is not 'the world' but a discourse, the discourse of someone else: criticism is discourse upon a discourse; it is a second language, or a *metalanguage* (as the logicians would say), which operates on a first language (or *language object*).[16]

Yet the relation of 'hors texte' (outside or extra-text), as Derrida puts it, to text is not quite so clear-cut. As Lacan announced, three years later:

> Language is language and there is only one sort of language: concrete language – English or French for instance – that people talk. The first thing to state in this context is that

there is no meta-language. For it is necessary that all so
called meta-language be presented to you with language . . . .
It is necessary to speak an ordinary language that is understood.[17]

A somewhat ironic statement from one of the most difficult and
obscure of post-structuralist thinkers, but the point remains.
The establishment of a critical, even scientific, vocabulary is
bound to produce falsification - for criticism, as language, has
no ground from which to view its object, language, objectively.
By 1970, Barthes, characteristically, had reversed his position:

Theory, precisely if one conceives of it as a permanent autocritique, ceaselessly dissolves the signified which is always
ready to reify behind science.[18]

Theory has now become precisely that which prevents the formation of a stable metalanguage by a constant self-subversion. Just
as poetry became self-reflexive with Romanticism, so criticism
becomes self-reflexive with post-structuralism.
  As a self-reflexive discourse, which constantly divides itself
against itself and transgresses its own systems, post-structuralist
criticism avoids becoming fixed, avoids becoming an established
method. It is this self-critical, self-transforming aspect that is
often found so irritating and so confusing in post-structuralist
thinkers. Looking (mistakenly) for a completed system, the
reader finds it impossible to pin down and systematise a series of
texts. Instead, all he gets is the uncertainty of, for instance,
Lacan's 'Ecrits' ('Writings'). Once this aspect is recognised, however, the reader can feel less bewildered, and reassured that at
least his being at sea is to the point. The breakthrough occurs
when he realises that his unease and uncertainty are not the
product of a failure to understand, but an anticipated critique of
the terms of his own will to knowledge.
  The shift, or mutation, from structuralism to post-structuralism
is clearest in the work of Barthes. In an interview given in 1971
he suggests that for him it occurred between the -Introduction
to the Structural Analysis of Narratives- (1966) and 'S/Z' (1970):

In the former text I appealed to a general structure from which
would then be derived analyses of contingent texts . . . I
postulated the profit there would be in reconstructing a sort
of grammar of narrative, or a logic of narrative, (and at that
period, I believed in the possibility of such a grammar - I do
not wish to deny it) . . . . In 'S/Z', I reversed this perspective: there I refused the idea of a model transcendent to several
texts (and thus, all the more so, of a model transcendent to
every text) in order to postulate . . . that each text is in some
sort its own model, that each text, in other words, must be
treated in its difference, 'difference' being understood precisely
in a Nietzschean or a Derridean sense.[19]

Barthes here puts the issues with an exemplary clarity. If, for
Barthes in 1966, theory was a 'hypothetical model of description',
post-structuralism characteristically challenges the suppositions
on which this remark is based: theory as dissociable from practice, the assumption of the status of the model, and the role of
criticism as description, commentary or representation. And if
criticism recognises its own status as 'text', so its regard may
be said to shift from the model 'behind' or 'within' the text to
the signifying surface of the text it criticises. At the same time,
whereas the model implies an already constituted product, the
more the surface of the text is analysed the more it can be seen
in terms of 'textuality' - the interaction of reader and text as a
productivity, the production of a multiplicity of signifying effects.
In turn this implies the questioning of the model of communication
as a closed system, and of the attempt to fix a unified theory of
sets of structural relations.[20]

Post-structuralism, then, involves a shift from meaning to
staging, or from the signified to the signifier. It may be seen
from this how the premises of post-structuralism disallow any
denominative, unified, or 'proper' definition of itself. Broadly,
however, it involves a critique of metaphysics (of the concepts
of causality, of identity, of the subject, and of truth), of the
theory of the sign, and the acknowledgment and incorporation of
psychoanalytic modes of thought.[21] In brief, it may be said that
post-structuralism fractures the serene unity of the stable sign
and the unified subject. In this respect, the 'theoretical' reference points of post-structuralism can be best mapped via the
work of Foucault, Lacan and Derrida, who in different ways
have pushed structuralism to its limits and shown how its most
radical premises open it up to its own deconstruction. The
writings for whom these names stand as points of authorship are
often spoken of in association with structuralism, but it would
be more accurate to say that they have been working within that
problematic in order to produce its own self-subversion. As a
result of this work, reading has lost its status as a passive consumption of a product to become a performance; and text has become, as Derrida puts it, 'wherever . . . discourse and its order
(essence, meaning, truth, intent, consciousness, ideality, etc.)
are exceeded and transgressed (débordées)'.[22]

II: CRISE DU *VERSUS*

A crisis of *versus:* these marks no longer allow themselves to
be resumed or 'decided' in the two of the binary opposition nor
sublated in the three of speculative dialectics (Jacques Derrida).

Foucault, Lacan, and Derrida are the names of problems, not
'authors' of doctrines. Their work is interrelated, but in no way
homogeneous. In spite of - or because of - this, it is their work
above all that has to be taken into account, both in a 'definition'

of post-structuralism and in any work that can be called 'post-structuralist'.[23] Their autocritical modes give the (shifting) ground for the possibilities of criticism. Thus post-structuralist criticism either takes its point of departure from them or is measured against their critiques of other positions. It remains to show how the heterogeneity of Saussure's work both enabled and demanded their work, and, within this structure, to suggest the implications of this work for literary criticism.

The effect of Saussure's work is to undercut its own positions, and thus to pose new problems. The distinction, for instance, between 'langue' and 'parole' has been criticised on a number of grounds. First because, as Macherey argues, it produces an abstract, idealist system that lacks any relation to its exercise in specific historical and institutional practices.[24] This does not imply the necessity of a sociology of language or a crude Marxist determinism, but rather that Saussure's dualism omits a third element in language formation, which Foucault calls 'discourse'.[25] Within 'the apparent embrace of words and things', Foucault suggests, one can see rules that determine and enable specific discursive practices. These rules define not the 'dumb existence of reality' nor a particular use of vocabulary, but the formulation and ordering of the objects themselves. Commenting on the title of his own 'Les Mots et les choses' ('The Order of Things') Foucault remarks:

> 'Words and Things' is the entirely serious title of a problem; it is the ironic title of a work that modifies its own form, displaces its own data, and reveals, at the end of the day, a quite differ-ent task. A task that consists of not - of no longer - treating discourses as groups of signs (signifying elements referring to contents or representations) but as practices that system-atically form the objects of which they speak. Of course, dis-courses are composed of signs; but what they do is more than use these signs to designate things. It is this *more* that ren-ders them irreducible to language (*langue*) and to speech (*parole*). It is this 'more' that we must reveal and describe.[26]

Foucault has taken particular care to refuse his categorisation as a structuralist; the relation of his work on discourse to Saussure substantiates Colin Gordon's claim that Foucault's work has always consisted of an interrogation of the whole precept upon which structuralism was based. As Gordon has pointed out in one of the best essays on Foucault's work, structuralism itself may be seen as the apex of the 'sciences de l'homme':

> for all the aggressively 'anti-humanist' ideology of some of its manifestations, [structuralism's] overall effect was emphatically one of reinforcing the implicit claims of the human sciences to constitute something like the self-evident rationality of the age.[27]

The focus of Foucault's attention on the decades around 1800 may
be seen as especially significant in so far as this was the period
in which the 'sciences of man' - the sciences which privilege man
as the centre and telos of their domain - were originally constituted. It is in this perspective that Foucault's famous pronounce-
ment about 'the end of man' should be judged:

> [The appearance of the figure of man] was not the liberation
> of an old anxiety, the transition into luminous consciousness
> of an age-old concern, the entry into objectivity of something
> that had long remained trapped within beliefs and philosophies:
> it was the effect of a change in the fundamental arrangements
> of knowledge. As the archaeology of our thought easily shows,
> man is an invention of recent date. And one perhaps nearing
> its end.
>   If those arrangements [of knowledge] were to disappear as
> they appeared . . . then one can certainly wager that man
> would be erased, like a face drawn in sand at the edge of the
> sea.[28]

For Foucault, structuralism is merely the last attempt to represent
the world to consciousness 'as if the world were made to be read
by man'. It may have realised the death of 'man', but not the
death of a subject-centred discourse.
    Foucault's early work, Gordon suggests, was in effect asking
two questions: 'how are the human sciences historically possible,
and what are the historical consequences of their existence?'
Foucault, as Edward Said has pointed out, is interested in knowledge whose practice conceals its own fabrication; his investigation of the categories of the human sciences is comparable in aim
to Barthes's interpretation of the semiotics of Realism and contemporary (ideological) practices.[29] In the foreword to the English
edition of 'The Order of Things', Foucault suggests that what
he has been looking for is 'to reveal a *positive unconscious* of
knowledge' - in other words, all the discursive rules and categories that are an a priori constituent and formative part of any discourse, and so fundamental to its existence that they remain unvoiced and unthought.[30] This is the object of his 'archaeology':
to articulate the rules and procedures which determine the different forms of our knowledge. Foucault's later work has shifted in
emphasis but has not abandoned its earlier terrain. As with
Macherey, this movement is largely ascribable to the events of
May 1968.[31] Whereas for Macherey this meant a move towards an
examination of literature's ideological effects in the practices in
which it figures, for Foucault it meant a move towards the analysis
of the relation between knowledge and power, at the level of
social practices within the functioning of specific discursive/
institutional apparatuses. This can be seen clearly in -The Order
of Discourse- where the organisation of discourse is related to
the exercise of power, and where Foucault specifies the practices
of control and restraint that mark discourse at every point. This

is the other side of the coin of Foucault's earlier description of
'immanent principles of regularity' within discourse, and it is in
this way that we can judge Foucault's claim that his work has always been, whether he knew it or not, about forms of power.

There are several related aspects of Foucault's work that literary criticism has to take into account. Foucault began by wishing
to articulate precisely that which reason excluded: madness,
chance, discontinuity, difference.[32] His early interest in literature of a certain sort (Sade, Nerval, Nietzsche, Freud, Artaud)
relates to the way in which he finds that the literary text allows
otherness, 'madness', to speak, when elsewhere, in philosophy,
law or medicine for instance, this otherness is either silent or
not listened to. It is no coincidence that one of Foucault's books
is an analysis of the aleatory, 'reversed' style of Raymond
Roussel;[33] in the vacant surrealistic spaces of novels like 'Locus
Solus' or 'Impressions of Africa' what Foucault finds is a non-
discursive language, which refuses to fix meaning or representation, and thus reason, science, or the logos. In 'The Order of
Things' he describes the appearance of this sort of writing (at
the beginning of the nineteenth century) at the very moment
when language was becoming an object of knowledge. From then
on

> literature becomes progressively more differentiated from the
> discourse of ideas, and encloses itself within a radical intransi-
> tivity; it becomes detached from all values that were able to
> keep it in circulation during the Classical age (taste, pleasure,
> naturalness, truth), and creates within its own space every-
> thing that will ensure a ludic denial of them (the scandalous,
> the ugly, the impossible) (p. 300).

This transgressive sort of writing maintains a disruptive existence within a predominant culture which needs to use language
as representation, as reason, for the mastery of meaning. Instead,
literature is permeated by difference, its movement a curving
back upon itself, a questioning of its own limits, and an affirmation of its own exhaustion and excess. This positive emphasis on
literature as transgression, as able to subvert the constraints
of all other forms of discourse by its 'difference', has been
developed less in the work of Foucault than in that of Deleuze;
it provides the basis for Barthes's later claim in 'Lecture' (1978)
that literature alone, by its self-reflexiveness, can evade the
exercise of power.[34] Foucault's own work is more inclined toward
the negative, toward the analysis of literature itself as a discursive practice in terms of its relation to the institutional sites of
its production and consumption. Perhaps most significant of all
in the present context, his archaeology can be used as a method
of questioning our own preconceptions about the object and methodology of the discipline 'literary criticism'. This self-criticism
can begin, for instance, by subjecting the notion of the author
to the same process of interrogation as 'man' or discourse itself.

The author's name, Foucault suggests, 'is not a function of man's civil status, nor is it fictional; it is situated in the breach, among the discontinuities, which gives rise to new groups of discourse and their singular mode of existence.'[135] The role of the author in literary criticism is precisely to resolve the discontinuities of discourse into a harmonious totality. A simple example of this would be the use of chronology to explain away radically dissimilar parts of a poem, or of different works. A Foucaldian analysis would highlight and analyse these differences. It would also question the concept of literary history as a continuity, as a genealogy, even the concept of 'literature' itself: its constitution as an object, its limits and exclusions, its political functions and its investiture with power in the society and institutions which constitute it. At all levels, the exercise of limitation and control are to be encountered, for, as Said puts, it we find that in our society 'the will to knowledge . . . is an effort made to exclude that which is not suitable as knowledge.'[136]

Foucault's stress on the necessity for the separation of the various functions of the author is closely related to his stress on the subject's dispersal in language, his loss at the site of unconscious desire. The subject may inhabit language, but not

the whole of his language like a secret and perfectly fluent god. Next to himself, he discovers the existence of another language that also speaks and that he is unable to dominate, one that strives, fails, and falls silent and that he cannot manipulate, the language he spoke at one time and that has now separated itself from him, now gravitating in a space increasingly silent.[37]

This understanding, derived from psychoanalysis, of the dispersal of subjectivity in language is crucial to Foucault's analysis of the relation of the subject to discourse. Foucault, Lacan and Derrida in their different ways have all produced a critique of the classical conception of the unitary subject, to which we now turn.

Discussion in this case is dominated by the psychoanalytic description, and it is in relation to this that a further critique of Saussure's differentiation between 'langue' and 'parole' can be made.[38] By separating off any consideration of specific speech acts, Saussure effectively evaded any consideration of the positioning and construction of the subject in discourse, exiling it to the unanalysable realm of 'parole'. The effect of this, however, was more than a negation or exclusion. The removal of the human subject from the centre of the stage can be said to have enabled the interrogation of what Stephen Heath has called 'the mythic site par excellence in our society' - the subject/author as originating consciousness, authority for meaning and truth.[39] Foucault's analysis of the subject as author shows the dependence of literary criticism upon the concept of the originating subject for the stability of meaning and the homogeneity of experience 'prior' to its representation in language. Saussure may have elided the subject by his attention to 'langue', but this denial or death of the subject in Saussure, and hence structuralism, has precisely led to its reappearance – not as a unified consciousness, but structured by language as difference according to Saussure's formulation of the sign. This is the radical effect of Lacan's thesis that 'the unconscious is structured like a language'. It could be said that it was only the decentring, indeed exclusion, of the subject in Saussure's own formulations that allowed the subject's reintroduction – not as a plenitude, a full imaginary unity, but as a serial movement, an effect of language.

The subject's relegation to ex-centricity in Saussure has allowed the re-reading of the Freudian description of the division of the subject as *a construction in language*, with the subject 'always a fading thing that runs under the chain of signifiers'.[40] Lacan's work can be focused on this description of the subject as (a) subject to the desire of the Other (the unconscious of another), which is to say that he becomes a signifier in the linguistic or 'Symbolic' system. This description is formulated through a reading of the Freudian concept of castration; as Jeffrey Mehlman puts it, 'Lacan and those around him were distinguished by their willingness to take seriously Freud's remark that the castration complex was the "bedrock" beyond which one could not go'.[41] The desire of the subject is constituted by lack (of the phallus, hence 'castration'). This inscribes the subject in and as a circulating system of substitutions (signifiers) for the lost object (lack) in the field of the Other. Hence Lacan's aphorism, 'man's desire is the desire of the Other'. The following is perhaps his simplest exposition of this very difficult description:

Where is the subject? It is necessary to find the subject as a lost object. More precisely this lost object is the support of the subject . . . . The question of desire is that the fading subject yearns to find itself again by means of some sort of encounter with this miraculous thing defined by the phantasm. In its endeavour it is sustained by that which I call the lost object . . . which is such a terrible thing for the imagination. That which is produced and maintained here, and which in my vocabulary I call the *objet petit a*, is well known by all psychoanalysts as all psychoanalysis is founded on the existence of this peculiar object. But the relation between the subject and this *objet petit a* is the structure which is always found in the phantasm which supports desire, in as much as desire is only that which I have called the metonymy of signification.[42]

Metonymy is the structure of displacement, the circulating system of exchange of phantasied objects which constitutes the subject: 'above all he *is* these objects, according to the place where they function in his fundamental phantasy.'[43] With the description, psychoanalytic criticism no longer contents itself with mapping unconscious processes across texts, but becomes a glimpsing of 'bizarre interactions between word and process which owe their possibility to (a reading of) Freud.[44]

A somewhat different but powerful description of what psycho-analytic criticism might be is to be found in Shoshana Felman's essay, -Turning the Screw of Interpretation-.[45] Considering the question, 'What is a Freudian reading?' Felman suggests that a Freudian reading would, logically, focus around the problem of sexuality, and, specifically, sexuality in a text. Yet if, in the past, it has been a text's ambiguity that has demanded a 'Freudian' reading, it is precisely the literalisation of the answer of a vulgar Freudian reading ('sex') that has effaced this very quality:

> The literal is 'vulgar' because it *stops* the *movement* constitu-tive of meaning, because it blocks and interrupts the endless process of metaphorical substitution. The vulgar is anything which misses, or falls short of, the dimension of the symbolic, anything which rules out, or excludes, meaning as a loss and as a flight - anything which strives . . . to eliminate from language its inherent silence (p. 107).

In fact, Felman points out, sexuality far from being the answer to the riddle of a text, is composed of two dynamically opposed forces, and is therefore 'precisely *what rules out simplicity as such*':

> If, far from implying the simplicity of a self-present literal meaning, sexuality points rather to a multiplicity of conflicting forces, to the complexity of its own divisiveness and contradic-tion, its meaning can by no means be univocal or unified, but must necessarily be *ambiguous*. It is thus not rhetoric which disguises and hides sex; sexuality *is* rhetoric, since it essen-tially consists of ambiguity: it is the coexistence of dynamically antagonistic meanings. Sexuality is the *division and divisiveness of meaning;* it is meaning *as* division, meaning *as* conflict (p. 112).

The problem, also encountered in Jeffrey Mehlman's -Trimethyl-amin-, is precisely that interpretation and ambiguity make up an impossible contrary: it is impossible to interpret ambiguity in a text without reducing it in the process. In this sense, interpreta-tion *is* repression, and to avoid it we need Mehlman's psychic troping, or Felman's different question - 'not "*what* does the story mean?" but rather "*how* does the story mean?" How does the meaning of the story, whatever it may be, rhetorically take place through permanent displacement, textually take shape and take effect: *take flight*' (p. 119). The opposition between 'a self-present literal meaning' and 'meaning as a loss and as a flight' significantly repeats the opposition already described between the subject as a self-present consciousness and the subject as 'always a fading thing that runs under the chain of signifiers.' In both cases, Lacanian psychoanalysis criticises the terms of the

first description to propose a radical alternative: another locality, another space, another scene.
The self-presence of meaning and consciousness is also the object of the philosophical critique of Jacques Derrida. It is Derrida who is often associated most closely with post-structuralism, precisely because it is he who has most carefully investigated and exposed the contradictions and paradoxes upon which structuralism is formed. His basic criticism is quite simple:

> In Western and notably French thought, the dominant discourse - let us call it 'structuralism' - remains caught, by an entire layer, sometimes the most fecund, of its stratification, within . . . metaphysics - logocentrism.[46]

Derrida can be seen as part of a history of attempts to produce a materialist philosophy. Like Marx, Nietzsche, and Heidegger before him, he is trying to remove all vestiges of idealism from thought. What he finds is that in doing so he has also, like Nietzsche, to remove 'philosophy', to be left only with language. For Derrida, structuralism is simply one episode in the whole of Western thought that remains grounded on metaphysical concepts. If he is most associated with post-structuralism, nevertheless a straightforward identification of deconstruction with post-structuralism puts the issue too simply. In particular, his own relation to psychoanalysis is complex and remains largely unexplored.[47] At the very least Derrida has the distinction of producing a revolutionary mode of textual criticism (which includes 'philosophy' and 'literary criticism'), and of turning attention away from structures and relations as such to the strange movements discernible in language itself. It is only to be expected, then, that his most polemical and influential book, 'Of Grammatology', should open with a critique of Saussure.[48]

Typically, Derrida uses Saussure to deconstruct Saussure. He produces a critique of Saussure's theory of the sign by pushing Saussure's formulation of difference to its limits. Derrida denies the very possibility of literal meaning. This is because the literal assumes the absolute self-presence of meaning, whereas in fact, according to Saussure's own formulation, language is constituted by différance - it is 'form and not a substance'. The sign must always involve the silent play of 'spacing' - the absence of everything from which it is differentiated.[49] At the same time, the sign cannot literally represent that which it signifies, produce the signified as present, precisely because a sign for something must imply that thing's absence (just as a copy must be different from an original in order to be a copy, or a repetition can never be an exact repetition, otherwise it would be the thing itself). Representation never re-presents, but always defers the presence of the signified. The sign, therefore, always differs and defers, a curious double movement that Derrida calls 'différance'.

The 'associative bond' between signifier and signified which for Saussure made up the unity of the sign is thus by no means so assured and complicitous. Derrida's interest is precisely in the movement of passage that always defers the arrival of the signified. A perpetual play and instability occurs in the unending drift across the traverse. This flickering of the signifier, fissuring and retarding any signified, is beautifully illustrated in Derrida's essay on Mallarmé - La Double séance - where the signifiers OR and EUR (cf. hORa, hEURe) are shown to be playing across the first chapter of 'Igitur', dissolving finally into reverie in the glitter of the word 'ORfEVRERIE'.[50] These glimmering letters produce the refraction of a signifying process without recourse to the conventional concepts of representation and meaning.

If Derrida thus shows that Saussure's theory of difference itself enables a powerful critique of 'logocentrism' or the metaphysics of presence, in other respects Saussure's theories remain clearly within the logocentric tradition. In particular, Derrida points to the way in which Saussure privileges speech over writing. In the 'Course', for instance, Saussure remarks:

> Language and writing are two distinct systems of signs; *the second exists for the sole purpose of representing the first.* The linguistic object is not both the written and the spoken forms of words; the spoken forms alone constitute the object. But the spoken word is so intimately bound to its written image that the *latter manages to usurp the main role.* People attach even more importance to the written image of a vocal sign than to the sign itself. A similar mistake would be in thinking that more can be learned about someone by looking at his photograph than by viewing him directly ('Course,', pp. 23-4, my italics).

What Derrida points out is that Saussure's comments are in fact simply a part of the 'logocentric' tradition of the West, the involvement of all Western thought in the metaphysics of presence. This motif of presence and the present as being true is nicely illustrated by Saussure's own comparison: to privilege writing over speech would be to commit the same mistake as to think one could learn more about someone by looking at their representation in a photograph than by experiencing their presence in the present. For Saussure, as for Aristotle and Plato, speech is privileged because it seems closest to the self-presence of consciousness, to what *is*:

> It is not by chance that the thought of being, as the thought of this transcendental signified, is manifested above all in the voice . . . . It is the unique expression of the signified producing itself spontaneously, from within the self . . . . This effacement of the signifier in the voice is not merely one illusion among many . . . it is the condition of the very idea of truth (p. 20).

So too, for Descartes, the pure self-presence of the 'cogito' was the one moment of certitude, truth itself. Writing, on the other hand, as Saussure's remark shows, is considered to be merely secondary, a falling away of thought or a feeble copy of speech. As a representation of the originary presence of consciousness, it is considered a perversion of it, a corrupting and alienating element. 'The letter killeth.' This hierarchy can be clearly seen in Romantic poetry, which privileges consciousness to the extent that the actual activity of writing poetry often disappears from consideration. George Eliot makes the point nicely in 'Middlemarch'; Dorothea suggests to Will Ladislaw that he might become a poet and Will replies:

> 'That depends. To be a poet is to have a soul so quick to discern, that no shade of quality escapes it, and so quick to feel, that discernment is but a hand playing with finely ordered variety on the chords of emotion – a soul in which knowledge passes instantaneously into feeling, and feeling flashes back as a new organ of knowledge. One may have that condition by fits only.'
> 'But you leave out the poems,' said Dorothea. 'I think they are wanted to complete the poet' (Chapter 22).

In 'Of Grammatology', Derrida's example is from Rousseau, who, like Saussure, considers writing to be 'nothing but the representation of speech'. Rousseau privileges speech, since he too considers it to be closest to self-consciousness and self-presence. Writing is condemned 'as destruction of presence and as disease of speech' (p. 142). Yet, in spite of this, Rousseau finds that speech never quite achieves the fulness of presence which it seems to promise. 'In the "Confessions", when Jean-Jacques tries to explain how he became a writer, he describes the passage to writing as a restoration, by a certain absence and by a sort of calculated effacement, of presence disappointed of itself in speech' (p. 142). If speech is lacking it is necessary to supplement this lack by writing, the very medium which also seems to destroy presence.

> Writing is dangerous from the moment that representation there claims to be presence and the sign of the thing itself. And there is a fatal necessity, inscribed in the very functioning of the sign, that the substitute makes one forget the vicariousness of its own function and makes itself pass for the plenitude of a speech whose deficiency and infirmity it nevertheless only *supplements*. For the concept of the supplement . . . harbors within itself two significations whose cohabitation is as strange as it is necessary (p. 144).

The supplement is both a surplus, 'a plenitude enriching another plenitude, the fullest measure of presence', but also adds 'only to replace'. It adds to speech, but also displaces it as a substitute. Derrida's analysis explores the strange logic involved here. An inside/outside opposition (speech/writing) has to introduce a

third term (the supplement) in order to produce a sense of the
very thing that the supplement defers (presence). Yet the supplement is not in fact a third term at all, since it partakes of
and transgresses both sides of the 'opposition'. This supplementary logic, another name for 'différance', is the peculiar
characteristic that Derrida isolates of writing. Its effect is to undo the closure of the 'logocentric' oppositions of texts, letting
loose 'false' verbal units which

> escape from inclusion in the philosophical (binary) opposition,
> and which nonetheless inhabit it, resist and disorganize it,
> but *without ever* constituting a third term.[51]

Derrida calls these units 'brisures' or 'hinge-words'. Their effect
is to break down the oppositions by which we are accustomed to
think and which ensure the survival of metaphysics in our thinking: matter/spirit, subject/object, signifier/signified, veil/truth,
body/soul, text/meaning, interior/exterior, representation/pres-
ence, appearance/essence, etc. Writing transgresses these oppositions, erupts as the outside within the inside. To deconstruct a
text is to make such units subvert the text's own assumptions by
tracing the paradoxical movements within its own language.
Derrida has taken apart our presuppositions about the way in
which language works, and shown us what he calls 'the crevice
through which the yet unnameable glimmer beyond the closure
can be glimpsed' (p. 14). Undoing the values of truth, unequivocal meaning and presence, deconstruction shows the possibilities for writing no longer as a representation of something else,
but as the limitlessness of its own 'play'. To deconstruct a text
is not to search for its 'meaning', but to follow the paths by
which writing both sets up and transgresses its own terms, producing instead an asemantic 'drift' (dérive) of differance. As
Barthes describes it,

> In the multiplicity of writing, everything is to be *disentangled,*
> nothing *deciphered;* the structure can be followed, 'run' (like
> the thread of a stocking) at every point and at every level, but
> there is nothing beneath: the space of writing is to be ranged
> over, not pierced; writing ceaselessly posits meaning cease-
> lessly to evaporate it, carrying out a systematic exemption of
> meaning.[52]

Derrida's interest in so-called 'literary' texts stems from the
fact that, most obviously in the case of modernist texts, certain
'literary' texts transgress the commonly accepted representation
of literature. This representation is of course a philosophical and
a critical one: one of the effects of Derrida's work is to articulate
the complicity between critical and philosophical positions. Against
this, certain texts 'mark and . . . organize a structure of resistance to the philosophical conceptuality which might have claimed to
dominate, to understand them.'[53] The 'philosophical conceptuality'

consists of the values of meaning, form, truth, representation, etc. which are customarily used to account for the effects and significance of literature. For literary critics the emphasis of deconstruction tends perhaps to be slightly different: whereas for Derrida the interest of any text is that it subverts the categories of Western metaphysics, for literary criticism the interest tends to be in the properties of writing per se. For the unsympathetic literary critic these same procedures may seem merely 'the mystifications of a degenerate problematic of textuality'.[54]

But deconstructive criticism can be more than a mere textual aestheticism. There are, as Derrida points out, no logocentric texts, only logocentric readings. This puts the onus and emphasis on criticism and its institutions, and gives significance to deconstruction's dispersal of the quest for homogeneity and final meaning. To break through and from truth is not to substitute polysemy for unequivocal meanings. The force of writing as 'dissemination' breaks through all semantic horizons. It is not 'the inexhaustible richness of meaning or the transcendence of semantic excess', for this itself would reduce the text back to a polyvalence of things, reality, plenitude, content, reference. Rather, deconstruction demands the conclusion that is so contrary to the assumptions of orthodox criticism, namely that 'what opens meaning and language is writing as the disappearance of natural presence' (p. 159).

There is then a strategy for deconstruction, and that strategy occurs within institutions and institutional practices. A text for analysis can be strategically chosen, to show how, in Derrida's words,

> the text overruns all the limits assigned to it so far . . . all the limits, everything that was to be set up in opposition to writing (speech, life, the world, the real, history, and what not, every field of reference - to body or mind, conscious or unconscious, politics, economics, and so forth).[55]

This description also shows, however, that deconstruction poses a challenge which goes beyond the limits of literary criticism; its claims go beyond those with which literary critics generally feel comfortable. Its position is particularly powerful because it is clear that whether one likes it or not, approves of it or not, as a mode of textual analysis deconstruction certainly *works*. It cannot simply be wished away. The 'dangers' that Saussure saw contained in writing may no longer be suppressed, but, for literary criticism, writing's 'liberation' also poses new difficulties and new problems - problems which, in the broadest sense, may be termed political. Deconstruction does not remove 'the world', but it demands that we rethink the terms in which we formulate it.

NOTES

1   Clearly a detailed analysis of 'structuralism' would also have
    to include a consideration of the work of the Russian Formal-
    ists, Propp, Mauss and Bourbaki, to name only a few
    associated with its early manifestations. The reader who
    wishes for more detailed information is referred to the works
    on structuralism in the bibliography. Within the space of a
    single essay much simplification has been inevitable; through-
    out my criteria have been to present significant forms of
    thought rather than, necessarily, individual contributions.
    On the crucial importance of Saussure, however, cf. Lacan:
    'the revolution of the sciences and a regrouping of them
    around [Saussurian linguistics] signals, as is usually the
    case, a revolution in knowledge' ('Ecrits, A Selection', trans.
    Alan Sheridan, London, 1977, p. 149), and also Derrida:
    'Most of the semiological or linguistic research currently
    dominating the field of thought (whether due to the results
    of its own investigations or due to its role as a generally re-
    cognised regulative model) traces its genealogy, rightly or
    wrongly, to Saussure as its common founder.' ('Speech and
    Phenomena, and Other Essays on Husserl's Theory of Signs',
    trans. David B. Allison, Evanston, Northwestern University
    Press, 1973, p. 152).
2   Claude Lévi-Strauss, 'Structural Anthropology 1', trans.
    Claire Jacobson and Brooke Grundfest Schoepf, Harmonds-
    worth, Penguin, 1972, p. 34.
3   References are to the 'Course in General Linguistics', trans.
    Wade Baskin, London, Fontana, 1974. The most significant
    parts of the 'Course' are the Introduction, and Parts One
    and Two. For a comparison of Saussure's langue/parole with
    Chomsky's competence/performance, see Jonathan Culler,
    'Structuralist Poetics', pp. 9, 20-4. For Saussure, see also Jean
    Starobinski, 'Words upon Words, the Anagrams of Ferdinand
    Saussure', trans. Olivia Emmet, New Haven, Yale University
    Press, 1979; and 'Semiotext(e)'s The Two Saussures, 1:2,
    1974, and Saussure's Anagrams, 2:1, 1975. Critical work on
    Saussure also includes Jonathan Culler, 'Saussure', London,
    Fontana, 1976; Sylvère Lotringer, The Game of the Name, in
    'Diacritics', 3:2, Summer 1973, pp. 2-9; and Samuel Weber,
    Saussure and the Apparition of Language: The Critical Per-
    spective, in 'Modern Language Notes', 91, 1976, pp. 913-38.
    Cf. also Derrida, as cited in note 48, below.
4   The way in which language works by difference is best illus-
    trated by Saussure's own well-known example:

    For instance, we speak of the identity of two '8:25 p.m.
    Geneva-to-Paris' trains that leave at twenty-four hours
    intervals. We feel that it is the same train each day, yet
    everything - the locomotive, coaches, personnel - is
    probably different. . . . What makes the express is its

hour of departure, its route, and in general every circumstance that sets it apart from other trains. Wherever the same conditions are fulfilled, the same entities are obtained. Still, the entities are not abstract since we cannot conceive of a . . . train outside its material realization (pp. 108-9).

5 'Structural Anthropology 1', p. 33.
6 See the 'Course', p. 16, and cf. Derrida's substitution of 'grammatology' for 'semiology' in the same passage, in 'Of Grammatology', trans. G.C. Spivak, Baltimore, Johns Hopkins University Press, 1976, p. 51.
7 Tzvetan Todorov, Structuralism and Literature, in Seymour Chatman, ed, 'Approaches to Poetics', New York, Columbia University Press, 1973, p. 154. One of the most prolific of critics, Todorov's writings include 'The Fantastic: A Structural Approach to a Literary Genre', trans. Richard Howard, Cleveland, Case Western Reserve University Press, 1973; 'The Poetics of Prose', trans. Richard Howard, Ithaca, Cornell University Press, 1977; 'Théories du symbole', Paris, Seuil, 1977; and 'Les Genres du discours', Paris, Seuil, 1978.
8 Introduction to the Structural Analysis of Narratives, in Roland Barthes, 'Image-Music-Text', essays selected and translated by Stephen Heath, London, Fontana, 1977, p. 81.
9 A clear analysis of this failure is given in Nathaniel Wing's review of A.J. Greimas, ed, 'Essais de sémiotique poetique' (1972), Semiotics of Poetry: The Meaning of Form, in 'Diacritics', Fall 1974, pp. 20-7.
10 Louis Althusser, Jacques Rancière and Pierre Macherey, 'Lire le Capital I', Paris, Maspero, 1967. (Macherey's contribution is not included in the English selection, 'Reading Capital', trans. Ben Brewster, London, New Left Books, 1970.)
11 Macherey's essay is translated in 'A Theory of Literary Production', trans. Geoffrey Wall, London, Routledge & Kegan Paul, 1978, pp. 136-56 (hereafter cited by page number). Cf. Fredric Jameson, The Ideology of the Text, 'Salmagundi', 31-2, Fall 1975/Winter 1976, pp. 204-46.
12 Quoted by Macherey (pp. 142-3) from 'Essais critiques', Paris, Seuil, 1964, p. 214; translated as The Structuralist Activity, in 'Critical Essays', trans. Richard Howard, Evanston, Northwestern University Press, 1972, pp. 213-20 (translation here slightly modified).
13 Louis Althusser, 'For Marx,' trans. Ben Brewster, London, New Left Books, 1977, p. 251 (Glossary). Cf. also Marxism and Humanism, pp. 219-47, or Lenin and Philosophy, and Lenin before Hegel, in 'Lenin and Philosophy and Other Essays', trans. Ben Brewster, London, New Left Books, 1971, pp. 29-68, 105-20, especially pp. 48-55, 114-15.
14 Jean Starobinski, 'Words upon Words', p. 43.
15 Michel Foucault, 'The Birth of the Clinic: An Archaeology of Medical Perception', London, Tavistock, 1973, p. xvi. Cf.

The Order of Discourse, Chapter 3, below.
16 What is Criticism? in 'Critical Essays', p. 258.
17 Jacques Lacan, Of Structure as an Inmixing of an Otherness
    Prerequisite to Any Subject Whatever, in 'The Structuralist
    Controversy, The Languages of Criticism and the Sciences
    of Man', ed Richard Macksey and Eugenio Donato, Baltimore,
    Johns Hopkins University Press, 1970 (1972), p. 188. Cf.
    also 'Ecrits', pp. 310-11:

> Let us set out from the conception of the Other as the locus
> of the signifier. Any statement of authority has no other
> guarantee than its very enunciation, and it is pointless for
> it to seek it in another signifier, which could not appear
> outside this locus anyway. Which is what I mean when I
> say that no metalanguage can be spoken, or more aphoristi-
> cally, that there is no Other of the Other. And when the
> Legislator (he who claims to lay down the Law) presents
> himself to fill the gap, he does so as an impostor.

18 Quoted by Stephen Heath from La théorie (interview) in 'VH
    101',2, Summer 1970, p. 9, in 'Vertige du déplacement, lec-
    ture de Barthes', Paris, Fayard, 1974, p. 79 (my translation).
19 A Conversation with Roland Barthes, in 'Signs of the Times:
    Introductory Readings in Textual Semiotics', ed Stephen
    Heath, Colin MacCabe and Christopher Prendergast, Cam-
    bridge, Granta, 1971, p. 44. Cf. Barthes's distinction be-
    tween 'structural' and 'textual' analysis, p. 135 below, and
    Barbara Johnson on 'S/Z', Chapter 7, below.
20 But cf. Wing, Semiotics of Poetry, p. 27: 'If the aim of a
    total reading can be acknowledged as misplaced, vitiated at
    its origin, the structuralist description could be accepted as
    a tentative formalization, a moment of sense which cannot be.'
21 Hence Culler's omission of any consideration of psycho-
    analysis in 'Structuralist Poetics' is, in a strict sense, histor-
    ically accurate. The acceptation of psychoanalysis after 1966
    (the year of the publication of Lacan's 'Ecrits') came most
    directly via Althusser, Derrida and Kristeva, or, in institu-
    tional terms via 'Tel Quel' (and in England, via 'Screen').
22 Jacques Derrida, 'Positions', Paris, Minuit, 1972, p. 82. Parts
    of this book have been translated; I follow the reference
    system of Spivak in 'Of Grammatology'; hence Pos E I refers
    to 'Diacritics', 2:4, Winter 1972, pp. 35-43, Pos E II to
    'Diacritics', 3:1, Spring 1973, pp. 33-46. The present quota-
    tion is at Pos E I, p. 43.
23 For the sake of exposition, I will not be dealing with the
    specific arguments between these writers (which generally take
    the form of an initial critique by Derrida), although these
    are obviously of the greatest interest. Cf. n.2, pp. 76-7, and
    The Frame of Reference, Chapter 11, below.
24 Contrast, for instance, V.N. Vološinov's 'Marxism and the
    Philosophy of Language', trans. Ladislav Matejka and I.R.

Titunik, New York, Seminar Press, 1973, for a view of
language as a terrain of ideological struggle.
25 The present essay has space only to consider the work of
Foucault. Discourse analysis, however, has also been developed from a position more compatible with Althusserian Marxism in the work of Michel Pêcheux. See his 'Stating the
Obvious: From Semantics to Discourse', London, Macmillan,
1980; and Colin MacCabe, On Discourse, 'Economy and
Society', 8:4, August 1979, pp. 279-307.
26 Michel Foucault, 'The Archaeology of Knowledge', trans. A.M.
Sheridan Smith, London, Tavistock, 1972, p. 49.
27 Colin Gordon, Other Inquisitions, 'Ideology and Consciousness', 6, Autumn 1979, p. 24. On the 'anti-humanism' of poststructuralism, cf. Paul Hirst, The Necessity of Theory,
'Economy and Society', 8:4, November 1979, pp. 431-2:

> The 'anti-humanism' I am concerned to defend does not
> seek to *abolish* men, or to appropriate their experience of
> subjectivity, but to problematise the category of the subject. It does not challenge the reality of 'experience', but
> asks what are its conditions, its forms and effects. It
> challenges the notion of the subject as a unitary self-experience, a presence-to-self in the single and continuous
> space of consciousness. It is this very presence which
> makes both the subject and a stable, continuous body of
> experience possible. In humanist philosophies the subject
> is a unity as consciousness and as agent, it is capable of
> knowing itself (through reflection on that unity) and of
> being the source of its actions. It is this centredness in
> consciousness that philosophical anti-humanism in its various
> forms (not only Althusser but Nietzsche and Freud) challenges.

Cf. Foucault's discussion in Revolutionary Action: 'Until Now',
in 'Language, Counter-Memory, Practice: Selected Essays
and Interviews', edited and translated by Donald F. Bouchard
and Sherry Simon, Ithaca, Cornell University Press, 1977,
pp. 221-2.
28 Michel Foucault, 'The Order of Things: An Archaeology of
the Human Sciences', trans. anonymous, London, Tavistock,
1970, p. 387. Cf. p. 342; and Jacques Derrida, The Ends of
Man, trans. E. Morot-Sir, W.C. Piersol, H.L. Dreyfus, and
B. Reid, in 'Philosophy and Phenomenological Research', 30,
1969, pp. 31-57.
29 Edward Said, An Ethics of Language, in 'Diacritics', 4:2,
Summer 1974, p. 32; Roland Barthes, 'Mythologies', selected
and trans. Annette Lavers, London, Cape, 1972; 'S/Z', trans.
Richard Miller, London, Cape, 1975.
30 'The Order of Things', p. xi. It is this description which
seems to suggest Foucault's alleged structuralism most clearly;
cf. Edward Said's description of Foucault as structuralist in

'Beginnings', New York, Basic Books, 1975, pp. 284-5; Daniel Silverman and Brian Torode, 'The Material Word, Some Theories of Language and its Limits', London, Routledge & Kegan Paul, 1980, pp. 332-7; and Foucault's objections to the categorisation in the discussion printed after What is an Author? in 'Screen', 20:1, Spring 1979, pp. 29-33; cf. also the Conclusion to 'The Archaeology of Knowledge', pp. 199-211.

31   See, for instance, Intellectuals and Power, in 'Language, Counter-Memory, Practice', pp. 205-17; and The History of Sexuality: Interview, in 'The Oxford Literary Review', 4:2, 1980, pp. 3-19. For Macherey, see the interview in 'Red Letters', 5, 1967, p. 5; (cf. also his praise of Foucault and dismissal of Lacan, Derrida, and Deleuze, p. 8).

32   This is the area of Derrida's attack. See n.2, pp. 76-7, below for details of the debate. The best discussion of the status of literature in Foucault's work is in Shoshana Felman's essay Madness and Philosophy or Literature's Reason, in 'Yale French Studies', 52, 1975, pp. 206-28.

33   'Raymond Roussel', Paris, Gallimard, 1963.

34   Foucault's admiration for Deleuze - 'perhaps one day, this century will be known as Deleuzian' - is not always shared by admirers of Foucault. For Deleuze's work, see his 'Proust and Signs', trans. Richard Howard, London, Allen Lane, 1973; his two books on Nietzsche ('Nietzsche et la philosophie', Paris, Presses Universitaires de France, 1962, and 'Nietzsche', Paris, P.U.F., 1965); 'Différence et répétition', Paris, P.U.F., 1969; 'Logique du sens', Paris, Minuit, 1969 (a section of this is translated in Josué V. Harari, ed, 'Textual Strategies', Ithaca, Cornell University Press, 1979, pp. 277-95); and with Félix Guattari, 'Anti-Oedipus, Capitalism and Schizophrenia', trans. Robert Hurley, Mark Seem and Helen R. Lane, New York, Viking Press, 1977, and 'Rhizôme', Paris, Minuit, 1976. See also 'Semiotext(e)'s Anti-Oedipus issue (2:3, 1977); and Foucault's essay on 'Différence et répétition' and 'Logique du sens', Theatrum Philosophicum, in 'Language, Counter-Memory, Practice', pp. 165-96. Roland Barthes's 'Lecture', trans. Richard Howard, is printed in 'October', 8, Spring 1979, pp. 3-16, and 'The Oxford Literary Review', 4:1, 1979, pp. 31-44.

35   What is an Author?, in 'Language Counter-Memory, Practice', p. 123.

36   Said, An Ethics of Language, p. 35.

37   Preface to Transgression, in 'Language, Counter-Memory, Practice', pp. 41-2.

38   See for instance, Colin MacCabe, On Discourse, p. 289, and Diana Adlam et al., Psychology, Ideology and the Human Subject, 'Ideology and Consciousness', 1, Spring 1977, p. 48.

39   Heath, 'Vertige du déplacement', p. 69 (my translation).

40   Lacan, Of Structure as an Inmixing of an Otherness Prerequisite to any Subject Whatever, p. 194.

41 Jeffrey Mehlman, 'Revolution and Repetition: Marx/Hugo/ Balzac', Berkeley, University of California Press, 1977, pp. 93-94; Mehlman continues: 'Much of the aftermath of structuralism may be read in terms of degrees of ambivalence toward the duplicity of castration: at once a radical theory of *difference* and medium through which subject is made to adapt to structure.' In the pages that follow, Mehlman discusses Jean Laplanche's lectures on castration, contrasting Laplanche's engagement with the intricacies of Freud's texts with Deleuze and Guattari's attempt 'to laugh away castration' in 'Anti-Oedipus' (e.g., pp. 59-61).

42 Lacan, Of Structure, pp. 189, 194 (translation slightly modified). See also 'Ecrits', Chapters 5, 8, 9, and 'The Four Fundamental Concepts of Psycho-Analysis', trans. Alan Sheridan, London, Hogarth Press, 1977 (throughout). For details of some of Kristeva's writings on the 'subject as process', see p. 47.

43 'Ecrits', pp. 251-2.

44 Ann Wordsworth, Derrida and Criticism, 'The Oxford Literary Review', 3:2, 1978, p. 51. For an example of the possibilities for this sort of criticism, see Maud Ellmann's Disremembering Dedalus, Chapter 9, below.

45 'Yale French Studies', 55/56, 1977, pp. 94-207.

46 'Of Grammatology', p. 99. For extended critiques of structuralism, see Force and Signification, and Structure, Sign, and Play in the Discourse of the Human Sciences, in 'Writing and Difference', trans. Alan Bass, London, Routledge & Kegan Paul, 1978, pp. 3-30, 278-93.

47 The structure of the supplement has obvious similarities with Lacan's *objet a*; in 'Of Grammatology' Derrida remarks, 'in spite of appearances, the locating of the word *supplement* is here not at all psychoanalytical' (p. 99), but it all hinges on his qualification, 'if by that we understand . . .'. Cf. Pos E II, 'the concept of castration is in fact inseparable . . . from that of dissemination' (p. 42ff.), and the longer version of Barbara Johnson's The Frame of Reference, in 'Yale French Studies', 55/56, 1977, pp. 457-505.

48 For other analyses, see Différance, in Derrida, 'Speech and Phenomena', pp. 129-60; and the interview with Kristeva, Sémiologie et grammatologie, in 'Positions', pp. 27-50. Page references in the text hereafter will be to 'Of Grammatology'.

49 Cf. 'Speech and Phenomena', p. 133: 'Saussure had only to remind us that the play of difference was the functional condition, the condition of possibility, for every sign; and it itself is silent.' For Derrida on 'spacing', see note 50.

50 La Double séance, in 'La Dissémination', Paris, Seuil, 1972, pp. 199-317. Cf. also Saussure's work on anagrams, 'Words upon Words' (note 3).

51 Pos E I, p. 36. These '"false" verbal units' are always found in the text under analysis, and thus always manifest themselves differently (e.g., 'pharmakon', 'hymen', 'grammè',

'parergon', etc.).
52   'Image-Music-Text', p. 147.
53   Pos E II, p. 37.
54   Jeffrey Mehlman, Teaching Reading: The Case of Marx in
     France, 'Diacritics', 6:4, Winter 1976, p. 18.
55   Living On, in Harold Bloom et al., 'Deconstruction and
     Criticism', London, Routledge & Kegan Paul, 1979, p. 84.

FURTHER READING

1   *Structuralism*
CULLER, JONATHAN, 'Structuralist Poetics: Structuralism,
   Linguistics, and the Study of Literature', London, Routledge
   & Kegan Paul, 1975.
DE GEORGE, RICHARD and FERNANDE, (eds), 'The Structural-
   ists: From Marx to Lévi-Strauss', New York, Doubleday
   Anchor, 1972.
DONATO, EUGENIO, Of Structuralism and Literature, in Richard
   Macksey (ed), 'Veolcities of Change: Critical Essays from
   MLN', Baltimore, Johns Hopkins University Press, 1974, pp.
   153–78.
— Structuralism: The Aftermath, in 'Sub-Stance', 7, 1973, pp.
   9–26.
EHRMANN, JACQUES, 'Structuralism', New York, Doubleday
   Anchor, 1970 (reprint of 'Yale French Studies', 36–37, 1966).
HAWKES, TERENCE, 'Structuralism and Semiotics', London,
   Methuen, 1977.
JAMESON, FREDRIC, 'The Prison-House of Language: A Critical
   Account of Structuralism and Russian Formalism', Princeton,
   Princeton University Press, 1972.
LANE, MICHAEL (ed), 'Structuralism: A Reader', London, Cape,
   1970.
MACKSEY, RICHARD and DONATO, EUGENIO (eds), 'The
   Structuralist Controversy: The Languages of Criticism and the
   Sciences of Man', Baltimore, Johns Hopkins University Press,
   1970.
PIAGET, JEAN, 'Structuralism', trans. Chaninah Maschler,
   London, Routledge & Kegan Paul, 1971.
SCHOLES, ROBERT, 'Structuralism in Literature: An Introduc-
   tion', New Haven, Yale University Press, 1974.
WAHL, FRANÇOIS (ed), 'Qu'est-ce que le structuralisme?', Paris,
   Seuil, 1968.

2   *Post-Structuralism*
HARARI, JOSUE V. (ed), 'Textual Strategies: Perspectives in
   Post-Structuralist Criticism', Ithaca, Cornell University Press,
   1979 (contains comprehensive bibliography, pp. 421–63).
'Tel Quel', 'Théorie d'ensemble', Paris, Seuil, 1968.
'Yale French Studies', French Freud: Structural Studies in
   Psychoanalysis, ed Jeffrey Mehlman, 48, 1972.

— Graphesis: Perspectives in Literature and Philosophy, ed
Marie-Rose Logan, 52, 1975.
— Literature and Psychoanalysis: The Question of Reading:
Otherwise, ed Shoshana Felman, 55/56, 1977.

3 *Jacques Derrida*
In addition to the books and essays by and about Derrida cited
elsewhere, the following essays on his work are helpful:
CULLER, JONATHAN, Jacques Derrida, in John Sturrock (ed),
'Structuralism and Since: From Lévi-Strauss to Derrida',
Oxford, Oxford University Press, 1979, pp. 154-80 (the best
short introduction).
FERGUSON, FRANCES C., Reading Heidegger: Paul de Man and
Jacques Derrida, in 'Boundary 2', 4:2, Winter 1976, pp. 593-
610.
HARTMAN, GEOFFREY, Monsieur Texte: On Jacques Derrida,
His 'Glas', and Monsieur Texte II: Epiphany in Echoland, in
'The Georgia Review', 29:4, Winter 1975, pp. 759-97, and
30:1, Spring 1976, pp. 169-204.
RIDDEL, JOSEPH N., From Heidegger to Derrida to Chance:
Doubling and (Poetic) Language, in 'Boundary 2', 4:2, Winter
1976, pp. 571-92.
RORTY, RICHARD, Philosophy as a Kind of Writing: An Essay
on Derrida, in 'New Literary History', 10:1, Autumn 1978,
pp. 141-60.
SPIVAK, GAYATRI C., Translator's Preface to 'Of Grammatology',
· Baltimore, Johns Hopkins University Press, 1976.
There is a useful bibliography of Derrida's work in his 'Edmund
Husserl's Origin of Gemoetry: An Introduction', trans. John P.
Leavey, Hassocks, Harvester Press, 1978, pp. 181-93 (contains
also details of translations and critical works on Derrida).

4 *Michel Foucault*
See Further Reading to The Order of Discourse, Chapter 3, below.

5 *Jacques Lacan/Psychoanalysis*
ADAMS, PARVEEN, Representation and Sexuality, in 'm/f', 1,
1978, pp. 65-82.
ALTHUSSER, LOUIS, Freud and Lacan, in 'Lenin and Philosophy
and Other Essays', trans. Ben Brewster, London, New Left
Books, 1971, pp. 177-202.
COWARD, ROSALIND and ELLIS, JOHN, 'Language and Material-
ism: Developments in Semiology and the Theory of the Subject',
London, Routledge & Kegan Paul, 1977.
GREEN, ANDRÉ, 'The Tragic Effect: The Oedipus Complex in
Tragedy', trans. Alan Sheridan, Cambridge, Cambridge
University Press, 1979.
HEATH, STEPHEN, Anata Mo, in 'Screen', 17:4, 1976, pp. 49-66.
IRIGARAY, LUCE, 'Speculum de l'autre femme', Paris, Minuit,
1974.
— 'Ce Sexe qui n'en est pas un', Paris, Minuit, 1977 (excerpts

have been translated in 'The New French Feminisms', ed Elaine
Marks and Isabelle De Courtivron, Amherst, University of
Massachusetts Press, 1980, pp. 99-110.
— Woman's Exile (interview), in 'Ideology and Consciousness', 1,
1977, pp. 62-76.
LACAN, JACQUES, Le Seminaire, Paris, Seuil, 1973- (Lacan's
Lectures; in addition to 'The Four Fundamental Concepts of
Psycho-Analysis (XI)', the following have been published:
'Les Ecrits techniques de Freud (I)', 1975; 'Le Moi dans la
théorie de Freud et dans la technique de la psychanalyse (II)',
1977; 'Encore (XX)', 1975.)
LACOUE-LABARTHE, PHILIPPE and NANCY, JEAN-LUC, 'Le Titre
de la lettre', Paris, Galilée, 1973.
LAPLANCHE, JEAN and PONTALIS, JEAN-BAPTISTE, 'The
Language of Psycho-Analysis', trans. Donald Nicholson-Smith,
London, Hogarth Press, 1973.
LE GALLIOT, JEAN, 'Psychanalyse et langages littéraires:
Théorie et pratique', Paris, Nathan, 1977.
LYOTARD, JEAN-FRANÇOIS, 'Economie libidinale', Paris, Minuit,
1974.
MANNONI, MAUD, 'The Child, His "Illness", and the Others',
trans. anonymous, Harmondsworth, Penguin, 1973.
MITCHELL, JULIET, 'Psychoanalysis and Feminism', London,
Allen Lane, 1974.
MONTRELAY, MICHÈLE, 'L'Ombre et le nom', Paris, Minuit, 1977
(an excerpt has been translated in 'm/f', 1, pp. 83-101).
'Nouvelle revue de psychanalyse' Ecrire la psychanalyse, 16, 1977.
VERDIGLIONE, ARMANDO (ed), 'Psychanalyse et politique',
Paris, Seuil, 1974.
WILDEN, ANTHONY, 'The Language of the Self', Baltimore, Johns
Hopkins University Press, 1968. (Still the best introduction to
Lacan.)
— 'System and Structure: Essays in Communication and Exchange',
London, Tavistock, 1972; 2nd edition, 1980.

Part One

TEXT, DISCOURSE, IDEOLOGY

A 'text' is henceforth no longer a finished corpus of writing, some content enclosed in a book or its margins, but a differential network, a fabric of traces referring endlessly to something other than itself, to other differential traces (Jacques Derrida).

Power is everywhere (Michel Foucault).

2 THEORY OF THE TEXT

Roland Barthes

['That is the pleasure of the text: value shifted to the sumptuous rank of the signifier.' Barthes's disarmingly hedonistic statement captures the issues involved in his shift from the analysis of structures to the analysis of processes of signification. Published in the same year as 'The Pleasure of the Text' (1973), -Theory of the Text- elaborates the new object of post-structuralist criticism - except that it is not, strictly, an 'object', or even a 'concept'. Text is produced in the space of the relations between the reader and the written, and that space is the site of a productivity: 'écriture' ('writing').

The theory of the text was developed by those associated with the journal 'Tel Quel' in the late 1960s and early 1970s (Barthes, Derrida, Kristeva and Sollers). In their formulations, text displaces the conventional notion of the literary work, even of 'literature' itself. Whereas the work is a finished object, consisting of a body of writing enclosed within the covers of a book, 'the Text', in Barthes's words, 'is a methodological field . . . experienced only in an activity of production' (-From Work to Text-). The difference between the two can be conceived in terms of the difference between a thing and a process, a product and productivity, signified and signifier, or 'truth' and 'play'. But they are not, strictly, in opposition to each other, for to compare the two is to compare an object with a practice. Text functions as a transgressive activity which disperses the author as the centre, limit, and guarantor of truth, voice and pre-given meaning. Instead, it produces a performative writing, which fissures the sign and 'ceaselessly posits meaning endlessly to evaporate it'. The theory of the text, it is also claimed, enunciates a signifying practice that can be rearticulated with the social practices in which it participates.

Just as text is not a stable object, so the word 'text' does not reify into a metalanguage. Part of the theory of the text involves the destruction of metalanguage, and its replacement by a 'criticism' conceived as a practice of writing also. So, in Barthes's essay, the word enacts its own meanings, a wandering of signification which is, precisely, text. The word and the 'concept' text refuse to rest at any level of arrested meaning, performing instead a play, a trembling and overflowing of the signifiers, a stereographic shifting of signification. This 'hesitense', to use Joyce's word, occurs also in the movement between the appearance of 'text', 'the text', and 'some text'; the word never reaches its point of limit, but wanders and redoubles upon itself in its

meanings of text as a critical value, text as a replacement for
the work, text as pleasure, text as a discursive unit, textuality
as a tissue of signifying practices, text as the (critical) activity
which textualises and analyses these movements in the following
essay.

Two French terms are retained in this translation. Heath's use
of the term 'signifiance' is followed, since no English word adequately invokes its sense of a continual process of signification.
The word, which comes from Benveniste via Kristeva, is exten-
sively defined in the essay itself. The term with which it is
identified, 'jouissance', seems by now sufficiently well known in
its French usage to allow its retrieval from the OED's 'obsolete'
classification. It is commonly agreed that neither 'bliss' nor
'pleasure' are adequate translations. The closest word to 'jouissance' in English would be 'enjoyment' if the English word had a
little more frisson. 'Jouissance' means enjoyment in the sense of
enjoyment of a right, of a pleasure, and, most of all, of sexual
climax. 'Jouissance' and 'signifiance' invoke the sense of an
ecstatic loss of the subject in a sexual or textual coming – a
textasy.]

What is a text, for current opinion? It is the phenomenal surface
of the literary work; it is the fabric of the words which make up
the work and which are arranged in such a way as to impose a
meaning which is stable and as far as possible unique. In spite
of the partial and modest character of the notion (it is, after all,
only an object, perceptible to the visual sense), the text partakes
of the spiritual glory of the work, of which it is the prosaic but
necessary servant. Constitutively linked with writing (the text
is *what is written*), perhaps because the very graphics of the
letter – although remaining linear – suggest not speech, but the
interweaving of a tissue (etymologically speaking, 'text' means
'tissue'), the text is, in the work, what secures the guarantee
of the written object, bringing together its safe-guarding functions: on the one hand the stability and permanence of inscription, designed to correct the fragility and imprecision of the
memory, and on the other hand the legality of the letter, that
incontrovertible and indelible trace, supposedly, of the meaning
which the author has intentionally placed in his work; the text
is a weapon against time, oblivion and the trickery of speech,
which is so easily taken back, altered, denied. The notion of
the text is historically linked to a whole world of institutions:
the law, the Church, literature, education. The text is a moral
object: it is the written in so far as the written participates in
the social contract. It subjects us, and demands that we observe
and respect it, but in return it marks language with an inestim-
able attribute which it does not possess in its essence: security.

1   THE CRISIS OF THE SIGN

From the epistemological point of view, the text, in this classical
acceptation, is part of a conceptual set whose centre is the sign.
We are beginning to understand now that the sign is a historical
concept, an analytic (and even ideological) artefact. We know
that there is a civilisation of the sign, namely our own Western
civilisation from the Stoics to the middle of the twentieth century.[1]
The notion of text implies that the written message is articulated
like the sign: on one side the signifier (the materiality of the
letters and of their connection into words, sentences, paragraphs,
chapters), and on the other side the signified, a meaning which
is at once original, univocal, and definitive, determined by the
correctness of the signs which carry it. The classical sign is a
sealed unit, whose closure arrests meaning, prevents it from
trembling or becoming double, or wandering. The same goes for
the classical text: it closes the work, chains it to its letter, rivets
it to its signified. It thus commits us to two types of operation,
both intended to repair the holes which a thousand causes (historical, material, human causes) can punch in the integrity of
the sign. These two operations are those of restoration and interpretation.
   As the repository of the very materiality of the signifier (the
order and exactitude of the letters), the text demands to be
rediscovered, 'restored', if it should come to be lost or changed
for some historical reason. It is then taken in hand by a science,
philology, and by a technique, textual criticism. But that is
not all: the literal exactitude of the written, defined by the conformity of its successive versions to its original version, is
metonymically confused with its semantic exactitude. In the
classical universe, a law of the signified is deduced from the law
of the signifier, and vice versa. The two legalities coincide, and
each confirms the other: the literality of the text is made the
repository of its origin, of its intention, and of a canonical meaning which has to be maintained or rediscovered. The text then
becomes the very object of all hermeneutics. From the 'restitution' of the signifier one passes naturally to the canonical interpretation of the signified: the text is the name of the work in so
far as it is inhabited by one, and one only, meaning, a 'true'
meaning, a definitive meaning. It is that scientific 'instrument'
which defines in an authoritarian way the rules of an eternal
reading.
   This conception of the text (the classical, institutional, and
current conception) is obviously linked to a metaphysics, that of
truth. Just as the oath authenticates speech, so the text authenticates writing: its literalness, its origin, its meaning, that is to
say, its 'truth'. For centuries, how many battles for truth, and
also, concurrently, how many battles in the name of one meaning
against another, how many attacks of anguish at the uncertainty
of signs, how many rules as an attempt to make them firm! One
and the same history, bloody at times and always bitter, has

linked together truth, the sign, and the text. But also, one and
the same crisis, which started last century in the metaphysics of
truth (Nietzsche), is being opened up again today in the theory
of language and literature, by the ideological critique of the sign
and by the substitution of a new text for the old one, that of
the philologists.

This crisis was initiated by linguistics itself. In an ambiguous
(or dialectical) manner, (structural) linguistics scientifically
consecrated the concept of sign (articulated into signifier and
signified); this may be regarded as the triumphant culmination
of a metaphysics of meaning. At the same time, by its very imper-
ialism, it necessitated the displacement, deconstruction, and
subversion of the apparatus of signification. At the apogee of
structural linguistics (around 1960) certain new researchers, who
in many cases had emerged from linguistics itself, began to
enunciate a critique of the sign and a new theory of the text
(formerly known as 'literary').[2]

Linguistics played a triple role in this mutation. First, by moving closer to logic, at a time when logic, with Carnap, Russell
and Wittgenstein, was thinking of itself as a language, linguistics gave its researchers the habit of substituting the criterion
of validity for that of truth; of withdrawing the whole language
from the sanction of content; of exploring the richness, the subtlety and shall we say infinitude of the tautological transformations
of discourse. Through the practice of formalisation, a full apprenticeship in the signifier, in its autonomy and the amplitude of
its unfolding, was carried out. Then, thanks to the work of the
Prague circle and of Jakobson, these researchers were encouraged
to rework the traditional division of discourses: a whole section
of literature passed over to linguistics (at the level of research,
if not of teaching) under the name of 'poetics' (Valéry had seen
the necessity of this shift), and thereby escaped from the juris-
diction of literary history, conceived as a mere history of ideas
and genres. Finally, semiology, a new discipline postulated by
Saussure at the beginning of the century but which began to
develop only around 1960, applied itself, at least in France,
principally to the analysis of literary discourse. Linguistics stops
at the sentence and certainly defines the units which compose it
(syntagms, monemes, phonemes); but beyond the sentence? What
are the structural units of discourse (if we give up the normative
divisions of classical rhetoric)? Literary semiotics here needed
the notion of text, a discursive unit higher than or interior to
the sentence, yet still structurally different from it. 'The notion
of *text* is not situated on the same plane as that of *sentence* . . .;
in this sense, the text must be distinguished from the *paragraph*,
the typographic unit of several sentences. The text may coincide
with a phrase or with an entire book; . . . it constitutes a system
which must not be identified with the linguistic system but put in
relation to it: a relation both of contiguity and of resemblance'
(T. Todorov).[3]

In strict literary semiotics, the text is in a manner of speaking

that which formally includes linguistic phenomena; it is at the
level of the text that the semantics of signification (and no longer
only of communication), together with narrative or poetic syntax,
are studied. This new conception of the text, which is much
closer to rhetoric than to philology, is however meant to be subject to the principles of positive science: the text is studied in
an immanent way, since one abstains from any reference to content and (sociological, historical, psychological) determinations,
yet in an external way, since the text, as in any positive science,
is only an object, submitted to the distant inspection of a knowing
subject. Hence one cannot speak, at this level, of an epistemological mutation; such a mutation begins when the gains of linguistics and of semiology are deliberately placed (relativised:
destroyed-reconstructed) in a new field of reference, essentially
defined by the intercommunication of two different epistemes:
dialectical materialism and psychoanalysis. The dialectical-
materialist reference (Marx, Engels, Lenin, Mao) and the Freudian
reference (Freud, Lacan) enable us to identify with certainty the
adherents of the new theory of the text. For there to be a new
science it is not enough, in effect, for the old science to become
deeper or wider (which is what happens when one passes from
the linguistics of the sentence to the semiotics of the work);
there has to be a meeting of different epistemes, indeed ones
that normally know nothing of each other (as is the case with
Freudianism, Marxism, and structuralism), and this meeting has
to produce a new object (it is no longer a question of a new
approach to an old object): in the event, it is this new object
that we call text.

2 THE THEORY OF THE TEXT

The language we decide to use to define the text is not a matter
of indifference, for it is a part of the theory of the text to
plunge any enunciation, including its own, into crisis. The
theory of the text is directly critical of any metalanguage: revis-
ing the discourse of scientificity, it demands a mutation in science
itself, since the human sciences have hitherto never called into
question their own language, which they have considered as a
mere instrument or as purely transparent. The text is a fragment
of language, itself placed in a perspective of languages. To communicate some knowledge or some theoretical reflection about the
text pre-supposes, then, that one is oneself in some way or other
engaging in textual practice. The theory of the text can, of
course, be enunciated in the mode of a coherent and neutral
scientific discourse, but then at least it is for the sake of being
circumstantial and didactic; alongside this mode of exposition we
are entitled to place under the theory of the text the great
variety of texts (whatever their genre, whatever their form)
which treat of the reflexivity of language and the circuit of enunciation: the text can be approached by definitions, but also

(and perhaps above all) by metaphors.

The definition of the text has been elaborated for epistemological purposes principally by Julia Kristeva: 'We define the
Text as a translinguistic apparatus which redistributes the order
of the language by putting a communicative utterance, aiming to
inform directly, in relation with different utterances, anterior
to or synchronic with it.'[4] It is to Julia Kristeva that we owe the
principal theoretical concepts which are implicitly present in this
definition: signifying practices, productivity, 'signifiance',
phenotext and genotext, intertextuality.

Signifying practices
The text is a signifying practice, which semiology privileges because it shows in an exemplary way the work by means of which
the meeting between subject and language is produced: it is the
'function' of the text to dramatize this work, in a certain sense.
What is a signifying practice? It is first of all a differentiated
signifying system, dependent on a typology of significations (and
not on a universal matrix of the sign). This requirement of differentiation was laid down by the Prague School; it implies that
signification is not produced in a uniform way, but according to
the material of the signifier (this diversity founds semiology),
and also according to the plurality which makes the enunciating
subject (whose enunciation – unstable – is always made under the
gaze – under the discourse – of the Other).[5] Second, it is a practice; that means that signification is produced not at the level of
an abstraction (langue), as postulated by Saussure, but through
an operation, a labour in which both the debate of the subject
and the Other, and the social context, are invested in the same
movement. The notion of signifying practice restores to language
its active energy; but the act which it implies is not an act of
understanding (already described by the Stoics and by Cartesian
philosophy), and therein lies the epistemological mutation: the
subject no longer has the fine unity of the Cartesian 'cogito';
it is a plural subject, which so far only psychoanalysis has been
able to approach. No one can claim to reduce communication to the
simplicity of the classical schema postulated by linguistics: sender,
channel, receiver, except by relying implicitly on a metaphysics
of the classical subject or on an empiricism whose (sometimes
aggressive) 'naivety' is just as metaphysical.[6] In fact the plural
is directly at the heart of signifying practice, in the form of
contradiction; signifying practices, even if it be provisionally
permitted to isolate one of them, always belong to a dialectic, not
to a classification.

Productivity
The text is a productivity. This does not mean that it is the
product of a labour (such as could be required by a technique
of narration and the mastery of style), but the very theatre of a
production where the producer and reader of the text meet: the
text 'works', at each moment and from whatever side one takes it.

Even when written (fixed), it does not stop working, maintaining
a process of production. The text works what? Language. It
deconstructs the language of communication, representation, or
expression (where the individual or collective subject may have
the illusion that he is imitating something or expressing himself)
and reconstructs another language, voluminous, having neither
bottom nor surface, for its space is not that of the figure, the
painting, the frame, but the stereographic space of the combina-
tive play, which is infinite once one has gone outside the limits
of current communication (subjected to opinion, to the 'doxa') and
of narrative or discursive verisimilitude. Productivity is triggered
off, the redistribution is carried out, the text comes about, as
soon as, for example, the scriptor and/or the reader begin to
play with the signifier, either (in the case of the author) by
ceaselessly producing 'word-plays', or (in the case of the reader)
by inventing ludic meanings, even if the author of the text had
not foreseen them, and even if it was historically impossible for
him to foresee them: the signifier belongs to everybody; it is the
text which, in fact, works tirelessly, not the artist or the con-
sumer. The analysis of productivity cannot be reduced to a linguistic description; we must - or at least we can - add to it other
paths of analysis: that of mathematics (inasmuch as it gives
account of the play of sets and subsets, that is to say, of the
multiple relation of signifying practices), that of logic, that
of Lacanian psychoanalysis (inasmuch as it explores a logic of the
signifier), and that of dialectical materialism (which recognises
contradiction).

'Signifiance'
One can attribute a unique and in some sense canonical signification to a text; this is attempted in detail by philology, and in
general by interpretative criticism, which seeks to demonstrate
that the text possesses a total and secret signified, varying
according to critical doctrine: a biographical sense, for psychoanalytical criticism; a project, for existential criticism; a socio-
historical sense, for Marxist criticism, etc.[7] The text is treated
as if it were the repository of an objective signification, and this
signification appears as embalmed in the work-as-product. But
once the text is conceived as production (and no longer as product), 'signification' is no longer an adequate concept. As soon
as the text is conceived as a polysemic space where the paths of
several possible meanings intersect, it is necessary to cast off
the monological, legal status of signification, and to pluralise it.
It was for this liberation that the concept of connotation was
used: the volume of secondary or derived, associated senses, the
semantic 'vibrations' grafted on to the denoted message. A fortiori,
when the text is read (or written) as a mobile play of signifiers,
with no possible reference to one or several fixed signifieds, it
becomes necessary to distinguish carefully between signification,
which belongs to the level of the product, of the statement, of
communication, and the signifying work, which belongs to the

level of production, enunciation, symbolisation: it is this work
that we call the 'signifiance'. 'Signifiance' is a process, in the
course of which the 'subject' of the text, escaping the logic of
the ego-cogito and engaging other logics (that of the signifier
and that of contradiction), struggles with meaning and is deconstructed ('is lost'). 'Signifiance' - and this is what immediately
distinguishes it from signification - is thus work, not the work
by which the subject (intact and external) might try to master
the language (for example the work of style), but that radical
work (which leaves nothing intact) through which the subject
explores how language works him and undoes him as soon as he
stops observing it and enters it. 'Signifiance' is 'the without-end-
ness of the possible operations in a given field of language'.[8]
'Signifiance', unlike signification, cannot be reduced to communication, to representation, to expression: it puts the (writing
or reading) subject into the text, not as a projection, not even a
fantasmatic one (there is no 'transport' of a constituted subject),
but as a 'loss' (in the sense which the word 'perte' can have in
speleology[9]); whence its identification with 'jouissance': it is
through the concept of 'signifiance' that the text becomes erotic
(and for that it does not have to represent any erotic 'scenes').

Phenotext and genotext

It is also to Julia Kristeva that we owe the distinction between
phenotext and genotext. The phenotext is 'the verbal phenomenon
as it presents itself in the structure of the concrete statement'.[10]
The infinite 'signifiance' is in fact given through a contingent
work, and this level of contingency corresponds to the phenotext.
The methods of analysis as ordinarily practised (before and outside of semanalysis) are applied to the phenotext. Phonological,
structural, semantic descriptions - in short, structural analysis -
are suited to the phenotext, because this analysis poses no questions about the subject of the text: it bears on statements, not on
enunciations. The phenotext can, then, come under a theory of
the sign and of communication, without any incoherence: it is
the privileged object of semiology. Whereas the genotext 'sets out
the grounds for the logical operations proper to the constitution
of the subject of the enunciation'; it is 'the place of structuration
of the phenotext'; it is a heterogeneous domain: at the same time
verbal and of the nature of drives ('pulsionnel') (it is the domain
'where signs are cathected by drives').[11] The genotext does not,
therefore, belong exclusively to the domain of structuralism (it
is a structuration, not a structure), nor to that of psychoanalysis
(it is not the place of the unconscious, but of the 'scions' of the
unconscious); it belongs to the realm of a general, multiple logic,
which is no longer solely the logic of understanding. The genotext
is, of course, the field of 'signifiance'. From the epistemological
point of view, it is through the concept of genotext that semanalysis exceeds classical semiology, which merely seeks to structure
statements, but does not seek to find out how the subject displaces
himself, turns aside, and is lost when enunciating.

Intertext

The text redistributes language (it is the field of this redistribution). One of the paths of this deconstruction-reconstruction is to permute texts, scraps of texts that have existed or exist around and finally within the text being considered: any text is an intertext; other texts are present in it, at varying levels, in more or less recognisable forms: the texts of the previous and surrounding culture. Any text is a new tissue of past citations. Bits of codes, formulae, rhythmic models, fragments of social languages, etc. pass into the text and are redistributed within it, for there is always language before and around the text. Intertextuality, the condition of any text whatsoever, cannot, of course, be reduced to a problem of sources or influences; the intertext is a general field of anonymous formulae whose origin can scarcely ever be located; of unconscious or automatic quotations, given without quotation-marks. Epistemologically, the concept of intertext is what brings to the theory of the text the volume of sociality: the whole of language, anterior or contemporary, comes to the text, not following the path of a discoverable filiation or a willed imitation, but that of a dissemination - an image which makes sure the text has the status not of a reproduction but of a productivity.

These principal concepts, which are the articulations of the theory, are all concordant, on the whole, with the image suggested by the very etymology of the word 'text': it is a tissue, something woven. But whereas criticism (to date the only known form, in France, of a theory of literature) hitherto unanimously placed the emphasis on the finished 'fabric' (the text being a 'veil' behind which the truth, the real message, in a word the 'meaning', had to be sought), the current theory of the text turns away from the text as veil and tries to perceive the fabric in its texture, in the interlacing of codes, formulae and signifiers, in the midst of which the subject places himself and is undone, like a spider that comes to dissolve itself into its own web. A lover of neologisms might therefore define the theory of the text as a 'hyphology' ('hyphos' is the fabric, the veil, and the spider's web).

3   THE TEXT AND THE WORK

The text must not be confused with the work. A work is a finished object, something computable, which can occupy a physical space (take its place, for example, on the shelves of a library); the text is a methodological field. One cannot, therefore, count up texts, at least not in any regular way: all one can say is that in such-and-such a work, there is, or there isn't, some text. 'The work is held in the hand, the text in language.' We can put it another way by saying that if the work can be defined in terms that are heterogeneous to language (everything from the format of the book to the socio-historical determinations which produced that

book), the text, for its part, remains homogeneous to language
through and through: it is nothing other than language and can
exist only through a language other than itself. In other words,
'the text can be felt only in a work, a production': that of
'signifiance'.[12]

'Signifiance' invokes the idea of an infinite labour (of the
signifier upon itself): the text can therefore no longer coincide
exactly (nor by right) with the linguistic or rhetorical units
hitherto recognised by the sciences of language, the singling-
out of which always implied the idea of a finished structure. The
text does not necessarily contradict these units, but it overflows
them, or, to be more precise, it does not have to fit itself to
them. Since the text is a massive (rather than numerative) concept, we can find text from one end to the other of the discursive spectrum. We know that this spectrum is traditionally divided
into two distinct and heterogeneous regions: any manifestation of
language whose dimensions are less than or equal to the sentence
belongs by right to linguistics; everything beyond the sentence
belongs to 'discourse', the object of an ancient normative science,
rhetoric. Of course, stylistics and rhetoric itself can treat of
phenomena internal to the sentence (choice of words, assonances,
figures of speech); and in addition, certain linguists have tried
to found a linguistics of discourse (speech analysis);[13] but these
attempts cannot be compared to the work of textual analysis, because they are either outmoded (rhetoric) or else very limited
(stylistics), or else tainted with a metalinguistic spirit, placing
themselves externally to the statement and not internally to the
enunciation.

'Signifiance', which is the text at work, does not recognise the
domains imposed by the sciences of language (these domains can
be recognised at the level of the phenotext but not at that of the
genotext). 'Signifiance' - the glow, the unpredictable flash of the
infinities of language - is at all the levels of the work without
distinction: in the sounds, which are thus no longer considered
as units meant to determine the meaning (phonemes) but as drive-
movements; in the monemes, which are not so much semantic units
as networks of associations, produced by connotation, by latent
polysemy, in a generalised metonymy; in the syntagms, whose
impact, whose intertextual resonance, is more important than their
lawful meaning; and finally, in the discourse, whose 'readability'
is either overflowed or overlaid by a plurality of logics other than
mere predicative logic. This running-together of the scientific
'fields' of language makes 'signifiance' (the text in its textual
specificity) closely resemble the dream-work, such as Freud began
to describe it. However, we must here note that it is not a priori
the 'strangeness' of a work which necessarily brings it close to
dreams, but rather the signifying *work*, whether it be strange or
not. What 'dream-work' and 'text-work' have in common (other
than certain operations and certain figures, noted by Benveniste)
is that they are a labour outside exchange, inaccessible to
'calculation'.[14]

We can henceforth understand that the text is a scientific (or at the very least, epistemological) concept and at the same time a critical value, permitting an evaluation of works according to the degree of intensity of the 'signifiance' which is in them. Hence the privilege accorded by the theory of the text to the texts of modernity (from Lautréamont to Philippe Sollers) is double: these texts are exemplary because they present (in a state never previously attained) 'the labour of semiosis in language and with the subject', and because they constitute a de facto claim against the constraints of the traditional ideology of meaning ('verisimilitude', 'readability', 'expressivity' of an imaginary subject, imaginary because constituted as a 'person', etc.).[15] However, just because the text is massive (and not numerative), because it is not necessarily the same as the work, it is possible to find 'text', though no doubt to a lesser extent, in earlier productions. A classical work (Flaubert, Proust, and why not Bossuet?) can comprise levels or fragments of 'écriture': the play, the plays of the signifier may be present (at work) in it, particularly if we permit, as is prescribed by the theory, the inclusion of the activity of reading in textual practice - and not only the activity of fabricating the written. In the same way, still in the domain of the written, the theory of the text will not regard itself as bound to observe the customary distinction between 'good' and 'bad' literature. The principal criteria of the text may be found, at least singly, in works rejected or disdained by noble, humanist culture (whose norms are fixed by the education system, criticism, histories of literature, etc.). The intertext, the plays of word (of signifiers) may be present in very popular works; 'signifiance' may be present in so-called 'delirious' writings, traditionally excluded from 'literature'.

Furthermore, we cannot by right restrict the concept of 'text' to what is written (to literature). No doubt the presence of articulated language (or, if you like, of the mother-tongue) in a production gives that production a greater richness of 'signifiance'; highly constructed, because of having come out of a very coded system, linguistic signs offer themselves up to a deconstruction that is all the more penetrating; but it is sufficient for there to be a signifying overflow for there to be text. 'Signifiance' depends on the material (the 'substance') of the signifier only in its mode of analysis, not in its being. If our consideration of 'signifiance' is to be extended beyond all limits, it is enough (taking up a saying of Claudel's concerning Mallarmé) to 'put oneself in front of the outside world, not as before a spectacle . . . , but as before a text'. All signifying practices can engender text: the practice of painting pictures, musical practice, filmic practice, etc. The works, in certain cases, themselves prepare the subversion of the genres, of the homogeneous classes to which they have been assigned: we can adduce the striking example of contemporary painting, which in many cases is no longer, strictly speaking, either painting or sculpture, but the production of 'objects'; not to mention melody, for example, which the theory will treat as a text (a hybrid of voice, which is a pure corporeal signifier, and language) much more than as a musical genre. It is true - and to be expected - that textual analysis is currently much more developed in the domain of written (literary) 'substance' than in that of other substances (visual, auditory). This head start arises partly from the existence of a pre-existing science of signification (though not of 'signifiance'), which is linguistics, and partly from the very structure of articulated language (in relation to the other 'languages'): there the sign is distinct and directly signifying (it is the 'word'), and language is the only semiotic system which has the power to interpret the other signifying systems and itself.

If the theory of the text tends to abolish the separation of genres and arts, this is because it no longer considers works as mere 'messages', or even as 'statements' (that is, finished products, whose destiny would be sealed as soon as they were uttered), but as perpetual productions, enunciations, through which the subject continues to struggle; this subject is no doubt that of the author, but also that of the reader. The theory of the text brings with it, then, the promotion of a new epistemological object: the reading (an object virtually disdained by the whole of classical criticism, which was essentially interested either in the person of the author, or in the rules of manufacture of the work, and which never had any but the most meagre conception of the reader, whose relation to the work was thought to be one of mere projection). Not only does the theory of the text extend to infinity the freedoms of reading (authorising us to read works of the past with an entirely modern gaze, so that it is legitimate, for example, to read Sophocles' 'Oedipus' by pouring Freud's Oedipus back into it, or to read Flaubert on the basis of Proust), but it also insists strongly on the (productive) equivalence of writing and reading. No doubt there are readings which are mere acts of consumption: precisely the ones in which the 'signifiance' is censored all the way along. Full reading, on the contrary, is the kind in which the reader is nothing less than the one who desires to write, to give himself up to an erotic practice of language. The theory of the text can find historical indications in the use of reading; it is certain that contemporary civilisation tends to flatten reading out, by making it into a simple consumption, entirely separated from writing. Not only does the school system boast that it teaches reading, and no longer as in former times writing (even if the pupil or student of those days had to write according to a highly conventional rhetorical code), but also writing itself is driven off and confined in a caste of technicians (writers, teachers, intellectuals). The economic, social and institutional conditions no longer permit us to recognise, either in art or in literature, that particular practitioner, who once existed and might do so yet, in a liberated society - the amateur/lover.

4 TEXTUAL PRACTICE

Traditionally the work of art may belong, broadly, to two
sciences: history and philology. These sciences - or rather,
these 'discourses' - have in common the constraint (which,
incidentally, they share with all positive sciences) that they constitute the work as a closed object placed at a distance from an
observer who inspects it from the outside. It is essentially this
exteriority which textual analysis puts in question, not at all in
the name of the rights of a more or less impressionistic 'subjectivity', but on the grounds of the infinitude of languages. No
language has an edge over any other; there is no metalanguage
(a proposition established by psychoanalysis), and the subject
of writing and/or of reading does not have to do with objects
(works, statements), but with fields (texts, enunciations). He is
himself caught in a topology (a science of the places of speaking).
In place of the conception of a positive science, which was that
of literary history and of literary criticism, and which still is
that of semiology, textual analysis tends to substitute the idea of
a critical science, that is, a science which calls into question its
own discourse.

This methodological principle does not necessarily oblige us to
reject the results of the canonical sciences of the work (history,
sociology, etc.), but it leads us to use them partially, freely,
and above all relatively. Thus, textual analysis will not in the
least impugn the information provided by literary history or
general history; what it will contest is the critical myth according
to which the work is caught in a purely evolutionary movement,
as if it always had to be attached to, appropriated by, the (civil,
historical, affective) person of an author, who would be its
father. To the metaphor of filiation, of organic 'development',
textual analysis prefers the metaphor of the network, of the intertext, of an overdetermined, plural field. The same correction,
and the same displacement, apply in respect of philological
science (to which we assign, for present purposes, interpretative
commentaries): criticism seeks in general to discover the meaning
of the work, a meaning which is more or less hidden and which
is assigned to diverse levels, depending on the critic; textual
analysis impugns the idea of a final signified. The work does not
stop, does not close. It is henceforth less a question of explaining
or even describing, than of entering into the play of the signifiers; of enumerating them, perhaps (if the text allows), but not
hierarchising them. Textual analysis is pluralist.

Julia Kristeva proposed to call textual analysis 'semanalysis'.
It was indeed necessary to distinguish the analysis of 'text' (in
the sense we have here given to that word) from literary semiotics.
The most evident difference is in the reference to psychoanalysis,
present in semanalysis, absent from literary semiotics (which
merely classifies statements and describes their structural functioning, without concerning itself with the relation between the
subject, the signifier, and the Other). Semanalysis is not merely

a method of classification. To be sure, it is interested in the
typology of genres, but precisely in order to replace it by a
typology of texts: its object, dialectically, is the intersection
of phenotext and genotext. This intersection constitutes what
is called, in the wake of the Russian post-Formalists and Kristeva,
an 'ideologeme', a concept which allows us to articulate the text
on to the intertext and to 'think it in the texts of society and
of history'.

However, whatever the methodological or merely operative concepts which the theory of the text seeks to focus under the name
of semanalysis or textual analysis, the exact development of this
theory, the blossoming which justifies it, is not this or that
recipe for analysis, it is *writing itself. Let the commentary be
itself a text:* that is, in brief, what the theory of the text demands. The subject of the analysis (the critic, the philologist,
the scholar) cannot in fact, without bad faith and smugness,
believe he is external to the language he is describing. His
exteriority is only quite provisional and apparent: he too is in
language, and he must assume his insertion, however 'rigorous'
and 'objective' he may wish to be, into the triple knot of the subject, the signifier, and the Other - an insertion which writing
(the text) fully accomplishes, without having recourse to the
hypocritical distance of a fallacious metalanguage. *The only
practice that is founded by the theory of the text is the text
itself.* The consequence is evident: all in all, it is the whole of
criticism (as a discourse held 'on' a work) which is outdated. If
an author comes to speak of a past text, he can only do so by
himself producing a new text (by entering into the undifferentiated proliferation of the intertext). There are no more critics,
only writers. We can put it still more precisely: from its very
principles, the theory of the text can produce only theoreticians
or practitioners (writers), but absolutely not 'specialists' (critics
or teachers); as a practice, then, it participates itself in the subversion of the genres which as a theory it studies.

The real taking-up of the theory of the text is the practice of
textual writing. Thus it is intended more for the subjects/pro-
ducers of writing than for critics, researchers, students. This
practice (if we wish to differentiate it from the mere work of
style) presupposes that one has passed the descriptive or communicative level of language, and that one is ready to produce
its generative energy. It thus implies that one accepts a certain
number of procedures: generalised recourse to anagrammatical
distortions of the enunciation ('word-plays'), polysemy, dialogue-
writing, or inversely 'l'écriture blanche', which thwarts and
deceives connotations;[16] 'irrational' (implausible) variations of
person and tense; the continuous subversion of the relation between writing and reading, between the sender and the receiver
of the text. It is thus a practice which is strongly transgressive
in relation to the main categories which found our current sociality: perception, intellection, the sign, grammar, and even science.
It is clear from then on that the theory of the text is 'ill-placed'

in the contemporary picture of gnoseology (but also that it draws its force and its historical meaning from this displacement). In relation to the traditional sciences of the work, which were – and are – sciences of the content and/or of the letter, its discourse is formalist; but in relation to the formalist sciences (classical logic, semiology, aesthetics) it reintroduces into its field history, society (in the form of the intertext), and the subject (but it is a cloven subject, ceaselessly displaced – and undone – by the presence-absence of his unconscious). The critical science postulated by this theory is paradoxical: it is not a science of the general (a nomothetic science); there is no 'model' of the text; nor is it a science of the singular (an idiographic science), for the text is never appropriated, it is situated in the infinite intercourse of codes, and not at the end-point of a 'personal' (identifiable in civil law) activity of the author. In conclusion, two predicative statements will give account of the particularity of this science: it is a science of 'jouissance', any 'textual' text (one that has entered into the field of 'signifiance') tends ultimately to provoke or to live the loss of consciousness (the annulment) that the subject assumes fully in erotic enjoyment; and it is a science of becoming (of that subtle becoming which Nietzsche demanded that we perceive beyond the gross form of things):

We are not *subtle* enough to perceive the probably absolute *flow* of *becoming;* the *permanent* exists only thanks to our coarse organs which summarise things and reduce them to common levels, when in fact nothing exists in that form. The tree is at each instant a new thing; we assert *form* because we do not grasp the subtlety of an absolute movement.

The text is likewise this tree to which we can (provisionally) give a name only because of the coarseness of our organs.

Translated by Ian McLeod

NOTES

(All notes are by the editor)
1   Cf. Julia Kristeva, 'Semeiotikè, Recherches pour une sémanalyse', Paris, Seuil, 1969, p.69: 'the subject *is* the sign, and cannot be constituted outside the sign. The civilization of the sign is the civilization of the subject; in a dictionary of the society of exchange, the sign would be the synonym of the subject, of communication and of speech' (my translation).
2   Notably, perhaps, Barthes himself. See, for instance, 'Mythologies', 1957, trans. Annette Lavers, London, Cape, 1972, and 'Elements of Semiology', 1964, trans. Annette Lavers, London, Cape, 1967.
3   O. Ducrot and T. Todorov (eds), 'Encyclopedic Dictionary

of the Sciences of Language', trans. Catherine Porter, Baltimore, Johns Hopkins University Press, 1979, p. 294.

4 Julia Kristeva, 'Le Texte du roman, Approche sémiologique d'une structure discursive transformationnelle', The Hague, Mouton, 1970, p. 12.

5 Cf. Lacan's seminar, Of the Gaze as Objet Petit a, in 'The Four Fundamental Concepts of Psycho-Analysis', trans. Alan Sheridan, London, Hogarth Press, 1977, pp. 67-119. Lacan's description is not strictly compatible with Barthes's 'split subject, who simultaneously enjoys *(jouisse)*, through the text, the consistency of his selfhood and its collapse, its fall' ('The Pleasure of the Text', trans. Richard Miller, London, Cape, 1976, p. 21). 'The fine unity of the Cartesian "cogito"' will always be lost; but this dissolve has here a positive value, for it is precisely at this site of loss that text is to be found.

6 Barthes is here referring to Jakobson's model of verbal communication:

CONTEXT

ADDRESSER   MESSAGE   ADDRESSEE
....

CONTACT

CODE

See Closing Statement: Linguistics and Poetics, in Thomas A. Sebeok (ed), 'Style in Language', New York, MIT, 1960, pp. 350-77.

7 Barthes is presumably here referring to the historical rather than contemporary versions of psychoanalytic and Marxist criticism.

8 'Le sans-fin des opérations possibles dans un champ donné de la langue': the play on 'fin' is important here, meaning both that there are unlimited possible operations, and that their non-teleological quality is here stressed.

9 'Perte' of a water-course, in geology, refers to the place where it disappears, only to reappear again somewhere else; e.g. 'la perte du Rhône,' near Bellegarde.

10 Julia Kristeva, Sémanalyse: Conditions d'une sémiotique scientifique (interview with J.-Cl.Coquet), in 'Semiotica', 5:4, 1972, p. 335.

11 Kristeva, Sémanalyse, pp. 335-6.

12 Roland Barthes, From Work to Text, 1971, in 'Image-Music-Text', essays selected and translated by Stephen Heath, London, Fontana, 1977, p. 157.

13 See, for instance, Emile Benveniste, 'Problems in General Linguistics', chapter 10, The Levels of Linguistic Analysis, pp. 101-11; Z. Harris, Discourse Analysis, in 'Language', 28, 1952, pp. 1-30, 474-94.

14 See Benveniste, 'Problems in General Linguistics', chapter 7, Remarks on the Function of Language in Freudian Theory, pp. 65-75.
15 Kristeva, Sémanalyse, p. 334.
16 For Barthes's discussion of Sartre's phrase (first used to describe the neutral, colourless style of Camus), see 'Writing Degree Zero', trans. Annette Lavers and Colin Smith, London, Cape, 1967, pp. 76-8.

FURTHER READING

BARTHES, ROLAND, 'The Pleasure of the Text', trans. Richard Miller, London, Cape, 1976.
— The Death of the Author, and From Work to Text, in 'Image-Music-Text', essays selected and translated by Stephen Heath, London, Fontana, 1977, pp. 142-8, 155-64.
— Jeunes chercheurs, in 'Communications', 19, 1972, pp. 1-5.
BOUAZIS, CHARLES (ed), 'Essais de la théorie du texte', Paris, Galilée, 1973.
DERRIDA, JACQUES, The End of the Book and the Beginning of Writing, in 'Of Grammatology', trans. G.C. Spivak, Baltimore, Johns Hopkins University Press, 1976, pp. 6-26.
— Tympan, in 'Marges-de la philosophie', Paris, Minuit, 1972, pp. I-XXV.
DUCROT, OSWALD and TODOROV, TZVETAN, 'Encyclopedic Dictionary of the Sciences of Language', trans. Catherine Porter, Baltimore, Johns Hopkins University Press, 1979.
HEATH, STEPHEN, 'Vertige du déplacement, lecture de Barthes', Paris, Fayard, 1974, pp. 136-76.
KRISTEVA, JULIA, 'Semeiotikè: Recherches pour une sémanalyse', Paris, Seuil, 1969.
— 'La Révolution du langage póetique: L'Avant-garde à la fin du dix-neuvième siècle; Lautréamont et Mallarmé', Paris, Seuil, 1974.
— 'Polylogue', Paris, Seuil, 1977.
— The Semiotic Activity, trans Stephen Heath and Christopher Prendergast, in 'Screen', 14:1/2, Spring/Summer 1973, pp. 25-39.
— Four Types of Signifying Practices, trans. anonymous, in 'Semiotext(e)', 1:1, 1974, pp. 65-74.
— The Subject in Signifying Practice, trans. anonymous, in 'Semiotext(e)', 1:3, 1975, pp. 19-26.
— The System and the Speaking Subject, in Thomas A. Sebeok (ed), 'The Tell-Tale Sign: A Survey of Semiotics', Lisse, The Peter de Ridder Press, 1975, pp. 47-55.
SOLLERS, PHILIPPE, Programme, in 'Logiques', Paris, Seuil, 1968, pp. 9-14.
UNGAR, STEPHEN, Doing and Not Doing Things with Barthes, in 'Enclitic', 2:2, Fall 1978, pp. 86-109.

3 THE ORDER OF DISCOURSE

Michel Foucault
Inaugural Lecture at the Collège de France, given
2 December 1970

[Together with 'The Archaeology of Knowledge' (1969), -The
Order of Discourse- is an outstanding example of that characteristic post-structuralist genre, the autocritique. Described by
Edward Said as Foucault's most important work, -The Order of
Discourse- was written in 1970 at the turning point of Foucault's
shift from 'archaeology', his method for the synchronic analyses
and representation of the history of systems of thought, to
'cartography', a more directly political mapping of the forms of
power exercised in discursive and other practices.

    Foucault's work is best approached in relation to his earlier
attempt to speak the unspoken language of otherness, of madness,
in 'Madness and Civilization' ('Histoire de la folie', 1961). The
difficulty of that book was how to avoid repeating the habitual
exclusion of madness by making it once again an *object* for
analysis, without ever allowing the disclosure of its own voice.
Foucault, therefore, himself attempted to produce a new form of
discourse, an 'ungrounded language', in which the inclusion/
exclusion, inside/outside, opposition of reason and madness
would be effaced. The attempt to hear the silence of madness led
Foucault to turn to literature (to Sade, Nietzsche, Artaud) in
search of its authentic voice. The difficulty, even impossibility,
of finding its form of discourse elsewhere led to reflection on all
those rules, systems and procedures which constitute, and are
constituted by, our 'will to knowledge'. These, Foucault argues,
comprise a discrete realm of discursive practices - the 'order
of discourse' - a conceptual terrain in which knowledge is formed
and produced. What is analysed is not simply what was thought
or said per se, but all the discursive rules and categories that
were a priori, assumed as a constituent part of discourse and
therefore of knowledge, and so fundamental that they remained
unvoiced and unthought. Discursive practices are characterised
by 'a delimitation of a field of objects, the definition of a legitimate perspective for the agent of knowledge, and the fixing of
norms for the elaboration of concepts and theories' ('Language,
Counter-Memory, Practice', p. 199). Their effect is to make it
virtually impossible to think outside them. To think outside them
is, by definition, to be mad, to be beyond comprehension and
therefore reason. It is in this way that we can see how discursive
rules are linked to the exercise of power; how the forms of discourse are both constituted by, and ensure the reproduction of,
the social system, through forms of selection, exclusion and
domination. 'In every society,' Foucault writes, 'the production

of discourse is controlled, organised, redistributed, by a certain
number of procedures whose role is to ward off its powers and
dangers, to gain mastery over its chance events, to evade its
materiality.'

Foucault's shift, then, is a shift of emphasis – which is clearly
manifesting itself in -The Order of Discourse-. In view of the
length and complexity of the essay, it may be helpful here to
provide a brief skeleton of Foucault's argument, at the same time
clarifying some of its references. Discourse itself is playfully
analysed in terms of a model reminiscent of the ego and the id (or
perhaps the pleasure principle and the death drive). It is constituted by a relation between desire, which wants discourse to be
unrestricted, 'infinitely open', and the institutions, which assert
that discourse comes into formation through constraint and control,
and that it is in this way that it possesses power. In other words,
the two are inseparable: discourse is formed and exists through
the operation of both, exactly in the way that ego and id are
constitutive of each other. Analysis, on the other hand, separates
the two: the 'critical' analysis (which examines the functions of
exclusion, the processes of depletion, that is, the institutional
role), and the 'genealogical' analysis (which examines the formation of discourses, the constituting processes of desire).

Foucault divides the procedures for mastery into three main
groups. First, the social procedures of exclusion, prohibition,
comprising the forbidden speech of politics and sexuality, the
division between reason and its other, madness, and the distinction between 'truth' and 'falsehood' which forms the way in which
knowledge is put to work in our society. Second, there are internal procedures of 'rarefaction'. The French term 'rarefaction'
includes not only the meaning of the rarefaction of gases, but
also the sense of depletion (of supplies), of growing scarcity, of
dwindling, dying out and exhaustion. The effect of an analysis
of forms of discourse is to reveal not a plenitude of meaning,
but a scarcity. Thus the internal procedures of rarefaction consist in discourses which exercise their own control, which limit
themselves, through principles such as the commentary, the
author, the 'discipline'. Third, neither exterior nor interior to
the discourse itself, are the determining conditions of application,
the imposition of roles on speaking subjects, and the restrictions
of access (for instance, education: 'any system of education is
a political way of maintaining or modifying the appropriation of
discourses, along with the power and knowledge they carry.')

If these are the three principles of restraint, Foucault argues
that a certain number of themes in philosophy collude with this.
First, philosophy's exclusion of discourse from its consideration
of the processes of thought and speech, and thus also the exclusion of the relation of the individual subject to the institution;
second, phenomenology's perpetuation of the idea of the founding,
originating subject; third, the idea, to be found in hermeneutics,
of originating experience, or meaning and signification as pre-
given; and fourth, the 'universal mediation' of neo-Hegelianism

which produces not the reality of discourse but a movement of transcendence, in which things or events 'imperceptibly turn themselves into discourse as they unfold the secret of their own essence.' In order to think round these collusive conceptual structures, Foucault suggests that we must call into question our will-to-truth, restore to discourse its character as an event, and throw off our acceptance of 'the sovereignty of the signifier,' of the sign, of 'the reduction of discursive practices to textual traces; the elision of the events produced therein and the retention only of marks for a reading.' Derrida is clearly included in this attack on philosophy, but for Foucault he is merely 'the most decisive modern representative' of a very traditional system.

The tasks that Foucault advocates require certain methodological principles. First, a principle of reversal, in the sense of an overturning, or a subversion. This could be compared to the way in which Foucault suggests that madness undermines philosophy and thought. Here it is a question of reversing the systems and figures which are customarily seen as the sources of discourses in the history of ideas. The event must be opposed to the idea of creation. Second, a principle of discontinuity - the fact that there are systems of rarefaction and depletion does not mean that somewhere else there is 'a vast unlimited discourse', 'a great unsaid'. Instead, 'discourses must be treated as discontinuous practices, which cross each other, are juxtaposed to each other, but can just as well exclude each other and be unaware of each other.' These series of discourses must be put in opposition to the assumption of the 'unity of a work, an epoch, or a theme'. Third, a principle of specificity: we must not imagine that discourse can be resolved simply into a 'play of pre-existing significations'. Discourse is 'a violence that we do to things, or in any case a practice that we impose on them'. Fourth, a principle of exteriority: the analysis of the 'external conditions of possibility' for a discourse, that which gives rise to its appearance and fixes its limits. To this Foucault opposes the idea of the hidden essence, meaning, 'the infinite treasure of buried signification'.

For Foucault, the fundamental philosophical concepts are no longer consciousness and continuity, with their corollary of freedom and causality (existentialism), nor even sign and structure (structuralism), but the event and the series, 'along with the play of the notions that are linked to them: "alea", regularity, discontinuity, dependence, transformation'. Thus in later work, the implication of a powerful determinism in -The Order of Discourse- shifts towards emphasis on the instability of the discontinuous segments of discourse, and the possibility of the resistance as well as the exercise of power. As Foucault puts it in 'The History of Sexuality' ('La Volonté de savoir'):

> Discourses are not once and for all subservient to power or raised up against it, any more than silences are. We must make allowances for the complex and unstable process whereby dis-

course can be both an instrument and an effect of power, but also a hindrance, a stumbling-block, a point of resistance and a starting point for an opposing strategy. Discourse transmits and produces power; it reinforces it, but also undermines and exposes it, renders it fragile and makes it possible to thwart it (pp. 100-1).]

I

I wish I could have slipped surreptitiously into this discourse which I must present today, and into the ones I shall have to give here, perhaps for many years to come. I should have preferred to be enveloped by speech, and carried away well beyond all possible beginnings, rather than have to begin it myself. I should have preferred to become aware that a nameless voice was already speaking long before me, so that I should only have needed to join in, to continue the sentence it had started and lodge myself, without really being noticed, in its interstices, as if it had signalled to me by pausing, for an instant, in suspense. Thus there would be no beginning, and instead of being the one from whom discourse proceeded, I should be at the mercy of its chance unfolding, a slender gap, the point of its possible disappearance.

I should have liked there to be a voice behind me which had begun to speak a very long time before, doubling in advance everything I am going to say, a voice which would say: 'You must go on, I can't go on, you must go on, I'll go on, you must say words, as long as there are any, until they find me, until they say me, strange pain, strange sin, you must go on, perhaps it's done already, perhaps they have said me already, perhaps they have carried me to the threshold of my story, before the door that opens on my story, that would surprise me, if it opens.'[1]

I think a good many people have a similar desire to be freed from the obligation to begin, a similar desire to be on the other side of discourse from the outset, without having to consider from the outside what might be strange, frightening, and perhaps maleficent about it. To this very common wish, the institution's reply is ironic, since it solemnises beginnings, surrounds them with a circle of attention and silence, and imposes ritualised forms on them, as if to make them more easily recognisable from a distance.

Desire says: 'I should not like to have to enter this risky order of discourse; I should not like to be involved in its peremptoriness and decisiveness; I should like it to be all around me like a calm, deep transparence, infinitely open, where others would fit in with my expectations, and from which truths would emerge one by one; I should only have to let myself be carried, within it and by it, like a happy wreck.' The institution replies: 'You should not be afraid of beginnings; we are all here in order to show you that discourse belongs to the order of laws, that we have long

been looking after its appearances; that a place has been made
ready for it, a place which honours it but disarms it; and that if
discourse may sometimes have some power, nevertheless it is
from us and us alone that it gets it.'

But perhaps this institution and this desire are nothing but two
contrary replies to the same anxiety: anxiety about what discourse
is in its material reality as a thing pronounced or written; anxiety
about this transitory existence which admittedly is destined to
be effaced, but according to a time-scale which is not ours;
anxiety at feeling beneath this activity (despite its greyness and
ordinariness) powers and dangers that are hard to imagine;
anxiety at suspecting the struggles, victories, injuries, domina-
tions and enslavements, through so many words even though long
usage has worn away their roughness.

What, then, is so perilous in the fact that people speak, and
that their discourse proliferates to infinity? Where is the danger
in that?

II

Here is the hypothesis which I would like to put forward tonight
in order to fix the terrain - or perhaps the very provisional
theatre - of the work I am doing: that in every society the
production of discourse is at once controlled, selected, organised
and redistributed by a certain number of procedures whose role
is to ward off its powers and dangers, to gain mastery over its
chance events, to evade its ponderous, formidable materiality.

In a society like ours, the procedures of exclusion are well
known. The most obvious and familiar is the prohibition. We know
quite well that we do not have the right to say everything, that
we cannot speak of just anything in any circumstances whatever,
and that not everyone has the right to speak of anything whatever. In the taboo on the object of speech, and the ritual of the
circumstances of speech, and the privileged or exclusive right
of the speaking subject, we have the play of three types of prohibition which intersect, reinforce or compensate for each other,
forming a complex grid which changes constantly. I will merely
note that at the present time the regions where the grid is
tightest, where the black squares are most numerous, are those
of sexuality and politics; as if discourse, far from being that transparent or neutral element in which sexuality is disarmed and politics
pacified, is in fact one of the places where sexuality and politics
exercise in a privileged way some of their most formidable powers.
It does not matter that discourse appears to be of little account,
because the prohibitions that surround it very soon reveal its
link with desire and with power. There is nothing surprising
about that, since, as psychoanalysis has shown, discourse is not
simply that which manifests (or hides) desire - it is also the
object of desire; and since, as history constantly teaches us,
discourse is not simply that which translates struggles or systems

of domination, but is the thing for which and by which there is struggle, discourse is the power which is to be seized.

There exists in our society another principle of exclusion, not another prohibition but a division and a rejection. I refer to the opposition between reason and madness.[2] Since the depths of the Middle Ages, the madman has been the one whose discourse cannot have the same currency as others. His word may be considered null and void, having neither truth nor importance, worthless as evidence in law, inadmissible in the authentification of deeds or contracts, incapable even of bringing about the trans-substantiation of bread into body at Mass. On the other hand, strange powers not held by any other may be attributed to the madman's speech: the power of uttering a hidden truth, of telling the future, of seeing in all naivety what the others' wisdom cannot perceive. It is curious to note that for centuries in Europe the speech of the madman was either not heard at all or else taken for the word of truth. It either fell into the void, being rejected as soon as it was proffered, or else people deciphered in it a rationality, naive or crafty, which they regarded as more rational than that of the sane. In any event, whether excluded, or secretly invested with reason, the madman's speech, strictly, did not exist. It was through his words that his madness was recognised; they were the place where the division between reason and madness was exercised, but they were never recorded or listened to. No doctor before the end of the eighteenth century had ever thought of finding out what was said, or how and why it was said, in this speech which nonetheless determined the difference. This whole immense discourse of the madman was taken for mere noise, and he was only symbolically allowed to speak, in the theatre, where he would step forward, disarmed and reconciled, because there he played the role of truth in a mask.

You will tell me that all this is finished today or is coming to an end; that the madman's speech is no longer on the other side of the divide; that it is no longer null and void; on the contrary, it puts us on the alert; that we now look for a meaning in it, for the outline or the ruins of some oeuvre; and that we have even gone so far as to come across this speech of madness in what we articulate ourselves, in that slight stumbling by which we lose track of what we are saying. But all this attention to the speech of madness does not prove that the old division is no longer operative. You have only to think of the whole framework of knowledge through which we decipher that speech, and of the whole network of institutions which permit someone - a doctor or a psychoanalyst - to listen to it, and which at the same time permit the patient to bring along his poor words or, in desperation, to withhold them. You have only to think of all this to become suspicious that the division, far from being effaced, is working differently, along other lines, through new institutions, and with effects that are not at all the same. And even if the doctor's role were only that of lending an ear to a speech that is free at last, he still does this listening in the context of the same division. He is listening to a discourse which is invested with desire, and which – for its greater exaltation or its greater anguish – thinks it is loaded with terrible powers. If the silence of reason is required for the curing of monsters, it is enough for that silence to be on the alert, and it is in this that the division remains.

It is perhaps risky to consider the opposition between true and false as a third system of exclusion, along with those just mentioned. How could one reasonably compare the constraint of truth with divisions like those, which are arbitrary to start with or which at least are organised around historical contingencies; which are not only modifiable but in perpetual displacement; which are supported by a whole system of institutions which impose them and renew them; and which act in a constraining and sometimes violent way?

Certainly, when viewed from the level of a proposition, on the inside of a discourse, the division between true and false is neither arbitrary nor modifiable nor institutional nor violent. But when we view things on a different scale, when we ask the question of what this will to truth has been and constantly is, across our discourses, this will to truth which has crossed so many centuries of our history; what is, in its very general form, the type of division which governs our will to know (notre volonté de savoir), then what we see taking shape is perhaps something like a system of exclusion, a historical, modifiable, and institutionally constraining system.

There is no doubt that this division is historically constituted. For the Greek poets of the sixth century BC, the true discourse (in the strong and valorised sense of the word), the discourse which inspired respect and terror, and to which one had to submit because it ruled, was the one pronounced by men who spoke as of right and according to the required ritual; the discourse which dispensed justice and gave everyone his share; the discourse which in prophesying the future not only announced what was going to happen but helped to make it happen, carrying men's minds along with it and thus weaving itself into the fabric of destiny. Yet already a century later the highest truth no longer resided in what discourse was or did, but in what it said: a day came when truth was displaced from the ritualised, efficacious and just act of enunciation, towards the utterance itself, its meaning, its form, its object, its relation to its reference. Between Hesiod and Plato a certain division was established, separating true discourse from false discourse: a new division because henceforth the true discourse is no longer precious and desirable, since it is no longer the one linked to the exercise of power. The sophist is banished.

This historical division probably gave our will to know its general form. However, it has never stopped shifting: sometimes the great mutations in scientific thought can perhaps be read as the consequences of a discovery, but they can also be read as the appearance of new forms in the will to truth. There is doubtless a will to

truth in the nineteenth century which differs from the will to
know characteristic of Classical culture in the forms it deploys,
in the domains of objects to which it addresses itself, and in
the techniques on which it is based. To go back a little further:
at the turn of the sixteenth century (and particularly in England),
there appeared a will to know which, anticipating its actual contents, sketched out schemas of possible, observable, measurable,
classifiable objects; a will to know which imposed on the knowing
subject, and in some sense prior to all experience, a certain
position, a certain gaze and a certain function (to see rather
than to read, to verify rather than to make commentaries on);
a will to know which was prescribed (but in a more general manner than by any specific instrument) by the technical level
where knowledges had to be invested in order to be verifiable
and useful. It was just as if, starting from the great Platonic
division, the will to truth had its own history, which is not that
of constraining truths: the history of the range of objects to be
known, of the functions and positions of the knowing subject, of
the material, technical, and instrumental investments of knowledge.

   This will to truth, like the other systems of exclusion, rests
on an institutional support: it is both reinforced and renewed by
whole strata of practices, such as pedagogy, of course; and the
system of books, publishing, libraries; learned societies in the
past and laboratories now. But it is also renewed, no doubt more
profoundly, by the way in which knowledge is put to work,
valorised, distributed, and in a sense attributed, in a society.
Let us recall at this point, and only symbolically, the old Greek
principle: though arithmetic may well be the concern of democratic cities, because it teaches about the relations of equality,
geometry alone must be taught in oligarchies, since it demonstrates the proportions within inequality.

   Finally, I believe that this will to truth - leaning in this way
on a support and an institutional distribution - tends to exert a
sort of pressure and something like a power of constraint (I am
still speaking of our own society) on other discourses. I am
thinking of the way in which for centuries Western literature
sought to ground itself on the natural, the 'vraisemblable', on
sincerity, on science as well - in short, on 'true' discourse. I am
thinking likewise of the manner in which economic practices,
codified as precepts or recipes and ultimately as morality, have
sought since the sixteenth century to ground themselves, rationalise themselves, and justify themselves in a theory of wealth
and production. I am also thinking of the way in which a body
as prescriptive as the penal system sought its bases or its justi-
fication, at first of course in a theory of justice, then, since the
nineteenth century, in a sociological, psychological, medical, and
psychiatric knowledge: it is as if even the word of the law could
no longer be authorised, in our society, except by a discourse
of truth.

   Of the three great systems of exclusion which forge discourse -
the forbidden speech, the division of madness and the will to truth,

I have spoken of the third at greatest length. The fact is that it is towards this third system that the other two have been drifting constantly for centuries. The third system increasingly attempts to assimilate the others, both in order to modify them and to provide them with a foundation. The first two are constantly becoming more fragile and more uncertain, to the extent that they are now invaded by the will to truth, which for its part constantly grows stronger, deeper, and more implacable.

And yet we speak of the will to truth no doubt least of all. It is as if, for us, the will to truth and its vicissitudes were masked by truth itself in its necessary unfolding. The reason is perhaps this: although since the Greeks 'true' discourse is no longer the discourse that answers to the demands of desire, or the discourse which exercises power, what is at stake in the will to truth, in the will to utter this 'true' discourse, if not desire and power? 'True' discourse, freed from desire and power by the necessity of its form, cannot recognise the will to truth which pervades it;[3] and the will to truth, having imposed itself on us for a very long time, is such that the truth it wants cannot fail to mask it.

Thus all that appears to our eyes is a truth conceived as a richness, a fecundity, a gentle and insidiously universal force, and in contrast we are unaware of the will to truth, that prodigious machinery designed to exclude. All those who, from time to time in our history, have tried to dodge this will to truth and to put it into question against truth, at the very point where truth undertakes to justify the prohibition and to define madness, all of them, from Nietzsche to Artaud and Bataille, must now serve as the (no doubt lofty) signs for our daily work.

III

There are, of course, many other procedures for controlling and delimiting discourse. Those of which I have spoken up to now operate in a sense from the exterior. They function as systems of exclusion. They have to do with the part of discourse which puts power and desire at stake.

I believe we can isolate another group: internal procedures, since discourses themselves exercise their own control; procedures which function rather as principles of classification, of ordering, of distribution, as if this time another dimension of discourse had to be mastered: that of events and chance.

In the first place, commentary. I suppose – but without being very certain – that there is scarcely a society without its major narratives, which are recounted, repeated, and varied; formulae, texts, and ritualised sets of discourses which are recited in well-defined circumstances; things said once and preserved because it is suspected that behind them there is a secret or a treasure. In short, we may suspect that there is in all societies, with great consistency, a kind of gradation among discourses: those which are said in the ordinary course of days and exchanges, and which

vanish as soon as they have been pronounced; and those which
give rise to a certain number of new speech-acts which take them
up, transform them or speak of them, in short, those discourses
which, over and above their formulation, are said indefinitely,
remain said, and are to be said again. We know them in our own
cultural system: they are religious or juridical texts, but also
those texts (curious ones, when we consider their status) which
are called 'literary'; and to a certain extent, scientific texts.
This differentiation is certainly neither stable, nor constant,
nor absolute. There is not, on the one side, the category of
fundamental or creative discourses, given for all time, and on
the other, the mass of discourses which repeat, gloss, and
comment. Plenty of major texts become blurred and disappear,
and sometimes commentaries move into the primary position. But
though its points of application may change, the function remains;
and the principle of a differentiation is continuously put back in
play. The radical effacement of this gradation can only ever be
play, utopia, or anguish. The Borges-style play of a commentary
which is nothing but the solemn and expected reappearance word
for word of the text that is commented on; or the play of a
criticism that would speak forever of a work which does not exist.
The lyrical dream of a discourse which is reborn absolutely new
and innocent at every point, and which reappears constantly in
all freshness, derived from things, feelings or thoughts. The
anguish of that patient of Janet's for whom the least utterance
was gospel truth, concealing inexhaustible treasures of meaning
and worthy to be repeated, re-commenced, and commented on
indefinitely: 'When I think,' he would say when reading or listening, 'when I think of this sentence which like the others will go
off into eternity, and which I have perhaps not yet fully understood.'[4]
But who can fail to see that this would be to annul one of the
terms of the relation each time, and not to do away with the
relation itself? It is a relation which is constantly changing with
time; which takes multiple and divergent forms in a given epoch.
The juridical exegesis is very different from the religious commentary (and this has been the case for a very long time). One
and the same literary work can give rise simultaneously to very
distinct types of discourse: the 'Odyssey' as a primary text is
repeated, in the same period, in the translation by Bérard, and
in the endless 'explications de texte', and in Joyce's 'Ulysses'.
For the moment I want to do no more than indicate that, in what
is broadly called commentary, the hierarchy between primary and
secondary text plays two roles which are in solidarity with each
other. On the one hand it allows the (endless) construction of
new discourses: the dominance of the primary text, its permanence, its status as a discourse which can always be re-actualised,
the multiple or hidden meaning with which it is credited, the
essential reticence and richness which is attributed to it, all this
is the basis for an open possibility of speaking. But on the other
hand the commentary's only role, whatever the techniques used,

is to say at last what was silently articulated 'beyond', in the
text. By a paradox which it always displaces but never escapes,
the commentary must say for the first time what had, nonetheless, already been said, and must tirelessly repeat what had,
however, never been said. The infinite rippling of commentaries
is worked from the inside by the dream of a repetition in disguise:
at its horizon there is perhaps nothing but what was at its point
of departure – mere recitation. Commentary exorcises the chance
element of discourse by giving it its due; it allows us to say
something other than the text itself, but on condition that it is
this text itself which is said, and in a sense completed. The open
multiplicity, the element of chance, are transferred, by the principle of commentary, from what might risk being said, on to the
number, the form, the mask, and the circumstances of the repetition. The new thing here lies not in what is said but in the
event of its return.

I believe there exists another principle of rarefaction of a discourse, complementary to the first, to a certain extent: the
author. Not, of course, in the sense of the speaking individual
who pronounced or wrote a text, but in the sense of a principle
of grouping of discourses, conceived as the unity and origin of
their meanings, as the focus of their coherence. This principle
is not everywhere at work, nor in a constant manner: there exist
all around us plenty of discourses which circulate without deriving their meaning or their efficacity from an author to whom they
could be attributed: everyday remarks, which are effaced immediately; decrees or contracts which require signatories but no
author; technical instructions which are transmitted anonymously.
But in the domains where it is the rule to attribute things to an
author – literature, philosophy, science – it is quite evident that
this attribution does not always play the same role. In the order
of scientific discourse, it was indispensable, during the Middle
Ages, that a text should be attributed to an author, since this
was an index of truthfulness. A proposition was considered as
drawing even its scientific value from its author. Since the
seventeenth century, this function has steadily been eroded in
scientific discourse: it now functions only to give a name to a
theorem, an effect, an example, a syndrome. On the other hand,
in the order of literary discourse, starting from the same epoch,
the function of the author has steadily grown stronger: all those
tales, poems, dramas or comedies which were allowed to circulate
in the Middle Ages in at least a relative anonymity are now asked
(and obliged to say) where they come from, who wrote them. The
author is asked to account for the unity of the texts which are
placed under his name. He is asked to reveal or at least carry
authentification of the hidden meaning which traverses them. He
is asked to connect them to his lived experiences, to the real
history which saw their birth. The author is what gives the dist-
urbing language of fiction its unities, its nodes of coherence, its
insertion in the real.

I know that I will be told: 'But you are speaking there of the author as he is reinvented after the event by criticism, after he is dead and there is nothing left except for a tangled mass of scribblings; in those circumstances a little order surely has to be introduced into all that, by imagining a project, a coherence, a thematic structure that is demanded of the consciousness or the life of an author who is indeed perhaps a trifle fictitious. But that does not mean he did not exist, this real author, who bursts into the midst of all these worn-out words, bringing to them his genius or his disorder.[15]

It would of course, be absurd to deny the existence of the individual who writes and invents. But I believe that – at least since a certain epoch – the individual who sets out to write a text on the horizon of which a possible oeuvre is prowling, takes upon himself the function of the author: what he writes and what he does not write, what he sketches out, even by way of provisional drafts, as an outline of the oeuvre, and what he lets fall by way of commonplace remarks – this whole play of differences is prescribed by the author-function, as he receives it from his epoch, or as he modifies it in his turn. He may well overturn the traditional image of the author; nevertheless, it is from some new author-position that he will cut out, from everything he could say and from all that he does say every day at any moment, the still trembling outline of his oeuvre.

The commentary-principle limits the chance-element in discourse by the play of an identity which would take the form of repetition and sameness. The author-principle limits this same element of chance by the play of an identity which has the form of individuality and the self.

We must also recognise another principle of limitation in what is called, not sciences but 'disciplines': a principle which is itself relative and mobile; which permits construction, but within narrow confines.

The organisation of disciplines is just as much opposed to the principle of commentary as to that of the author. It is opposed to the principle of the author because a discipline is defined by a domain of objects, a set of methods, a corpus of propositions considered to be true, a play of rules and definitions, of techniques and instruments: all this constitutes a sort of anonymous system at the disposal of anyone who wants to or is able to use it, without their meaning or validity being linked to the one who happened to be their inventor. But the principle of a discipline is also opposed to that of commentary: in a discipline, unlike a commentary, what is supposed at the outset is not a meaning which has to be rediscovered, nor an identity which has to be repeated, but the requisites for the construction of new statements. For there to be a discipline, there must be the possibility of formulating new propositions, ad infinitum.

But there is more; there is more, no doubt, in order for there to be less: a discipline is not the sum of all that can be truthfully said about something; it is not even the set of all that can be accepted about the same data in virtue of some principle of

coherence or systematicity. Medicine is not constituted by the
total of what can be truthfully said about illness; botany cannot
be defined by the sum of all the truths concerning plants. There
are two reasons for this: first of all, botany and medicine are
made up of errors as well as truths, like any other discipline –
errors which are not residues or foreign bodies but which have
positive functions, a historical efficacity, and a role that is often
indissociable from that of the truths. And besides, for a proposition to belong to botany or pathology, it has to fulfil certain
conditions, in a sense stricter and more complex than pure and
simple truth: but in any case, other conditions. It must address
itself to a determinate plane of objects: from the end of the
seventeenth century, for example, for a proposition to be 'botanical' it had to deal with the visible structure of the plant, the
system of its close and distant resemblances or the mechanism of
its fluids; it could no longer retain its symbolic value, as was the
case in the sixteenth century, nor the set of virtues and properties
which were accorded to it in antiquity. But without belonging
to a discipline, a proposition must use conceptual or technical
instruments of a well-defined type; from the nineteenth century,
a proposition was no longer medical – it fell 'outside medicine'
and acquired the status of an individual phantasm or popular
imagery – if it used notions that were at the same time metaphorical, qualitative, and substantial (like those of engorgement,
of overheated liquids or of dried-out solids). In contrast
it could and had to make use of notions that were equally metaphorical but based on another model, a functional and physiological one (that of the irritation, inflammation, or degeneration
of the tissues). Still further: in order to be part of a discipline,
a proposition has to be able to be inscribed on a certain type of
theoretical horizon: suffice it to recall that the search for the
primitive language, which was a perfectly acceptable theme up
to the eighteenth century, was sufficient, in the second half
of the nineteenth century, to make any discourse fall into – I
hesitate to say error – chimera and reverie, into pure and simple
linguistic monstrosity.
    Within its own limits, each discipline recognises true and false
propositions; but it pushes back a whole teratology of knowledge
beyond its margins. The exterior of a science is both more and
less populated than is often believed: there is of course immediate experience, the imaginary themes which endlessly carry and
renew immemorial beliefs; but perhaps there are no errors in the
strict sense, for error can only arise and be decided inside a
definite practice; on the other hand, there are monsters on the
prowl whose form changes with the history of knowledge. In
short, a proposition must fulfil complex and heavy requirements
to be able to belong to the grouping of a discipline; before it
can be called true or false, it must be 'in the true', as Canguilhem
would say.
    People have often wondered how the botanists or biologists of
the nineteenth century managed not to see that what Mendel was

saying was true. But it was because Mendel was speaking of objects, applying methods, and placing himself on a theoretical horizon which were alien to the biology of his time. Naudin, before him, had of course posited the thesis that hereditary traits are discrete; yet, no matter how new or strange this principle was, it was able to fit into the discourse of biology, at least as an enigma. What Mendel did was to constitute the hereditary trait as an absolutely new biological object, thanks to a kind of filtering which had never been used before: he detached the trait from the species, and from the sex which transmits it; the field in which he observed it being the infinitely open series of the generations, where it appears and disappears according to statistical regularities. This was a new object which called for new conceptual instruments and new theoretical foundations. Mendel spoke the truth, but he was not 'within the true' of the biological discourse of his time: it was not according to such rules that biological objects and concepts were formed. It needed a complete change of scale, the deployment of a whole new range of objects in biology for Mendel to enter into the true and for his propositions to appear (in large measure) correct. Mendel was a true monster, which meant that science could not speak of him; whereas about thirty years earlier, at the height of the nineteenth century, Scheiden, for example, who denied plant sexuality, but in accordance with the rules of biological discourse, was merely formulating a disciplined error.

It is always possible that one might speak the truth in the space of a wild exteriority, but one is 'in the true' only by obeying the rules of a discursive 'policing' which one has to reactivate in each of one's discourses.

The discipline is a principle of control over the production of discourse. The discipline fixes limits for discourse by the action of an identity which takes the form of a permanent re-actuation of the rules.

We are accustomed to see in an author's fecundity, in the multiplicity of the commentaries, and in the development of a discipline so many infinite resources for the creation of discourses. Perhaps so, but they are nonetheless principles of constraint; it is very likely impossible to account for their positive and multiplicatory role if we do not take into consideration their restrictive and constraining function.

IV

There is, I believe, a third group of procedures which permit the control of discourses. This time it is not a matter of mastering their powers or averting the unpredictability of their appearance, but of determining the condition of their application, of imposing a certain number of rules on the individuals who hold them, and thus of not permitting everyone to have access to them. There is a rarefaction, this time, of the speaking subjects; none

shall enter the order of discourse if he does not satisfy certain
requirements or if he is not, from the outset, qualified to do so.
To be more precise: not all the regions of discourse are equally
open and penetrable; some of them are largely forbidden (they
are differentiated and differentiating), while others seem to be
almost open to all winds and put at the disposal of every speaking subject, without prior restrictions.

In this regard I should like to recount an anecdote which is so
beautiful that one trembles at the thought that it might be true.
It gathers into a single figure all the constraints of discourse:
those which limit its powers, those which master its aleatory
appearances, those which carry out the selection among speaking
subjects. At the beginning of the seventeenth century, the
Shogun heard tell that the Europeans' superiority in matters of
navigation, commerce, politics, and military skill was due to their
knowledge of mathematics. He desired to get hold of so precious
a knowledge. As he had been told of an English sailor who
possessed the secret of these miraculous discourses, he sum-
moned him to his palace and kept him there. Alone with him, he
took lessons. He learned mathematics. He retained power, and
lived to a great old age. It was not until the nineteenth century
that there were Japanese mathematicians. But the anecdote does
not stop there: it has its European side too. The story has it
that this English sailor, Will Adams, was an autodidact, a carpen-
ter who had learnt geometry in the course of working in a ship-
yard. Should we see this story as the expression of one of the
great myths of European culture? The universal communication
of knowledge and the infinite free exchange of discourses in
Europe, against the monopolised and secret knowledge of Oriental
tyranny?

This idea, of course, does not stand up to examination.
Exchange and communication are positive figures working inside
complex systems of restriction, and probably would not be able
to function independently of them. The most superficial and
visible of these systems of restriction is constituted by what can
be gathered under the name of ritual. Ritual defines the qualification which must be possessed by individuals who speak (and
who must occupy such-and-such a position and formulate such-
and-such a type of statement, in the play of a dialogue, of
interrogation or recitation); it defines the gestures, behaviour,
circumstances, and the whole set of signs which must accompany
discourse; finally, it fixes the supposed or imposed efficacity of
the words, their effect on those to whom they are addressed, and
the limits of their constraining value. Religious, judicial, therapeutic, and in large measure also political discourses can scarcely
be dissociated from this deployment of a ritual which determines
both the particular properties and the stipulated roles of the
speaking subjects.

A somewhat different way of functioning is that of the 'societies
of discourse', which function to preserve or produce discourses,
but in order to make them circulate in a closed space, distributing

them only according to strict rules, and without the holders being dispossessed by this distribution. An archaic model for this is provided by the groups of rhapsodists who possessed the knowledge of the poems to be recited or potentially to be varied and transformed. But though the object of this knowledge was after all a ritual recitation, the knowledge was protected, defended and preserved within a definite group by the often very complex exercises of memory which it implied. To pass an apprenticeship in it allowed one to enter both a group and a secret which the act of recitation showed but did not divulge; the roles of speaker and listener were not interchangeable.

There are hardly any such 'societies of discourse' now, with their ambiguous play of the secret and its divulgation. But this should not deceive us: even in the order of 'true' discourse, even in the order of discourse that is published and free from all ritual, there are still forms of appropriation of secrets, and non-interchangeable roles. It may well be that the act of writing as it is institutionalised today, in the book, the publishing-system and the person of the writer, takes place in a 'society of discourse', which though diffuse is certainly constraining. The difference between the writer and any other speaking or writing subject (a difference constantly stressed by the writer himself), the intransitive nature (according to him) of his discourse, the fundamental singularity which he has been ascribing for so long to 'writing', the dissymmetry that is asserted between 'creation' and any use of the linguistic system – all this shows the existence of a certain 'society of discourse', and tends moreover to bring back its play of practices. But there are many others still, functioning according to entirely different schemas of exclusivity and disclosure: e.g., technical or scientific secrets, or the forms of diffusion and circulation of medical discourse, or those who have appropriated the discourse of politics or economics.

At first glance, the 'doctrines' (religious, political, philosophical) seem to constitute the reverse of a 'society of discourse', in which the number of speaking individuals tended to be limited even if it was not fixed; between those individuals, the discourse could circulate and be transmitted. Doctrine, on the contrary, tends to be diffused, and it is by the holding in common of one and the same discursive ensemble that individuals (as many as one cares to imagine) define their reciprocal allegiance. In appearance, the only prerequisite is the recognition of the same truths and the acceptance of a certain rule of (more or less flexible) conformity with the validated discourses. If doctrines were nothing more than this, they would not be so very different from scientific disciplines, and the discursive control would apply only to the form or the content of the statement, not to the speaking subject. But doctrinal allegiance puts in question both the statement and the speaking subject, the one by the other. It puts the speaking subject in question through and on the basis of the statement, as is proved by the procedures of exclusion and the mechanisms of rejection which come into action when a speaking subject has formulated one or several unassimilable statements; heresy and orthodoxy do not derive from a fanatical exaggeration of the doctrinal mechanisms, but rather belong fundamentally to them. And conversely the doctrine puts the statements in question on the basis of the speaking subjects, to the extent that the doctrine always stands as the sign, manifestation and instrument of a prior adherence to a class, a social status, a race, a nationality, an interest, a revolt, a resistance or an acceptance. Doctrine binds individuals to certain types of enunciation and consequently forbids them all others; but it uses, in return, certain types of enunciation to bind individuals amongst themselves, and to differentiate them by that very fact from all others. Doctrine brings about a double subjection: of the speaking subjects to discourses, and of discourses to the (at least virtual) group of speaking individuals.

On a much broader scale, we are obliged to recognise large cleavages in what might be called the social appropriation of discourses. Although education may well be, by right, the instrument thanks to which any individual in a society like ours can have access to any kind of discourse whatever, this does not prevent it from following, as is well known, in its distribution, in what it allows and what it prevents, the lines marked out by social distances, oppositions and struggles. Any system of education is a political way of maintaining or modifying the appropriation of discourses, along with the knowledges and powers which they carry.

I am well aware that it is very abstract to separate speech-rituals, societies of discourse, doctrinal groups and social appropriations, as I have just done. Most of the time, they are linked to each other and constitute kinds of great edifices which ensure the distribution of speaking subjects into the different types of discourse and the appropriation of discourses to certain categories of subject. Let us say, in a word, that those are the major procedures of subjection used by discourse. What, after all, is an education system, other than a ritualisation of speech, a qualification and a fixing of the roles for speaking subjects, the constitution of a doctrinal group, however diffuse, a distribution and an appropriation of discourse with its powers and knowledges? What is 'écriture' (the writing of the 'writers') other than a similar system of subjection, which perhaps takes slightly different forms, but forms whose main rhythms are analogous? Does not the judicial system, does not the institutional system of medicine likewise constitute, in some of their aspects at least, similar systems of subjection of and by discourse?

V

I wonder whether a certain number of themes in philosophy have not come to correspond to these activities of limitation and exclusion, and perhaps also to reinforce them.

They correspond to them first of all by proposing an ideal truth as the law of discourse and an immanent rationality as the principle of their unfolding, and they re-introduce an ethic of knowledge, which promises to give the truth only to the desire for truth itself and only to the power of thinking it.

Then they reinforce the limitations and exclusions by a denial of the specific reality of discourse in general.

Ever since the sophists' tricks and influence were excluded and since their paradoxes have been more or less safely muzzled, it seems that Western thought has taken care to ensure that discourse should occupy the smallest possible space between thought and speech. Western thought seems to have made sure that the act of discoursing should appear to be no more than a certain bridging (apport) between thinking and speaking – a thought dressed in its signs and made visible by means of words, or conversely the very structures of language put into action and producing a meaning-effect.

This very ancient elision of the reality of discourse in philosophical thought has taken many forms in the course of history. We have seen it again quite recently in the guise of several familiar themes.

Perhaps the idea of the founding subject is a way of eliding the reality of discourse. The founding subject, indeed, is given the task of directly animating the empty forms of language with his aims; it is he who in moving through the density and inertia of empty things grasps by intuition the meaning lying deposited within them; it is likewise the founding subject who founds horizons of meaning beyond time which history will henceforth only have to elucidate and where propositions, sciences and deductive ensembles will find their ultimate grounding. In his relation to meaning, the founding subject has at his disposal signs, marks, traces, letters. But he does not need to pass via the singular instance of discourse in order to manifest them.

The opposing theme, that of originating experience, plays an analogous role. It supposes that at the very basis of experience, even before it could be grasped in the form of a cogito, there were prior significations – in a sense, already said – wandering around in the world, arranging it all around us and opening it up from the outset to a sort of primitive recognition. Thus a primordial complicity with the world is supposed to be the foundation of our possibility of speaking of it, in it, of indicating it and naming it, of judging it and ultimately of knowing it in the form of truth. If there is discourse, then, what can it legitimately be other than a discreet reading? Things are already murmuring meanings which our language has only to pick up; and this language, right from its most rudimentary project, was already speaking to us of a being of which it is like the skeleton.

The idea of universal mediation is yet another way, I believe, of eliding the reality of discourse, and despite appearances to the contrary. For it would seem at first glance that by rediscovering everywhere the movement of a logos which elevates particularities

to the status of concepts and allows immediate consciousness
to unfurl in the end the whole rationality of the world, one puts
discourse itself at the centre of one's speculation. But this logos,
in fact, is only a discourse that has already been held, or rather
it is things themselves, and events, which imperceptibly turn
themselves into discourse as they unfold the secret of their own
essence. Thus discourse is little more than the gleaming of a
truth in the process of being born to its own gaze; and when
everything finally can take the form of discourse, when everything can be said and when discourse can be spoken about everything, it is because all things, having manifested and exchanged
their meaning, can go back into the silent interiority of their
consciousness of self.

Thus in a philosophy of the founding subject, in a philosophy
of originary experience, and in a philosophy of universal mediation alike, discourse is no more than a play, of writing in the
first case, of reading in the second, and of exchange in the
third, and this exchange, this reading, this writing never put
anything at stake except signs. In this way, discourse is
annulled in its reality and put at the disposal of the signifier.

What civilisation has ever appeared to be more respectful of
discourse than ours? Where has it ever been more honoured, or
better honoured? Where has it ever been, seemingly, more radically liberated from its constraints, and universalised? Yet it
seems to me that beneath this apparent veneration of discourse,
under this apparent logophilia, a certain fear is hidden. It is just
as if prohibitions, barriers, thresholds and limits had been set
up in order to master, at least partly, the great proliferation of
discourse, in order to remove from its richness the most dangerous part, and in order to organise its disorder according to
figures which dodge what is most uncontrollable about it. It is as
if we had tried to efface all trace of its irruption into the activity
of thought and language. No doubt there is in our society, and,
I imagine, in all others, but following a different outline and
different rhythms, a profound logophobia, a sort of mute terror
against these events, against this mass of things said, against
the surging-up of all these statements, against all that could be
violent, discontinuous, pugnacious, disorderly as well, and
perilous about them - against this great incessant and disordered
buzzing of discourse.

And if we want to - I would not say, efface this fear, but -
analyse it in its conditions, its action and its effects, we must, I
believe, resolve to take three decisions which our thinking today
tends to resist and which correspond to the three groups of
functions which I have just mentioned: we must call into question
our will to truth, restore to discourse its character as an event,
and finally throw off the sovereignty of the signifier.

VI

These are the tasks, or rather some of the themes, which govern
the work I should like to do here in the coming years. We can
see at once certain methodological requirements which they imply.

First of all, a principle of reversal: where tradition sees the
source of discourses, the principle of their swarming abundance
and of their continuity, in those figures which seem to play a
positive role, e.g., those of the author, the discipline, the will
to truth, we must rather recognise the negative action of a
cutting-up and a rarefaction of discourse.

But once we have noticed these principles of rarefaction, once
we have ceased to consider them as a fundamental and creative
instance, what do we discover underneath them? Must we admit
the virtual plenitude of a world of uninterrupted discourses?
This is where we have to bring other methodological principles
into play.

A principle of discontinuity, then: the fact that there are
systems of rarefaction does not mean that beneath them or beyond them there reigns a vast unlimited discourse, continuous
and silent, which is quelled and repressed by them, and which
we have the task of raising up by restoring the power of speech
to it. We must not imagine that there is a great unsaid or a great
unthought which runs throughout the world and intertwines with
all its forms and all its events, and which we would have to
articulate or to think at last. Discourses must be treated as discontinuous practices, which cross each other, are sometimes
juxtaposed with one another, but can just as well exclude or be
unaware of each other.

A principle of specificity: we must not resolve discourse into
a play of pre-existing significations; we must not imagine that
the world turns towards us a legible face which we would have
only to decipher; the world is not the accomplice of our knowledge; there is no prediscursive providence which disposes the
world in our favour. We must conceive discourse as a violence
which we do to things, or in any case as a practice which we
impose on them; and it is in this practice that the events of discourse find the principle of their regularity.

The fourth rule is that of exteriority: we must not go from discourse towards its interior, hidden nucleus, towards the heart
of a thought or a signification supposed to be manifested in it;
but, on the basis of discourse itself, its appearance and its
regularity, go towards its external conditions of possibility, towards what gives rise to the aleatory series of these events, and
fixes its limits.

Four notions, then, must serve as the regulating principle of
the analysis: the event, the series, the regularity, the condition
of possibility. Term for term we find the notion of event opposed
to that of creation, series opposed to unity, regularity opposed
to originality, and condition of possibility opposed to signification. These other four notions (signification, originality, unity,

creation) have in a general way dominated the traditional history
of ideas, where by common agreement one sought the point of
creation, the unity of a work, an epoch or a theme, the mark of
individual originality, and the infinite treasure of buried significations.

I will add only two remarks. One concerns history. It is often
entered to the credit of contemporary history that it removed the
privileges once accorded to the singular event and revealed the
structures of longer duration. That is so. However, I am not sure
that the work of these historians was exactly done in this direction. Or rather I do not think there is an inverse ratio between
noticing the event and analysing the long durations. On the contrary, it seems to be by pushing to its extreme the fine grain of
the event, by stretching the resolution-power of historical analysis
as far as official price-lists (les mercuriales), title deeds, parish
registers, harbour archives examined year by year and week by
week, that these historians saw - beyond the battles, decrees,
dynasties or assemblies - the outline of massive phenomena with
a range of a hundred or many hundreds of years. History as
practised today does not turn away from events; on the contrary,
it is constantly enlarging their field, discovering new layers of
them, shallower or deeper. It is constantly isolating new sets of
them, in which they are sometimes numerous, dense and interchangeable, sometimes rare and decisive: from the almost daily
variations in price to inflations over a hundred years. But the
important thing is that history does not consider an event without defining the series of which it is part, without specifying
the mode of analysis from which that series derives, without
seeking to find out the regularity of phenomena and the limits of
probability of their emergence, without inquiring into the variations, bends and angles of the graph, without wanting to determine the conditions on which they depend. Of course, history
has for a long time no longer sought to understand events by the
action of causes and effects in the formless unity of a great becoming, vaguely homogeneous or ruthlessly hierarchised; but
this change was not made in order to rediscover prior structures,
alien and hostile to the event. It was made in order to establish
diverse series, intertwined and often divergent but not autonomous, which enable us to circumscribe the 'place' of the event,
the margins of its chance variability, and the conditions of its
appearance.

The fundamental notions which we now require are no longer
those of consciousness and continuity (with their correlative
problems of freedom and causality), nor any longer those of sign
and structure. They are those of the event and the series, along
with the play of the notions which are linked to them: regularity,
dimension of chance (aléa), discontinuity, dependence, transformation; it is by means of a set of notions like this that my projected analysis of discourses is articulated, not on the traditional
thematics which the philosophers of yesterday still take for 'living' history, but on the effective work of historians.

Yet it is also in this regard that this analysis poses philosophical, or theoretical, problems, and very likely formidable
ones. If discourses must be treated first of all as sets of discursive events, what status must be given to that notion of event
which was so rarely taken into consideration by philosophers?
Naturally the event is neither substance nor accident, neither
quality nor process; the event is not of the order of bodies. And
yet it is not something immaterial either; it is always at the level
of materiality that it takes effect, that it is effect; it has its
locus and it consists in the relation, the coexistence, the dispersion,
the overlapping, the accumulation, and the selection of material
elements. It is not the act or the property of a body; it is produced as an effect of, and within, a dispersion of matter. Let us
say that the philosophy of the event should move in the at first
sight paradoxical direction of a materialism of the incorporeal.

Furthermore, if discursive events must be treated along the
lines of homogeneous series which, however, are discontinuous
in relation to each other, what status must be given to this discontinuity? It is of course not a matter of the succession of in-
stants in time, nor of the plurality of different thinking subjects.
It is a question of caesurae which break up the instant and dis-
perse the subject into a plurality of possible positions and functions. This kind of discontinuity strikes and invalidates the
smallest units that were traditionally recognised and which are
the hardest to contest: the instant and the subject. Beneath
them, and independently of them, we must conceive relations between these discontinuous series which are not of the order of
succession (or simultaneity) within one (or several) conscious-
nesses; we must elaborate - outside of the philosophies of the
subject and of time - a theory of discontinuous systematicities.
Finally, though it is true that these discontinuous discursive
series each have, within certain limits, their regularity, it is undoubtedly no longer possible to establish links of mechanical
causality or of ideal necessity between the elements which constitute them. We must accept the introduction of the aléa as a
category in the production of events. There once more we feel
the absence of a theory enabling us to think the relations between
chance and thought.

The result is that the narrow gap which is to be set to work in
the history of ideas, and which consists of dealing not with the
representations which might be behind discourse, but with discourses as regular and distinct series of events - this narrow gap
looks, I'm afraid, like a small (and perhaps odious) piece of
machinery which would enable us to introduce chance, the discontinuous, and materiality at the very roots of thought. This is
a triple peril which a certain form of history tries to exorcise by
narrating the continuous unravelling of an ideal necessity. They
are three notions that should allow us to connect the history of
systems of thought to the practice of historians. And they are
three directions which the work of theoretical elaboration will
have to follow.

VII

The analyses which I propose to make, following these principles
and making this horizon my line of reference, will fall into two
sets. On the one hand the 'critical' section, which will put into
practice the principle of reversal: trying to grasp the forms of
exclusion, of limitation, of appropriation of which I was speaking
just now; showing how they are formed, in response to what
needs, how they have been modified and displaced, what constraint they have effectively exerted, to what extent they have
been evaded. On the other hand there is the 'genealogical' set,
which puts the other three principles to work: how did series of
discourses come to be formed, across the grain of, in spite of,
or with the aid of these systems of constraints; what was the
specific norm of each one, and what were their conditions of
appearance, growth, variation.
    First, the critical set. A first group of analyses might deal
with what I have designated as functions of exclusion. I formerly
studied one of them, in respect of one determinate period: the
divide between madness and reason in the classical epoch. Later,
I might try to analyse a system of prohibition of language, the
one concerning sexuality from the sixteenth to the nineteenth
century. The aim would be to see not how this interdiction has
been progressively and fortunately effaced, but how it has been
displaced and re-articulated from a practice of confession in
which the forbidden behaviour was named, classified, hierarchised
in the most explicit way, up to the appearance, at first very timid
and belated, of sexual thematics in nineteenth-century medicine
and psychiatry; of course these are still only somewhat symbolic
orientation-points, but one could already wager that the rhythms
are not the ones we think, and the prohibitions have not always
occupied the place that we imagine.
    In the immediate future, I should like to apply myself to the
third system of exclusion; this I envisage in two ways. On the
one hand, I want to try to discover how this choice of truth,
inside which we are caught but which we ceaselessly renew, was
made - but also how it was repeated, renewed, and displaced. I
will consider first the epoch of the Sophists at its beginning,
with Socrates, or at least with Platonic philosophy, to see how
efficacious discourse, ritual discourse, discourse loaded with
powers and perils, gradually came to conform to a division between true and false discourse. Then I will consider the turn of
the sixteenth century, at the time when there appears, especially
in England, a science of the gaze, of observation, of the established fact, a certain natural philosophy, no doubt inseparable
from the setting-up of new political structures, and, inseparable,
too, from religious ideology; this was without a doubt a new form
of the will to know. Finally, the third orientation-point will be the
beginning of the nineteenth century, with its great acts that
founded modern science, the formation of an industrial society
and the positivist ideology which accompanied it. These will be my

three cross-sections in the morphology of our will to know, three stages of our philistinism.

I would also like to take up the same question again, but from a quite different angle: to measure the effect of a discourse with scientific claims – a medical, psychiatric, and also sociological discourse – on that set of practices and prescriptive discourses constituted by the penal system. The starting point and basic material for this analysis will be the study of psychiatric expertise and its role in penal practices.

Still looking at it from this critical perspective, but at another level, the procedures of limitation of discourses should be analysed. I indicated several of these just now: the principle of the author, of commentary, of the discipline. A certain number of studies can be envisaged from this perspective. I am thinking, for example, of an analysis of the history of medicine from the sixteenth to the nineteenth century. The objective would be not so much to pinpoint the discoveries made or the concepts put to work, but to grasp how, in the construction of medical discourse, and also in the whole institution that supports, transmits and reinforces it, the principle of the author, of the commentary, and of the discipline were used. The analysis would seek to find out how the principle of the great author operated: Hippocrates and Galen, of course, but also Paracelsus, Sydenham, or Boerhaave. It would seek to find out how the practice of the aphorism and the commentary were carried on, even late into the nineteenth century, and how they gradually gave place to the practice of the case, of the collection of cases, of the clinical apprenticeship using a concrete case. It would seek to discover, finally, according to what model medicine tried to constitute itself as a discipline, leaning at first on natural history, then on anatomy and biology.

One could also consider the way in which literary criticism and literary history in the eighteenth and nineteenth centuries constituted the person of the author and the figure of the oeuvre, using, modifying, and displacing the procedures of religious exegesis, biblical criticism, hagiography, historical or legendary 'lives', autobiography, and memoirs. One day we will also have to study the role played by Freud in psychoanalytic knowledge, which is surely very different from that of Newton in physics (and of all founders of disciplines), and also very different from the role that can be played by an author in the field of philosophical discourse (even if, like Kant, he is at the origin of a different way of philosophising).

So there are some projects for the critical side of the task, for the analysis of the instances of discursive control. As for the genealogical aspect, it will concern the effective formation of discourse either within the limits of this control, or outside them, or more often on both sides of the boundary at once. The critical task will be to analyse the processes of rarefaction, but also of regrouping and unification of discourses; genealogy will study their formation, at once dispersed, discontinuous, and regular. In truth these two tasks are never completely separable:

there are not, on one side, the forms of rejection, exclusion,
regrouping and attribution, and then on the other side, at a
deeper level, the spontaneous surging-up of discourses which,
immediately before or after their manifestation, are submitted to
selection and control. The regular formation of discourse can
incorporate the procedures of control, in certain conditions and
to a certain extent (that is what happens, for instance, when a
discipline takes on the form and status of a scientific discourse);
and conversely the figures of control can take shape within a
discursive formation (as is the case with literary criticism as the
discourse that constitutes the author): so much so that any
critical task, putting in question the instances of control, must
at the same time analyse the discursive regularities through which
they are formed; and any genealogical description must take into
account the limits which operate in real formations. The difference
between the critical and the genealogical enterprise is not so much
a difference of object or domain, but of point of attack, perspective, and delimitation.

Earlier on I mentioned one possible study, that of the taboos
which affect the discourse of sexuality. It would be difficult, and
in any case abstract, to carry out this study without analysing
at the same time the sets of discourses - literary, religious or
ethical, biological or medical, juridical too - where sexuality is discussed, and where it is named, described, metaphorised, explained, judged. We are very far from having constituted a unitary and regular discourse of sexuality; perhaps we never will,
and perhaps it is not in this direction that we are going. No matter.
The taboos do not have the same form and do not function in the
same way in literary discourse and in medical discourse, in that
of psychiatry or in that of the direction of conscience. Conversely,
these different discursive regularities do not have the same way of
reinforcing, evading, or displacing the taboos. So the study can be
done only according to pluralities of series in which there are taboos
at work which are at least partly different in each.

One could also consider the series of discourses which in the sixteenth and seventeeth centuries dealt with wealth and poverty,
money, production, commerce. We are dealing there with sets of very
heterogeneous statements, formulated by the rich and the poor, the
learned and the ignorant, protestants and catholics, officers of the
king, traders or moralists. Each one has its own form of regularity,
likewise its own systems of constraint. None of them exactly pre-
figures that other form of discursive regularity which will later take
on the air of a discipline and which will be called 'the analysis of
wealth', then 'political economy'. Yet it is on the basis of this
series that a new regularity was formed, taking up or excluding,
justifying or brushing aside this one or that one of their utterances.

We can also conceive of a study which would deal with the discourses concerning heredity, such as we can find them, up to the
beginning of the twentieth century, scattered and dispersed
through various disciplines, observations, techniques and
formulae. The task would then be to show by what play of articu-

lation these series in the end recomposed themselves, in the
epistemologically coherent and institutionally recognised figure
of genetics. This is the work that has just been done by François
Jacob with a brilliance and an erudition which could not be
equalled.

Thus the critical and the genealogical descriptions must alternate, and complement each other, each supporting the other by
turns. The critical portion of the analysis applies to the systems
that envelop discourse, and tries to identify and grasp these
principles of sanctioning, exclusion, and scarcity of discourse.
Let us say, playing on words, that it practises a studied casual-
ness. The genealogical portion, on the other hand, applies to
the series where discourse is effectively formed: it tries to grasp
it in its power of affirmation, by which I mean not so much a
power which would be opposed to that of denying, but rather
the power to constitute domains of objects, in respect of which
one can affirm or deny true or false propositions. Let us call
these domains of objects positivities, and let us say, again playing on words, that if the critical style is that of studious casual-
ness, the genealogical mood will be that of a happy positivism.

In any event, one thing at least has to be emphasised: discourse
analysis understood like this does not reveal the universality of
a meaning, but brings to light the action of imposed scarcity,
with a fundamental power of affirmation. Scarcity and affirmation; ultimately, scarcity *of* affirmation, and not the continuous
generosity of meaning, and not the monarchy of the signifier.

And now, let those with gaps in their vocabulary say - if they
find the term more convenient than meaningful - that all this is
structuralism.

VIII

I know that but for the aid of certain models and supports I
would not have been able to undertake these researches which I
have tried to sketch out for you. I believe I am greatly indebted
to Georges Dumézl, since it was he who urged me to work, at an
age when I still thought that to write was a pleasure. But I also
owe a great deal to his work. May he forgive me if I have stretched
the meaning or departed from the rigour of those texts which are
his and which dominate us today. It was he who taught me to
analyse the internal economy of a discourse in a manner quite
different from the methods of traditional exegesis or linguistic
formalism. It was he who taught me to observe the system of
functional correlations between discourses by the play of com-
parisons from one to the other. It was he who taught me how to
describe the transformations of a discourse and its relations to
institutions. If I have tried to apply this method to discourses
quite different from legendary or mythical narratives, it was
probably because I had in front of me the works of the historians
of science, especially Georges Canguilhem. It is to him that I

owe the insight that the history of science is not necessarily caught in an alternative: either to chronicle discoveries or to describe the ideas and opinions that border science on the side of its indeterminate genesis or on the side of its later expulsions, but that it was possible and necessary to write the history of science as a set of theoretical models and conceptual instruments which is both coherent and transformable.

But I consider that my greatest debt is to Jean Hyppolite. I am well aware that in the eyes of many his work belongs under the aegis of Hegel, and that our entire epoch, whether in logic or epistemology, whether in Marx or Nietzsche, is trying to escape from Hegel: and what I have tried to say just now about discourse is very unfaithful to the Hegelian logos.

But to make a real escape from Hegel presupposes an exact appreciation of what it costs to detach ourselves from him. It presupposes a knowledge of how close Hegel has come to us, perhaps insidiously. It presupposes a knowledge of what is still Hegelian in that which allows us to think against Hegel; and an ability to gauge how much our resources against him are perhaps still a ruse which he is using against us, and at the end of which he is waiting for us, immobile and elsewhere.

If so many of us are indebted to Jean Hyppolite, it is because he tirelessly explored, for us and ahead of us, this path by which one gets away from Hegel, establishes a distance, and by which one ends up being drawn back to him, but otherwise, and then constrained to leave him once again.

First of all Jean Hyppolite took the trouble to give a presence to the great and somewhat ghostly shadow of Hegel which had been on the prowl since the nineteenth century and with which people used to wrestle obscurely. It was by means of a translation (of the 'Phenomenology of Mind') that he gave Hegel this presence. And the proof that Hegel himself is well and truly present in this French text is the fact that even Germans have consulted it so as to understand better what, for a moment at least, was going on in the German version.

Jean Hyppolite sought and followed all the ways out of this text, as if his concern was: can we still philosophise where Hegel is no longer possible? Can a philosophy still exist and yet not be Hegelian? Are the non-Hegelian elements in our thought also necessarily non-philosophical? And is the anti-philosophical necessarily non-Hegelian? So that he was not merely trying to give a meticulous historical description of this presence of Hegel: he wanted to make it into one of modernity's schemata of experience (is it possible to think science, history, politics and everyday suffering in the Hegelian mode?); and conversely he wanted to make our modernity the test of Hegelianism and thereby of philosophy. For him the relation to Hegel was the site of an experiment, a confrontation from which he was never sure that philosophy would emerge victorious. He did not use the Hegelian system as a reassuring universe; he saw in it the extreme risk taken by philosophy.

Hence, I believe, the displacements he carried out, not so
much within Hegelian philosophy but upon it, and upon philosophy
as Hegel conceived it. Hence also a whole inversion of themes.
Instead of conceiving philosophy as the totality at last capable
of thinking itself and grasping itself in the movement of the
concept, Jean Hyppolite made it into a task without end set
against an infinite horizon: always up early, his philosophy was
never ready to finish itself. A task without end, and consequently
a task forever re-commenced, given over to the form and the
paradox of repetition: philosophy as the inaccessible thought of
the totality was for Jean Hyppolite the most repeatable thing in
the extreme irregularity of experience; it was what is given and
taken away as a question endlessly taken up again in life, in
death, in memory. In this way he transformed the Hegelian theme
of the closure on to the consciousness of self into a theme of
repetitive interrogation. But philosophy, being repetition, was
not ulterior to the concept; it did not have to pursue the edifice
of abstraction, it had always to hold itself back, break with its
acquired generalities and put itself back in contact with non-
philosophy. It had to approach most closely not the thing that
completes it but the thing that precedes it, that is not yet
awakened to its disquiet. It had to take up the singularity of
history, the regional rationalities of science, the depth of memory
within consciousness – not in order to reduce them but in order
to think them. Thus there appears the theme of a philosophy that
is present, disquieted, mobile all along its line of contact with
non-philosophy, yet existing only by means of non-philosophy
and revealing the meaning it has for us. If philosophy is in this
repeated contact with non-philosophy, what is the beginning of
philosophy? Is philosophy already there, secretly present in
what is not itself, starting to formulate itself half-aloud in the
murmur of things? But then perhaps philosophical discourse no
longer has a raison d'être; or must it begin from a foundation
that is at once arbitrary and absolute? In this way the Hegelian
theme of the movement proper to the immediate is replaced by
that of the foundation of philosophical discourse and its formal
structure.
    And finally the last displacement that Jean Hyppolite carried
out on Hegelian philosophy: if philosophy must begin as an
absolute discourse, what about history? And what is this beginning which begins with a single individual, in a society, in a
social class, and in the midst of struggles?
    These five displacements, leading to the extreme edge of
Hegelian philosophy, and no doubt pushing it over on to the
other side of its own limits, summon up one by one the great
figures of modern philosophy, whom Hyppolite never ceased confronting with Hegel: Marx with the questions of history, Fichte
with the problem of the absolute beginning of philosophy, Bergson
with the theme of contact with the non-philosophical, Kierkegaard
with the problem of repetition and truth, Husserl with the theme
of philosophy as an infinite task linked to the history of our

rationality. And beyond these philosophical figures we perceive all the domains of knowledge that Jean Hyppolite invoked around his own questions: psychoanalysis with the strange logic of desire; mathematics and the formalisation of discourse; information-theory and its application in the analysis of living beings; in short, all those domains about which one can ask the question of a logic and an existence which never stop tying and untying their bonds.

I believe that Hyppolite's work, articulated in several major books, but invested even more in his researches, in his teaching, in his perpetual attention, in his constant alertness and gener-osity, in his responsibilities which were apparently administrative and pedagogic but in reality doubly political, came upon and for-mulated the most fundamental problems of our epoch. There are many of us who owe him an infinite debt.

It is because I have no doubt borrowed from him the meaning and possibility of what I am doing, and because he very often gave me illumination when I was working in the dark, that I wanted to place my work under his sign, and that I wanted to conclude this presentation of my plans by evoking him. It is in his direction, towards this lack - in which I feel both his absence and my own inadequacy - that my questionings are now converging.

Since I owe him so much, I can well see that in choosing to invite me to teach here, you are in large part paying homage to him. I am grateful to you, profoundly grateful, for the honour that you have done me, but I am no less grateful for the part he plays in this choice. Though I do not feel equal to the task of succeed-ing him, I know that, on the other hand, if such a happiness could have been granted us tonight, he would have encouraged me by his indulgence.

And now I understand better why I found it so difficult to be-gin just now. I know now whose voice it was that I would have liked to precede me, to carry me, to invite me to speak, to lodge itself in my own discourse. I know what was so terrifying about beginning to speak, since I was doing so in this place where I once listened to him, and where he is no longer here to hear me.

Translated by Ian McLeod

NOTES

(All notes are by the editor)
1   Samuel Beckett, 'The Unnamable', in 'Trilogy', London, Calder and Boyars, 1959, p. 418.
2   The subject of the debate between Foucault and Derrida. Derrida's review of 'Madness and Civilization' is reprinted in 'Writing and Difference', trans. Alan Bass, London, Routledge & Kegan Paul, 1978, pp. 31-63. Foucault's reply, an appendix to the second edition of 'Madness and Civilization' (1972), is translated as My Body, This Paper, This Fire in 'The Oxford

Literary Review', 4:1, 1979, pp. 9-28. Foucault's remarks
here continue the debate. In 'Madness and Civilization'
Foucault had argued that an 'epistemological break' had
occurred between the medieval and classical eras; the pivot
of this shift was Descartes, the effect of it was to change
the 'free exchange' of reason and madness in the medieval
period into the privileging of reason and the exclusion of
madness in the classical period. Derrida argues that this
implies a metaphysics of presence or origins, and attempts
to show that the division is constitutive of language itself.
Here Foucault claims that it is possible to see the division
occurring during the history of Greek thought, so disputing
Derrida's claim that the Logos was always already split, even
for the Greeks. The effect of Foucault's remarks is to imply
a structure of repetition, which avoids any notion of an
original presence, or origins in general. For further discussion by Derrida, see 'L'Archéologie du frivole', first published as a preface to Condillac's 'Essai sur l'origine des
connaissances humaines', Paris, Galilée, 1973, republished
as a separate volume by Denöel/Gonthier, 1976. For further
discussions of the debate, see Edward Said, The Problem of
Textuality: Two Exemplary Positions, 'Critical Inquiry', 4:4,
Summer 1978, pp. 673-714; and Shoshana Felman, Madness
and Philosophy or Literature's Reason, 'Yale French Studies',
52, 1975, pp. 206-28.

3   'The necessity of its form': that is, discourse in its form as
    constituted by Plato, viz., the laws of logic.
4   Pierre Janet (1859-1947), clinical psychologist, best known
    for 'L'état mental des hystériques' (1892). Janet was Charcot's
    pupil and successor at the Salpêtrière, the famous Paris
    hospital where Freud studied in 1885-6.
5   Foucault here alludes to Alexandre Dumas *fils*, 'Kean, ou
    Désordre génie'ie' (1836). The play was adapted by Jean-
    Paul Sartre in 1954: 'Kean', Paris, Gallimard.

FURTHER READING

ADAMS, PARVEEN and MINSON, JEFF, The 'Subject' of Feminism,
    in 'm/f', 2, 1978, pp. 43-61.
BAUDRILLARD, JEAN, 'Oublier Foucault', Paris, Galilée, 1977.
BERSANI, LEO, The Subject of Power, in 'Diacritics', 7:3, Fall
    1977, pp. 2-21.
CARROLL, DAVID, The Subject of Archeology or the Sovereignty
    of the Episteme, in 'Modern Language Notes', 93:4, May 1978,
    pp. 695-722.
DELEUZE, GILLES, Ecrivain non: Un nouveau cartographe (re-
    view of 'Discipline and Punish'), in 'Critique', 31, no. 343,
    December 1975, pp. 1207-27.
FELMAN, SHOSHANA, Madness and Philosophy or Literature's
    Reason, in 'Yale French Studies', 52, 1975, pp. 206-28.

— Women and Madness: The Critical Phallacy, in 'Diacritics', 5:4, Winter 1975, pp. 2-10.
— 'La Folie et la chose littéraire', Paris, Seuil, 1978.
FOUCAULT, MICHEL, 'Madness and Civilization: A History of Insanity in the Age of Reason', trans. Richard Howard, New York, Pantheon, 1965. (Translation of the abridged edition (10/18, 1961); a translation of the original Plon edition (1961) is in preparation).
— 'The Birth of the Clinic: An Archaeology of Medical Perception', trans. A.M. Sheridan Smith, London, Tavistock, 1973.
— 'Raymond Roussel', Paris, Gallimard, 1963.
— 'The Order of Things', trans. anonymous, London, Tavistock, 1970.
— 'The Archaeology of Knowledge', trans. A.M. Sheridan Smith, London, Tavistock, 1972.
— 'Discipline and Punish', trans. A.M. Sheridan Smith, London, Allen Lane, 1977.
— 'The History of Sexuality. Volume 1: An Introduction', trans. Robert Hurley, London, Allen Lane, 1979. (As Colin Gordon suggests, it would be more accurate to refer to this volume as 'The Will to Know'.)
(Collections:) 'Language, Counter-Memory, Practice', ed and trans. Donald F. Bouchard and Sherry Simon, Ithaca, Cornell University Press, 1977.
— 'Power/Knowledge, Selected Interviews and Other Writings, 1972-1977', ed and trans. Colin Gordon, Hassocks, Harvester, 1980.
MINSON, JEFF, Strategies for Socialists? Foucault's Conception of Power, in 'Economy and Society', 9:1, February 1980, pp. 1-43.
MORRIS, MEAGHAN and PATTON, PAUL (eds), 'Michel Foucault: Power, Truth, Strategy', Sydney, Feral Publications, 1979 (contains useful bibliography, pp. 92-100).
SAID, EDWARD, An Ethics of Language, in 'Diacritics', 4:2,pp. 28-37.
— Abecedarium Culturae, in 'Beginnings: Intention and Method', New York, Basic Books, 1975, pp. 283-315.
— The Problem of Textuality: Two Exemplary Positions, in 'Critical Inquiry': 4:4, Summer 1978, pp. 673-714.
— 'Orientalism', London, Routledge & Kegan Paul, 1978.
— (ed), 'Literature and Society', Baltimore, Johns Hopkins University Press, 1979.
SEEM, MARK D., Liberation of Difference: Toward a Theory of Antiliterature, in 'New Literary History', 5:1, Autumn 1975, pp. 119-33.

4 ON LITERATURE AS AN IDEOLOGICAL FORM

Etienne Balibar and
Pierre Macherey

[Macherey's 'A Theory of Literary Production' (first published in
1966) outlined a critical strategy which focused on the conditions
of a text's production as inscribed 'silently' within the text itself.
This strategy was a development of the Althusserian concept of
the 'symptomatic reading' (from 'Reading Capital'), which reconstructs a field of discourse in order to locate the conditions of a
text's possibility. In 'A Theory' Macherey aimed at articulating
the hidden effects of ideological contradiction within a text, contradictions masked by various formal devices such as resolutions
at the level of plot and character.

In an interview in 'Red Letters' (5, 1977), Macherey explains
that the difference between that formalistic early work and the
present essay, -On Literature as an Ideological Form-, should be
seen in terms of the effect of Althusser's -On Ideology and Ideological State Apparatuses- (1969). Althusser's essay was,
Macherey suggests, a theoretical development that resulted from
reflection on the events of May 1968 in France. The importance
of Althusser's essay lay in the fact that it broke with the 'essentialist' concept of ideology which sees ideology in terms of
'illusion' versus 'reality', a system of (false) ideas masking the
'real' material structure. Against this notion of 'false consciousness', which had been particularly influential through the work
of Georg Lukács, Althusser's essay proposed that ideology is
the material system of social practices. To study ideology is to
study not ideas, but the material practices of certain (religious,
educational, familial, legal, etc.) ideological state apparatuses
and the processes by which subjects become constituted in
ideology.

The effect of this essay on Macherey's work was that his attention shifted from the problem of the relation of the work to its
historical conditions of production, to that work's specific historical (or contemporary) ideological effects in the society in which
it is read. Renée Balibar's 'Les français fictifs', to which this
essay constituted a preface, tests Althusser's hypothesis in an
analysis of the specific uses of literature as a part of the schooling system; it concludes that the differences between literary
and spoken French are used for a materially discernible effect
of ideological domination through language.

Althusser, in fact, had considered art to be a special case,
existing 'mid-way' between ideology and science (i.e. 'knowledge').
He saw its peculiar effect as that of the 'internal distancing' of
the ideological, so making us 'see'. Balibar and Macherey reject

this view, arguing that any study of art from the point of view of aesthetics (and they would characterise most literary criticism in this way) is necessarily implicated in the process of ideological domination. Calling for a complete break with aesthetics, Balibar and Macherey also reject the category of 'literature'. As Foucault points out in 'The Order of Things' (p. 300), the concept of 'literature' was specifically invented for the bourgeois epoch in the nineteenth century. Balibar and Macherey argue that the literary phenomenon does not exist outside its historical and social conditions. Literary works do not exist as transcendent objects, eternal and immutable. And just as they are produced under determinate historical conditions, so they are reproduced under different conditions in each epoch. The idea of the literary work as an object-in-itself is meaningless. This is because it can never be considered apart from its specific effects - effects which are determined materially within social practices.]

Is there a Marxist theory of literature? In what could it consist? This is a classic question, and often purely academic. We intend to reformulate it in two stages and suggest new propositions.

1   MARXIST THESES ON LITERATURE AND THE CATEGORY OF 'REFLECTION'

1.1 *Can there be a 'Marxist aesthetic'?*

It is not our intention to give an account of the attempts which have been made to substantiate this idea nor the controversies which have surrounded it. We will merely point out that to constitute an aesthetic (and particularly a literary aesthetic) has always presented Marxism with two kinds of problem, which can be combined or held separate: (i) How to explain the specific ideological mode for 'art' and the 'aesthetic' effect. (ii) How to analyse and explain the class position (or the class positions, which may be contradictory in themselves) of the author and more materially the 'literary text', within the ideological class struggle.

The first problem is obviously brought in, imposed on Marxism by the dominant ideology so as to force the Marxist critic to produce his own aesthetic and to 'settle accounts' with art, the work of art, the aesthetic effect, just like Lessing, or Hegel, or Taine, or Valéry, et al. Since the problem is imposed on Marxism from outside, it offers two alternatives: to reject the problem and so be 'proved' unable to explain, not so much a 'reality' as an absolute 'value' of our time, which is now supreme since it has replaced religious value; or to recognise the problem and therefore be forced to acknowledge aesthetic 'values', i.e., to submit to them. This is an even better result for the dominant ideology since it thereby makes Marxism concede to the 'values' of the dominant class within its own problematic - a result which has great political significance in a period when Marxism becomes the ideology of the working class.

The second problem meanwhile is induced from within the theory and practice of Marxism, on its own terrain, but in such a way that it can remain a formal and mechanical presentation. In this case the necessary criterion is that of practice. In the first place, of scientific practice: the question for Marxism should be, does the act of confronting literary texts with their class positions result in the opening of new fields of knowledge and in the first place simply in the siting of new problems? The proof of the right formulation would be whether it makes objectively clear within historical materialism itself whole sets of unsolved and sometimes as yet unrecognised problems.[1]

In the second place, of political practice itself, in so much as it is operative within literature. The least one should therefore ask a Marxist theory is that it should bring about real transformation, new practice, whether in the production of texts and 'works of art' or in their social 'consumption'. But is this a real transformation, even if at times it does have an immediate political effect - the simple fact of instilling the practitioners of art (writers and artists, but also teachers and students) with a Marxist ideology of the form and social function of art (even if this operation may sometimes have a certain immediate political interest)? Is it enough simply to give Marxism and its adherents their turn to taste and consume works of art in their own way? In effect experience proves that it is perfectly possible to substitute new 'Marxist' themes, i.e. formulated in the language of Marxism, for the ideological notions dominant in 'cultural life', notions that are bourgeois or petit-bourgeois in origin, and yet not alter at all the place of art and literature within social practice, nor therefore the practical relationship of individuals and classes to the works of art they produce and consume. The category of art in general dominates production and consumption, which are conceived and practised within this mode - whether 'committed', 'socialist', 'proletarian', or whatever.

Yet in the Marxist classics there were elements which can open a path (frayer la voie) - not an 'aesthetic', nor a 'theory of literature', any more than a 'theory of knowledge'. Yet through their mode of practising literature and the implications of a theoretical position based ultimately on revolutionary class practice, they pose certain theses about literary effects, which, worked within the problematic of historical materialism, make theses for a scientific and therefore historical analysis of literary effects.[2]

These very general premises are enough to show at once that the two types of problem between which Marxist attempts are divided, are really one and the same. To be able to analyse the nature and expression of class positions in literature and its output (the 'texts', 'works' perceived as literature) is simultaneously to be able to define and know the ideological mode of literature. But this means that the problem must be posed in terms of a theory of the history of literary effects, clearly showing the primary elements of their relation to their material base,

their progressions (for they are not eternal) and their tendential
transformations (for they are not immutable).

1.2 The materialist category of reflection

Let us be clear. The classic Marxist theses on literature and art
set out from the essential philosophical category of the reflection.
To understand this category fully is therefore the key to the
Marxist conception of literature.

In the Marxist texts on this materialist concept, Marx and Engels
on Balzac, Lenin on Tolstoy, it is qua material reflection, reflection of objective reality, that literature is conceived as an historic
reality - in its very form, which scientific analysis seeks to grasp.

In the 'Talks at the Yenan Forum on Literature and Art', Mao
Tse-Tung writes, 'Works of literature and art, as ideological
forms, are the product of the reflection in the human brain of the
life of a given society.'[3] So the first implication of the category
of reflection for Marxist theoreticians is to provide an index of
reality of literature. It does not 'fall from the heavens', the product of a mysterious 'creation', but is the product of social practice (rather a particular social practice); neither is it an 'imaginary' activity, albeit it produces imaginary effects, but inescap-
ably part of a material process, 'the product of the reflection . . .
of the life of a given society'.

The Marxist conception thus inscribes literature in its place in
the unevenly determined system of real social practices: one of
several ideological forms within the ideological superstructures,
corresponding to a base of social relations of production which
are historically determined and transformed, and historically
linked to other ideological forms. Be sure that in using the term
ideological forms no reference to formalism is intended - the historical materialist concept does not refer to 'form' in opposition
to 'content', but to the objective coherence of an ideological formation - we shall come back to this point. Let us note too that
this first, very general but absolutely essential premise, has no
truck with queries about what ideological form is taken by literature within the ideological instance. There is no 'reduction' of
literature to morality, religion, politics, etc.

The Marxist concept of reflection has suffered from so many mis-
interpretations and distortions that we must stop here for a
mement. The conclusions reached by Dominique Lecourt through
an attentive reading of Lenin's 'Materialism and Empiriocriticism'
will be useful to us.[4]

Dominique Lecourt shows that the Marxist and Leninist category
of reflection contains two propositions which are combined within
a constitutive order - or better, two articulated successive problems. (Thus according to Lecourt there is not one simple thesis,
but a double thesis of the reflection of things in thought.)

The first problem, which materialism always re-establishes in
its priority, is the problem of the objectivity of the reflection. It
poses the question: 'Is there an existent material reality reflected
in the mind which determines thought?' And consequently it has

the rider, 'Is thought itself a materially determined reality?'
Dialectical materialism asserts the objectivity of the reflection
and the objectivity of thought as reflection, i.e., the determinance of the material reality which precedes thought and is irreducible to it, and the material reality of thought itself.

The second problem, which can only be posed correctly on the
basis of the first, concerns the scientific knowledge of the exactitude of the reflection. It poses the question, '*If* thought reflects
an existent reality how accurate is its reflection?' or better,
'Under what conditions (i.e. historical conditions whereby the
dialectic between "absolute truth" and "relative truth" intervenes)
can it provide an accurate reflection?' The answer lies in the
analysis of the relatively autonomous process of the history of
science. In the context, it is clear that this second problem poses
the question, 'What form does the reflection take?' But it only has
a materialist implication once the first question has been posed
and the objectivity of the reflection affirmed.

The result of this analysis, which we have only given in outline,
is to show that the Marxist category of the 'reflection' is quite
separate from the empiricist and sensualist concept of the image,
reflection as 'mirroring'. The reflection, in dialectical materialism,
is a 'reflection without a mirror'; in the history of philosophy this
is the only effective destruction of the empiricist ideology which
calls the relation of thought to the real a speculary (and therefore
reversible) reflection. This is thanks to the complexity of the
Marxist theory of 'reflection': it poses the separate nature of two
propositions and their articulation in an irreversible order within
which the materialist account is realised.

These observations are central to the problem of the 'theory of
literature'. A rigorous use of this complex structure eliminates
the seeming opposition of two contrary descriptions: that between
formalism and the 'critical' or 'normative' use of the notion of
'realism'. That is, on one side an intention to study the reflection
'for itself', independent of its relationship to the material world;
on the other, a confusion of both aspects and an assertion of the
primacy of thought, a reversal of the materialist order.[5]

Hence the advantage of a rigorous definition like Lenin's, for it
is then possible to articulate, in theory as in fact, two aspects
which must be both kept separate and in a constitutive order:
literature as an ideological form (amongst others), and the specific
process of literary production.

1.3 *Literature as an ideological form*

It is important to 'locate' the production of literary effects historically as part of the ensemble of social practices. For this to be
seen dialectically rather than mechanically, it is important to
understand that the relationship of 'history' to 'literature' is not
like the relationship or 'correspondence' of two 'branches', but
concerns the developing forms of an internal contradiction. Literature and history are not each set up externally to each other
(not even as the history *of* literature versus social and political

history), but are in an intricate and connected relationship, the
historical conditions of existence of anything like a literature.
Very generally, this internal relationship is what constitutes the
definition of literature as an ideological form.

But this definition is significant only in so far as its implications are then developed. Ideological forms, to be sure, are not
straightforward systems of 'ideas' and 'discourses', but are manifested through the workings and history of determinate practices
in determinate social relations, what Althusser calls the Ideological State Apparatuses (ISA). The objectivity of literary production therefore is inseparable from given social practices in a given
ISA. More precisely, we shall see that it is inseparable from a given
linguistic practice (there is a 'French' literature because there is
a linguistic practice 'French', i.e. a contradictory ensemble making a national tongue), in itself inseparable from an academic or
schooling practice which defines both the conditions for the consumption of literature and the very conditions of its production
also. By connecting the objective existence of literature to this
ensemble of practices, one can define the material anchoring
points which make literature an historic and social reality.

First, then, literature is historically constituted in the bourgeois epoch as an ensemble of language - or rather of specific
linguistic practices - inserted in a general schooling process so
as to provide appropriate fictional effects, thereby reproducing
bourgeois ideology as the dominant ideology. Literature submits
to a threefold determination: 'linguistic', 'pedagogic', and 'fictive'
(imaginaire) (we must return to this point, for it involves the
question of a recourse to psychoanalysis for an explanation of
literary effects). There is a linguistic determinance because the
work of literary production depends on the existence of a common
language codifying linguistic exchange, both for its material and
for its aims - in so much as literature contributes directly to the
maintenance of a 'common language'. That it has this starting
point is proved by the fact that divergences from the common
language are not arbitrary but determined. In our introduction
to the work of R. Balibar and D. Laporte, we sketched out an
explanation of the historical process by which this 'common
language' is set up.[6] Following their thought, we stressed that
the common language, i.e. the national language, is bound to
the political form of 'bourgeois democracy' and is the historical
outcome of particular class struggles. Like bourgeois right, its
parallel, the common national language is needed to unify a new
class domination, thereby universalising it and providing it with
progressive forms throughout its epoch. It refers therefore to a
social contradiction, perpetually reproduced via the process which
surmounts it. What is the basis of this contradiction?

It is the effect of the historic conditions under which the bourgeois class established its political, economic and ideological
dominance. To achieve hegemony, it had not only to transform the
base, the relations of production, but also radically to transform
the superstructure, the ideological formations. This transforma-

tion could be called the bourgeois 'cultural revolution' since it
involves not only the formation of a new ideology, but its realisation
as the dominant ideology, through new ISA and the remoulding
of the relationships between the different ISA. This revolutionary
transformation, which took more than a century but which was
preparing itself for far longer, is characterised by making
the school apparatus the means of forcing submission to the dominant ideology - individual submission, but also, and more importantly, the submission of the very ideology of the dominated
classes. Therefore in the last analysis, all the ideological contradictions rest on the contradictions of the school apparatus, and
become contradictions subordinated to the form of schooling,
within the form of schooling itself.

We are beginning to work out the form taken by social contradictions in the schooling apparatus. It can only establish itself
through the formal unity of a unique and unifying educational
system, the product of this same unity, which is itself formed
from the co-existence of two systems or contradictory networks:
those which, by following the institutional division of 'levels of
teaching' which in France has long served to materialise this contradiction, we could call the apparatus of 'basic education'
(primaire-professionnel) and that of 'advanced education'
(secondaire-supérieur).[7]

This division in schooling, which reproduces the social division
of a society based on the sale and purchase of individual labour-
power, while ensuring the dominance of bourgeois ideology through
asserting a specifically national unity, is primarily and throughout based on a linguistic division. Let us be clear: there as well,
the unifying form is the essential means of the division and of the
contradiction. The linguistic division inherent in schooling is not
like the division between different 'languages' observable in certain pre-capitalist social formations - those languages being a
'language of the common people' (dialect, patois or argot), and a
'language of the bourgeoisie' - on the contrary, the division presupposes a common language, and is the contradiction between
different practices of the same language. Specifically, it is in and
through the educational system that the contradiction is instituted
- through the contradiction between the basic language (français
elementaire), as taught at primary school, and the literary
language (français littéraire) reserved for the advanced level of
teaching. This is the basis of the contradiction in schooling techniques, particularly between the basic exercise of 'rédaction-
narration', a mere training in 'correct' usage and the reporting of
'reality', and the advanced exercise of comprehension, the
'dissertation-explication de textes', so-called 'creative' work which
presupposes the incorporation and imitation of literary material.
Hence the contradictions in schooling practice, and in ideological
practice and in social practice. What thus appears as the basis of
literary production is an unequal and contradictory relation
to the same ideology, the dominant one. But this contradiction
would not exist if the dominant ideology did not have to

struggle all the time for its priority.

From this analysis, given in mere outline, there is an essential point to be grasped: the objectivity of literature, i.e. its relation to objective reality by which it is historically determined, is not a relation to an 'object' which it represents, is not representative. Nor is it purely and simply the instrument for using and transforming its immediate material, the linguistic practices determined within the practice of teaching. Precisely because of their contradictions, they cannot be used as a simple primary material: thus all use is an intervention, made from a standpoint, a declaration (in a general sense) from within the contradiction and hence a further development of it. So, the objectivity of literature is its necessary place within the determinate processes and reproduction of the contradictory linguistic practices of the common tongue, in which the effectivity of the ideology of bourgeois education is realised.

This siting of the problem abolishes the old idealist question, 'What is literature?', which is not a question about its objective determinance, but a question about its universal essence, human and artistic.[8] It abolishes it because it shows us directly the material function of literature, inserted within a process which literature cannot determine even though it is indispensable to it. If literary production has for its material and specific base the contradictions of linguistic practices in schooling taken up and internalised (through an indefinitely repeated labour of fiction), it is because literature itself is one of the terms of the contradiction whose other term is determinately bound to literature. Dialectically, literature is simultaneously product and material condition of the linguistic division in education, term and effect of its own contradictions. Not surprising therefore that the ideology of literature, itself a part of literature, should work ceaselessly to deny this objective base: to represent literature supremely as 'style', as individual genius, conscious or natural, as creativity, etc., as something outside (and above) the process of education, which is merely able to disseminate literature, and to comment on it exhaustively, though with no possibility of finally capturing it. The root of this constitutive repression is the objective status of literature as an historic ideological form, its relation to the class struggle. And the first and last commandment in its ideology is: 'Thou shalt describe all forms of class struggle, save that which determines thine own self.'

By the same token, the question of the relation of literature to the dominant ideology is posed afresh – escaping a confrontation of universal essences, in which many Marxist discussions have been trapped. To see literature as ideologically determined is not – cannot be – to 'reduce' it to moral ideologies or to political, religious, even aesthetic ideologies which are definable outside literature. Nor is it to make ideology the content to which literature brings form – even when there are themes and ideological statements which are more or less perfectly separable. Such a pairing is thoroughly mechanical, and, moreover, serves to corroborate the way in which the ideology of literature by displacement misconstrues its historic determinance. It merely prolongs the endless false dialectic of 'form' and 'content' whereby the artifically imposed terms alternate so that literature is sometimes perceived as content (ideology), sometimes as form ('real' literature). To define literature as a particular ideological form is to pose quite another problem: the specificity of ideological effects produced by literature and the means (techniques) of production. This returns us to the second question involved in the dialectical materialist concept of reflection.

2 THE PROCESS OF PRODUCTION OF AESTHETIC EFFECTS IN LITERATURE

By now, thanks to the proper use of the Marxist concept of reflection, we are able to avoid the false dilemma of the literary critic (should he analyse literature on its own ground - search out its essence, - or from an external standpoint - find out its function?). Once we know better than to reduce literature either to something other than itself or to itself, but instead analyse its ideological specificity,[9] helped by the conclusions of R. Balibar, we can attempt to trace the material concepts which appear in this analysis. Of course such a sketch has only a provisional value - but it helps us to see the consistency of the material concept of literature and its conceptual place within historical materialism.

As we see it, these concepts have three moments. They refer simultaneously to (i) the contradictions which ideological literary formations (texts) realise and develop; (ii) the mode of ideological identification produced by the action of fiction; and (iii) the place of literary aesthetic effects in the reproduction of the dominant ideology. Let us deal with each one schematically.

2.1 *The specific complexity of literary formations - ideological contradictions and linguistic conflicts*
The first principle of a materialist analysis would be: literary productions must not be studied from the standpoint of their unity which is illusory and false, but from their material disparity. One must not look for unifying effects but for signs of the contradictions (historically determined) which produced them and which appear as unevenly resolved conflicts in the text.

So, in searching out the determinant contradictions, the materialist analysis of literature rejects on principle the notion of 'the work' - i.e., the illusory presentation of the unity of a text, its totality, self-sufficiency and perfection (in both senses of the word: success and completion). More precisely, it recognises the notion of 'the work' (and its correlative, 'the author') only in order to identify both as necessary illusions written into the ideology of literature, the accompaniment of all literary production. The text is produced under conditions which represent it as a finished work, providing a requisite order, expressing

either a subjective theme or the spirit of the age, according to
whether the reading is a naive or a sophisticated one. Yet in itself the text is none of these things: on the contrary, it is materially incomplete, disparate and diffuse from being the outcome
of the conflicting contradictory effect of superimposing real processes which cannot be abolished in it except in an imaginary way.[10]

To be more explicit: literature is produced finally through the
effect of one or more ideological contradictions precisely because
these contradictions cannot be solved within the ideology, i.e.,
in the last analysis through the effect of contradictory class positions within the ideology, as such irreconcilable. Obviously these
contradictory ideological positions are not in themselves 'literary' -
that would lead us back into the closed circle of 'literature'. They
are ideological positions within theory and practice, covering the
whole field of the ideological class struggle, i.e. religious, judicial, and political, and they correspond to the conjunctures of
the class struggle itself. But it would be pointless to look in the
texts for the 'original' bare discourse of these ideological positions, as they were 'before' their 'literary' realisations, for these
ideological positions can only be formed in the materiality of the
literary text. That is, they can only appear in a form which provides their imaginary solution, or better still, which displaces
them by substituting imaginary contradictions soluble within the
ideological practice of religion, politics, morality, aesthetics and
psychology.

Let us approach this phenomenon more closely. We shall say
that literature 'begins' with the imaginary solution of implacable
ideological contradictions, with the representation of that solution:
not in the sense of representing i.e. 'figuring' (by images, allegories, symbols or arguments) a solution which is really there (to
repeat, literature is produced because such a solution is impossible)
but in the sense of providing a 'mise en scène', a presentation
as solution of the very terms of an insurmountable contradiction,
by means of various displacements and substitutions. For
there to be a literature, it must be the very terms of the contradiction (and hence of the contradictory ideological elements) that
are enunciated in a special language, a language of 'compromise',
realising in advance the fiction of a forthcoming conciliation. Or
better still it finds a language of 'compromise' which presents the
conciliation as 'natural' and so both necessary and inevitable.

In 'A Theory of Literary Production', with reference to Lenin's
work on Tolstoy, and Verne and Balzac, the attempt was made to
use materialist principles to show the complex contradictions which
produce the literary text: in each case, specifically, what can be
identified as the ideological project of the author, the expression
of one determinate class position, is only one of the terms of the
contradiction of whose oppositions the text makes an imaginary
synthesis despite the real oppositions which it cannot abolish.
Hence the idea that the literary text is not so much the expression
of ideology (its 'putting into words' [sa mise en mots]) as its
staging (mise en scène), its display, an operation which has an

inbuilt disadvantage since it cannot be done without showing its
limits thereby revealing its inability to subsume a hostile ideology.
But what remained unclear in 'A Theory' is the process of literary production, the textual devices which present the contradictions of an ideological discourse at the same as the fiction of its
unity and its reconciliation, conditionally upon this same fiction.
What still evades us, in other words, is the specific mechanism of
the literary 'compromise', in so much as the materialist account is
still too general. The work of R. Balibar makes it possible to sur-
mount this difficulty and so not only complete the account but also
to correct and transform it.
   What does R. Balibar show us? That the discourse, literature's
own special 'language', in which the contradictions are set out,
is not outside ideological struggles as if veiling them in a neutral,
neutralising way. Its relation to these struggles is not secondary
but constitutive; it is always ready implicated in producing them.
Literary language is itself formed by the effects of a class contradiction. This is fundamental, bringing us back to the material
base of all literature. Literary language is produced in its specificity (and in all permitted individual variants) at the level of
linguistic conflicts, historically determined in the bourgeois epoch
by the development of a 'common language' and of an educational
system which imposes it on all, whether cultured or not.
   This, schematically put, is the principle of the complex nature
of literary formations, the production of which shares the material
conditions necessary to the bourgeois social formation and transforms itself accordingly. It is the imaginary solution of ideological
contradictions in so much as they are formulated in a special
language which is both different from the common language and
within it (the common language itself being the product of an internal conflict), and which realises and masks in a series of com-
promises the conflict which constitutes it. It is this displacement
of contradictions which R. Balibar calls 'literary style' and whose
dialectic she has begun to analyse. It is remarkable dialectic, for
it succeeds in producing the effect and the illusion of an imaginary
reconciliation of irreconcilable terms by displacing the ensemble
of ideological contradictions on to a single one, or a single aspect,
the linguistic conflict itself. So the imaginary solution has no
other 'secret' than the development, the redoubling of the contradiction: this is surely if one knows how to analyse it and work it
out, the proof of its irreconcilable nature.
   We are now ready to outline the principal aspects of the aesthetic
effect of literature as an ideological device.

2.2   *Fiction and realism: the mechanism of identification in*
      literature
Here we must pause, even if over-schematically, to consider a
characteristic literary effect which has already been briefly mentioned: the identification effect. Brecht was the first Marxist
theoretician to focus on this by showing how the ideological effects
of literature (and of the theatre, with the specific transformations

that implies) materialise via an identification process between the reader or the audience and the hero or anti-hero, the simultaneous mutual constitution of the fictive 'consciousness' of the character with the ideological 'consciousness' of the reader.[11]

But it is obvious that any process of identification is dependent on the constitution and recognition of the individual as 'subject' - to use a very common ideological notion lifted by philosophy from the juridical and turning up under various forms in all other levels of bourgeois ideology. Now all ideology, as Althusser shows in his essay -Ideology and Ideological State Apparatuses-, must in a practical way 'hail or interpellate individuals as subjects': so that they perceive themselves as such, with rights and duties, the obligatory accompaniments. Each ideology has its specific mode: each gives to the 'subject' - and therefore to other real or imaginary subjects who confront the individual and present him with his ideological identification in a personal form - one or more appropriate names. In the ideology of literature, the nomenclature is: Authors (i.e. signatures), Works (i.e. titles), Readers, and Characters (with their social background, real or imaginary).

But in literature, the process of constituting subjects and setting up their relationships of mutual recognition necessarily takes a detour via the fictional world and its values, because that process (i.e. of constitution and setting-up) embraces within its circle the 'concrete' or 'abstract' 'persons' which the text stages. We now reach a classic general problem: what is specifically 'fictional' about literature? We shall preface our solution with a parenthesis.

Mostly when one speaks of fiction in literature it means the singling out of certain 'genres' privileged as fiction: the novel, tale, short story. More generally, it indicates something which, whatever its traditional genre, can be appealed to as novelistic, it 'tells a story', whether about the teller himself or about other characters, about an individual or an idea. In this sense, the idea of fiction becomes allegorically the definition of literature in general, since all literary texts involve a story or a plot, realistic or symbolic, and arrange in a 'time', actual or not, chronological or quasi-chronological, an unrolling of events which do or do not make sense (in formalist texts, order can be reduced to a verbal structure only). All description of literature in general, as of fiction, seems to involve a primary element: the dependence on a story which is analogous to 'life'.

But this characteristic involves another, more crucial still: the idea of confronting a model. All 'fiction', it seems, has a reference point, whether to 'reality' or to 'truth', and takes its meaning from that. To define literature as fiction means taking an old philosophical position, which since Plato has been linked with the establishing of a theory of knowledge, and confronting the fictional discourse with a reality, whether in nature or history, so that the text is a transposition, a reproduction, adequate or not, and valued accordingly and in relation to standards of verisimilitude and artistic licence.

No need to go further into details: it is enough to recognise
the consistency which links the definition of literature as fiction
with a particular appropriation of the category realism.
As everyone knows, realism is the key-word of a school: that
in favour of a realist 'literature' in place of 'pure fiction', i.e.
bad fiction. This too implies a definition of literature in general:
all literature must be realist, in one way or another, a representation of reality, even and especially when it gives reality an image
outside immediate perception and daily life and common experience.
The 'shores' of reality can stretch to infinity.
And yet the idea of realism is not the opposite of fiction: it
scarcely differs from it. It too has the idea of a model and of its
reproduction, however complex that may be – a model outside the
representation, at least for the fleeting instant of evaluation –
and of a norm, even if it is nameless.
After this digression we can get back to the problem we had
set ourselves. Marxist propositions, provisory and immature as
they may be, are nevertheless bound to carry out a profound
critical transformation of the classic idealist problematic. Let us
have no doubt, for instance, that the classics of Marxism, no
more than Brecht and Gramsci who can be our guides here, never
dealt with literature in terms of 'realism'. The category of reflection, central to the Marxist problematic as we have shown, is not
concerned with realism but with materialism, which is profoundly
different. Marxism cannot define literature in general as fiction
in the classic sense.
Literature is not fiction, a fictive image of the real, because it
cannot define itself simply as a figuration, an appearance of
reality. By a complex process, literature is the production of a
certain reality, not indeed (one cannot over-emphasise this) an
autonomous reality, but a material reality, and of a certain social
effect (we shall conclude with this). Literature is not therefore
fiction, but the production of fictions: or better still, the production of fiction-effects (and in the first place the provider of the
material means for the production of fiction-effects).
Similarly, as the 'reflection of the life of a given society', historically given (Mao), literature is still not providing a 'realist'
reproduction of it, even and least of all when it proclaims itself
to be such, because even then it cannot be reduced to a straight
mirroring. But it is true that the text does produce a reality-
effect. More precisely it produces simultaneously a reality-effect
and a fiction-effect, emphasising first one and then the other,
interpreting each by each in turn but always on the basis of their
dualism.
So, it comes to this once more: fiction and realism are not the
concepts for the production of literature but on the contrary the
notions produced by literature. But this leads to remarkable consequences for it means that the model, the real referent 'outside'
the discourse which both fiction and realism presuppose, has no
function here as a non-literary non-discursive anchoring point
predating the text. (We know by now that this anchorage, the

primacy of the real, is different from and more complex than a
'representation'.) But it does function as an effect of the discourse. So, the literary discourse itself institutes and projects
the presence of the 'real' in the manner of an hallucination.
How is this materially possible? How can the text so control
what it says, what it describes, what it sets up (or 'those' it
sets up) with its sign of hallucinatory reality, or contrastingly,
its fictive sign, diverging, infinitesimally perhaps, from the
'real'? On this point too, in parts of their deep analysis, the
works we have used supply the material for an answer. Once
more they refer us to the effects and forms of the fundamental
linguistic conflict.

In a study of 'modern' French literary texts, carefully dated
in each case according to their place in the history of the common
language and of the educational system, R. Balibar refers to the
production of 'imaginary French' (français fictif). What does this
mean? Clearly not pseudo-French, elements of a pseudo-language,
seeing that these literary instances do also appear in certain contexts chosen by particular individuals, e.g. by compilers of dic-
tionaries who illustrate their rubrics only with literary quotations.
Nor is it simply a case of the language being produced in fiction
(with its own usages, syntax and vocabulary), i.e. that of
characters in a narrative making an imaginary discourse in an imaginary language. Instead, it is a case of expressions which always di-
verge in one or more salient details from those used in practice
outside the literary discourse, even when both are grammatically
'correct'. These are linguistic 'compromise formations', compromis-
ing between usages which are socially contradictory in practice and
hence mutually exclude each other. In these compromise formations there is an essential place, more or less disguised but recognisable, for the reproduction of 'simple' language, 'ordinary'
language, French 'just like that', i.e. the language which is
taught in elementary school as the 'pure and simple' expression
of 'reality'. In R. Balibar's book there are numerous examples
which 'speak' to everyone, re-awakening or reviving memories
which are usually repressed (it is their presence, their reproduction - the reason for a character or his words and for what the
'author' makes himself responsible for without naming himself -
which produces the effect of 'naturalness' and 'reality', even if
it is only by a single phrase uttered as if in passing). In comparison, all other expressions seem 'arguable', 'reflected' in a
subjectivity. It is necessary that first of all there should be
expressions which seem objective: these are the ones which in the
text itself produce the imaginary referent of an elusive 'reality'.

Finally, to go back to our starting point: the ideological effect
of identification produced by literature or rather by literary texts,
which Brecht, thanks to his position as a revolutionary and
materialist dramatist, was the first to theorise. But there is only
ever identification of one subject with another (potentially with
'oneself': 'Madame Bovary, c'est moi', familiar example, signed
Gustave Flaubert). And there are only ever subjects through the

interpellation of the individual into a subject by a Subject who
names him, as Althusser shows: 'tu es Un tel, et c'est à toi que
Je m'adresse'; 'Hypocrite lecteur, mon semblable, mon frère',
another familiar example, signed Charles Baudelaire. Through
the endless functioning of its texts, literature unceasingly 'produces' subjects, on display for everyone. So paradoxically using
the same schema we can say: literature endlessly transforms
(concrete) individuals into subjects and endows them with a
quasi-real hallucinatory individuality. According to the fundamental mechanism of the whole of bourgeois ideology, to produce
subjects ('persons' and 'characters') one must oppose them to
objects, i.e. to things, by placing them in and against a world
of 'real' things, outside it but always in relation to it. The realistic effect is the basis of this interpellation which makes characters or merely discourse 'live' and which makes readers take up
an attitude towards imaginary struggles as they would towards
real ones, though undangerously. They flourish here, the subjects we have already named: the Author and his Readers, but
also the Author and his Characters, and the Reader and his
Characters via the mediator, the Author – the Author identified
with his Characters, or 'on the contrary' with one of their
Judges, and likewise for the Reader. And from there, the Author,
the Reader, the Characters opposite their universal abstract subjects: God, History, the People, Art. The list is neither final
nor finishable: the work of literature is by definition to prolong
and expand it indefinitely.

2.3   *The aesthetic effect of literature as ideological domination-
      effect*
The analysis of literature (its theory, criticism, science etc.) has
always had as its given object either – from a spiritualist perspective – the essence of Works and Authors, or better of the
Work (of Art) and of Writing, above history, even and especially
when seeming its privileged expression; or – from an empiricist
(but still idealist) perspective – the ensemble of literary 'facts',
the supposedly objective and documentary givens which lend
biographical and stylistic support to 'general facts,' the 'laws' of
genres, styles and periods. From a materialist point of view, one
would analyse literary effects (more precisely, aesthetic literary
effects) as effects which cannot be reduced to ideology 'in general'
because they are particular ideological effects, in the midst of others
(religious, juridical, political) to which they are linked but from
which they are separate.
   This effect must finally be described at a threefold level, re-
lating to the three aspects of one social process and its successive
historical forms:- (1) its production under determinate social
conditions; (2) its moment in the reproduction of the dominant
ideology; (3) and consequently as in itself an ideological
domination-effect. To demonstrate this: the literary effect is
socially produced in a determined material process. This is the
process of constitution, i.e. the making and composing of texts,

the 'work' of literature. Now, the writer is neither supreme creator, founder of the very conditions to which he submits (in particular, as we have seen, certain objective contradictions within ideology), nor its opposite - expendable medium, through whom is revealed the nameless power of inspiration, or history, or period, or even class (which comes to the same thing). But he is a material agent, an intermediary inserted in a particular place, under conditions he has not created, in submission to contradictions which by definition he cannot control, through a particular social division of labour, characteristic of the ideological superstructure of bourgeois society, which individuates him.[12]

The literary effect is produced as a complex effect, not only, as shown, because its determinant is the imaginary resolution of one contradiction within another, but because the effect produced is simultaneously and inseparably the materiality of the text (the arrangement of sentences), and its status as a 'literary' text, its 'aesthetic' status. That is, it is both a material outcome and a particular ideological effect, or rather the production of a material outcome stamped with a particular ideological effect which marks it ineradicably. It is the status of the text in its characteristics - no matter what the terms, which are only variants: its 'charm', 'beauty', 'truth', 'significance', 'worth', 'profundity', 'style', 'writing', 'art', etc. Finally, it is the status of the text per se, quite simply, for in our society only the text is valid in itself, revealer of its true form; equally, all texts once 'written' are valid as 'literary'. This status extends as well to all the historic dissimilar modes of reading texts: the 'free' reading, reading for the pure 'pleasure' of letters, the critical reading giving a more or less theorised, more or less 'scientific' commentary on form and content, meaning, 'style', 'textuality' (revealing neologism!) - and behind all readings, the explication of texts by academics which conditions all the rest.

Therefore, the literary effect is not just produced by a determinate process, but actively inserts itself within the reproduction of other ideological effects: it is not only itself the effect of material causes, but is also an effect on socially determined individuals, constraining them materially to treat literary texts in a certain way. So, ideologically, the literary effect is not just in the domain of 'feeling', 'taste', 'judgment', and hence of aesthetic and literary ideas; it sets up a process itself: the rituals of literary consumption and 'cultural' practice.

That is why it is possible (and necessary) when analysing the literary effect as produced qua text and by means of the text, to treat as equivalents the 'reader' and the 'author'. Equivalent too are the 'intentions' of the author - what he expresses whether in the text itself (integrated within the 'surface' narrative) or alongside the text (in his declarations or even in his 'unconscious' motives as sought out by literary psychoanalysis) - and the interpretations, criticism and commentaries evoked from readers, whether sophisticated or not.

It is not important to know whether the interpretation 'really' identifies the author's intention (since the latter is not the cause of literary effects but is one of the effects). Interpretations and commentaries reveal the (literary) aesthetic effect, precisely, in full view. Literariness is what is recognised as such, and it is recognised as such precisely in the time and to the extent that it activates the interpretations, the criticisms and the 'readings'. This way a text can very easily stop being literary or become so under new conditions.

Freud was the first to follow this procedure in his account of the dream-work and more generally in his method of analysing the compromise formations of the unconscious; he defined what must be understood by the 'text' of the dream. He gave no import-ance to restoring the manifest content of the dream – to a careful isolated reconstruction of the 'real' dream. Or at least he accedes to it only through the intermediary of the 'dream narrative', which is already a transposition through which via condensation, dis-placement, and dream symbolism, repressed material makes its play. And he posited that the text of the dream was both the object of analysis and explanation simultaneously, through its own contradictions, the means of its own explanation: it is not just the manifest text, the narrative of the dream, but also all the 'free' associations (i.e., as one well knows, the forced asso-ciations, imposed by the psychic conflicts of the unconscious), the 'latent thoughts' for which the dream (or symptom) can serve as a pretext and which it arouses.

In the same way, criticism, the discourse of literary ideology, an endless commentary on the 'beauty' and 'truth' of literary texts, is a train of 'free' associations (in actuality forced and predetermined) which develops and realises the ideological effects of a literary text. In a materialist account of the text one must take them not as located above the text, as the beginnings of its explication, but as belonging to the same level as the text, or more precisely to the same level as the 'surface' narrative whether that is figurative, allegorically treating with certain general ideas (as in the novel or autobiography) or straightforwardly 'abstract', non-figurative (as in the moral or political essay). They are the tendential prolongation of this facade. Free from all question of the individuality of the 'writer', the 'reader' or the 'critic', these are the same ideological conflicts, resulting in the last instance from the same historic contradictions, or from their transformations, that produce the form of the text and of its commentaries.

Here is the index of the structure of the process of reproduc-tion in which the literary effect is inserted. What is in fact 'the primary material' of the literary text? (But a raw material which always seems to have been already transformed by it). It is the ideological contradictions which are not specifically literary but political, religious, etc.; in the last analysis, contradictory ideological realisations of determinate class positions in the class struggle. And what is the 'effect' of the literary text? (at least on those readers who recognise it as such, those of the dominant cultured class). Its effect is to provoke other ideological dis-courses which can sometimes be recognised as literary ones but which are usually merely aesthetic, moral, political, religious discourses in which the dominant ideology is realised.

We can now say that the literary text is the agent for the reproduction of ideology in its ensemble. In other words, it induces by the literary effect the production of 'new' discourses which always reproduce (under constantly varied forms) the same ideology (with its contradictions). It enables individuals to appropriate ideology and make themselves its 'free' bearers and even its 'free' creators. The literary text is a privileged operator in the concrete relations between the individual and ideology in bourgeois society and ensures its reproduction. To the extent that it induces the ideological discourse to leave its subject matter which has always already been invested as the aesthetic effect, in the form of the work of art, it does not seem a mechanical imposition, forced, revealed like a religious dogma, on individuals who must repeat it faithfully. Instead it appears as if offered for interpretations, a free choice, for the subjective private use of individuals. It is the privileged agent of ideological subjection, in the democratic and 'critical' form of 'freedom of thought'.[13]

Under these conditions, the aesthetic effect is also inevitably an effect of domination: the subjection of individuals to the dominant ideology, the dominance of the ideology of the ruling class.

It is inevitably therefore an uneven effect which does not operate uniformly on individuals and particularly does not operate in the same way on different and antagonistic social classes. 'Subjection' must be felt by the dominant class as by the dominated but in two different ways. Formally, literature as an ideological formation realised in the common language, is provided and destined for all and makes no distinctions between readers but for their own differing tastes and sensibilities, natural or acquired. But concretely, subjection means one thing for the members of the educated dominant class: 'freedom' to think within ideology, a submission which is experienced and practised as if it were a mastery, another for those who belong to the exploited classes: manual workers or even skilled workers, employees, those who according to official statistics never 'read' or rarely. These find in reading nothing but the confirmation of their inferiority: subjection means domination and repression by the literary discourse of a discourse deemed 'inarticulate' and 'faulty' and inadequate for the expression of complex ideas and feelings.

This point is vital to an analysis. It shows that the difference is not set up after the event as a straightforward inequality of reading power and assimilation, conditioned by other social inequalities. It is implicit in the very production of the literary effect and materially inscribed in the constitution of the text.

But one might say, how is it clear that what is implicit in the structure of the text is not just the discourse of those who practise literature but also, most significantly, the discourse of those who do not know the text and whom it does not know; i.e. the discourse of those who 'write' (books) and 'read' them, and the discourse of those who do not know how to do it although quite

simply they 'know how to read and write' – a play of words and a
profoundly revealing double usage. One can understand this
only by reconstituting and analysing the linguistic conflict in its
determinant place as that which produces the literary text and
which opposes two antagonistic usages, equal but inseparable,
of the common language: on one side, 'literary' French which is
studied in higher education (l'enseignement secondaire et supér-
ieur) and on the other 'basic', 'ordinary' French which far from
being natural, is also taught at the other level (à l'école primaire).
It is 'basic' only by reason of its unequal relation to the other,
which is 'literary' by the same reason. This is proved by a comparative and historical analysis of their lexical and syntactical
forms – which R. Balibar is one of the first to undertake system-
atically.

So, if in the way things are, literature can and must be used
in secondary education both to fabricate and simultaneously dominate, isolate and repress the 'basic' language of the dominated
classes, it is only on condition that that same basic language
should be present in literature, as one of the terms of its constitutive contradiction – disguised and masked, but also necessarily given away and exhibited in the fictive reconstructions.
And ultimately this is because literary French embodied in literary texts is both tendentially distinguished from (and opposed
to) the common language and placed within its constitution and
historic development, so long as this process characterises general education because of its material importance to the development of bourgeois society. That is why it is possible to assert
that the use of literature in schools and its place in education is
only the converse of the place of education in literature, and
that therefore the basis of the production of literary effects is
the very structure and historical role of the currently dominant
ideological state apparatus. And that too is why it is possible to
denounce as a denial of their own real practice the claims of the
writer and his cultured readers to rise above simple classroom
exercises, and evade them.

The effect of domination realised by literary production presupposes the presence of the dominated ideology within the dominant ideology itself. It implies the constant 'activation' of the
contradiction and its attendant ideological risk – it thrives on
this very risk which is the source of its power. That is why,
dialectically, in bourgeois democratic society, the agent of the
reproduction of ideology moves tendentially via the effects of
literary 'style' and linguistic forms of compromise. Class struggle
is not abolished in the literary text and the literary effects which
it produces. They bring about the reproduction, as dominant, of
the ideology of the dominant class.

Translated by Ian McLeod, John Whitehead and Ann Wordsworth

NOTES

1   [In the Althusserian formulation, 'science' is distinguished
    from 'ideology' not so much by what it 'knows' as by the fact
    that it produces new 'problematics', new objects of possible
    knowledge and new problems about them. The effect of
    ideology, according to Althusser, is the reverse of this; it
    contains any problems or contradictions by masking them with
    fictional or imaginary resolutions.]
2   Lenin shows this clearly in his articles on Tolstoy. [Lenin's
    articles on Tolstoy, written 1908-11, are reprinted as an
    appendix to Macherey's 'A Theory of Literary Production',
    pp. 299-323.]
3   'Selected Readings from the Works of Mao Tse-Tung (A)',
    Peking, Foreign Language Press, 1971, p. 250.
4   Dominique Lecourt, 'Une crise et son enjeu (Essai sur la
    position de Lénine en philosophie)', collection Theorie, Paris,
    Maspero, 1973.
5   [Macherey and Balibar here refer to structuralism (and also,
    by implication, to the journal 'Tel Quel'), and to the concept
    of realism, as espoused by Lukács.]
6   R. Balibar and D. Laporte, 'Le français national (constitution
    de la langue nationale commune à l'époque de la révolution
    démocratique bourgeoise)', Paris, Hachette, 1974. [Introduced
    by E. Balibar and P. Macherey].
7   Readers are referred to the first two chapters of J. Baudelot
    and R. Establet, 'L'Ecole capitaliste en France', Paris, Maspero,
    1972.
8   [Macherey and Balibar are referring here to Sartre's 'What is
    Literature?' (1948). In the 'Red Letters' interview, Macherey adds
        He was looking for a definition, a theory of what literature
        is, and in my view, this sort of enterprise is really very
        traditional and not very revolutionary. The question 'what
        is literature?' is as old as the hills; it revives . . . an
        idealist and conservative aesthetic. If I had a single clear
        idea when I began my work, it was that we must abandon
        this kind of question because 'what is literature?' is a false
        problem. Why? Because it is a question which already con-
        tains an answer. It implies that literature is *something*,
        that literature exists as a *thing*, as an eternal and unchange-
        able thing with an essence.]
9   See Pierre Macherey, 'A Theory of Literary Production', 1966.
10 Rejecting the mythical unity and completeness of a work of
    art does not mean adopting a reverse position - that of see-
    ing the work of art as anti-nature, a violation of order (as in
    'Tel Quel'). Such reversals are characteristic of conservative
    ideology: 'For oft a fine disorder stems from art' (Boileau)!
11 [See 'Brecht on Theatre', trans. John Willett, London,
    Methuen, 1964.]
12 [On the category of the author, see also Michel Foucault, The
    Order of Discourse, Chapter 3, above; What Is an Author?,

in 'Language, Counter-Memory, Practice', ed and trans.
Donald F. Bouchard, Ithaca, Cornell, 1977, pp.
113–38; and Roland Barthes, The Death of the Author, in 'Image-Music-Text', essays selected and translated by Stephen Heath, London, Fontana, 1977, pp. 142–8.]
13 One could say that there is no proper religious literature; at least there was not before the bourgeois epoch, by which time religion had been instituted as a form (subordinant and contradictory) of the bourgeois ideology itself. Rather, literature itself and the aesthetic ideology played a decisive part in the struggle against religion, the ideology of the dominant feudal class.

FURTHER READING

ALTHUSSER, LOUIS, Ideology and Ideological State Apparatuses (Notes towards an Investigation), and A Letter on Art in Reply to Andre Daspré, in 'Lenin and Philosophy and Other Essays', trans. Ben Brewster, London, New Left Books, 1971, pp. 121–73, 203–8.

BALIBAR, RENÉE, 'Les français fictifs: le rapport des styles littéraires au français national', Paris, Hachette, 1974.
— An Example of Literary Work in France: George Sand's 'La mare au diable'/'The Devil's Pool' of 1846, in F. Barker et al. (eds), 'The Sociology of Literature: 1848', Essex Conference Proceedings, 1978, pp. 27–46.

BENNETT, TONY, 'Formalism and Marxism', London, Methuen, 1979.
COUSINS, MARK, Material Arguments and Feminism, in 'm/f', 2, 1978, pp. 62–70.

EAGLETON, TERRY, 'Criticism and Ideology, A Study in Marxist Literary Theory', London, New Left Books, 1976.
HIRST, PAUL Q., Althusser and the Theory of Ideology, in 'Economy and Society', 5:4, November 1976, pp. 385–412.
JAMESON, FREDRIC, Imaginary and Symbolic in Lacan: Marxism, Psychoanalytic Criticism, and the Problem of the Subject, in 'Yale French Studies', 55/56, 1977, pp. 338–95.

MACHEREY, PIERRE, 'A Theory of Literary Production' (1966), trans. Geoffrey Wall, London, Routledge & Kegan Paul, 1978.
— Problems of Reflection, in Francis Barker et al. (eds), 'Literature, Society and the Sociology of Literature', Essex Conference Proceedings, 1977, pp. 41–54.
— Histoire et romans dans 'Les Paysans' de Balzac, in 'Socio-critique', Claude Duchet (ed), Paris, Nathan, 1979, pp. 137–46.

PÊCHEUX, MICHEL, 'Stating the Obvious: From Semantics to Discourse', London, Macmillan, 1980.
'Sub-Stance', Socio-Criticism, 15, 1976.
WILLIAMS, RAYMOND, 'Keywords: A Vocabulary of Culture and Society', London, Fontana, 1976 (see pp. 150–4 for a history of the concept of 'Literature'; cf. also Tony Davies, Education, Ideology and Literature, in 'Red Letters', 7, 1978, pp. 4–15).

Part Two

STRUCTURALISMS WAKE

What is being called in question here, where the limitations of a familiar conception of semiotics are concerned, is not merely the theoretical presupposition on which the conception is based and which biases it towards discovering in every kind of field analogues of the system of language. Such rigidity has merely served to throw into relief a shortcoming of linguistics itself: established as a science in as much as it focuses on language as a social code, the science of linguistics has no way of apprehending anything in language which belongs not with the social contract but with play, pleasure or desire. . . .

Thus we reach a crucial point in semiotic research: of its possible deployment as a critique of its own presuppositions (Julia Kristeva).

5 INTERPRETATION AND DESCRIPTIVE POETRY:

A Reading of Wordsworth's 'Yew-Trees'

Michael Riffaterre

[The effect of the work of Michael Riffaterre is to shift stylistic criticism towards a theory of reading and of the production of meaning. The literary phenomenon that he seeks to isolate is the relationship between text and reader, not that between author and text (the traditional area for historical enquiry). The reader is, as Riffaterre points out, 'the only one who makes the connections between text, interpretant, and intertext, the one in whose mind the semiotic transfer from sign to sign takes place' ('Semiotics of Poetry', p. 164).

Just as for Chomsky a speaker/hearer's competence is specified by a set of rules which 'generate' an (infinite) set of sentences, so for Riffaterre the language of a text functions according to predictable patterns within the semiotic system of poetry. The effect of these patterns in the system is to overdetermine the occurrence of a given sign in any text. Thus the functioning of a poetic text is defined by Riffaterre as follows:

Poetic discourse is the equivalence established between a word and a text, or a text and another text.

The poem results from the transformation of the matrix, a minimal and literal sentence, into a longer, complex and non-literal periphrasis. The matrix is hypothetical, being only the grammatical and lexical actualisation of a structure. The matrix may be epitomized in one word, in which case the word will not appear in the text. It is always actualised in successive variants; the form of these variants is governed by the first or primary actualisation, the model. Matrix, model, and text are variants of the same structure ('Semiotics of Poetry', p. 19).

The poem's content and form are created by a constant tension and shifting away from the matrix, which is usually repressed. Effectively, any poem in Riffaterre's system becomes a deviation from a single image, cliché or stereotype, and is only understood and gives pleasure in so far as it is a variation from such a norm. The reader rationalises the poem back into its hypothetical pre-detour, pre-transformation stage, and thus perceives its contents - the matrix. Riffaterre adds, 'the paradox is that while the poetic text is interpreted as a departure from the norm, that imaginary . . . norm is in effect deduced, or even retroactively fantasised, from the text perceived as departure' ('Semiotics of Poetry', p. 164). There is a problem here, which revolves around the question of whether the matrix is in fact a 'kernel' which produced the poem, or whether it really is only a retrospective deduction, a 'norm'. Riffaterre suggests that the correct answer is that it is a retrospective deduction, but this in itself poses new problems which can be illustrated by the fact that the 'norm' comes to resemble rather closely Freud's Primal Scene. If it does work in the same way – as a hypothetical deduction that is only retrospectively fantasised – then it must also be stressed that this will inevitably be some sort of interpretation, and that the analysis will thus be caught, as ever, within the hermeneutic circle. The matrix, or kernel word, that is chosen will still depend on what the reader wishes to find, and will, in effect, depend upon his interpretation of the poem as a whole.

It might be objected that in so far as the text works within an ascertainable semiotic system, then any variation ought to be impossible. In this respect, Riffaterre works within the tradition of E.D. Hirsch, and, like Hirsch, wants to find a valid, unequivocally correct interpretation. This in fact tends to lead him to imply that the matrix *is* a kernel which produced the poem. In 'Yew-Trees', Riffaterre chooses 'yew-tree' as his matrix: darkness, growth, mortality, ghosts, etc. are all overdetermined syntagms that necessarily follow. Yet this reading does assume that a poem grows from a kernel word and develops toward a final single statement of significance. It is unable to deal with any sort of dialectical structure. The possibility of a dialectical reading is given in Brooks and Warren's banal summary of the subject-matter of the poem in 'Understanding Poetry': 'There is in Lorton Vale a single yew-tree of enormous age and size. But even more remarkable is the grove of four yew-trees at Borrowdale' (p. 274). Despite the platitude of this description, it shows how the poem is both split, and divided against itself (one against four). In Riffaterre's description, the significance of this is effaced.

It is, however, precisely this which is developed in Geoffrey Hartman's reply to Riffaterre's essay, punningly entitled – The Use and Abuse of Structural Analysis –. Hartman argues that Riffaterre's conclusion – 'sensation is all' – is inadequate to 'the spiritual and historical complexity of Romantic poetry'. For Hartman, poetry not only conveys knowledge, but is itself a cognitive activity. He argues that Riffaterre's method is limited because it cannot follow the movement of a poem if it should deviate from the expected pattern. Thus Riffaterre does not find the absence of consciousness in the poem at all problematic or strange either. In fact, Hartman suggests, the absence of consciousness is more an elision than an absence of the human intermediary or observer. The effect of this impersonal structure is to negate self-reference and make a ghost of the speaker. Where Riffaterre puts only language, Hartman as a phenomenologist wishes to put 'the subjectivity or consciousness of the poet' – even if here that consciousness is only a ghostly or imagined death.

The subtlety of Hartman's reading is itself an argument against what Riffaterre calls 'the sin of brilliance'. Riffaterre's present position is that criticism should limit itself to what is available to

the average reader. Hartman, on the other hand, builds his
whole reading on what would be scarcely available to an 'average
reader' (if such a person exists). He suggests that in the sudden
pre-eminence of the word 'united' we also in a ghostly way hear
the dream-word 'yew-nited'. The four yew trees that make up the
single grove of Borrowdale themselves become figurations of the
'esemplastic' imagination, the 'unity in multeity'. Emphasising the
element of darkness in the grove, Hartman links this to the per-
sephonic shade of the Romantic imagination in general, and to
the series of melancholy tree poems of Wordsworth and Coleridge
in particular - a series that began, fittingly enough, with
Wordsworth's -Lines Left Upon a Seat in a Yew-Tree-.
 Faced with Riffaterre's 'materialism of the word', Hartman ad-
mits to missing what he calls the

> chastening and sceptical attitude towards meaning in Valéry and
> the later semioticians. For them, a text or a meaning is a residue,
> an abandoned series of transformations, an incomplete or frozen
> metamorphosis. Each interpreter is a new Ovid, translating the
> text into subtler surfaces (p. 185).

For Hartman as Ovid the question of the reader that we posit in
interpretation is crucial; for Hartman this simply means himself
('Confession - I have a superiority complex vis-à-vis other
critics') and few would deny the value of his own meteoric flight
that shades the text into subtler surfaces. On the other hand,
as with his more recent development and affirmation of the concept of 'voice' in the face of deconstruction, we may also detect
a certain defensiveness as well in his reassertion, against
Riffaterre, of a ghostly consciousness in the poem. It could be
argued that the effect of Hartman's phenomenological position is
that Wordsworth's poems are always translated back to a hypo-
stasised consciousness, an interpretation first projected in 'The
Unmediated Vision' (1954).
 Hartman points to the positivistic organicist assumptions in
Riffaterre's methodology; his whole essay is an argument against
the powerful determinism that Riffaterre claims for the reading
process. Other problems would seem to include the fact that there
is no recognition in Riffaterre's work of the ideology of a semiotic
system, nor any reflection on the functioning of that ideology. (A
very simple example of this would be that whereas he claims that
Wordsworth's references to 'Azincour . . . Crecy . . . Poictiers'
are simply markers for durability (history and fame), and that
any exotic names would do, it could be objected that there is a
significance in the fact that all these battles were English victories
against the French, in itself not insignificant in a poem written
between 1804 and 1814.) For Riffaterre, however, the system
that he describes is entirely self-referential. There is no place
for the connotative element analysed at such length by Barthes,
a concept that has been rejected by semioticians in general,
largely because it is not susceptible to the sort of precise analysis

and dissection that they require. For similar reasons, perhaps, there is no recognition in Riffaterre's work of the effects of the unconscious upon the processes of reading and writing (or vice versa). Finally, there is little engagement with the charge of essentialism which could be levelled against the concept of the matrix.

These problems, interesting though they are, should not be allowed to efface the more strategic usefulness of Riffaterre's work. For what is particularly valuable is Riffaterre's stress on the non-representational nature of poetry, and hence what he calls the 'referential fallacy' of criticism which presumes that we have to verify information about actual yew-trees, or research into the historical accuracy of Wordsworth's description, in order to read, appreciate, or understand the poem. As Riffaterre reminds us, 'texts are made of words, not things or ideas' (-A Stylistic Approach to Literary History-, p. 147). -Interpretation and Descriptive Poetry- is also included here both because it is an example of the very best kind of structuralist analysis, and also because the scrupulousness of its attention to the detail of the way in which language works in a text shows how such work produces and enables possibilities for post-structuralist criticism. Riffaterre has been more wary than some to move in that direction, but his movements have always come from the implications of his own work. Thus, in his most recent book in English, his insistence on self-referentiality is extended to the more complex concept of intertextuality ('the poem is made up of texts, of fragments of texts, integrated with or without conversion into a new system'). Similarly, his stress on the separation of 'meaning' and 'significance' in a poem produces a dialectical mode of reading based on the pun or syllepsis. This generates a flickering instability in the reader's mind - 'a continual recommencing, an indecisiveness resolved one moment and lost the next' - a development which, as Reinhard Kuhn remarks ('MLN' 94, 1979), belies the orthodoxy of the title 'Semiotics of Poetry'.]

Literary interpretation stands halfway between semantics and aesthetics. Traditional criticism emphasised the aesthetic aspect; today our attention has fortunately shifted to the more basic problem of meaning. Since poetry says one thing but means something else, the main thrust of interpretation is towards the second, the deep or 'true' meaning. What is more, the difference between the meaning of a literary utterance and the meaning of a non-literary utterance is found at the level of significance. The assumption is widespread that no difference of this kind can be observed on the surface, at the level of subject matter.[1] At that level, words in a given type of literary discourse are believed to carry meaning in relation to non-verbal referents, as they do in the corresponding type of non-literary discourse.

Nowhere would this seem to be more obviously the case than in descriptive, or nature, poetry, since everything in it rests upon

the representation of reality. The singularity and uniqueness
that must mark the poem are recognised, but these characteristics
are explained as a departure from reality or from the audience
consensus as to what reality should be. We speak of metaphor,
of ambiguity, of polysemy, or even of obscurity. Interpretation
and value judgment have a common postulate: they define
meaning as a relationship between words and things, and they
use the poem's consonance with or dissonance from reality as their
criterion. Two distinct types of discourse are recognised in a
descriptive poem (and poems are classified according to which
predominates): the plain record of facts or verification of data;
and symbolic discourse. Consonance is generally reserved for the
first type; aesthetic judgment calls it pictorialism, sometimes
realism. Dissonance is reserved for symbolic discourse and is
rationalised as imagination, this last usually being a positive
value.

Referentiality of literary meaning is thus so basic an assumption that it involves the whole frame of interpretation and the
very nature of descriptive poetry. I shall try to show that this
postulate is a fallacy, and that the representation of reality is a
verbal construct in which meaning is achieved by reference from
words to words, not to things.

A secondary weakness of this sort of interpretation is that in
defining significance as opposed to subject matter, it pays too
little attention to the verbal process whereby that significance is
actually perceived when the poem is read. This process too, I
think, can best be understood as an awareness of verbal structure, rather than in terms of referentiality. The form a text
imposes upon a meaning is also the key to decipherment of that
meaning.

I choose 'Yew-Trees' to test out my objections to referentiality
because at first glance it appears to confirm the supposed dichotomy between mimetic and symbolic discourse. It has the descriptive literality, the matter-of-factness that Coleridge deplored in
Wordsworth's depiction of objects. Yet Coleridge himself sets it
first among the texts where 'the gift of imagination' is most manifest. Ruskin's admiration reflects the same duality: 'the real and
high action of the imagination . . . in Wordsworth's Yew-Trees
(perhaps the most vigorous and solemn bit of forest landscape
ever painted).' There is another reason for choosing this text:
aside from their intrinsic interpretation, the allegorical personifications in the poem raise the question of whether they modify the
nature of representation or even the 'descriptiveness' of the
genre.

> There is a Yew-tree, pride of Lorton Vale,
> Which to this day stands single, in the midst
> Of its own darkness, as it stood of yore:
> Not loth to furnish weapons for the bands
> Of Umfraville or Percy ere they marched   5
> To Scotland's heaths; or those that crossed the sea

And drew their sounding bows at Azincour,
Perhaps at earlier Crecy, or Poictiers.
Of vast circumference and gloom profound
This solitary Tree! a living thing   10
Produced too slowly ever to decay;
Of form and aspect too magnificent
To be destroyed. But worthier still of note
Are those fraternal Four of Borrowdale,
Joined in one solemn and capacious grove;   15
Huge trunks! and each particular trunk a growth
Of interwisted fibres serpentine
Up-coiling, and inveterately convolved;
Nor uninformed with Phantasy, and looks
That threaten the profane;-a pillared shade,   20
Upon whose grassless floor of red-brown hue,
By sheddings from the pining umbrage tinged
Perennially - beneath whose sable roof
Of boughs, as if for festal purpose, decked
With rejoicing berries - ghostly Shapes   25
May meet at noontide; Fear and trembling Hope,
Silence and Foresight; Death the Skeleton
And Time the Shadow;- there to celebrate,
As in a natural temple scattered o'er
With altars undisturbed of mossy stone,   30
United worship; or in mute repose
To lie, and listen to the mountain flood
Murmuring from Glaramara's inmost caves.[2]

This poem is much, and deservedly, admired, but with the
exception of Brooks and Warren's masterly commentary,[3] no one
seems to have devoted more than some passing remarks to it. I
shall refer often to that commentary, both because I should have
been hard put to improve upon it, and because it occasionally
exemplifies the perils of the referential definition of poetic meaning.

1 THE REFERENTIAL FALLACY

There is no denying that this description refers to actual trees,
that readers believe in its fidelity, that literary pilgrims have
verified it on the spot. We also know that Wordsworth changed
or omitted certain facts about these yews because they did not
suit his purpose. But the locus of the literary phenomenon is
limited to the text-reader relationship which includes such reactions as a belief in its likeness to reality. While interpretation cannot take into account the genesis of the text, it must account for
the reader's reaction. The pertinent question is, therefore,
whether this reaction presupposes a relationship between the
words of the description and the actual trees, or whether such a
relationship is just an appearance and a rationalisation; also, whether
it helps interpretation if we compare representation and reality.

Certainly no reference is more specific than that of place names,
yet none can more obviously do without the reader's ever going
beyond the text. In fact any name will do as a place name, so
long as grammar introduces it as such and it is italicised. Put dots
or an X after a preposition like 'at' or before a noun like 'Valley',
and you have conventionally but irrefutably localised your story
within a setting. Spelling out names only adds to verisimilitude,
especially when a component of the name happens to make sense
as a noun and that noun denotes a place – like 'dale' in 'Borrowdale'. In 'pride of Lorton Vale', the encomiastic words localise as
effectively as 'vale'; this conforms to an aesthetic convention of
the era for descriptive poetry: the poem must aggrandise its subject, and any representation of Nature must be laudatory. The
meaning of the place names thus flows entirely from syntax, and
the reader needs nothing more than the context to sense their
evocative power: in 'Glaramara,' syntax demands that we understand 'mountain' or 'hill', and the non-English repeated 'a' also
points to some peripheral province of Britain: this name is simply
an index of verisimilitude, with the exoticism marker required for
a text about the Lakes region.

The same holds true of historical names. Say Brooks and Warren:
'the substance of the great tree has . . . become a part of history. . . . Centuries after the bows which it contributed to
Percy's soldiers and centuries after the soldiers themselves have
become dust, the tree is still alive, its continuity with the past
unbroken' (p. 275). Nothing truer, but then why should the
commentary have to explain the actual historical circumstances
the names hark back to? The important factor, indeed, is the
wealth of suggestive historical associations; that is the chief merit
in this way of treating the motif of a long-lived tree. But adding
philological information to the text does not enrich it, or demonstrate how rich the associations are, but only obscures what
makes for its literariness: namely, that a poem is self-sufficient.
As for place names, the text is all you need to understand the
historical allusions: 'drew their sounding bows' (7) suffices to
make 'Azincour' a battle and 'bows' suffices to set it back in the
depths of the Middle Ages. The argument that everyone knows
about Agincourt is irrelevant: how long will people still know?
And when Agincourt has disappeared from the reader's mythology,
will the text be less evocative? Certainly not, and this is the more
important point, again obscured by historical, that is, referential,
interpretation. Associations here do not work from outside history
to text, but the other way around. The text builds up a phantasm
of history. Shift the sentence from general to particular, from
nouns to names, and in terms of time or space you create an
effect of reality. And if the reality be distant in time, then the
effect of a reality that deserves not to be forgotten. The whole
'weapons' motif serves only as a time marker, but a periphrastic
one. In accordance with the principles of the genre, it dates the
tree by describing activities of yore, instead of just stating that
it is very old. The description of dated activities is the more

effective if the text adds a marker of fame, since in a time code *fame* is the equivalent of *durability*, and is therefore a hyperbole of *ancient* if the time code is actualised in the past tense. Names are such a marker not because they are famous per se, but because a name sounds more specific than a noun, its distribution potentialities being more limited. In a descriptive context, this limitation leaves only one possible function: the specific term is a paragon, an exemplar. Transposed into a time code, this forces the presumption that the name is memorable. This verbal mechanism merely particularises the general rule that in any paradigm of synonyms, the word with the most aberrant or peculiar shape hyperbolises the meaning it receives from the context: in a narrative, you fall harder on a granite floor than on a stone floor, and it would hurt still worse on a basalt floor. 'At Azincour' is thus more suggestive than, say, 'on a distant battlefield', and it is all the more suggestive because Wordsworth chooses a French spelling rather than 'Agincourt', the accepted English version. Likewise, forgotten 'Umfraville' matches 'Percy', whom we still remember as Hotspur; because of its form, it will probably be more effective than 'Percy' once that link has vanished from our memories.

History, and referentiality, are thus all at the verbal level. Names anchor the description solidly in time because of their metonymic function, their ability to stand for a whole complex of representations. Suggestiveness is circular: the descriptive sentence finds its reference in a name whose referent need only be the preceding part of the sentence leading up to it.

Next to names, what seems to be most squarely founded upon referential meaning is the so-called descriptive or picturesque detail. Infallibly, it is interpreted and evaluated by comparison with a standard of reality. The striking description of the yew trunks (16-18), for instance, is singled out because the poem here 'appears to content itself with description for its own sake,' and at the same time it is extolled for the 'magnificence of the phrasing'.[4] Whereby two poles are neatly separated: one, reality, is interesting in itself and is faithfully represented; the other, the fact that the poet has done a beautiful job of representation. It does look as though the style, faced with a challenging subject, has risen to the occasion, and as though the text's formal complexity is merely mirroring a reality of especial intricacy.

But a closer look, I believe, reveals that this textual complexity simply indicates the interpretation demanded of the reader, and that the apparent emphasis upon the picturesque is a deliberate effort to orient him towards a change in the nature of the object represented – from ideogram to symbol. At first blush, indeed, you might think that here reality is all. The bark and trunk of a yew tree are really distinctive. This sudden crowding of adjectives and participles seems to be Wordsworth's verbal reaction to an exceptional, involved group of contours. Each individual word seems to stand for one physical detail. Even were this true, such a one-to-one referentiality would not suffice per se to turn a faithful account of reality into a literary text – or, to put it differently, it would not endow a recording of reality with literariness. But what actually happens in this sentence is that adjectives and participles all spring from one word. They do seem to progress, as a description should, from feature to feature of the trunk. But being synonyms, they actually repeat the same meaning through a modulation from code to code. First we have a wood code, or living-matter code, represented by 'intertwisted fibres' (17). 'Intertwisted' not so much adds to 'fibre' as it activates and singles out the most important feature in the semantic complex of 'fibre'. That is to say 'fibre' as a part of an organic, living fabric, 'fibre' as a component incapable of independent existence (except under autopsy), tied to other fibres by something that is not mere contiguity or mere mechanical function, for that would be mineral or metallic or artificial. 'Fibre' as bound to other fibres by links complex enough, and labyrinthine enough, to become a kind of image within an image of the complexity of life. Hence 'intertwisted'. But then 'serpentine' takes up 'intertwisted' by a variation of transformation into 'snake code'. All the more effective because many stereotypes do describe vegetable life in terms of slow, crawling progress, like vines creeping up tree trunks or walls – that is, reptilian terms. 'Up-coiling' (18) confirms the snake code, but brings it back closer to the verticality characteristic of vegetable life; and this confirms also the image of the tree as a striving upwards through centuries. 'Inveterately convolved' summarises what precedes.

Now, all these details are but a grammatical expansion of the meaning of the word 'growth' (16), which is in itself only a generalisation of 'trunk'. In a quite comparable passage, Wordsworth expands a single statement of *fantastic shape* in a string of adjectives describing clouds:

> Confused, commingled, mutually inflamed,
> Molten together, and composing thus,
> Each lost in each . . . and huge
> Fantastic pomp of structure without name.[5]

So that lines 16-18 mean not in relation to the particular experience of a yew-tree and do not depend upon our verifying them against such an actual tree. They mean as a formal variation on one semantic feature. As if to say, a trunk is a trunk is a trunk, in words that all share the same characteristic: complex, irresistible mobility.

Thus the descriptive sentence in the poem is not built like the same sentence in cognitive language. In cognitive language, a 'vertical' semantic axis supports every word and links it to things or to commonplace concepts about things. The truth test of a cognitive message is whether or not it conforms to these commonplaces. In a poem, the descriptive sentence is a chain of derivations. Each word is generated by positive or negative conformity with the preceding one – that is, either by synonymy or by antonymy - and the sequence is thus tautological or oxymoric. 'Desert', for instance, comprises 'barrenness' (with or without sand), 'aridity' (with or without heat), 'space' (usually empty). These components generate tautologically a line of Milton's:

> . . . there was room
> For barren *desert* fountainless and dry
> (my italics)[6]

A tautological sequence enumerates some or most of the semantic features making up the meaning of a kernel word (the initial word, or any word emphasised by a stylistic structure); it may be a string of synonyms like 'fountainless and dry' or, in 'Yew-Trees', lines 16-18. An oxymoric sequence enumerates antonyms of the kernel word's semantic features: e.g., 'natural temple' (29). Each variant will then look as if it verified the preceding one from a different viewpoint, or by setting it within a new frame of reference. The truth test of such a sequence cannot be whether or not each component corresponds to a referent, but whether or not the sequence is well constructed, that is, exemplary in establishing word-to-word relationships of similarity or dissimilarity, duplicating the grammatical sequence with a string of semantic associations. The description has verisimilitude because it in fact confirms again and again the same statement in various codes. The relation of literary description to its subject matter is not the relation of language to its non-verbal context, but that of metalanguage to language.

So that interpretation does not start with a judgment as to whether there is consistency with a hypothetical consensus about reality. It starts with a judgment as to whether there is compatibility or incompatibility among the words distributed along the syntagm. There may be incompatibilities that would be unacceptable in context, let alone in reality. And yet they make sense. This is the case when they do not occur within one sequence, but between two parallel sequences derived jointly from the same kernel. Thus the oxymoric 'natural temple' generates two tautological sequences - they describe the sacred grove:

> . . . a natural temple scattered o'er
> With altars undisturbed of mossy stone (29-30).

The regular procedures of a religious ritual are incompatible with 'undisturbed', or with 'mossy', which in a human context ('temple') is normally associated with abandonment and disuse. But the kernel is the group 'natural temple', rather than just 'temple' (a frequent topos, powerful enough to start a sequence because it is a transformation of the basic opposition Nature v. Artifact into an equivalence of the two). 'Altars' and 'of stone' consequently develop 'temple'. As for 'natural', it generates 'scattered' (that would be incompatible with the ritual significance of the position of real altars), and 'undisturbed', the adjective

par excellence for regions free of man, in Wordsworth one of the
clichés in his descriptions of Virgin Nature. Thus is achieved a
compound representation: the grove is a 'fane' though it remains
a copse.

Interpretation, therefore, does not need much philology or
erudition. It does not need to know norms of thought, or the conventions of a society at a given time, so long as it knows the
lexicon in which they are encoded. Interpretation is sufficiently
informed by a consideration of the two possible (and in no way
mutually exclusive) organisations of that lexicon: semantic (which
is inseparable from the consideration of grammar), and rhetorical.
Hence the interpreter's first step is to ascertain which semantic
features of the trigger word are being activated. And this is the
advantage of discarding the referential fallacy. When you are
seeking the author's intention, 'real meaning' can only be guesswork if the critic attempts a psychological or sociological or historical reconstruction of the norms. Finding out which violation
is or is not meaningful can only lead to more guesswork. Here,
on the contrary, interpretation starts from an incontrovertible
fact independent of the critic's own bent, safe from the whims of
his attention - which is to say, it starts from the shape of the
sentence. The very way the descriptive sentence is generated,
that is, the way a kernel statement is expanded into its semantic
components, or homonyms or antonyms (a word being transformed,
in the generative sense, into a phrase, a phrase into a sentence),
this precisely enables the critic to interpret what the text is aiming at, to watch the description changing into the sign of something else.

Thus even though the description of the tree trunks happens
to be true to life (that is, would be accurate in a purely cognitive context), the significant factor is that it is a fugue-like
variation upon one basic, unchanging statement. The space
occupied by the sentence so produced creates the textual imbalance which is relevant to interpretation (whereas the distortion
of reality would be irrelevant). The repetitive sequence is like a
hymn to the (hyperbolised) concept of Vegetable Life, as opposed
to Mineral Life (fibreless, growthless), and as opposed to Animal
Life. The yew is not described in relation to the tree of that name,
but as an image of an existence closer to Eternity than ours - or,
in Wordsworth's terms, more impervious to 'decay' than ours. It
simply carries on in a new language the first part of the poem,
which stated this poetic vision in terms of human life transcended.

2   TEXTUAL OVERDETERMINATION

Thus a description is deflected from its surface meaning and
makes the reader aware of a symbolic significance. This phenomenon, however, is the more compelling because it extends beyond sentence boundaries. It extends to an entire descriptive
system. But the first rule of nature poetry is that a poem is

coterminal with a descriptive system - from the title to the last
word. Thus reorientation involves the complete poem. Instead of
simply actualising the semantic features of a word, verbal sequences are simultaneously generated in accordance with the
higher probabilities of verbal association in the system. By that
term I mean a network of words related to one another around a
central concept embodied in a kernel word. The concept of 'tree',
with its various literal or metaphorical implications, provides the
speakers of a language with an ideal model for various chains of
commonplace associations. The model is like an imaginary space in
which its components are distributed so as to define their reciprocal functions. Cumulative meaning is bound to develop along such
lines as predetermined by the system: strings of semantic equivalences start from one component of the system and use other
components as their lexical material. Equivalences are the more
powerful because any systemic component can be a metonymic
substitute for the whole system ('shade' for 'tree', for example).
Which also means that the entire complex of that system (or at
least those components actualised in the text) can be made to
represent only one meaning originally connected with a single
feature of the system (perhaps even a featuer of secondary importance). The description will therefore emphasise such features as
are connected in more than one way with that meaning.

Interpretation must, then, be a statement of these equivalences.
Since these equivalences are deduced from the features selected
by the text, such a reading, by definition, allows the reader no
freedom of choice in his understanding of descriptive details. All
these converge and concur irresistibly towards the one single
significance, once the sequence has started moving - all function
as structural variants of that obsessive, rapidly overwhelming
semantic variant.

The starter, the system component which triggers the sequence,
must have stylistic features that make it so compellingly noticeable that the reader's attention is kept under control and his
further decoding of what follows is firmly directed. In this respect
as in all others, the interpreter is only a more conscious reader.
But he has to start with the same experiences as the most ordinary
reader.

The system's components and their combinatory rules are simply
language level restrictions upon use; translated into an actual
description, these rules lend it verisimilitude. But they are not
realised together, necessarily, or in a given sequence. Because
of the metonymic relationships among the system components, there
can be descriptions where one component or its periphrastic substitute is enough to achieve the mimesis of reality: quite a few
literary trees are represented only by their foliage. Here is the
all-important consequence: naming a component is never just stating it, writing about it; naming it means making it significant
and attention-compelling.

Since a tree can be stated as a separate thing or as part of a
group, or as a single individual within or without a forest, the

fact that a text realises the first option is significant twice over:
at the language level, since certain associative possibilities have
been selected to the exclusion of others; and within the text,
since this choice has now become an element of the text's
'heterocosm'. It also means that no reader can help noticing this
particular slant of the description.

This is precisely what happens in our poem, where the tree's
first modality of existence expressed and made stylistically prominent is its isolation. Yew-trees do grow singly or in small
clumps, so this first trait would seem plainly referential. But
only for a reader who already knows about yews; and the accuracy of the remark cannot justify the extremely heavy emphasis
laid upon singleness. The isolation is a modality of 'descriptiveness' not because it coincides with a possible or common reality
of the woods, but because it is an unavoidable fact of the text,
because it is stated again and again in a cumulative sequence:
with the proud 'stands single . . . as it stood of yore' (2-3),
with 'solitary Tree', with the underlining of an exclamation and
the use of the capital letter. All culminates in the naming of the
grove of Borrowdale, four yews described as a oneness ('fraternal
Four . . . joined in one' [14-15]). Not only is all this remarkable
in itself; the loneness of a tree cannot be emphasised in any text
without implicit antithesis to 'forest', a powerful antithesis the
more striking because it is a variant of the structural opposition
Solitude v. Multitude. Singleness, moreover, is linked to three
more tree-traits which in turn inform the entire poem. Or rather,
this singleness is restated in three different ways (each of them
in turn serving as reference to the others and thus appearing to
be proof of existence, of the genuineness of the descriptions).

First, the tree's isolation is expressed as individuality (the
capital letter already mentioned, the humanisation, 'those fraternal Four', already implied by the suggestion that it has a will of
its own - 'not loth' [4]). All this ties in with the description of
the tree as slow, quasi-animal life, growing matter, on which I
commented above in my discussion of lines 16-18. The notation of
singleness is thus also an affirmation of independent life.

Second, isolation linked to durability implies survival, as is
apparent from everyday-language clichés like 'the last one left',
lone survivor. A statement that turns the tree into a *sole witness* (another cliché, which shows how easy the association is),
a living monument to the past. Survival, that is, the disappearance of all shorter-lived contemporaries, spells loneliness. The
ability to witness and remember, and ultimately to perpetuate
and celebrate rituals of awareness of the past and present, on
the one hand; on the other, isolation - these are linked together
in a verbal stereotype. Wordsworth's poems offer several examples
of this, from 'The Oak of Guernica' ('a most venerable natural
monument' says the foreword) to commemorative columns, even
to a maypole standing 'forlorn Of song and dance and games',
and hence a monument to bygone Maydays[7].

Third, and most strikingly, there is a syntagmatic variant of 'isolation' - the revealing expansion of *single* into the appositive 'in the midst / Of its own darkness' (2-3). If its meaning were referential, this would just refer to the shade. Here, however, the functional element is not a mimetic detail but the symbolic circularity of the phrase. Not only because 'shade', as a *tree*-system component, would be a metonym for the whole tree, the tree therefore standing 'in the midst / Of its own self', in solitary splendour, so to speak, but because the phrase reverses a characteristic representation of epiphany as a self-sufficiency of light emitted and received. For example, Milton's apparition:

> . . . this is she alone,
> Sitting like a Goddess bright,
> *In the centre of her light,* (my italics)

or Keats's encomium on Mary Frogley's beauty:

> And thy humid eyes that dance
> *In the midst of their own brightness,*
> In the very fane of lightness.[8] (my italics)

This circularity (acting - acted upon) makes the solitariness of the tree look like a microcosm, or at the very least a space marked out by sacred confines; it leads inevitably, as it does also and not by coincidence in Keats's verse, to the interpretation of the described object as a 'templum'. This syntagmatic tautology can be verified in other Wordsworthian variants, as in his comparison of Memory with mountain rivers 'to their own far-off murmurs listening'.[9] Blissful life as a contemplative accord with oneself is expressed by the motif of self-containment, whose form is literally a grammatical 'uroboros'.

At this point in our reading that particular potential is not activated, though it will be retroactively, when we reach the end of the poem. Right here and now, by implicit comparison with the polar opposite of the single tree, that is, the forest, and by a shift from opposition to equivalence, the tree is like a forest, a world unto itself, 'vast circumference and gloom profound'.[10]

From the beginning of the poem, overdetermination has consistently opposed the Lorton tree to man. The tree's living immortality underscores the mortality of human life. Now that the description shifts to the grove, and that the emphasis on isolation activates its potential as hallowed ground, two associative sequences merge. Those features they may have in common are thereby reinforced. 'Shade' is one of them. Its 'darkness' can thus represent equally well the tree as tree, the tree as a place of meditation, and the tree as a reminder of man's doom.

It is the first time that one systemic component is so powered and primed that its influence pervades the entire representation. Instead of limited derivations from separate kernels, an all-encompassing permutation is taking place.

Brooks and Warren sense this, of course, but they still try to

explain the heightening of effects by an increased contrast between mere recording (it is more strikingly mimetic) and imaginary construct (it is more suggestive). For instance:

> 'Pining umbrage' would mean literally 'wilting foliage'. But a
> common meaning of 'pine' applies to a human being's failing in
> vitality from longing or regret, and 'umbrage' is powerfully
> associated with shade and shadow. . . . So the suggestions
> build up the sense of melancholy gloom, *yet at no expense to
> the pictorial detail, for 'pining' in its echo of 'pine tree'
> accords with the pinelike foliage of needles that is 'tinged/Per-
> ennially' from darkest green to reddish-brown* (p. 276; my
> italics).

Reality is offered as the index of accuracy (hence praise for
Wordsworth's outer eye) and as a standard of minimal factual recording (hence relative appraisal of what his imagination has
added; and Wordsworth being looked upon with favour anyway,
there follows praise for the poet's inner eye). Unfortunately,
what they call imagined rather than seen may be praised by another reader as seen rather than imagined. Ruskin pounces upon
the same sheddings from the pining umbrage tinged, but he sees
no suggestion, only objective reality, detail worthy of a painter's
note, a pure touch of colour. And I suspect that the model is not
Nature but Milton. The 'pillared shade' of Wordsworth's yew-trees
was first the 'Pillar'd shade' of our first parents' fig tree; just
before Adam finally decides to hide his newborn shame within its
thickest shade, he longs for shelter

> where highest Woods impenetrable
> To Star or Sun-light, spread thir *umbrage broad,*
> And *brown* as Evening: Cover me ye *Pines.*[11]

I have italicised the words found again in Wordsworth. Milton's
text functions independently of meaning, as a lexical paragram[12]
to Wordsworth's. Brooks and Warren are probably right in their
interpretation of these words in 'Yew-Trees'; but they cannot be
sure reality is the reference. On the other hand, even if the
reader were aware that Wordsworth's phrasing was inspired by
Milton, the Miltonian flavour certain words might seem to take on
would at most contribute to their literariness (for instance, would
set them at the lexical level characteristic of a lofty genre like
the ode). Their relationships within the context would not be
modified.
    In any case, there is no need to extol the double aptness of
'pining', as if there were a double reference to the yew-tree as a
conifer symbolising sadness, and to the pine as a conifer related
to the yew (which means that in order to make the relationship
closer, Brooks and Warren have to reconstruct two whole trees
by including the very details excluded by the description). All
that is needed is a contextual overdetermination of 'pining', fully

observable within the verbal sequence. Within that sequence,
'pining' is semantically apt because it belongs to a lexicon of
'sadness', and mythologically apt because it is a pun and therefore looks as if it belonged to a lexicon of 'treeness'.[13]
But then, every word in the description is just as overdetermined as 'pining', because every word is selected to represent a
grove and at the same time its symbolic gloom. This overdetermination can be ascribed to an overall semantic transformation of the
descriptive system into a code carrying its true meaning. Consider how Shelley conveys the idea that Liberty is not of this
world: the metaphorical vehicle is exile. A basic landscape ('glen'/
'hill'; 'piny promontory' / 'islet') is transformed into exile code
by the addition to each topographical detail of negative markers.
These markers (adjectives expressing cold and remoteness) are
readily associated with Siberia, but they have connoted exile
ever since Ovid's 'Tristia' and 'Ex Ponto Epistulae'. Thus:

> From what Hyrcanian glen or frozen hill,
>   Or piny promontory of the Arctic main,
>   Or utmost islet inaccessible,
>   Didst thou lament the ruin of thy reign?[14]

This type of transformation is governed by what we might call
a conversion rule; given a matrix (here, the sentences actualising
the *tree* system), the descriptive text is generated through a
simultaneous modification of all the semantic components of that
matrix by one constant factor (here, a *sadness* marker).
One of the two meanings is obtained by the progressive decoding of the sentence (the subject matter); the other results from
the overall effect of the marker on sentence components (the
significance).
The entire lexicon belongs to the descriptive system of *tree*, in
various metonymical degrees, from mere contiguity (*grass* in
relation to 'umbrage', 'sheddings') to synecdoche ('umbrage',
'boughs', 'berries', and, formally, 'pining'). But the tree system
in itself is aesthetically and 'morally' neutral, in fact preferably
even positive, because of the favourable connotations of unspeci-
fied *tree*. The starting point of the sequence, however, is not an
elm or an oak, but a tree that botanical mythology makes into a
powerfully negative sign. The realisation of the system will therefore be negative throughout, each component being modified by
synonymous indicia of gloom. In fact, the cue given by the title
has already been taken by the 'darkness' (3), 'gloom' (9), 'shade'
(20) series. Hence 'grassless floor': the detail is descriptive not
because 'the earth is carpeted with needles' (p. 276), and actual
sheddings have caused actual grass to wither, but because the
suffix is as negative and mournful as the yew – *joyless* in vegetable code. Hence 'red-brown', which in a context of vegetation
annuls *green*, descriptively normal, but symbolically joyful[15] –
what Ruskin saw as merely pictorial is indeed symbolic and spiritual. And hence, of course, 'pining umbrage' and 'sable roof'. One

dark meaning invades and takes over words foreign to it, the way
a hermit crab settles into any shell available – to such an extent
that one inversion from a plus sign to a minus sign may reverse
semantically the meaning of a whole sentence. For instance: 'as if
for festal purpose, decked/With unrejoicing berries'. Brooks
and Warren detect two stages here: first, the berries remind the
speaker of an English hall at Christmastime, until he realises that
these berries are from the wrong tree. Actually there is no such
dichotomy. We do have a representation of joyous festivity (hypo-
thesised first by 'as if', corroborated by 'decked', confirmed by
'berries', a truly meliorative word, whose positiveness is actualised by 'rejoicing') – but with a minus sign (the 'un' prefix)
which makes it a celebration of Death. If anyone argues that an
actual absence of grass, and a deep shade, and a claustral grove,
are negative by their very nature, and that the meanings of these
details may still be referential – I will retort that they are not
separated in context but sequential. Proof that no natural symbolism can prevail against formal conversion is the following:

> A stately Fir-grove, whither I was not
> To hasten, for I found, beneath the roof
> Of that perennial shade, a cloistral place
> Of refuge, with an unincumbered floor.[16]

The topography is strikingly similar to that of our poem, the
details are physically the same, their natural symbolism is potentially just as negative; and the actual tree is just as coniferous
and wont to shed needles. But the sequence-starter is *fir*, that
is, a noun with positive connotations: consequently every word
thereafter is positively indexed. Grasslessness itself, instead of
remaining barren as referential description would dictate, is
metamorphosed by sequential description into a cute variant of
the wishy-washy animals-my-brethren theme: ' . . . sometimes
on a speck of visible earth,/The redbreast near me hopped.'[17]
    As far as the theory of interpretation is concerned, we must
conclude that one cannot distinguish between plain descriptive
details and descriptive details that would also carry symbolism.
Everything pertaining to subject matter, every actualised systemic
component, is also marked with significance. Nothing in the description escapes symbolic orientation.
    As for the poem itself, we have seen that the *shade* code and
the *temple* code were necessarily derived from the *darkness* invariant, since it was overdetermined by the fusion of the two associative sequences: tree as mortality, and tree as place of worship.
The new *ghost* variant is just as imperatively derived from the
first two codes. For ghosts are components of both descriptive
systems, as well as being negative in both. *Shade* is darkness
and death, but then *ghosts* entertain a metonymic relationship
(from shade to Shapes) with darkness in the literal sense, and a
metaphoric one with darkness as death. *Temple* begets worshippers, but, if it becomes a symbol of mortality, the conversion rule

turns these worshippers into ghosts. Furthermore, *haunted* is a
component of the *architecture* system. Since the architecture
here is natural architecture, there is an inevitable association
with the mythological tradition of ghosts haunting sacred groves.
Vergil has an elm inhabited by the shadows of mythological monsters at the gates of his Hell. My reaction is to see this coincidence as proof of the power of these potential derivations. The
reaction of Wordsworth's editors is to see the 'Aeneid' as a source
for 'Yew-Trees'. A likely hypothesis, but irrelevant to interpretation. Vergil's phantoms may form part of the poem's intertext
for learned readers, including Wordsworth. This is no longer an
important factor, for the days are long past when the average
reader brought to his reading a mind full of Latin.

An important factor for today's reader is that personifications
embarrass him, and this does warp his understanding of the text.[18]
Whether we like them or not, we should not be tempted to dismiss
them as a purely ornamental trope reflecting a dated aesthetics.
We cannot separate a trope from its context, any more than we
can separate other groups of words. In fact, especially not a
trope, for it is by definition more visible and must therefore play
a role in the stylistic system. The personifications, as we have
seen, are the top of the paradigm of *darkness* variants. They are
thus not gratuitous as style.

They certainly were not incompatible with the rules of the genre:
the River Duddon sonnets, for instance, are ample proof of their
frequency in nature poetry. We may think that they are not in
keeping with the 'realist' simplicity of the first lines. The description of the trees, however, includes a viewer who is telling about
his experience of the yews, speaking aloud (witness the exclama-
tions of lines 10 and 16, which cannot be interpreted as vocatives,
and the change of intonation audible in 'but worthier still of note').
The descriptive poem, like most of Wordsworth's texts of this kind,
is also a narrative in the first person (implicit here). Part of the
description therefore consists of the speaker's reactions to what
he sees. These reactions take the form of fancy: which is what
the narrator's voice explicitly says - 'nor uninformed with Phantasy'.
Fancy, aroused by the dark, readily begets ghosts. This is commonplace, part of our verbal code, hence enough to make us follow the speaker and accept his account of his experience. Moreover, Wordsworth addicts will find confirmation of how natural
and likely all this is in other personal-experience narratives of
his, e.g., the visit to a cave, where the traveller

> sees, or thinks
> He sees, erelong, the roof above his head,
> Which instantly unsettles and recedes
> Substance and shadow, light and darkness, all
> Commingled, making up a Canopy
> Of Shapes and Forms and Tendencies to Shape
> That shift and vanish, change and interchange
> Like Spectres, ferment quiet and sublime.[19]

The vision of 'Yew-Trees' is altogether likely and acceptable
as descriptive style because personifications belong to the mimesis
of the viewer's emotions – in Wordsworth's own words, 'they are,
indeed, a figure of speech occasionally prompted by passion, and
I have made use of them as such.'[20] Better yet, within that mimesis,
it is as natural that a character should see ghosts in a tree as in a
cave.[21] Especially when the tree is a yew. The ghosts are part of
the special *yew* variety within the *tree* system, just as they would
be part of the Gothic variant within a *castle* system. Here again
Wordsworth testifies to the wilfulness of fancy and conceit that
beautified natural objects during an early period of his inspiration:

> . . . From touch of this new power
> Nothing was safe . . .
> . . . the Yew-Tree had its Ghost,
> That took its station there for ornament.[22]

This quotation, to be sure, does keep its ironical distance from
impetuous fancy. But so does our poem, though without irony.
The clincher: 'beneath whose sable roof . . . ghostly Shapes /
May meet at noontide.' Both 'may' and the inversion of the normal ghostly hour banish all doubt that this phrase is on the model
of 'the moon is so bright that you could read by it'. What we have
here is simply the equivalent (in *yew* code) of a superlative: the
shade is so dense that ghosts could carry on their business here
at high noon instead of midnight.

Up to this point, the 'Shapes' are not metaphorical, or allegorical. They are represented 'things', the tree's shade in an hallucinatory code. Each one of the variants of *darkness*, in fact, can
be classified under Wordsworth's aesthetic category of Fancy.

However, since their sequence has now reached its apex,
Imagination picks up Fancy's visionary material as an allegory,
with intent to draw conclusions and elaborate the poem's significance. Hence symbolic names are given to the Shapes, and equally
symbolic actions. We now move from the purely descriptive to
the meditative descriptive (and so back to the level of the Lorton
yew passage):

> . . . Thus sometimes were the shapes
> Of wilful fancy grafted upon feelings
> Of the imagination, and they rose
> In worth accordingly.[23]

In a sense, the descriptions leading to this turning point have
only been a descriptive-symbolic preparation for a moral that will
now be directly stated.

3   THE STRUCTURE OF SIGNIFICANCE

The chains of association that started with the first line end when they culminate in the *ghost* variant. While every image up to this point in the text was subordinated to the *tree* system, that system retroactively appears to have been the symbolic and material prop of a stage. The text now focuses on the ghostly Shapes, and its language changes accordingly.

Meaning is no longer being conveyed the way it was before. Up to line 25, it was expressed figuratively through the description of natural objects. Devices like the metaphors for describing the tree trunks simply amounted to a second level of deviation in the descriptive code, with a straightforward relationship subsisting between the variants and their invariant, the descriptive system. Now, on the contrary, meaning becomes literal, or so it seems, because personification[24] permits the integration of concepts as such (their meaning being abstract, general and idealised, but not metaphorical) into descriptive or narrative forms by means of a conventional trick: make-believe animation. The animism of the personifications does not blunt the analytical power of the personified abstract nouns. There is no ambiguity, no double or multiple meaning at the lexical level. To understand, we just have to allow grammar to guide us along the sentence.

But the directness of expression that seems to be gained at the lexical level is lost at the syntactic. For the personifications generate verbs ('celebrate united worship' [28]; 'listen' [32]) that do not clearly lend themselves to metaphorical interpretation. And yet, their literal meaning seems unsatisfactory, because the object of worship remains unnamed. Also, plain listening somehow defeats the high expectations awakened by personification. These verbs must occupy some intermediate status between literal and figurative meaning.

It would seem that we must discover a symbolism that fits Time, Death, Fear, Hope, Silence, and Foresight all equally well: a concept that can both serve as object of 'united worship' and take a stream as its own symbol. Thus the interpreter is tempted to treat lines 25-33 as a periphrasis of the riddle class,[25] as a circuitous series of pointers surrounding a semantic hole; the hole is to be filled by the reader's participation and ingenuity.

A glance at two commentaries will show that, despite the distance that separates them in language and thought, their principle is the same and the results frustrating:

An ideal grove, in which the ghostly masters of mankind meet, and sleep, and offer worship to the Destiny that abides above them, while the mountain flood, as if from another world, makes music to which they dimly listen.

Time the Shadow and Death the Skeleton excite in man alternately Fear and trembling Hope, demand his Foresight and often awe him into silent contemplation. . . . Time is frequently likened to a stream, and a stream that runs murmuring through 'inmost caves' is a sufficiently apt symbol of the flowing of time, especially conceived of as issuing from a dim and inaccessible past.[26]

Both interpretations commit that sin of brilliance, enticing to all literary critics. The cleverest carries the day. Literature does indeed aim at an elite, but not necessarily an elite made up exclusively of meteors. Interpretation should never go beyond that in the text which is within the reach of just about any sensible reader. The first interpretation, Stopford Brooke's, tries to solve the *worship* riddle by superimposing Greek concepts onto Wordsworth's text; his own preoccupation with metaphysics makes him dismiss the stream as the mere decor of a well appointed park. Brooks and Warren prefer to solve the *river* riddle, but they create their own contradiction: for if the river is Time, how can Time also be one of the listeners?

The solutions proposed in both cases are hypotheses. I suspect they would not have been proposed in the first place, if the critics had not been bothered by irrelevancies. First, an aesthetic preconception: evidently they are troubled by the gap between the stylistic build-up of the personifications and the idle listening to the river in countryboy fashion. As a remedy, one makes it more ornamental than it is, while the others elevate it to the rank of symbol. Second, a logical preconception: a sentence about *worship* is incomplete, if it does not specify of what. Third, the referential fallacy again, with a further nuance: the hypothetical referent here is a literary topos; therefore, the river must be a representation of time, since there is such a tradition.

But a word refers to a theme or topos only if its context makes the figurative reading imperative or at least likely. There is nothing here, in the grammar, to prevent us from accepting the literal sense. If, on the other hand, figurative meaning is possible, the context will orient the reader's choice. Since the contradiction mentioned before eliminates the river as Time, perhaps Timelessness will do instead.

> *Still glides the Stream, and shall for ever glide;*
> *The Form remains, the Function never dies.*[27]

This reading leaves out important, although not essential, features of the context, but its main defect is that it does not lead to a conclusion. We shall have to try harder.

'Celebrate . . . United worship' may be an incomplete statement in prose, but in poetry, it yields all the information needed. The phrase results from the conversion of a kernel sentence, *they stand under the tree*, into a *temple* code. Only one word is not part of that code: *united*. Since it cannot be explained away as a descriptive variant (such as *celebrate worship*, a variant of *stand*), it must carry a new meaning at the narrative level. Coming, as it does, after an enumeration of strongly differentiated characters (some of them mutual enemies), 'united' describes unexpected unison: their alliance in spite of themselves, perhaps, or recognition of the fact that they have something in common. Even though some, like Death, necessarily rule over the others, they are all equal in one respect. They do share an inferiority, since worshipping of course presupposes that the worshippers are dependent upon and dominated by the object of their worship. United they stand, under some god. Not Time, this much we now know. Nor Destiny, because it could not possibly be associated with a river image. Perhaps an identification of this type is not necessary at all, for the text does not really create a semantic void. When André Breton speaks of 'le bruit de paupières de l'eau dans l'ombre',[28] comparing the lapping noise of water at night to the noise of shutting eyelids we understand: *silent water*, expressed in *sleep* code. *Eyelid* is hyperbolic substitute for the negative in the phrase *no noise*. In a similar way, the rituals of worship are but a descriptive, periphrastic way to state: *they are united*.

Let us return to the aesthetic preconception. We modern readers tend to believe that tropes attract tropes. Once we find a personification we expect more figures, while, conversely, not expecting plain literalness. Moreover, we have trouble visualising allegories. We are still familiar with the figures of Death and Time, they are rather popular; but we think of foresight as a quality of the intelligent mind and forget Foresight, a Virtue, the Prudentia of Christian tradition. Wordsworth knew the emblems well - for example, Foresight and Memory as the two faces of the Janus of Time.[29] Memory has been kept faintly alive by the easy identification with Mnemosyne, but Silence, having no Muse to sustain it and hence no ready visual delineation, is harder today to imagine as a person. Our problem, however, is but a time wrought infirmity, an accident of history. Unfortunately, it causes us to miss the point, namely that personification, as language, is a sentence, not just a word. It has an abstract, clearly stated subject, and a concrete predicate. This rule of the trope is what transforms concepts into creatures that act as if they were of flesh and blood. Consequently, predicates such as *listen* can be taken quite literally.

Our initial reaction was a mistaken aesthetic rationalisation. It is nonetheless valid in that it testifies to a very real phenomenon, to the continued impact of a textual feature. The contrast between an involved, artificial subject and lowbrow verbs does not violate the aesthetics of the trope. Nevertheless, it is a contrast, and, as such, the surface manifestation of a powerful semantic structure. The imbalance we feel to exist between subject and predicate is also, as we will see, part of the message conveyed by that structure.

As with the variants *tree*, the features shared by all subjects point to their true meaning. First, they are Man's ghosts, or rather they *are* Man. The enumeration simply lists obsessive components of the human psyche.[30] Second, even if they were not the hyperbolic variants of the *shade* invariant, as is indeed suggested by 'ghostly', the 'Shapes' would all be negatives. Among the evil,

'Death' and 'Time' are made worse by their spooky raiment. 'Fear' and 'Hope' together normally balance each other: here, 'trembling' makes 'Hope' a close equivalent of 'Fear',[31] in fact annuls their normal antonymy. Within this context, 'Silence' paired up with 'Foresight' nullifies any positive connotation the latter may have. But then 'Foresight', 'Fear', and 'Hope' are three variants of consciousness turned towards the future. These ghosts are troubled ones, and they are troubled only by the future.

The immediate effect of the enumeration is to state clearly and literally the significance expressed symbolically and obscurely by the variants of *tree* in the first part of the poem. Personification brings significance to the fore in the same way that the viewer projects himself into the ghosts he imagines. The trope is thus doubly appropriate: as analysis, and as the iconic image of Fancy.

The other pole of the contrast is the predicate, which means that we shall not separate the verb from its object. 'Listen' is not alone. The verb 'lie' prepares and justifies it within the conventions of descriptiveness. And 'in mute repose'[32] functions as a hyperbole developing the semantic feature of *attentiveness* inherent in 'listen'. These modifiers are thus operating as verisimilitude factors, giving tangible reality to the scene. But they operate also as counters to the *troubled* semantic invariant of the subject group: listening soothes them.

As for the object, the 'flood', one descriptive feature – the sound it makes – is stylistically emphasised. 'Glaramara', aside from being a place name, is a phonetic variant of the onomatopoeic 'murmuring' which it echoes and amplifies. This element, both phonetic and semantic, is synonymous with the soothing component of the verb group; it is the agent of that action.

The text cumulatively establishes an image of Man beset by fear and refusing hope, shutting himself against the future in tight-lipped frustration. The components of the second sequence are derived from this stylistic overloading which generates its extreme opposites: simplicity is derived from and balances complexity, and literalness is derived from and balances allegory. As a literary representation, it rings true because it is overdetermined. It says that extreme anxiety, inescapable fear, rooted in an involved consciousness of our very humanness, may be lulled by means as material and elemental as the fear is metaphysical – the monotonous murmur of water.

We can rewrite lines 26-33 thus: *the sound of running water is enough to assuage Man's misery.* This matrix shows plainly the potential power of the *sound* v. *Man's fear* opposition, between which terms there is no common measure, and yet the former balances the latter. In structural terms, the overwhelming superiority of A over B is transformed into the equivalence of B and A, or even reversed, since B, the sound, annuls A, Man's fear. In semantic terms, this is tantamount to making the sound symbolic of a power stronger than Death.

I have simply analysed a geometry of functions and polarities that are found coded differently in other texts. Its significance

stems not from the fact that it is a common denominator of these
texts, and therefore a negation of their respective originalities.
Its significance lies in the relation of analogy it establishes between different verbal shapes, making them converge towards a
meaning none of them had separately, or could have outside the
text: this unique congruence is that which informs each poem.
Like any geometry, it is never perceived in its abstract form,
only through its variants. My analysis necessarily keeps within
the boundaries of the reading experience. Once I have somewhat
formalised the matrix, the interpretation can become comparative.
I do not mean a comparison of codes, as is usually made, but a
comparison of poems which despite the codal differences verify
again and again the existence of the matrix discovered in 'Yew-
Trees'. This recurrence in turn must be seen as a fundamental
feature of Wordsworth's poetic system.

The 'words' of that ideal sentence and the grammar of their un-
changeable relationships constitute a thematic[33] structure that we
might call the *sound of waters* structure, so named for its one
invariant that is always actualised with the same image. The
structure is characterised by the interaction between two insep-
erable poles, a spectator and a spectacle. The spectator is a
meditative witness, the spectacle an object of contemplation instead of mere perception. There is thus an essential link between
descriptive poetry as a genre and this structure, since contemplation is a transform of *looking at,* the defining function of
the genre (with the attendant transformation of the implicit or
explicit onlooker into an explicit, pensive observer). It is a bit
awkward for me to be using visual terms, but I am obliged to in
order to define the point of departure of the transformations. In
fact, however, the resulting transform, so far as the subject of
the sentence is concerned, is an ear witness, a contemplative
listener.

The structure clearly outlines the mimesis of a visionary act. It
will come as no surprise that the vision is one of the ear, Wordsworth being the poet who chose to call the ear an organ of vision
and compared its labyrinth with an oracular cave.[34]

The change from watching to contemplating results from the
combining of sensorial and inward perception, attentiveness and
thoughtfulness. This philosophical additive is a marker comparable to those I used in the conversion rule. It endows all components of a variant with the ability to connote a meditative attitude
at the same time that they denote a scene and a story. The actualisation of this invariant marker is always a setting, a locale
(usually but not always enclosed) of *isolation* or loneliness, therefore propitious to contemplation. In 'Yew-Trees' it is represented
by two variants: the shade of the Lorton tree, the fane of Borrowdale. Elsewhere, by groves and bowers. For example, in 'Nutting',
it is the 'dear nook / Unvisited . . . Where fairy water-breaks do
murmur on / For ever.' In 'Nunnery', if I may quote a negligible
piece after a great one, it is the convent near the river.

A deictic constituent represents Time, this meaning being determined through its relation to the subject. Time, therefore, is a reminder of mortality, since that subject is Man. In 'Yew-Trees', this deictic constituent, is represented by three variants: the age of the Lorton tree, whose life is to Man's what eternity is to transience; 'Death' and 'Time' among the 'Shapes'. In 'Nunnery' the variant is the emptiness of the long abandoned convent. In 'Lines left upon a Seat in a Yew-tree', the tree itself. In 'At Vallombrosa', the memory of a long-dead Milton, who once had listened to the same 'precipitous flood' as the narrator.

The object of our ideal sentence, the listened-to sound of waters, has zero variance (aside from changes in the surrounding landscape). There is never any suggestion that the 'unremitting voice of nightly streams'[35] has meaning.

The interaction of subject and object is a permutation by which the object becomes the agent of change in the subject, a change that is, or symbolises, a spiritual upheaval. This change is not necessarily expressed by a verb: in our text, the soothing effect of the water sounds on the ghostly Shapes is implied in their posture - 'mute repose' - while listening.

The listening subject is normally actualised in the person of the narrator. The difference in 'Yew-Trees' is of course that the narrator's thoughts, the ghosts, take his place as listener.

Of the variants I have compared, 'Resolution and Independence' unexpectedly offers the one closest to 'Yew-Trees'. The 'meditative' marker is the lonely moor. The deictic constituent is the Leech Gatherer himself, who represents Time in a way that awakens thoughts of death: not only does he closely resemble the allegory of Time itself, but in his first appearance he is also likened to a stone left stranded on the moor since ages immemorial. The listener is haunted by thoughts that recall our familiar ghosts: 'the fear that kills; / And hope that is unwilling to be fed'. The passage actualising the object is even more significant. It demonstrates the structure's power to transform any reality, no matter how unyielding, and to reshape it to its purpose. Although in the first lines of the poem, the 'pleasant noise of waters' was available, so to speak, the voice that soothes is that of the old man 'from some far region sent, / To give me human strength'. It is therefore the Leech Gatherer who is represented in the water code: 'But now his voice to me was like a stream / Scarce heard'. Further proof that our structure informs the image is the fact that the voice-stream gives comfort, and yet is not understood: 'nor word from word could I divide'. We recognise the motif of the lulling, meaningless sound of the stream.[36]

True, the river could be a gentle sound and a symbol at the same time. In 'Yew-Trees' the last words, 'inmost caves',[37] may tempt the reader to assume a symbolic meaning. The river's voice - the same muttering voice heard by the poet in the crags of the Simplon Pass[38] - rises from the depths. It is therefore, in Wordsworth's language, the voice of Nature.[39]

However, this reading of 'Yew-Trees' is more informed by contact with other Wordsworthian texts than it could be by our text

alone. Even if the reader adopts it, the association with Nature
will still be subordinated to the representation of a 'soundscape':[40]
this association is no more than part of a descriptive periphrasis
which expands the sound image.

There nevertheless remains the opposition *water murmuring*/
dulls the pangs of mortality, the imbalance between the mere
sound and the infinity of thought. This again points to two significant coincidences that I believe to be the key to the interpretation of the poem. First, the one invariant of the poem's structure
always actualised by the same variant - the image of the water
sounds - is also the one to which no symbolism is ever attached.
Second, this statement of meaningless sensation always coincides
with the disappearance of dire thoughts or fears. The dread of
the future vanishes during the moment of bliss. This progress
from meditative gloom to peaceful feeling, repeated from poem to
poem and so evidently central to Wordsworth's aesthetics, is his
strategy in 'Yew-Trees'.

The poem's verbal structure, and the grammar of personification
that mirrors this structure within the poem, is the iconic parallel
of that progress. The poem begins with meditation and foresight
to end with the mere recording of present experience. Far from
being a letdown after the symbolic meanings of the first part, the
strict literalness of the end is a climax. Its significance lies in the
meaninglessness of the sound. Sensation is all - which is exactly
what descriptive poetry is about.[41]

NOTES

1   On significance, see E.D. Hirsch, Jr., 'Validity in Interpre-
     tation', New Haven, 1967.
2   'Poems of the Imagination', V. (Figures in parentheses and
     brackets, unless otherwise designated, refer to line numbers
     of this poem.) Wordsworth himself thought that it was 'among
     the best [of his poems] for the imaginative power displayed'
     (Crabb Robinson's Diary for 9 May, 1815). Selincourt ('Poetical
     Works', II, pp. 209-10, 503-4) gives variants which would
     not modify my reading, if I took them under consideration.
     As I am exclusively concerned with the relationship of the
     reader to the text, they are irrelevant to my purpose.
3   Cleanth Brooks and Robert Penn Warren, 'Understanding
     Poetry', 3rd ed., New York, 1960, pp. 273-9. The most
     developed commentary aside from theirs is one page in R.D.
     Havens, 'The Mind of a Poet', Baltimore, 1941, I, 227.
4   Brooks and Warren, p. 274. (From now on, I shall refer to
     their commentary simply by giving the page number in paren-
     theses.)
5   'The Excursion', II, 855-9.
6   'Paradise Regained', III, 263-4. On oxymoric and tautological
     sequences, descriptive systems, and textual overdetermina-
     tion in general, see my paper, Modèles de la phrase littéraire,

in 'Problems of Textual Analysis', ed P.R. Léon, et al., Montreal, 1971, pp. 133-51. [Reprinted in 'La Production du texte', Paris, Seuil, 1979, pp. 45-60].

7   'While from the purpling east . . . ,' ll. 41-5; cf. the trophy-laden 'HART'S HORN TREE' ('Yarrow Revisited' XXII), The Pine of Monte Mario at Rome, The Haunted Tree, The Pillar of Trajan, etc.

8   Milton, Arcades, ll. 17-19. Keats, To Mary Frogley, ll. 4-6 (Garrod ed, p. 21); cf. the rising of Hyperion, where the circularity is complicated by an antithetical transformation of the kernel word (splendour → shade): 'Till suddenly a splendour . . .; Pervaded all. . . . It was Hyperion . . . Regal his shape majestic, a vast shade / *In midst of his own brightness*' ('Hyperion', ll. 357-8; 367; 372-3; my italics). The difference between Keats's and Wordsworth's texts is that Wordsworth gives only the transform. Cf. Coleridge, Hymn to the Earth, l. 26: 'Inly thou strovest to flee, and didst seek thyself at thy centre!' The light (shade) and spatial code variants are among the most frequent. In 'moral' codes, this circular structure generates edifying reversals of fate such as 'caught in his own trap', or Alice's comic and (or) nightmarish predicament: 'I shall be punished for it now, I suppose, by being drowned in my own tears!' ('Alice's Adventures in Wonderland', chapter 2). [Cf. 'The Prelude' (1805), III, 284-6.]

9   Memory, l. 29. Cf. 'The River Duddon', XIV, 12-13: '. . . through this wilderness a passage cleave / Attended but by thy own voice.'

10 And as is usual where such a structural change occurs, the representation contains echoes of literary tradition (witness, in Norse mythology, the tree Yggdrasil covering the world, or in French literature, Lamartine's Le Chêne ['Harmonies' XX] as a world within the universe); these echoes reinforce the effect if the tradition is part of the reader's culture.

11 'Paradise Lost', IX, 1086-88; 'Pillar'd shade' occurs at IX, 1106.

12 On the development of this concept by Saussure, see Jean Starobinski, 'Les Mots sous les mots', Paris, 1971. ['Words upon Words', trans. Olivia Emmet, New Haven, Yale University Press, 1979; cf. 'Semiotics of Poetry', pp. 39ff.] Cf. Julia Kristeva, 'Semeiotikê', Paris 1969, especially pp. 246 ff.

13 The sequence generates 'pining' as if by a kind of 'popular etymology'.

14 Ode to Liberty, ll. 106-9. 'Islet' as a transform of 'island' is an equivalent of 'inaccessible'.

15 So much so that Brooks and Warren, trying to reconcile the green of the real pine tree (which they extract from pining) with the sadness constant, have to qualify green as darkest (p. 276).

16 'When, to the attractions,' ll 9-12.

17 Finally, a speck is to earth what a redbreast is to man.

Smallness therefore means prettiness [ll. 14–15].

18   Brooks and Warren feel impelled to justify them as part of a mechanism of suspense that in effect involves the reader: 'The strategy is a sound one: the vaguely portentous statement of line 19 only gradually is given specific and concrete development *after* we who read the poem are made to visualize the scene and begin to participate in it' (p. 277).

One detects how defensive the critics feel when they are dealing with outmoded conventions and think they have to sell them to the modern audience: the foregoing interpretation really aims to prove that the convention here is functional.

19   'The Prelude', VIII, 716–23. [References are to the 1805 text.]

20   Preface to the Second Edition of 'Lyrical Ballads' (Selincourt, PW, II, p. 390).

21   There is, of course, ample evidence in all mythologies that ghosts dwell in trees. Vergil did not invent his phantoms: he just used them as allegories. Modern authors tend to make their ghosts more realistic than allegorical, e.g., Tennyson: 'Death, walking all alone beneath a yew' (Love and Death, I. 5).

22   'The Prelude', VIII, 525–6, 528–9.

23   'The Prelude', VIII, 583–5.

24   I have separated this analysis from my remarks in Part 2 on the Shapes, because we must distinguish between their meaning as derivations from shade (Fancy), and their grammatical function (Imagination). On personifications, see Morton W. Bloomfield, A Grammatical Approach to Personification Allegory, 'MP', 60, No. 3 (1963), pp. 161–71.

25   There are two classes: one in which the kernel word is given (the periphrasis is then a descriptive expansion); one, our type, in which the word has to be guessed from a circuitous description.

26   Stopford A. Brooke, 'Theology in the English Poets', 8th ed., London, 1896, p. 259; Brooks and Warren, pp. 277–8.

27   'The River Duddon', XXXIV, 5–6.

28   'Le Revolver à cheveux blancs' (1932), 'La Mort rose'.

29   E.g. 'The Excursion', V, 329–30: 'thoughtless peace, / By foresight, or remembrance, undisturbed'.

30   Cf. Preface to the Edition of 1815: 'the Imagination also shapes and creates . . . by innumerable processes; and in none does it more delight than in that of . . . dissolving and separating unity into number' (Selincourt, PW, II, pp. 438–9). Among the components, Death and Time motivate and determine Fear, trembling, and Silence.

31   The closer, because the bond between Fear and trembling Hope is strengthened by an implicit relationship in the language: the cliché fear and trembling.

32   A recurrent stereotype in Wordsworth, in this form or in variants such as 'mute', 'still', and 'hushed'. It is significant that they always emphasize silence. Cf. this sentence which could almost serve as a matrix for lines 26–32: 'Yet all is harmless – as the Elysian shades / Where Spirits dwell in un-

disturbed repose - ' (Sky-Prospect, ll. 9-10).
33 As opposed to both linguistic structure and the structure of
    descriptive systems (such as that of tree). I insist on thema-
    tic structure rather than theme, since thematology keeps con-
    fusing the invariant with its codes.
34 'On the Power of Sound', ll. 3, 6.
35 'Poems of Sentiment and Reflection', XXXII, 1.
36 The motif exists independently of the structure, of course.
    Wordsworth often uses it without a troubled listener and with-
    out a reminder of the flight of Time. In such cases, it is
    usually an element of the picturesque, e.g., 'The Prelude',
    V, 406-10.
37 The plural and the adjective actualize the archetypal 'depth'
    semantic feature of 'cave'; and because the *most* component
    makes the adjective look like a word stripped of its verbal
    flesh (something akin to 'inly'), all that remains is an 'abso-
    lute' superlative.
38 The Simplon Pass, ll. 10-12, 16-20. Cf. Humanity, ll. 8-9.
39 The same image (the 'blind cavern, whence is faintly heard /
    The sound of waters') expresses the birth of Imagination in
    'The Prelude', XIII, 174-5.
40 I borrow the term from G.H. Hartman, 'Wordsworth's Poetry
    1787-1814', New Haven, 1964, p. 96. Cf. J. Hollander, Words-
    worth and the Music of Sound, in 'New Perspectives on Coler-
    idge and Wordsworth', ed G.H. Hartman, New York, 1972,
    pp. 41ff.
41 'There is no object standing between the Poet and the image
    of things' (Preface to the Second Edition of 'Lyrical Ballads',
    Selincourt, PW, II, p. 395).

I wish to thank my Research Assistant, Miss Mary Ann
Richardson, for her help during the preparation of this paper.

FURTHER READING

BARTHES, ROLAND, 'Elements of Semiology', trans. Annette
    Lavers, London, Cape, 1967.
CHATMAN, SEYMOUR (ed), 'Literary Style: A Symposium',
    London, Oxford University Press, 1971.
ECO, UMBERTO, 'A Theory of Semiotics', Bloomington, Indiana
    University Press, 1976.
— 'The Role of the Reader: Explorations in the Semiotics of Texts',
    Bloomington, Indiana University Press, 1979.
FISH, STANLEY, What Is Stylistics and Why Are They Saying
    Such Terrible Things About It?: Part 1 in Seymour Chatman
    (ed), 'Approaches To Poetics', New York, Columbia University
    Press, 1973, pp. 109-52; Part 2 in 'Boundary 2', 8:1, 1979,
    pp. 129-45.
FREEMAN, DONALD C. (ed), 'Linguistics and Literary Style',
    New York, Holt, Rinehart and Winston, 1970.

GREIMAS, A.J., 'Essais de sémiotique poétique', Paris, Larousse, 1972.

HARTMAN, GEOFFREY, The Use and Abuse of Structural Analysis: Riffaterre's Interpretation of Wordsworth's 'Yew-Trees', 'New Literary History', 7:1, 1975, pp. 165-89.

ISER, WOLFGANG, 'The Act of Reading: A Theory of Aesthetic Response', London, Routledge & Kegan Paul, 1978.

RIFFATERRE, MICHAEL, 'Essais de Stylistique structurale', Paris, Flammarion, 1971.

— 'Semiotics of Poetry', Bloomington, Indiana University Press, 1978.

— 'La Production du texte', Paris, Seuil, 1979.

— Describing Poetic Structures: Two Approaches to Baudelaire's 'Les Chats', in 'Structuralism'. ed Jacques Ehrmann, New York, Anchor Books, 1970.

— The Self-Sufficient Text, 'Diacritics', 3:3, Fall 1973, pp. 39-45.

— The Stylistic Approach to Literary History, in 'New Directions in Literary History', ed Ralph Cohen, London, Routledge & Kegan Paul, 1974, pp. 147-64.

— Paragram and Significance, in 'Semiotext(e)', 1:2, 1974, pp. 72-87.

— La Syllepse intertextuelle, in 'Poétique', 40, 1979, pp. 496-501.

6 TEXTUAL ANALYSIS OF POE'S 'VALDEMAR'

Roland Barthes

[Barthes's 'semioclasm', first demonstrated in 'Mythologies' (1957), has always been directed against the naturalisation of the sign. For literature, this means an attack on the assumption that language is a transparent medium of communication, and that the novel provides simply 'a window on to the world'. Barthes's interest in realism stems from the fact that it masquerades as the form in which language achieves the state of direct representation of the real. The reverse, of course, is more the case: the 'real' can only be created and organised in language, in a particular society and at a particular time. Barthes's 'S/Z', his famous analysis of a Balzac short story, was an interrogation of the status of realist writing and the limits of realist discourse. Barthes shows how the self-effacing language that 'mirrors' the real constantly threatens to break down into the opacity of text, of layers or fragments of writing (écriture). The following essay, published three years later in 1973, has the advantage of representing and staging the method of 'S/Z' in a much more compact form, and yet at the same time, by emphasising those aspects of 'S/Z' that were most radical, forcing us to re-read and rethink 'S/Z' itself.

'S/Z' was the result of the mutation in Barthes's semiology, already discussed in terms of the shift 'from work to text'. Here Barthes begins by distinguishing between 'structural' and 'textual' analysis; whereas the former records a structure, a grammar or model of narrative, the latter produces instead 'a mobile structuration of the text', allowing the reader to stay within the symbolic, the plurality of the text, its 'signifiance'. Instead of the closed system of structural analysis, textual analysis substitutes the tissue of codes or voices and intertextual relations that traverse the space of the single text.

Refusing a rigorous methodology, Barthes advocates instead a number of 'operating tactics' which will be mobile enough to avoid positivism or closure. The most effective strategy is to refuse the story its 'totality' or 'unity' and to break it up into fragments, following instead the structuration as it unfolds and tracking down the moments of text. These fragments, or 'lexia', are units of any size, from a word to a paragraph or more. Unlike linguistics, which stops its analysis at the purely grammatical unit of the sentence (langue), Barthes's analysis operates at the level of discourse. The lexia are only hypothetical and arbitrary. The importance of this is that the reader himself is implicated as the divider of the text into units, and thus has to be aware of his own psychic involvement in the analysis. The reader himself produces the text,

and thus an identification between the notions of writing and
reading.

This step-by-step method, the 'decomposition' of the work of
reading, is structured via the play of 'codes'. The codes are not
part of a rigorous unified system: they operate simply as 'associative fields, a supra-textual organisation of notations which impose
a certain idea of structure.' Their realm is broadly that of connotation, polysemy:

> We use 'code' here not in the sense of a list, a paradigm that
> must be reconstituted. The code is a perspective of quotations,
> a mirage of structures; we know only its departures and re-
> turns; the units which have resulted from it (those we inven-
> tory) are themselves, always, ventures out of the text, the
> mark, the sign of a virtual digression toward the remainder of
> a catalogue (-The Kidnapping- refers to every kidnapping ever
> written); they are so many fragments of something that has
> always been already read, seen, done, experienced; the code
> is the wake of that *already*. . . . each code is one of the forces
> that can take over the text (of which the text is a network),
> one of the voices out of which the text is woven. Alongside
> each utterance, one might say that off-stage voices can be
> heard: they are the codes: in their interweaving, these voices
> (whose origin is 'lost' in the vast perspective of the already-
> written) de-originate the utterance ('S/Z', pp. 20-1).

In the convergence of the voices, text becomes volume, a stereo-
graphy.

In 'S/Z' Barthes began by grouping all the codes into five
major codes; here he allows the network, the process of structuration, to build up through the text before grouping them together
at the end. This has the advantage of highlighting the fact that
while it may be possible to group the codes for the purposes of
analysis, they do not make up a rigid system. The eventual grouping in the two essays differs at only one point: in -Valdemar-
there is also a code of communication or exchange, comprising
every relation stated as an address, including that of narrator
to reader. These codes traverse the text as departures of the
'déjà-lu', the frayed edges of intertextuality, providing explosions,
contracts, flashes of meaning, a 'broken or obliterated network -
all the movements and inflections of a vast "dissolve", which permits both the overlapping and loss of messages'.

All this 'volume' is pulled forward in the reading process by the
irreversible structure of the conventional realist narrative. But
Barthes is not keen to exaggerate the differences between the
classic and the modern text: 'what is specific to the text, once
it attains the quality of a text, is to constrain us to the undecidability of the codes.' Writing is the point of the obliteration of
origins, voices, in any text, the moment when 'one simply notes,
speaking has started'.]

TEXTUAL ANALYSIS

The structural analysis of narrative is at present in the course of full elaboration. All research in this area has a common scientific origin: semiology or the science of signification; but already (and this is a good thing) divergences within that research are appearing, according to the critical stance each piece of work takes with respect to the scientific status of semiology, or in other words, with respect to its own discourse. These divergences (which are constructive) can be brought together under two broad tendencies: in the first, faced with all the narratives in the world, the analysis seeks to establish a narrative model – which is evidently formal – , a structure or grammar of narrative, on the basis of which (once this model, structure or grammar has been discovered) each particular narrative will be analysed in terms of divergences. In the second tendency, the narrative is immediately subsumed (at least when it lends itself to being subsumed) under the notion of 'text', space, process of meanings at work, in short, 'signifiance' (we shall come back to this word at the end), which is observed not as a finished, closed product, but as a production in progress, 'plugged in' to other texts, other codes (this is the intertextual), and thereby articulated with society and history in ways which are not determinist but citational. We have then to distinguish in a certain way structural analysis and textual analysis, without here wishing to declare them enemies: structural analysis, strictly speaking, is applied above all to oral narrative (to myth); textual analysis, which is what we shall be attempting to practise in the following pages, is applied exclusively to written narrative.[1]

Textual analysis does not try to describe the structure of a work; it is not a matter of recording a structure, but rather of producing a mobile structuration of the text (a structuration which is displaced from reader to reader throughout history), of staying in the signifying volume of the work, in its 'signifiance'. Textual analysis does not try to find out what it is that determines the text (gathers it together as the end-term of a causal sequence), but rather how the text explodes and disperses. We are then going to take a narrative text, and we're going to read it, as slowly as is necessary, stopping as often as we have to (being at ease is an essential dimension of our work), and try to locate and classify without rigour, not all the meanings of the text (which would be impossible because the text is open to infinity: no reader, no subject, no science can arrest the text) but the forms and codes according to which meanings are possible. We are going to locate the avenues of meaning. Our aim is not to find *the* meaning, nor even *a* meaning of the text, and our work is not akin to literary criticism of the hermeneutic type (which tries to interpret the text in terms of the truth believed to be hidden therein), as are Marxist or psychoanalytical criticism. Our aim is to manage to conceive, to imagine, to live the plurality of the text, the opening of its 'signifiance'. It is clear then that

what is at stake in our work is not limited to the university treatment of the text (even if that treatment were openly methodological), nor even to literature in general; rather it touches on a
theory, a practice, a choice, which are caught up in the struggle
of men and signs.

In order to carry out the textual analysis of a narrative, we
shall follow a certain number of operating procedures (let us call
them elementary rules of manipulation rather than methodological
principles, which would be too ambitious a word and above all an
ideologically questionable one, in so far as 'method' too often
postulates a positivistic result). We shall reduce these procedures
to four briefly laid out measures, preferring to let the theory run
along in the analysis of the text itself. For the moment we shall
say just what is necessary to begin as quickly as possible the
analysis of the story we have chosen.

1   We shall cut up the text I am proposing for study into contiguous, and in general very short, segments (a sentence, part
of a sentence, at most a group of three or four sentences); we
shall number these fragments starting from 1 (in about ten pages
of text there are 150 segments). These segments are units of
reading, and this is why I have proposed to call them 'lexias'.[2]
A lexia is obviously a textual signifier; but as our job here is not
to observe signifiers (our work is not stylistic) but meanings, the
cutting-up does not need to be theoretically founded (as we are
in discourse, and not in 'langue', we must not expect there to be
an easily-perceived homology between signifier and signified; we
do not know how one corresponds to the other, and consequently
we must be prepared to cut up the signifier without being guided
by the underlying cutting-up of the signified). All in all the
fragmenting of the narrative text into lexias is purely empirical,
dictated by the concern of convenience: the lexia is an arbitrary
product, it is simply a segment within which the distribution of
meanings is observed; it is what surgeons would call an operating field: the useful lexia is one where only one, two or three
meanings take place (superposed in the volume of the piece of
text).

2   For each lexia, we shall observe the meanings to which that
lexia gives rise. By meaning, it is clear that we do not mean the
meanings of the words or groups of words which dictionary and
grammar, in short a knowledge of the French language, would be
sufficient to account for. We mean the connotations of the lexia,
the secondary meanings. These connotation-meanings can be
associations (for example, the physical description of a character,
spread out over several sentences, may have only one connoted
signified, the 'nervousness' of that character, even though the
word does not figure at the level of denotation); they can also
be relations, resulting from a linking of two points in the text,
which are sometimes far apart, (an action begun here can be completed, finished, much further on). Our lexias will be, if I can
put it like this, the finest possible sieves, thanks to which we
shall 'cream off' meanings, connotations.

3   Our analysis will be progressive: we shall cover the length
of the text step by step, at least in theory, since for reasons of
space we can only give two fragments of analysis here. This means
that we shan't be aiming to pick out the large (rhetorical) blocks
of the text; we shan't construct a plan of the text and we shan't
be seeking its thematics; in short, we shan't be carrying out an
explication of the text, unless we give the word 'explication' its
etymological sense, in so far as we shall be unfolding the text,
the foliation of the text. Our analysis will retain the procedure of
reading; only this reading will be, in some measure, filmed in
slow-motion. This method of proceeding is theoretically important:
it means that we are not aiming to reconstitute the structure of
the text, but to follow its structuration, and that we consider
the structuration of reading to be more important than that of
composition (a rhetorical, classical notion).
4   Finally, we shan't get unduly worried if in our account we
'forget' some meanings. Forgetting meanings is in some sense
part of reading: the important thing is to show departures of
meaning, not arrivals (and is meaning basically anything other
than a departure?). What founds the text is not an internal,
closed, accountable structure, but the outlet of the text on to
other texts, other codes, other signs; what makes the text is
the intertextual. We are beginning to glimpse (through other
sciences) the fact that research must little by little get used to
the conjunction of two ideas which for a long time were thought
incompatible: the idea of structure and the idea of combinational
infinity; the conciliation of these two postulations is forced upon
us now because language, which we are getting to know better,
is at once infinite and structured.
   I think that these remarks are sufficient for us to begin the
analysis of the text (we must always give in to the impatience
of the text, and never forget that whatever the imperatives of
study, the pleasure of the text is our law). The text which has
been chosen is a short narrative by Edgar Poe, in Baudelaire's
translation: -The Facts in the Case of M. Valdemar-.[3] My choice -
at least consciously, for in fact it might be my unconscious which
made the choice - was dictated by two didactic considerations: I
needed a very short text so as to be able to master entirely the
signifying surface (the succession of lexias), and one which was
symbolically very dense, so that the text analysed would touch
us continuously, beyond all particularism: who could avoid being
touched by a text whose declared 'subject' is death?
   To be frank, I ought to add this: in analysing the 'signifiance'
of a text, we shall abstain voluntarily from dealing with certain
problems; we shall not speak of the author, Edgar Poe, nor of
the literary history of which he is a part; we shall not take into
account the fact that the analysis will be carried out on a translation: we shall take the text as it is, as we read it, without
bothering about whether in a university it would belong to students of English rather than students of French or philosophers.
This does not necessarily mean that these problems will not pass

into our analysis; on the contrary, they will pass, in the proper sense of the term: the analysis is a crossing of the text; these problems can be located in terms of cultural quotations, of departures of codes, not of determinations.

A final word, which is perhaps one of conjuration, exorcism: the text we are going to analyse is neither lyrical nor political, it speaks neither of love nor society, it speaks of death. This means that we shall have to lift a particular censorship: that attached to the sinister. We shall do this, persuaded that any censorship stands for all others: speaking of death outside all religion lifts at once the religious interdict and the rationalist one.

ANALYSIS OF LEXIAS 1 - 17

(1) - The Facts in the Case of M. Valdemar -

(2) Of course I shall not pretend to consider it any matter for wonder, that the extraordinary case of M. Valdemar has excited discussion. It would have been a miracle had it not - especially under the circumstances. (3) Through the desire of all parties concerned, to keep the affair from the public, at least for the present, or until we had further opportunities for investigation - through our endeavours to effect this - (4) a garbled or exaggerated account made its way into society, and became the source of many unpleasant misrepresentations, and, very naturally, of a great deal of disbelief.

(5) It is now rendered necessary that I give the *facts* - as far as I comprehend them myself.

(6) They are, succinctly, these:

(7) My attention, for the last three years, had been repeatedly drawn to the subject of Mesmerism; (8) and, about nine months ago, it occurred to me, quite suddenly, that in a series of experiments made hitherto, (9) there had been a very remarkable and most unaccountable omission: (10) - no person had as yet been mesmerised 'in articulo mortis'. (11) It remained to be seen, (12) first, whether, in such condition, there existed in the patient any susceptibility to the magnetic influence; (13) secondly, whether if any existed, it was impaired or increased by the condition; (14) thirdly, to what extent, or for how long a period, the encroachments of Death might be arrested by the process. (15) There were other points to be ascertained, (16) but these most excited my curiosity (17) - the last in especial, from the immensely important character of its consequences.

(1) -The Facts in the Case of M. Valdemar- [-La vérité sur le cas de M. Valdemar-]

The function of the title has not been well studied, at least from

a structural point of view. What can be said straight away is that
for commercial reasons, society, needing to assimilate the text
to a product, a commodity, has need of markers: the function of
the title is to mark the beginning of the text, that is, to constitute the text as a commodity. Every title thus has several simultaneous meanings, including at least these two: (i) what it says
linked to the contingency of what follows it; (ii) the announcement itself that a piece of literature (which means, in fact, a
commodity) is going to follow; in other words, the title always
has a double function; enunciating and deictic.

(a) Announcing a truth involves the stipulation of an enigma.
The posing of the enigma is a result (at the level of the signifiers): of the word 'truth' [in the French title]; of the word
'case' (that which is exceptional, therefore marked, therefore
signifying, and consequently of which the meaning must be
found); of the definite article 'the' [in the French title] (there
is only one truth, all the work of the text will, then, be needed
to pass through this narrow gate); of the cataphorical form
implied by the title: what follows will realise what is announced,
the resolution of the enigma is already announced; we should
note that the English says: - The Facts in the Case . . . -: the
signified which Poe is aiming at is of an empirical order, that
aimed at by the French translator (Baudelaire) is hermeneutic:
the truth refers then to the exact facts, but also perhaps to
their meaning. However this may be, we shall code this first
sense of the lexia: 'enigma, position' (the enigma is the general
name of a code, the position is only one term of it).

(b) The truth could be spoken without being announced, without there being a reference to the word itself. If one speaks of
what one is going to say, if language is thus doubled into two
layers of which the first in some sense caps the second, then
what one is doing is resorting to the use of a metalanguage. There
is then here the presence of the metalinguistic code.

(c) This metalinguistic announcement has an aperitive function:
it is a question of whetting the reader's appetite (a procedure
which is akin to 'suspense'). The narrative is a commodity the
proposal of which is preceded by a 'patter'. This 'patter', this
'appetiser' is a term of the narrative code (rhetoric of narration).

(d) A proper name should always be carefully questioned, for
the proper name is, if I can put it like this, the prince of signifiers; its connotations are rich, social and symbolic. In the name
Valdemar, the following two connotations at least can be read:
(i) presence of a socio-ethnic code:is the name German? Slavic?
In any case, not Anglo-Saxon; this little enigma here implicitly
formulated, will be resolved at number 19 (Valdemar is Polish);
(ii) 'Valdemar' is 'the valley of the sea'; the oceanic abyss; the
depths of the sea is a theme dear to Poe: the gulf refers to what

is twice outside nature, under the waters and under the earth.
From the point of view of the analysis there are, then, the traces
of two codes: a socio-ethnic code and a (or the) symbolic code
(we shall return to these codes a little later).

(e) Saying 'M(onsieur) Valdemar' is not the same thing as saying
'Valdemar'. In a lot of stories, Poe uses simple christian names
(Ligeia, Eleonora, Morella). The presence of the 'Monsieur' brings
with it an effect of social reality, of the historically real: the
hero is socialised, he forms part of a definite society, in which he
is supplied with a civil title. We must therefore note: social code.

(2) 'Of course I shall not pretend to consider it any matter
for wonder, that the extraordinary case of M. Valdemar has
excited discussion. It would have been a miracle had it not -
especially under the circumstances.'

(a) This sentence (and those immediately following) have as
their obvious function that of exciting the reader's expectation,
and that is why they are apparently meaningless: what one wants
is the solution of the enigma posed in the title (the 'truth'), but
even the exposition of this enigma is held back. So we must code:
delay in posing the enigma.

(b) Same connotation as in (1c): it's a matter of whetting the
reader's appetite (narrative code).

(c) The word 'extraordinary' is ambiguous: it refers to that
which departs from the norm but not necessarily from nature (if
the case remains 'medical'), but it can also refer to what is supernatural, what has moved into transgression (this is the 'fantastic'
element of the stories - 'extraordinary', precisely [The French
title of Poe's Collected Stories is 'Histoires extraordinaires'] -
that Poe tells). The ambiguity of the word is here meaningful: the
story will be a horrible one (outside the limits of nature) which is
yet covered by the scientific alibi (here connoted by the 'discussion', which is a scientist's word). This bonding is in fact cultural:
the mixture of the strange and the scientific had its high-point in
the part of the nineteeth century to which Poe, broadly speaking,
belongs: there was great enthusiasm for observing the supernatural scientifically (magnetism, spiritism, telepathy, etc.); the
supernatural adopts a scientific, rationalist alibi; the cry from
the heart of that positivist age runs thus: if only one could believe scientifically in immortality! This cultural code, which for
simplicity's sake we shall here call the scientific code, will be of
great importance throughout the narrative.

(3) 'Through the desire of all parties concerned, to keep the
affair from the public, at least for the present, or until we had
further opportunities for investigation - through our endeavours
to effect this -'

(a) Same scientific code, picked up by the word 'investigation' (which is also a detective story word: the fortune of the detective novel in the second half of the nineteenth century - starting from Poe, precisely - is well known: what is important here, ideologically and structurally, is the conjunction of the code of the detective enigma and the code of science - scientific discourse -, which proves that structural analysis can collaborate perfectly well with ideological analysis).

(b) The motives of the secret are not given; they can proceed from two different codes, present together in reading (to read is also silently to imagine what is not said): (i) the scientific-deontological code: the doctors and Poe, out of loyalty and prudence, do not want to make public a phenomenon which has not been cleared up scientifically; (ii) the symbolic code: there is a taboo on living death: one keeps silent because it is horrible. We ought to say straight away (even though we shall come back and insist on this later) that these two codes are undecidable (we can't choose one against the other), and that it is this very undecidability which makes for a good narrative.

(c) From the point of view of narrative actions (this is the first one we have met), a sequence is here begun: 'to keep hidden' in effect implies, logically or pseudo-logically, consequent operations (for example: to unveil). We have then here to posit the first term of an actional sequence: to keep hidden, the rest of which we shall come across later.

(4) 'a garbled or exaggerated account made its way into society, and became the source of many unpleasant misrepresentations, and, very naturally, of a great deal of disbelief.'

(a) The request for truth, that is, the enigma, has already been placed twice (by the word 'truth' [in the French title] and by the expression 'extraordinary case'). The enigma is here posed a third time (to pose an enigma, in structural terms, means to utter: there is an enigma), by the invocation of the error to which it gave rise: the error, posed here, justifies retroactively, anaphorically, the [French] title (- La vérité sur . . . -). The redundancy operated on the position of the enigma (the fact that there is an enigma is repeated in several ways) has an aperitive value: it is a matter of exciting the reader, of procuring clients for the narrative.

(b) In the actional sequence 'to hide', a second term appears: this is the effect of the secret: distortion, mistaken opinion, accusation of mystification.

(5) 'It is now rendered necessary that I give the *facts* - as far as I comprehend them myself.'

(a) The emphasis placed on 'the facts' supposes the intrication of two codes, between which - as in (3b), it is impossible to decide: (i) the law, the deontology of science, makes the scientist, the observer, a slave to the fact; the opposition of fact and rumour is an old mythical theme; when it is invoked in a fiction (and invoked emphatically), the fact has as its structural function (for the real effect of this artifice fools no one) that of authenticating the story, not that of making the reader believe that it really happened, but that of presenting the discourse of the real, and not that of the fable. The fact is then caught up in a paradigm in which it is opposed to mystification (Poe admitted in a private letter that the story of M. Valdemar was a pure mystification: *it is a mere hoax*).[4] The code which structures the reference to the fact is then the scientific code which we have already met. (ii) However, any more or less pompous recourse to the fact can also be considered to be the symptom of the subject's being mixed up with the symbolic; protesting aggressively in favour of the fact alone, protesting the triumph of the referent, involves suspecting signification, mutilating the real of its symbolic supplement;[5] it is an act of censorship against the signifier which displaces the fact; it involves refusing the other scene, that of the unconscious. By pushing away the symbolical supplement, even if to our eyes this is done by a narrative trick, the narrator takes on an imaginary role, that of the scientist: the signified of the lexia is then the asymbolism of the subject of the enunciation: 'I' presents itself as asymbolic; the negation of the symbolic is clearly part of the symbolic code itself.[6]

(b) The actional sequence 'to hide' develops: the third term posits the necessity of rectifying the distortion located in (4b); this rectification stands for: wanting to unveil (that which was hidden). This narrative sequence 'to hide' clearly constitutes a stimulation for the narrative; in a sense, it justifies it, and by that very fact points to its value (its 'standing-for' ['valant-pour']), makes a commodity of it: I am telling the story, says the narrator, in exchange for a demand for counter-error, for truth (we are in a civilisation where truth is a value, that is, a commodity). It is always very interesting to try to pick out the 'valant-pour' of a narrative: in exchange for what is the story told? In the 'Arabian Nights', each story stands for a day's survival. Here we are warned that the story of M. Valdemar stands for the truth (first presented as a counter-distortion).

(c) The 'I' appears [in French] for the first time - it was already present in the 'we' in 'our endeavours' (3). The enunciation in fact includes three I's, or in other words, three imaginary roles (to say 'I' is to enter the imaginary): (i) a narrating 'I', an artist, whose motive is the search for effect; to this 'I' there corresponds a 'You', that of the literary reader, who is reading 'a fantastic story by the great writer Edgar Poe'; (ii) an I-witness, who has the power to bear witness to a scientific experiment; the corresponding 'You' is that of a panel of scientists, that of serious opinion, that of the scientific reader: (iii) an I-actor, experimenter, the one who will magnetise Valdemar; the 'You' is in this case Valdemar himself; in these two last instances, the motive for the imaginary role is the 'truth'. We have here the three terms of a code which we shall call, perhaps provisionally, the code of communication. Between these three roles, there is no doubt another language, that of the unconscious, which is spoken neither in science, nor in literature; but that language, which is literally the language of the interdict, does not say 'I': our grammar, with its three persons, is never directly that of the unconscious.

(6) 'They are, succinctly, these:'

(a) Announcing what is to follow involves metalanguage (and the rhetorical code); it is the boundary marking the beginning of a story in the story.

(b) 'Succinctly' carries three mixed and undecidable connotations: (i) 'Don't be afraid, this won't take too long': this, in the narrative code, is the phatic mode (located by Jakobson), the function of which is to hold the attention, maintain contact;[7] (ii) 'It will be short because I'll be sticking strictly to the facts'; this is the scientific code, allowing the announcement of the scientist's 'spareness', the superiority of the instance of the fact over the instance of discourse; (iii) to pride oneself on talking briefly is in a certain sense an assertion against speech, a limitation of the supplement of discourse, that is, the symbolic; this is to speak the code of the asymbolic.

(7) 'My attention, for the last three years, had been repeatedly drawn to the subject of Mesmerism;'

(a) The chronological code must be observed in all narratives; here in this code ('last three years'), two values are mixed; the first is in some sense naive; one of the temporal elements of the experiment to come is noted: the time of its preparation; the second does not have a diegetical, operative function (this is made clear by the test of commutation; if the narrator had said seven years instead of three, it would have had no effect on the story); it is therefore a matter of a pure reality-effect: the number connotes emphatically the truth of the fact: what is precise is reputed to be real (this illusion, moreover, since it does exist, is well known; a delirium of figures). Let us note that linguistically the word 'last' is a 'shifter': it refers to the situation of the speaker in time; it thus reinforces the *presence* of the following account.[8]

(b) A long actional sequence begins here, or at the very least a

sequence well-furnished with terms; its object is the starting-off
of an experiment (we are under the alibi of experimental science);
structurally, this setting-off is not the experiment itself, but an
experimental programme. This sequence in fact stands for the
formulation of the enigma, which has already been posed several
times ('there is an enigma'), but which has not yet been formulated. So as not to weigh down the report of the analysis, we
shall code the 'programme' separately, it being understood that
by procuration the whole sequence stands for a term of the
enigma-code. In this 'programme' sequence, we have here the
first term: the posing of the scientific field of the experiment,
magnetism.

(c) The reference to magnetism is extracted from a cultural code
which is very insistent in this part of the nineteenth century.
Following Mesmer (in English, 'magnetism' can be called 'mesmerism') and the Marquis Armand de Puységur, who had discovered that magnetism could provoke somnambulism, magnetisers
and magnetist societies had multiplied in France (around 1820);
in 1829, it appears that it had been possible, under hypnosis, to
carry out the painless ablation of a tumour; in 1845, the year of
our story, Braid of Manchester codified hypnosis by provoking
nervous fatigue through the contemplation of a shining object;
in 1850, in the Mesmeric Hospital of Calcutta, painless births
were achieved. We know that subsequently Charcot classified
hypnotic states and circumscribed hypnosis under hysteria (1882),
but that since then hysteria has disappeared from hospitals as a
clinical entity (from the moment it was no longer observed). The
year 1845 marks the peak of scientific illusion: people believed in
a psychological reality of hypnosis (although Poe, pointing out
Valdemar's 'nervousness', may allow the inference of the subject's
hysterical predisposition).

(d) Thematically, magnetism connotes (at least at that time) an
idea of fluid: something passes from one subject to another; there
is an exchange [un entrédit] (an interdict) between the narrator
and Valdemar: this is the code of communication.

(8) 'and, about nine months ago, it occurred to me, quite suddenly, that in a series of experiments made hitherto,'

(a) The chronological code ('nine months') calls for the same
remarks as those made in (7a).

(b) Here is the second term of the 'programme' sequence: in (7b)
a domain was chosen, that of magnetism; now it is cut up; a particular problem will be isolated.

(9) 'there had been a very remarkable and most unaccountable
omission:'

(a)   The enunciation of the structure of the 'programme' continues: here is the third term: the experiment which has not yet been tried - and which, therefore, for any scientist concerned with research, is to be tried.

(b)   This experimental lack is not a simple oversight, or at least this oversight is heavily significant; it is quite simply the oversight of death: there has been a taboo (which will be lifted, in the deepest horror); the connotation belongs to the symbolic code.

(10) ' - no person had as yet been mesmerised "in articulo mortis".'

(a)   Fourth term of the 'programme' sequence: the content of the omission (there is clearly a reduction of the link between the assertion of the omission and its definition, in the rhetorical code: to announce/to specify).

(b)   The use of Latin (in articulo mortis), a juridical and medical language, produces an effect of scientificity (scientific code), but also, through the intermediary of a euphemism (saying in a little-known language something one does not dare say in everyday language), designates a taboo (symbolic code). It seems clear that what is taboo in death, what is essentially taboo, is the passage, the threshold, the dying; life and death are relatively well-classified states, and moreover they enter into a paradigmatic opposition, they are taken in hand by meaning, which is always reassuring; but the transition between the two states, or more exactly, as will be the case here, their mutual encroachment, outplays meaning and engenders horror: there is the transgression of an antithesis, of a classification.

(11) 'It remained to be seen'

The detail of the 'programme' is announced (rhetorical code and action sequence 'programme').

(12) 'first, whether, in such conditions, there existed in the patient any susceptibility to the magnetic influence;'

(a)   In the 'programme' sequence, this is the first coining of the announcement made in (11): this is the first problem to elucidate.

(b)   This Problem I itself entitles an organised sequence (or a sub-sequence of the 'programme'): here we have the first term: the formulation of the problem; its object is the very being of magnetic communication: does it exist, yes or no? (there will be an affirmative reply to this in (78): the long textual distance separating the question and the answer is specific to narrative structure, which authorises and even demands the careful con-

struction of sequences, each of which is a thread which weaves
in with its neighbours).

(13) 'secondly, whether if any existed, it was impaired or increased by the condition;'

(a) In the 'programme' sequence, the second problem here takes
its place (it will be noted that Problem II is linked to Problem I
by a logic of implication: 'if yes . . . then'; if not, then the
whole story would fall down; the alternative, according to the
instance of discourse, is thus faked).

(b) Second sub-sequence of 'programme': this is Problem II:
the first problem concerned the being of the phenomenon; the
second concerns its measurement (all this is very 'scientific');
the reply to the question will be given in (82); receptivity is
increased: 'In such experiments with this patient I had never perfectly succeeded before . . . but to my astonishment, . . . '.

(14) 'thirdly, to what extent, or for how long a period, the encroachments of Death might be arrested by the process.'

(a) This is Problem III posed by the 'programme'.

(b) This Problem III is formulated, like the others – this formulation will be taken up again emphatically in (17); the formulation
implies two sub-questions: (i) to what extent does hypnosis allow
life to encroach on death? The reply is given in (110): *up to and
including language;* (ii) for how long? There will be no direct
reply to this question: the encroachment of life on death (the
survival of the hypnotized dead man) will end after seven months,
but only through the arbitrary intervention of the experimenter.
We can then suppose: infinitely, or at the very least indefinitely
within the limits of observation.

(15) 'There were other points to be ascertained,'

The 'programme' mentions other problems which could be posed
with respect to the planned experiment, in a global form. The
phrase is equivalent to 'etcetera'. Valéry said that in nature there
was no etcetera; we can add: nor in the unconscious. In fact the
etcetera only belongs to the discourse of pretence: on the one
hand it pretends to play the scientific game of the vast experimental programme; it is an operator of the pseudo-real: on the
other hand, by glossing over and avoiding the other problems,
it reinforces the meaning of the questions already posed: the
powerfully symbolic has been announced, and the rest, under
the instance of discourse, is only play acting.

(16) 'but these most excited my curiosity,'

Here, in the 'programme', it's a matter of a global reminder of
the three problems (the 'reminder', or the 'résumé', like the
'announcement', are terms in the rhetorical code).

(17) ' - this last in especial, from the immensely important
character of its consequences.'

(a) An emphasis (a term in the rhetorical code) is placed on
Problem III.

(b) Two more undecidable codes: (i) scientifically, what is at
stake is the pushing back of a biological given, death; (ii)
symbolically, this is the transgression of meaning, which opposes
life and death.

ACTIONAL ANALYSIS OF LEXIAS 18-102

Among all the connotations that we have met with or at least
located in the opening of Poe's story, we have been able to define some as progressive terms in sequences of narrative actions;
we shall come back at the end to the different codes which analysis has brought to light, including, precisely, the actional code.
Putting off this theoretical clarification, we can isolate these sequences of actions so as to account with less trouble (and yet
maintaining a structural import in our purpose) for the rest of
the story. It will be understood that in effect it is impossible to
analyse minutely (and even less exhaustively: textual analysis
is never, and never wants to be, exhaustive) the whole of Poe's
story: it would take too long; but we do intend to undertake
the textual analysis of some lexias again at the culminating point
of the work (lexias 103-110). In order to join the fragment we
have analysed and the one we are going to analyse, at the level
of intelligibility, it will suffice to indicate the principal actional
sequences which begin and develop (but do not necessarily end)
between lexia 18 and lexia 102. Unfortunately, through lack of
space, we cannot give the text which separates our two fragments,
nor the numeration of the intermediate lexias; we shall give only
the actional sequences (and moreover without even being able to
bring out the detail of them term by term), to the detriment of
the other codes, which are more numerous and certainly more
interesting. This is essentially because the actional sequences
constitute by definition the anecdotic framework of the story
(I shall make a slight exception for the chronological code, indicating by an initial and a final notation, the point of the narrative
at which the beginning of each sequence is situated).

I Programme: the sequence has begun and been broadly developed in the fragment analysed. The problems posed by the planned experiment are known. The sequence continues and closes
with the choice of the subject (the patient) necessary for the
experiment: it will be M. Valdemar (the posing of the programme

takes place nine months before the moment of narration).
II Magnetisation (or rather, if this heavy neologism is permitted:
magnetisability). Before choosing M. Valdemar as subject of the
experiment, P. tested his magnetic receptiveness; it exists, but
the results are nonetheless disappointing: M.V's obedience involves some resistances. The sequence enumerates the terms of
this test, which is anterior to the decision on the experiment
and whose chronological position is not specified.
III Medical death: actional sequences are most often distended,
and intertwined with other sequences. In informing us of M.V's
bad state of health and the fatal outcome predicted by the doctors,
the narrative begins a very long sequence which runs throughout
the story, to finish only in the last lexia (150), with the liquefaction of M.V's body. The episodes of this sequence are numerous, split up, but still scientifically logical: ill-health, diagnosis,
death-sentence, deterioration, agony, mortification (physiological
signs of death) - it is at this point in the sequence that our
second textual analysis is situated -, disintegration, liquefaction.
IV Contract: P. makes the proposal to M. Valdemar of hypnotising
him when he reaches the threshold of death (since he knows he is
to die) and M.V. accepts; there is a contract between the subject
and the experimenter: conditions, proposition, acceptance, conventions, decision to proceed, official registration in the presence of doctors (this last point constitutes a sub-sequence).
V Catalepsy (7 months before the moment of narration, a Saturday
at 7.55): as the last moments of M.V have come and the experimenter has been notified by the patient himself, P. begins the
hypnosis 'in articulo mortis', in conformity with the programme and
the contract. This sequence can be headed 'catalepsy'; among
other terms, it involves: magnetic passes, resistances from the
subject, signs of a cataleptic state, observation by the experimenter, verification by the doctor (the actions of this sequence
take up 3 hours: it is 10.55).
VI Interrogation I (Sunday, 3 o'clock in the moring): P. four
times interrogates M. Valdemar under hypnosis; it is pertinent
to identify each interrogative sequence by the reply made by the
hypnotised M. Valdemar. The reply to this first interrogation
is: 'I am asleep' (canonically, the interrogative sequences involve
the announcement of the question, the question, delay or resistance of the reply, and the reply).
VII Interrogation II: this interrogation follows shortly after the
first. This time M. Valdemar replies: 'I am dying.'
VIII Interrogation III: the experimenter interrogates the dying,
hypnotised M. Valdemar again ('do you still sleep?'); he replies
by linking the two replies already made: 'still asleep - dying'.
IX Interrogation IV: P. attempts to interrogate M.V a fourth
time; he repeats his question (M.V will reply beginning with
lexia 105, see below).
   At this point we reach the moment in the narrative at which we
are going to take up the textual analysis again, lexia by lexia.
Between Interrogation III and the beginning of the analysis to

follow, an important term of the sequence 'medical death' intervenes: this is the mortification of M. Valdemar (101-102). Under
hypnosis, M. Valdemar is henceforth dead, medically speaking.
We know that recently, with the transplantation of organs, the
diagnosis of death has been called into question: today the evidence of electro-encephalography is required. In order to certify
M.V's death, Poe gathers (in 101 and 102) all the clinical signs
which in his day certified scientifically the death of a patient:
open rolled-back eyes, corpse-like skin, extinction of hectic
spots, fall and relaxation of the lower jaw, blackened tongue,
a general hideousness which makes those present shrink back
from the bed (here again the weave of the codes should be noted:
all the medical signs are also elements of horror; or rather, horror is always given under the alibi of science: the scientific code
and the symbolic code are actualised at the same time, undecidably).

With M. Valdemar medically dead, the narrative ought to finish:
the death of the hero (except in cases of religious resurrection)
ends the story. The re-launching of the anecdote (beginning with
lexia 103) appears then at once as a narrative necessity (to allow
the text to continue) and a logical scandal. This scandal is that
of the supplement: for there to be a supplement of narrative,
there will have to be a supplement of life: once again, the narrative stands for life.

TEXTUAL ANALYSIS OF LEXIAS 103-110

(103) 'I feel that I have reached a point of this narrative at
which every reader will be startled into positive disbelief. It
is my business, however, simply to proceed.'

(a) We know that announcing a discourse to come is a term in the
rhetorical code (and the metalinguistic code); we also know the
'aperitive' value of this connotation.

(b) It being one's business to speak the facts, without worrying
about the unpleasantness, forms part of the code of scientific
deontology. [At this point the French text has 'mon devoir est
de continuer.']

(c) The promise of an unbelievable 'real' forms part of the field
of the narrative considered as a commodity; it raises the 'price'
of the narrative; here, then, in the general code of communication, we have a sub-code, that of exchange, of which every narrative is a term, cf. (5b).

(104) 'There was no longer the faintest sign of vitality in M.
Valdemar; and concluding him to be dead, we were consigning
him to the charge of the nurses,'

In the long sequence of 'medical death', which we have pointed
out, the mortification was noted in (101): here it is confirmed;
in (101), M. Valdemar's state of death was described (through a
framework of indices); here it is asserted by means of a metalanguage.

(105)   'when a strong vibratory motion was observable in the
tongue. This continued for perhaps a minute. At the expiration
of this period,'

(a)   The chronological code ('one minute') supports two effects:
an effect of reality-precision, cf. (7a), and a dramatic effect:
the laborious welling-up of the voice, the delivery of the cry
recalls the combat of life and death: life is trying to break free
of the bogging-down of death, it is struggling (or rather it is
here rather death which is unable to break free of life: we should
not forget that M.V is dead: it is not life, but death, that he has
to hold back).

(b)   Shortly before the point we have reached, P. has interro-
gated M.V (for the fourth time); and before M.V replies, he is
clinically dead. Yet the sequence Interrogation IV is not closed
(this is where the supplement we have mentioned intervenes): the
movement of the tongue indicates that M.V is going to speak. We
must, then, construct the sequence as follows: question (100)/
(medical death)/attempt to reply (and the sequence will continue).

(c)   There is quite clearly a symbolism of the tongue. The tongue
is speech (cutting off the tongue is a mutilation of language, as
can be seen in the symbolic ceremony of punishment of blas-
phemers); further, there is something visceral about the tongue
(something internal), and at the same time, something phallic.
This general symbolism is here reinforced by the fact that the
tongue which moves is (paradigmatically) opposed to the black,
swollen tongue of medical death (101). It is, then, visceral life,
the life of the depths, which is assimilated to speech, and speech
itself is fetishized in the form of a phallic organ which begins to
vibrate, in a sort of pre-orgasm: the one-minute vibration is the
desire to come ['le désir de la jouissance'] and the desire for
speech: it is the movement of desire to get somewhere.

(106)   'there issued from the distended and motionless jaws
a voice,'

(a)   Little by little the sequence Interrogation IV continues, with
great detail in the global term 'reply'. Certainly, the delayed
reply is well known in the grammar of narrative; but it has in
general a psychological value; here, the delay (and the detail it
brings with it) is purely physiological: it is the welling-up of
the voice, filmed and recorded in slow-motion.

(b) The voice comes from the tongue (105), the jaws are only
the gateway; it does not come from the teeth: the voice in preparation is not dental, external, civilised (a marked dentalism is
the sign of 'distinction' in pronunciation), but internal, visceral,
muscular. Culture valorises what is sharp, bony, distinct, clear
(the teeth); the voice of death, on the other hand, comes from
what is viscous, from the internal muscular magma, from the
depths. Structurally, we have here a term in the symbolic code.

> (107) ' – such as it would be madness in me to attempt describ-
> ing. There are, indeed, two or three epithets which might be
> considered as applicable to it in part; I might say, for example,
> that the sound was harsh, and broken and hollow; but the hid-
> eous whole is indescribable, for the simple reason that no similar
> sounds have ever jarred upon the ear of humanity.'

(a) The metalinguistic code is present here, through a discourse
on the difficulty of holding a discourse; hence the use of frankly
metalinguistic terms: epithets, describing, indescribable.

(b) The symbolism of the voice unfolds: it has two characteristics: the internal ('hollow'), and the discontinuous ('harsh',
'broken'): this prepares a logical contradiction (a guarantee of
the supernatural): the contrast between the 'broken-up' and the
'glutinous' (108), whilst the internal gives credit to a feeling of
distance (108).

> (108) 'There were two particulars, nevertheless, which I
> thought then, and still think, might be stated as character-
> istic of the intonation – as well adapted to convey some idea of
> its unearthly peculiarity. In the first place, the voice seemed
> to reach our ears – at least mine – from a vast distance, or from
> some deep cavern within the earth. In the second place, it im-
> pressed me (I fear, indeed, that it will be impossible to make
> myself comprehended) as gelatinous or glutinous matters impress
> the sense of touch.
>   I have spoken both of "sound" and of "voice". I mean to say
> that the sound was one of distinct – of even wonderfully, thrill-
> ingly distinct – syllabification.'

(a) Here there are several terms of the metalinguistic (rhetorical)
code: the announcement ('characteristic'), the résumé ('I have
spoken') and the oratorical precaution ('I fear that it will be impossible to make myself comprehended').

(b) The symbolic field of the voice spreads, through the taking-
up of the 'in part' expressions of lexia (107): (i) the far-off
(absolute distance): the voice is distant because/so that the distance between death and life is/should be total (the 'because'
implies a motive belonging to the real, to what is 'behind' the
paper; the 'so that' refers to the demand of the discourse which

wants to continue, survive as discourse; by noting 'because/so that' we accept that the two instances, that of the real and that of discourse are twisted together, and we bear witness to the structural duplicity of all writing). The distance (between life and death) is affirmed the better to be denied: it permits the transgression, the 'encroachment', the description of which is the very object of the story; (ii) 'under the earth'; the thematics of voice are in general double, contradictory: sometimes the voice is a light, bird-like thing that flies off with life, and sometimes a heavy, cavernous thing, which comes up from below: it is voice tied down, anchored like a stone: this is an old mythical theme: the chthonic voice, the voice from beyond the grave (as is the case here); (iii) discontinuity founds language; there is therefore a supernatural effect in hearing a gelatinous, glutinous, viscous language; the notation has a double value: on the one hand it emphasizes the strangeness of this language which is contrary to the very structure of language; and on the other hand it adds up the malaises and dysphorias: the broken-up and the clinging, sticking (cf. the suppuration of the eyelids when the dead man is brought round from hypnosis, that is, when he is about to enter real death, (133)); (iv) the distinct syllabification constitutes the imminent speech of the dead man as a full, complete, adult language, as an essence of language, and not as a mumbled, approximate, stammered language, a lesser language, troubled by non-language; hence the fright, the terror: there is a glaring contradiction between death and language; the contrary of life is not death (which is a stereotype), but language: it is undecidable whether Valdemar is alive or dead; what is certain, is that he speaks, without one's being able to refer his speech to life or death.

(c) Let us note here an artifice which belongs to the chronological code: 'I thought then and I still think': there is here a co-presence of three temporalities: the time of the story, the diegesis ('I thought then'), the time of writing ('I think it at the time at which I'm writing'), and the time of reading (carried along by the present tense of writing, we think it ourselves at the moment of reading). The whole produces a reality-effect.

(109) 'M. Valdemar *spoke* - obviously in reply to the question I had propounded to him a few minutes before. I had asked him, it will be rememered, if he still slept.'

(a) Interrogation IV is here in progress: the question is here recalled (cf.100), the reply is announced.

(b) The words of the hypnotised dead man are the very reply to Problem III, posed in (14): to what extent can hypnosis stop death? Here the question is answered: up to and including language.

(110) 'He now said: – "Yes; – no; – I *have been* sleeping – and now – now – *I am dead*." '

From the structural point of view, this lexia is simple: it is the term 'reply' ('I am dead') to Interrogation IV. However, outside the diegetical structure (i.e. the presence of the lexia in an actional sequence) the connotation of the words ('I am dead') is of inexhaustible richness. Certainly there exist numerous mythical narratives in which death speaks; but only to say: 'I am alive'. There is here a true hapax of narrative grammar, a staging of words impossible as such: I am dead. Let us attempt to unfold some of these connotations:

(i) We have already extracted the theme of encroachment (of life on death); encroachment is a paradigmatic disorder, a disorder of meaning; in the life/death paradigm, the bar is normally read as 'against' (versus); it would suffice to read it as 'on' for encroachment to take place and the paradigm to be destroyed. That's what happens here; one of the spaces bites unwarrantedly into the other. The interesting thing here is that the encroachment occurs at the level of language. The idea that, once dead, the dead man can continue to act is banal; it is what is said in the proverb 'the dead man seizes the living'; it is what is said in the great myths of remorse or of posthumous vengeance; it is what is said comically in Forneret's sally: 'Death teaches incorrigible people to live'.[9] But here the action of the dead man is a purely linguistic action; and, to crown all, this language serves no purpose, it does not appear with a view to acting on the living, it says nothing but itself, it designates itself tautologically. Before saying 'I am dead', the voice says simply 'I am speaking'; a little like a grammatical example which refers to nothing but language; the uselessness of what is proffered is part of the scandal: it is a matter of affirming an essence which is not in its place (the displaced is the very form of the symbolic).

(ii) Another scandal of the enunciation is the turning of the metaphorical into the literal. It is in effect banal to utter the sentence 'I am dead!': it is what is said by the woman who has been shopping all afternoon at Printemps, and who has gone to her hairdresser's, etc.[10] The turning of the metaphorical into the literal, precisely for this metaphor, is impossible: the enunciation 'I am dead', is literally foreclosed (whereas 'I sleep' remained literally possible in the field of hypnotic sleep). It is, then, if you like, a scandal of language which is in question.

(iii) There is also a scandal at the level of 'langue' (and no longer at the level of discourse). In the ideal sum of all the possible utterances of language, the link of the first person (I) and the attribute 'dead' is precisely the one which is radically impossible: it is this empty point, this blind spot of language which the story comes, very exactly, to occupy. What is said is no other than this impossibility: the sentence is not descriptive, it is not constative, it delivers no message other than its own enunciation. In a sense we can say that we have here a performative, but such, certainly, that neither Austin nor Benveniste had foreseen it in their analyses (let us recall that the performative is the mode of utterance according to which the utterance refers only to its enunciation: 'I declare war'; performatives are always, by force, in the first person, otherwise they would slip towards the constative: 'he declares war'); here, the unwarranted sentence performs an impossibility.[11]

(iv) From a strictly semantic point of view, the sentence 'I am dead' asserts two contrary elements at once (life, death): it is an enantioseme, but is, once again, unique: the signifier expresses a signified (death) which is contradictory with its enunciation. And yet, we have to go further still: it is not simply a matter of a simple negation, in the psychoanalytical sense, 'I am dead' meaning in that case 'I am not dead', but rather an affirmation-negation: 'I am dead and not dead'; this is the paroxysm of transgression, the invention of an unheard-of category: the 'true-false', the 'yes-no', the 'death-life' is thought of as a whole which is indivisible, uncombinable, non-dialectic, for the antithesis implies no third term; it is not a two-faced entity, but a term which is one and new.

(v) A further psychoanalytical reflection is possible on the 'I am dead'. We have said that the sentence accomplished a scandalous return to the literal. That means that death, as primordially repressed, irrupts directly into language; this return is radically traumatic, as the image of explosion later shows (147: 'ejaculations of "dead! dead!" absolutely bursting from the tongue and not from the lips of the sufferer'): the utterance 'I am dead' is a taboo exploded. Now, if the symbolic is the field of neurosis, the return of the literal, which implies the foreclosure of the symbol, opens up the space of psychosis: at this point of the story, all symbolism ends, and with it all neurosis, and it is psychosis which enters the text, through the spectacular foreclosure of the signifier: what is extraordinary in Poe is indeed madness.

Other commentaries are possible, notably that of Jacques Derrida.[12] I have limited myself to those that can be drawn from structural analysis, trying to show that the unheard-of sentence 'I am dead' is in no way the unbelievable utterance, but much more radically the impossible enunciation.

Before moving on to methodological conclusions, I shall recall, at a purely anecdotal level, the end of the story: Valdemar remains dead under hypnosis for seven months; with the agreement of the doctors, P. then decides to wake him; the passes succeed and a little colour returns to Valdemar's cheeks; but while P. attempts to activate the patient by intensifying the passes, the cries of 'Dead! dead' explode on his tongue, and all at once his whole body escapes, crumbles, rots under the experimenter's hands, leaving nothing but a 'nearly liquid mass of loathsome - of detestable putridity'.

METHODOLOGICAL CONCLUSIONS

The remarks which will serve as a conclusion to these fragments
of analysis will not necessarily be theoretical; theory is not
abstract, speculative: the analysis itself, although it was carried
out on a contingent text, was already theoretical, in the sense
that it observed (that was its aim) a language in the process of
formation. That is to say – or to recall – that we have not carried
out an explication of the text: we have simply tried to grasp the
narrative as it was in the process of self-construction (which
implies at once structure and movement, system and infinity).
Our structuration does not go beyond that spontaneously accomplished by reading. In concluding, then, it is not a question of
delivering the 'structure' of Poe's story, and even less that of all
narratives, but simply of returning more freely, and with less
attachment to the progressive unfolding of the text, to the principal codes which we have located.

The word 'code' itself should not be taken here in the rigorous,
scientific, sense of the term. The codes are simply associative
fields, a supra-textual organization of notations which impose a
certain idea of structure; the instance of the code is, for us,
essentially cultural: the codes are certain types of 'déjà-lu', of
'déjà-fait': the code is the form of this 'déjà', constitutive of all
the writing in the world.

Although all the codes are in fact cultural, there is yet one,
among those we have met with, which we shall privilege by calling it the cultural code: it is the code of knowledge, or rather
of human knowledges, of public opinions, of culture as it is
transmitted by the book, by education, and in a more general and
diffuse form, by the whole of sociality. We met several of these
cultural codes (or several sub-codes of the general cultural code):
the scientific code, which (in our story) is supported at once by
the principles of experimentation and by the principles of medical
deontology; the rhetorical code, which gathers up all the social
rules of what is said: coded forms of narrative, coded forms of
discourse (the announcement, the résumé, etc.); metalinguistic
enunciation (discourse talking about itself) forms part of this
code; the chronological code: 'dating', which seems natural and
objective to us today, is in fact a highly cultural practice – which
is to be expected since it implies a certain ideology of time ('historical' time is not the same as 'mythical' time); the set of chronological reference-points thus constitute a strong cultural code (a
historical way of cutting up time for purposes of dramatisation,
of scientific appearance, of reality-effect); the socio-historical
code allows the mobilisation in the enunciation, of all the inbred
knowledge that we have about our time, our society, our country
(the fact of saying 'M. Valdemar' and not 'Valdemar', it will be
remembered, finds its place here). We must not be worried by
the fact that we can constitute extremely banal notations into
code: it is on the contrary their banality, their apparent insignificance that predisposes them to codification, given our definition

of code: a corpus of rules that are so worn we take them to be
marks of nature; but if the narrative departed from them, it
would very rapidly become unreadable.

The code of communication could also be called the code of destination. Communication should be understood in a restricted sense;
it does not cover the whole of the signification which is in a text,
and still less its 'signifiance'; it simply designates every relationship in the text which is stated as an address (this is the case of
the 'phatic' code, charged with the accentuation of the relationship
between narrator and reader), or as an exchange (the narrative
is exchanged for truth, for life). In short, communication should
here be understood in an economic sense (communication, circulation of goods).

The symbolic field (here 'field' is less inflexible than 'code') is,
to be sure, enormous; the more so in that here we are taking the
word 'symbol' in the most general possible sense, without being
bothered by any of its usual connotations; the sense to which we
are referring is close to that of psychoanalysis: the symbol is
broadly that feature of language which displaces the body and
allows a 'glimpse' of a scene other than that of the enunciation,
such as we think we read it; the symbolic framework in Poe's
story is evidently the transgression of the taboo of death, the disorder of classification, that Baudelaire has translated (very well)
by the 'empiètement' ('encroachment') of life on death (and not,
banally, of death on life); the subtlety of the story comes in part
from the fact that the enunciation seems to come from an asymbolic
narrator, who has taken on the role of the objective scientist,
attached to the fact alone, a stranger to the symbol (which does
not fail to come back in force in the story).

What we have called the code of actions supports the anecdotal
framework of the narrative; the actions, or the enunciations which
denote them, are organized in sequences; the sequence has an
approximate identity (its contour cannot be determined rigorously,
nor unchallengeably); it is justified in two ways: first because one
is led spontaneously to give it a generic name (for example a certain number of notations, ill-health, deterioration, agony, the
mortification of the body, its liquefaction, group naturally under
a stereotyped idea, that of 'medical death'); and, second, because
the terms of the actional sequence are interlinked (from one to
the next, since they follow one another throughout the narrative)
by an apparent logic; we mean by that that the logic which institutes the actional sequence is very impure from a scientific point
of view; it is only an apparent logic which comes not from the
laws of formal reasoning, but from our habits of reasoning and
observing: it is an endoxal, cultural logic (it seems 'logical' to us
that a severe diagnosis should follow the observation of a poor
state of health); and what is more this logic becomes confused
with chronology: what comes 'after' seems to us to be 'caused by'.
Although in narrative they are never pure, temporality and
causality seem to us to found a sort of naturality, intelligibility,
readability for the anecdote: for example, they allow us to resume

it (what the ancients called the argument, a word which is at once
logical and narrative).

One last code has traversed our story from its beginning: that
of the enigma. We have not had the chance to see it at work, because we have only analysed a very small part of Poe's story. The
code of the enigma gathers those terms through the stringing-
together of which (like a narrative sentence) an enigma is posed,
and which, after some 'delays', make up the piquancy of the narrative, the solution unveiled. The terms of the enigmatic (or
hermeneutic) code are well differentiated: for example, we have
to distinguish the positing of the enigma (every notation whose
meaning is 'there is an enigma') from the formulation of the enigma
(the question is exposed in its contingency); in our story, the
enigma is posed in the [French] title itself (the 'truth' is announced, but we don't yet know about what question), formulated
from the start (the scientific account of the problems linked to the
planned experiment), and even, from the very start, delayed:
obviously it is in the interests of every narrative to delay the
solution of the enigma it poses, since that solution will toll its
death-knell as a narrative: we have seen that the narrator uses
a whole paragraph to delay the account of the case, under cover
of scientific precautions. As for the solution of the enigma, it is
not here of a mathematical order; it is in sum the whole narrative
which replies to the question posed at the beginning, the question
of the truth (this truth can however be condensed into two points:
the proffering of 'I am dead', and the sudden liquefaction of the
dead man when he awakes from hypnosis); the truth here is not
the object of a revelation, but of a revulsion.

These are the codes which traverse the fragments we have
analysed. We deliberately don't structure them further, nor do we
try to distribute the terms within each code according to a logical
or semiological schema; this is because for us the codes are only
departures of 'déjà-lu', beginnings of intertextuality: the frayed
nature of the codes does not contradict structure (as, it is
thought, life, imagination, intuition, disorder, contradict system
and rationality), but on the contrary (this is the fundamental
affirmation of textual analysis) is an integral part of structuration.
It is this 'fraying' of the text which distinguishes structure - the
object of structural analysis, strictly speaking - from structuration
- the object of the textual analysis we have attempted to practise
here.

The textile metaphor we have just used is not fortuitous. Textual
analysis indeed requires us to represent the text as a tissue (this
is moreover the etymological sense), as a skein of different voices
and multiple codes which are at once interwoven and unfinished. A
narrative is not a tabular space, a flat structure, it is a volume.
a stereophony (Eisenstein placed great insistence on the counter-
point of his directions, thus initiating an identity of film and text):
there is a field of listening for written narrative; the mode of
presence of meaning (except perhaps for actional sequences) is
not development, but 'explosion' [éclat]: call for contact, com-

munication, the positing of contracts, exchange, flashes [éclats]
of references, glimmerings of knowledge, heavier, more penetrating blows, coming from the 'other scene', that of the symbolic,
a discontinuity of actions which are attached to the same sequence
but in a loose, ceaselessly interrupted way.

All this 'volume' is pulled forward (towards the end of the narrative), thus provoking the impatience of reading, under the
effect of two structural dispositions: (a) distortion: the terms of
a sequence or a code are separated, threaded with heterogeneous
elements: a sequence seems to have been abandoned (for example,
the degradation of Valdemar's health), but it is taken up again
further on, sometimes much later; an expectation is created; we
can now even define the sequence: it is the floating micro-struc-
ture which constructs not a logical object, but an expectation
and its resolution; (b) irreversibility: despite the floating
character of structuration, in the classical, readable narrative
(such as Poe's story), there are two codes which maintain a
directional order; the actional code (based on a logico-temporal
order) and the code of the enigma (the question is capped by its
solution); and in this way an irreversibility of narrative is created.
It is clearly on this point that modern subversion will operate:
the avant-garde (to keep a convenient word) attempts to make the
text thoroughly reversible, to expel the logico-temporal residue,
to attack empiricism (the logic of behaviour, the actional code)
and truth (the code of the enigma).

We must not, however, exaggerate the distance separating the
modern text from the classical narrative. We have seen, in Poe's
story, that one sentence very often refers to two codes simultaneously, without one's being able to choose which is the 'true' one
(for example, the scientific code and the symbolic code): what is
specific to the text, once it attains the quality of a text, is to constrain us to the undecidability of the codes. In the name of what
could we decide? In the author's name? But the narrative gives us
only an enunciator, a performer caught up in his own production.
In the name of such and such a criticism? All are challengeable,
carried off by history (which is not to say that they are useless:
each one participates, but only as one voice, in the text's volume).
Undecidability is not a weakness, but a structural condition of
narration: there is no unequivocal determination of the enunciation: in an utterance, several codes and several voices are there,
without priority. Writing is precisely this loss of origin, this loss
of 'motives' to the profit of a volume of indeterminations or over-
determinations: this volume is, precisely, 'signifiance'. Writing
[écriture] comes along very precisely at the point where speech
stops, that is from the moment one can no longer locate who is
speaking and one simply notes that speaking has started.

Translated by Geoff Bennington

NOTES

1   I have attempted the textual analysis of a whole narrative
    (which could not be the case here for reasons of space) in my
    book 'S/Z', Seuil, 1970, [trans. Richard Miller, London,
    Cape, 1975.]
2   For a tighter analysis of the notion of the lexia, and moreover
    of the operating procedures to follow, I am obliged to refer
    to 'S/Z' [pp. 13ff].
3   'Histoires extraordinaires', trans. Charles Baudelaire, Paris,
    N.R.F.; Livre de poche, 1969, pp. 329–345 ['The Collected
    Works', 3 vols. ed T.O. Mabbott, Cambridge, Harvard
    University Press, 1978, III, 1233–43. Translator's note: The
    fact that Barthes is working on the translation of a text
    originally in English evidently causes some extra problems of
    translation. Naturally I have used Poe's text; the quality of
    Baudelaire's translation is such that most of Barthes's com-
    ments apply equally to the original. The notable exception to
    this is the title, and Barthes in fact explicitly comments on
    this, continuing, however, to use the word 'vérité' in the
    French title in support of his analysis. I have specified by
    notes in square brackets wherever this might lead to con-
    fusion.]
4   [Cf Shoshana Felman's discussion of James's comparable state-
    ment that The Turn of the Screw is a 'trap', in Turning the
    Screw of Interpretation, 'Yale French Studies', 55/6, 1977,
    pp. 101ff.]
5   [Barthes is here making use of Derrida's description of the
    supplementary structure of the sign. See Chapter 1, pp. 17–18,
    above.]
6   [According to Barthes, it was the inability to read the plural-
    ity of texts ('asymbolism') that was precisely the failure of
    his critical adversary Raymond Picard. See 'Critique et vérité'
    Paris, Seuil, 1966, pp. 35–42.]
7   [See Roman Jakobson, Closing Statement: Linguistics and
    Poetics, in 'Style in Language', ed Thomas A. Sebeok, New
    York, MIT, 1960, pp. 355–6.]
8   [In Jakobson's definition (Shifters, Verbal Categories, and
    the Russian Verb, in 'Selected Writings', 5 vols, The Hague,
    Mouton, 1962–, II, pp. 130–2) 'shifters' are the units in
    language which create the difference between the 'message'
    per se and the 'meaning' of a communication. Specifically, they
    refer to those units which refer to the mode of utterance or
    context, such as 'I', 'you', 'him', etc. But, typically, Barthes
    elsewhere modifies this to see 'shifting' as characteristic of
    all writing; see The Shifter as Utopia, in 'Roland Barthes by
    Roland Barthes', trans. Richard Howard, London, Macmillan,
    1977, pp. 165–6.]
9   [Xavier Forneret (1809–84), poet. His 'Vapeurs, ni vers ni
    prose' passed unnoticed when it was published in 1838, but
    was reissued in 1952 by André Breton, who situated him

in the tradition of Lautréamont and the Surrealists.]
10 [In French this metaphorical usage corresponds to the English expression 'I'm dead tired.']
11 [See J.L. Austin, 'Philosophical Papers', ed J.O. Urmson and G.J. Warnock, Oxford, Oxford University Press, 1961; 'How To Do Things With Words', ed J.O. Urmson and Marina Sbisa, Oxford, Oxford University Press, 1962; John R. Searle, 'Speech Acts: An Essay in the Philosophy of Language', Cambridge, Cambridge University Press, 1969. Cf. Stanley E. Fish, How To Do Things With Austin and Searle: Speech Act Theory and Literary Criticism, in 'Modern Language Notes', 91, 1976, pp. 983-1025; and Jacques Derrida, Signature Event Context, in 'Glyph' 1, 1977, pp. 172-97; John R. Searle, Reiterating the Differences: a Reply to Derrida, ibid., pp. 198-208; and Derrida's reply, Limited inc., in 'Glyph' 2, 1977, pp. 162-254. Cf. also, Paul de Man, Action and Identity in Nietzsche, Chapter 13, below.]
12 Jacques Derrida, 'La Voix et le phénomène', Paris, P.U.F., 1967, pp. 60-1, [Speech and Phenomena, trans. David B. Allison, Evanston, Northwestern University Press, 1973, pp. 54-5.]

FURTHER READING

BARTHES, ROLAND, 'S/Z', trans. Richard Miller, London, Cape, 1975.
— L'Effet de Réel, in 'Communications', 11, 1968, pp. 84-9.
— 'Prétexte: Roland Barthes', Colloque de Cerisy, Paris, 10/18, 1978: La Limite entre la vie et la mort, Dracula et Frankenstein, by François Flahault, and discussion with Barthes, pp. 65-86.
'Centrum', Forum: Speech Acts and Literature, 3:2, Fall 1975.
— A Speech-Act Theory Bibliography, by Robert B. Meyers and Karen Hopkins, 5:2, Fall 1977, pp. 73-108.
CHABROL, CLAUDE (ed), 'Sémiotique narrative et textuelle', Paris, Larousse, 1973.
CIXOUS, HÉLÈNE, Fiction and its Phantoms: A Reading of Freud's 'Das Unheimliche' ['The Uncanny'], in 'New Literary History', 7:3, Spring 1976, pp. 525-48.
— Ensemble Poe, in 'Prénoms de personne', Paris, Seuil, 1974, pp. 155-224.
DERRIDA, JACQUES, Entre Crochets [interview], in 'Digraphe', 8, 1976, pp. 107-9.
FOUCAULT, MICHEL, Theatrum Philosophicum, in 'Language, Counter-Memory, Practice', ed and trans. Donald F. Bouchard, Ithaca, Cornell, 1977, pp. 173-5.
GREIMAS, A.J, 'Maupassant, la sémiotique du texte: Exercices pratiques', Paris, Seuil, 1976.
— Elements of a Narrative Grammar, in 'Diacritics', 7:1, Spring 1977, pp. 23-40 (also contains a short Greimas bibliography).
GROSS, RUTH V., Rich Text/Poor Text: A Kafkan Confusion,

in 'PMLA', 95:2, March 1980, pp. 168-82.
OHMANN, RICHARD, Speech Acts and the Definition of Literature, in 'Philosophy and Rhetoric', 4:1, Winter 1971, pp. 1-19.
— Literature as Act, in Seymour Chatman (ed), 'Approaches to Poetics', New York, Columbia University Press, 1973, pp. 81-107.
RASTIER, FRANÇOIS, 'Essais de sémiotique discursive', Paris, Mame, 1973.
RIDDEL, JOSEPH N., The 'Crypt' of Edgar Poe, in 'Boundary 2', 7:3, Spring 1979, pp. 117-44.

7 THE CRITICAL DIFFERENCE:

Balzac's 'Sarrasine' and
Barthes's 'S/Z'

Barbara Johnson

[Barbara Johnson's exemplary reading of Barthes's 'S/Z' - and
of the story 'S/Z' reads, Balzac's 'Sarrasine' - needs little introduction, both because the essay explains itself with admirable
clarity, and because Barthes's -Textual Analysis of Poe's
'Valdemar'-, which demonstrates the method of 'S/Z', is included
in the present volume. This essay shows how deconstruction
works particularly well when dealing with a complex chain of
writings or intertexts, and also how psychoanalytic concepts can
be called into play for deconstructive analysis. 'S/Z' is a particularly interesting topic for investigation in so far as it seems to
have been read in two distinct ways. In -The Ideology of the Text-
Fredric Jameson specifically suggests that '"S/Z", like the novella
of which it is a study, may be said to be very much a mixed or
hybrid object, and just as "Sarrasine" will include elements of
textuality within an older "classical" or traditional form, so we
may suggest that "S/Z" itself combines both realistic and modern-
istic features' (p. 213). Jameson argues that it can be read as a
study of the relation between castration and artistic production
(as analysed in his own 'Prison-House of Language', p. 148), or
as a 'textualisation' of Balzac (as developed in his -The Ideology
of the Text-). Another way of putting it would be to say that
there are not two books in 'S/Z', but that a rigid appropriation or
schematisation of the codes, or emphasis on the story as a revelation of castration, produces a structuralist 'S/Z'; on the other
hand emphasis on its textuality, on its celebration of the transgression of the realist text, produces a post-structuralist 'S/Z'.

Barbara Johnson's reading inclines towards the former interpretation. A sense, derived from psychoanalysis, of the necessarily reductive nature of interpretation leads her to trace the
tactics of Barthes's own 'writerly' reading of a 'readerly' text,
and to discern a curious homology between Barthes's own critical
concerns and those of the story that he analyses. The collapse of
metalinguistic distance that Johnson describes is, however, perhaps equally appropriate for her own text. The following remarks
are offered more in the form of an afterword than as an introduction.

Johnson's argument is that Barthes only succeeds in making his
analysis 'writerly' or plural, by making the story 'readerly', or a
limit text, so that for Barthes, castration becomes *the* meaning of
the text - a closure which, she argues, the story itself refuses.
Barthes's 'Valdemar', however, prompts a re-analysis of this
description. Whereas 'S/Z's analysis seems to be moving toward

the final lifting of the veil of closure from a limit text, in 'Valde-mar' Barthes clearly finds a moment of text in the text itself. Focusing on the words 'I am dead', Barthes insists on their impos-sibility. If meant literally, as they are, then 'the tenor of the enounced . . . is strictly incompatible with the conditions of its enunciation.' This 'enantioseme', which is the very object of the story, reveals the narrative as producing its own transgression, partaking of the 'supplemental' space of writing. Here the 'en-croachment', the 'supplement of life that encroaches on death', is language: language which undoes meaning, which produces the impossible performative, the 'paroxysm of transgression', the words 'I am dead'. To find language defying all logic, producing two contradictory but positive opposites in the same place, is also to find 'the empty point, the blind spot of language that the story comes to occupy'. Why? Because this moment of transgression is the moment when representation breaks down; it produces a signi-fier which has no signified. The words of M. Valdemar erase the limit between life/death, producing an impossible representation, the breaking-point of realism: 'There is no recourse to an inside/ outside. You are there permanently. There is no reversal from one term to another. Hence, the horror' (Hélène Cixous, 'Fiction and Its Phantoms', 'NLH' 7, 1976, p. 545). In the story's own un-doing or deconstruction of the opposition life/death, Barthes finds the moment of breakthrough, of text.

To return to 'S/Z' after 'Valdemar' is to find that Barthes also stresses in this text (pp. 214-16) the moment at which 'Sarrasine' undoes itself. Not however, through the revelation of castration, but through the transgression of the axis of castration, Antithesis:

> Among all the figures, one of the most stable is the Antithesis; its apparent function is to consecrate (and domesticate) by a name, by a metalinguistic object, the division between opposites and the very irreducibility of this division. The antithesis separates for eternity . . . the antithesis is the battle between two plenitudes set ritually face to face like two fully armed warriors . . . . Every joining of two antithetical terms, every mixture, every conciliation - in short, every passage through the wall of the Antithesis - thus constitutes a transgression (pp. 26-7).

Whereas it is the axis of castration that enables meaning, it is the transgression of this opposition in 'S/Z' that undoes meaning, re-presentation, and realism. Such a scandal produces an explosion in the text:

> This is what happens when the arcana of meaning are subverted, when the sacred separation of the paradigmatic poles is abolished, when one removes the separating barrier, the basis of all 'per-tinence' . . . . Antithesis cannot be transgressed with impunity: *meaning* (and its classifying basis) is a question of life or death (pp. 65-6).

It is towards this crossing of the axis (the bar of 'S/Z') that the story moves. The revelation of Zambinella's castration is not simply the revelation of a secret per se:

> As for the castrato himself, we would be wrong to place him of necessity among the castrated: he is the blind and mobile flaw in this system (36).

> The coin is symbolic of the incommunicability of the two sides: like the paradigmatic slash mark of an antithesis, metal cannot be traversed: yet it will be, the Antithesis will be transgressed (48).

The castrato, therefore, is not the meaning of the text, but the 'blind and mobile flaw' in the system that undoes meaning, abolishes difference.

To produce a deconstructive reading of 'Sarrasine' then, Johnson is forced 'to cut the braid, to sketch the castrating gesture' (160) for 'S/Z'. The final transgression that makes meaning impossible explodes the (readerly) realism of 'Sarrasine', and perhaps also the force of Barbara Johnson's first question: 'Does Balzac's story really uphold the unambiguousness of the readerly values to which Barthes relegates it?' For this is hardly the way in which Barthes does seem to read it:

> It is fatal, the text says, to remove the dividing line, the paradigmatic slash mark which permits meaning to function (the wall of Antithesis), life to reproduce (the opposition of the sexes), property to be protected (rule of contract) . . . it is no longer possible to represent, to make things representative, individuated, separate, assigned; 'Sarrasine' represents the very confusion of representation, the unbridled (pandemic) circulation of signs, of fortunes (pp. 215-16).

It could be argued then, that just as Barbara Johnson accuses Barthes of relegating Balzac's text to the readerly, in order to produce his own writerly reading, so she herself relegates Barthes's 'S/Z' to the readerly in order to produce her own writerly reading. This, as she points out, is precisely what Sarrasine does to Zambinella in the story. At this point, we arrive (and end) with the problem of the reading-effect 'trap' which Shoshana Felman analyses (but does not herself escape from) in -The Turn of the Screw-:

> The scene of the critical debate is . . . a repetition of the scene dramatized in the text. The critical interpretation, in other words, not only elucidates the text but also reproduces it dramatically, unwittingly participates in it. Through its very reading, the text, so to speak, acts itself out. As a reading-effect, this inadvertent 'acting-out' is indeed uncanny: whichever way the reader turns, he can but be turned by the text, he can

but perform it by repeating it. (Turning the Screw of Interpretation, 'Yale French Studies', 55/56, 1977, p. 101.)

Thus not merely at the individual level, the proliferation of criticism reproduces the proliferation of narrative, each demanding
its own authenticity. This curious structure is analysed further
in Jeffrey Mehlman's -Trimethylamin-.]

Literary criticism as such can perhaps be called 'the art of re-
reading'. I would therefore like to begin by quoting the remarks
about re-reading made by Roland Barthes in 'S/Z'.

> Re-reading, an operation contrary to the commercial and ideo-
> logical habits of our society, which would have us 'throw away'
> the story once it has been consumed ('devoured'), so that we
> can then move on to another story, buy another book, and
> which is tolerated only in certain marginal categories of readers
> (children, old people, and professors), re-reading is here sug-
> gested at the outset, for it alone saves the text from repetition
> *(those who fail to re-read are obliged to read the same story*
> *everywhere)* (Roland Barthes, 'S/Z', translated by Richard
> Miller, New York: Hill and Wang, 1974, pp. 15-16; emphasis
> mine).

What does this paradoxical statement imply? First, it implies that
a single reading is composed of the already-read, that what we
can see in a text the first time is already in us, not in it, in us in
so far as we ourselves are a stereotype, an already-read text;
and in the text only to the extent that the already-read is that
aspect of a text which it must have in common with its reader in
order for it to be readable at all. When we read a text once, in
other words, we can see in it only what we have already learned
to see before.

Second, the statement that those who do not re-read must read
the same story everywhere involves a reversal of the usual properties of the words 'same' and 'different'. Here, it is the con-
suming of different stories which is equated with the repetition of
the same, while it is the re-reading of the same which engenders
what Barthes calls the 'text's difference'. This critical concept
of difference, which has been valorised both by Saussurian linguistics and by the Nietzschean tradition in philosophy - particularly the work of Jacques Derrida - is crucial to the practice of
deconstructive criticism. I would therefore like to examine here
some of its implications and functions.

In a sense, it could be said that to make a critical difference is
the object of all criticism as such. The very word 'criticism' comes
from the Greek verb 'krinein', 'to separate or choose', that is,
to differentiate. The critic not only seeks to establish standards
for evaluating the differences between texts, but also tries to
perceive something uniquely different within each text he reads

and in so doing to establish his own individual difference from
other critics. But this is not quite what Barthes means when he
speaks of the text's difference. On the first page of 'S/Z', he
writes:

This difference is not, obviously some complete, irreducible
quality (according to a mythic view of literary creation), it is
not what designates the individuality of each text, what names,
signs, finishes off each work with a flourish; on the contrary,
it is a difference which does not stop and which is articulated
upon the infinity of texts, of languages, of systems: a difference of which each text is the return (p. 3).

In other words, a text's difference is not its uniqueness, its
special identity. It is the text's way of differing from itself. And
this difference is perceived only in the act of re-reading. It is
the way in which the text's signifying energy becomes unbound,
to use Freud's term, through the process of repetition, which is
the return not of the same but of difference. Difference, in other
words, is not what distinguishes one identity from another. It is
not a difference between (or at least not between independent
units). It is a difference within. Far from constituting the text's
unique identity, it is that which subverts the very idea of identity, infinitely deferring the possibility of adding up the sum of
a text's part or meanings and reaching a totalised, integrated
whole.

Let me illustrate this idea further by turning for a moment to
Rousseau's 'Confessions'. Rousseau's opening statement about
himself is precisely an affirmation of difference: 'I am made unlike anyone I have ever met; I will even venture to say that I am
like no one in the whole world. I may be no better, but at least
I am different' (Penguin, 1954, p. 17). Now, this can be read as
an unequivocal assertion of uniqueness, of difference between
Rousseau and the whole rest of the world. This is the boast on
which the book is based. But in what does the uniqueness of this
self consist? It is not long before we find out: 'There are times
when I am so unlike myself that I might be taken for someone else
of an entirely opposite character' (p. 126). 'In me are united two
almost irreconcilable characteristics, though in what way I cannot
imagine' (p. 112). In other words, this story of the self's difference from others inevitably becomes the story of its own unbridgeable difference from itself. Difference is not engendered in the
space between identities; it is what makes all totalisation of the
identity of a self or the meaning of a text impossible.

It is this type of textual difference which informs the process
of deconstructive criticism. Deconstruction is not synonymous
with 'destruction', however. It is in fact much closer to the original meaning of the word 'analysis' itself, which etymologically
means 'to undo' - a virtual synonym for 'to de-construct'. The deconstruction of a text does not proceed by random doubt or arbitrary subversion, but by the careful teasing out of warring forces

of signification within the text itself. If anything is destroyed in
a deconstructive reading, it is not the text, but the claim to unequivocal domination of one mode of signifying over another. A
deconstructive reading is a reading which analyses the specificity
of a text's critical difference from itself.

I have chosen to approach this question of critical difference
by way of Barthes's 'S/Z' for three reasons: (1) Barthes sets up
a critical value system explicitly based on the paradigm of difference, and in the process works out one of the earliest, most influential, and most lucid and forceful syntheses of contemporary
French theoretical thought; (2) the Balzac story which Barthes
chooses to analyse in 'S/Z' is itself in a way a study of difference
– a subversive and unsettling formulation of the question of sexual
difference; (3) the confrontation between Barthes and Balzac may
have something to say about the critical differences between
theory and practice, on the one hand, and between literature and
criticism, on the other.

I shall begin by recalling the manner in which Barthes outlines
his value system:

> Our evaluation can be linked only to a practice, and this prac-
> tice is that of writing. On the one hand, there is what it is
> possible to write, and on the other, what it is no longer possible
> to write. . . . What evaluation finds is precisely this value:
> what can be written (rewritten) today: the 'writerly' (le script-
> ible). Why is the writerly our value? Because the goal of liter-
> ary work (of literature as work) is to make the reader no longer
> a consumer, but a producer of the text. . . . Opposite the
> writerly text is its countervalue, its negative, reactive value:
> what can be read, but not written: the 'readerly' (le lisible).
> We call any readerly text a classic text (p. 4).

Here, then, is the major polarity which Barthes sets up as a tool
for evaluating texts: the readerly versus the writerly. The
readerly is defined as a product consumed by the reader; the
writerly is a process of production in which the reader becomes a
producer: it is 'ourselves writing'. The readerly is constrained
by considerations of representation: it is irreversible, 'natural',
decidable, continuous, totalisable, and unified into a coherent
whole based on the signified. The writerly is infinitely plural
and open to the free play of signifiers and of difference, uncon-
strained by representative considerations, and transgressive of
any desire for decidable, unified, totalised meaning.

With this value system, one would naturally expect to find
Barthes going on to extol the play of infinite plurality in some
Joycean or Mallarméan piece of writerly obscurity, but no: he
turns to Balzac, one of the most readerly of readerly writers, as
Barthes himself insists. Why then does Barthes choose to talk
about Balzac? Barthes himself skilfully avoids confronting this
question. But perhaps it is precisely the way in which Barthes's
choice of Balzac doesn't follow logically from his value system –

that is, the way in which Barthes somehow differs from himself - which opens up the critical difference which we must analyse here.

Although Balzac's text apparently represents for Barthes the negative, readerly end of the hierarchy, Barthes's treatment of it does seem to illustrate all the characteristics of the positive, writerly end. In the first place, one cannot help but be struck by the plurality of Barthes's text itself with its numerous sizes of print, its 'systematic use of digression', and its successive superposable versions of the same but different story, from the initial reproduction of Girodet's Endymion to the four appendices which repeat the book's contents in different forms. The reading technique proper also obeys the demand for fragmentation and pluralisation, and consists in manhandling the text:

> What we seek is to sketch the stereographic space of writing (which will here be a classic, readerly writing). The comment-ary, based on the affirmation of the plural, cannot work with 'respect' to the text; the tutor text will ceaselessly be broken, interrupted without any regard for its natural divisions . . . ; the work of the commentary, once it is separated from any ideol-ogy of totality, consists precisely in manhandling the text, interrupting it (lui couper la parole). What is thereby denied is not the quality of the text (here incomparable) but its 'naturalness' (p. 15).

Barthes goes on to divide the story diachronically into 561 frag-ments called lexias and synchronically into five so-called voices or codes, thus transforming the text into a 'complex network' with 'multiple entrances and exits'.

The purpose of these cuts and codes is to pluralise the reader's intake, to effect a resistance to the reader's desire to restructure the text into large, ordered masses of meaning: 'If we want to re-main attentive to the plural of a text . . . , we must renounce structuring this text in large masses, as was done by classical rhetoric and by secondary-school explication: no construction of the text' [pp. 11-12]. In leaving the text as heterogeneous and discontinuous as possible, in attempting to avoid the repressive-ness of the attempt to dominate the message and force the text into a single ultimate meaning, Barthes thus works a maximum of disintegrative violence and a minimum of integrative violence.

The question to ask is whether this 'anti-constructionist' (as opposed to 'de-constructionist') fidelity to the fragmented signi-fier succeeds in laying bare the functional plurality of Balzac's text, or whether in the final analysis a certain systematic level of textual difference is not also lost and flattened by Barthes's refusal to reorder or reconstruct the text.

Let us now turn to Balzac's 'Sarrasine' itself. The story is divided into two parts, the story of the telling and the telling of the story. In the first part, the narrator attempts to seduce a beautiful Marquise by telling her the second part; that is, he wants to exchange narrative knowledge for carnal knowledge. The lady wants to know the secret of the mysterious old man at the party, and the narrator wants to know the lady. Story-telling, as Barthes points out, is thus not an innocent, neutral activity, but rather part of a bargain, an act of seduction. But here the bargain is not kept; the deal backfires. The knowledge the lady has acquired, far from bringing about her surrender, prevents it. The last thing she says is precisely: 'No one will have *known* me.'

It is obvious that the key to this failure of the bargain lies in the content of the story used to fulfil it. That story is about the passion of the sculptor Sarrasine for the opera singer La Zambinella, and is based not on knowledge but on ignorance: the sculptor's ignorance of the Italian custom of using castrated men instead of women to play the soprano parts on the operatic stage. The sculptor, who had seen in La Zambinella the perfect female body for the first time united in one person, a veritable Pygmalion's statue come to life, thus finds out that this image of feminine perfection literally has been carved by a knife, not in stone but in the flesh itself. He who had proclaimed his willingness to die for his love ends up doing just that, killed by La Zambinella's protector.

How is it that the telling of this sordid little tale ends up subverting the very bargain it was intended to fulfil? Barthes's answer to this is clear: 'castration is contagious'; 'contaminated by the castration she has just been told about, [the Marquise] impels the narrator into it' (p. 36).

What is interesting about this story of seduction and castration is the way in which it unexpectedly reflects upon Barthes's own critical value system. For in announcing that 'the tutor text will ceaselessly be broken, interrupted without any regard for its natural divisions', is Barthes not implicitly privileging something like castration over what he calls 'the ideology of totality'? 'If the text is subject to some form,' he writes, 'this form is not unitary . . . finite; it is the fragment, the slice, the cut up or erased network' (p. 20; translation modified). Indeed, might it not be possible to read Balzac's opposition between the ideal woman and the castrato as metaphorically assimilable to Barthes's opposition between the readerly and the writerly? Like the readerly text, Sarrasine's deluded image of La Zambinella is a glorification of perfect unity and wholeness:

At that instant he marvelled at the ideal beauty he had hitherto sought in life, seeking in one often unworthy model the roundness of a perfect leg; in another, the curve of a breast; in another, white shoulders: finally taking some girl's neck, some woman's hands, and some child's smooth knees, without ever having encountered under the cold Parisian sky the rich, sweet creations of ancient Greece. La Zambinella displayed to him, united, living, and delicate, those exquisite female forms he so ardently desired (pp. 237-8).

But like the writerly text, Zambinella is actually fragmented, un-natural, and sexually undecidable. Like the readerly, the soprano is a product to be 'devoured' ('With his eyes, Sarrasine devoured Pygmalion's statue, come down from its pedestal' [p. 238]), while, like the writerly, castration is a process of production, an active and violent indetermination. The soprano's appearance seems to embody the very essence of 'woman' as a signified ('This was woman herself' [p. 248]), while the castrato's reality, like the writerly text, is a mere play of signifiers, emptied of any ulti-mate signified, robbed of what the text calls a 'heart': 'I have no heart,' says Zambinella, 'the stage where you saw me . . . is my life, I have no other' (p. 247).

Here, then, is a first answer to the question of why Barthes might have chosen this text: it explicitly thematises the opposition between unity and fragmentation, between the idealised signified and the discontinuous empty play of signifiers, which underlies his opposition between the readerly and the writerly. The tradi-tional value system which Barthes is attempting to reverse is thus already mapped out within the text he analyses. Two ques-tions, however, immediately present themselves: (1) Does Bal-zac's story really uphold the unambiguousness of the readerly values to which Barthes relegates it? Does Balzac simply regard ideal beauty as a lost paradise and castration as a horrible tragedy? (2) If Barthes is really attempting to demystify the ideology of totality, and if his critical strategy implicitly gives a positive value to castration, why does his analysis of Balzac's text still seem to take castration at face value as an unmitigated and catastrophic horror?

In order to answer these questions, let us take another look at Balzac's story. To regard castration as the ultimate narrative revelation and as the unequivocal cause of Sarrasine's tragedy, as Barthes repeatedly does, is to read the story more or less from Sarrasine's point of view. It is in fact Barthes's very attempt to pluralise the text which thus restricts his perspective: however 'disrespectfully' he may cut up or manhandle the story, his read-ing remains to a large extent dependent on the linearity of the signifier, and thus on the successive unfoldings of the truth of castration to Sarrasine and to the reader. Sarrasine's ignorance, however, is not a simple lack of knowledge, but also a blindness to the injustice which is not only being done to him, but which he is also potentially doing to the other. This does not mean that Balzac's story is a plea for the prevention of cruelty to castrati, but that the failure of the couple to unite can perhaps not simply be attributed to the literal fact of castration. Let us therefore examine the nature of Sarrasine's passion more closely.

Upon seeing La Zambinella for the first time, Sarrasine exclaims: 'To be loved by her, or to die!' (p. 238). This alternative places all of the energy of the passion not on the object La Zambinella, but on the subject, Sarrasine himself. To be loved, or to die; to exist as the desired object, or not to exist at all. What is at stake is not the union between two people, but the narcissistic awakening of one. Seeing La Zambinella is Sarrasine's first experience of himself as an object of love. By means of the image of sculpturesque perfection, Sarrasine thus falls in love with none other than himself. Balzac's fictional narrator makes explicit the narcissistic character of Sarrasine's passion and at the same time nostalgically identifies with it himself when he calls it 'this golden age of love, during which we take pleasure in our own feeling and in which we are happy almost by ourselves' (p. 240). Sarrasine contents himself with La Zambinella as the product of his own sculptor's imagination ('This was more than a woman, this was a masterpiece!' [p. 238]), and does not seek to find out who she is in reality ('As he began to realise that he would soon have to act, . . . to ponder, in short, on ways to see her, speak to her, these great, ambitious thoughts made his heart swell so painfully that he put them off until later, deriving as much satisfaction from his physical suffering as he did from his intellectual pleasures' [p. 240]). When the sculptor is finally forced into the presence of his beloved, he reads in her only the proof of his own masculinity – she is the ideal woman, therefore he is the ideal man. When Sarrasine sees La Zambinella shudder at the pop of a cork, he is charmed by her weakness and says, 'My strength (puissance) is your shield' (p. 244). La Zambinella's weakness is thus the inverted mirror image of Sarrasine's potency. In this narcissistic system, the difference between the sexes is based on symmetry, and it is precisely the castrato that Sarrasine does indeed love – the image of the lack of what he thereby thinks he himself possesses. When Sarrasine says that he would not be able to love a strong woman, he is saying in effect that he would be unable to love anyone who was not his symmetrical opposite and the proof of his masculinity. This is to say that even if La Zambinella had been a real woman, Sarrasine's love would be a refusal to deal with her as a real other. This type of narcissism is in fact just as contagious in the story as castration: the Marquise sees the narcissistic delusion inherent in the narrator's own passion, and, banteringly foreshadowing one of the reasons for her ultimate refusal, protests: 'Oh, you fashion me to your own taste. What tyranny! You don't want me for myself!' (p. 233).

Sarrasine cannot listen to the other *as* other. Even when Zambinella suggests the truth by means of a series of equivocal remarks culminating in the question (directed toward Sarrasine's offers to sacrifice everything for love) – 'And if I were not a woman?' – Sarrasine cries: 'What a joke! Do you think you can deceive an artist's eye?' (p. 247). Sarrasine's strength is thus a shield against La Zambinella, not for her. He creates her as his own symmetrical opposite and through her loves only himself. This is why the revelation of the truth is fatal. The castrato is both outside the difference between the sexes and at the same time the literalisation of its illusory symmetry. He is that which subverts the desire for symmetrical, binary difference by fulfilling it. He is what destroys Sarrasine's reassuring masculinity by revealing that it is based on castration. But Sarrasine's realisation

that he himself is thereby castrated, that he is looking at his true
mirror image, is still blind to the fact that he had never been
capable of loving in the first place. His love was from the beginning the cancellation and castration of the other.

What Sarrasine dies of, then, is precisely a failure to re-read
in the exact sense with which we began this paper. What he
devours so eagerly in La Zambinella is actually located within
himself: a collection of sculpturesque clichés about feminine
beauty and his own narcissism. In thinking that he knows where
difference is located – between the sexes – what he is blind to is
precisely a difference that cannot be situated between, but only
within. In Balzac's story, the fact of castration thus stands as
the literalisation of the 'difference within' which prevents any
subject from coinciding with itself. In Derrida's terms, Sarrasine
reads the opera singer as pure Voice ('his passion for La Zambinella's voice' [p. 241]), as an illusion of imaginary immediacy
('The distance between himself and La Zambinella had ceased to
exist, he possessed her' [p. 239]), as a perfectly readable, motivated sign ('Do you think you can deceive an artist's eye?'), as
full and transparent logos, whereas she is the very image of the
empty and arbitrary sign, of writing inhabited by its own irreducible difference from itself. And it can thus be seen that the failure to re-read is hardly a trivial matter: for Sarrasine, it is fatal.

Balzac's text thus itself demystifies the logocentric blindness
inherent in Sarrasine's reading of the Zambinellian text. But if
Sarrasine's view of La Zambinella as an image of perfect wholeness
and unequivocal femininity is analogous to the classic, readerly
conception of literature according to Barthes's definition, then
Balzac's text has already worked out the same type of deconstruction of the readerly ideal as that which Barthes is trying to
accomplish as if it were in opposition to the classic text. In other
words, Balzac's text already 'knows' the limits and blindnesses
of the readerly, which it personifies in Sarrasine. Balzac has
already in a sense done Barthes's work for him. The readerly text
is itself nothing other than a deconstruction of the readerly text.

But at the same time, Balzac's text does not operate a simple
reversal of the readerly hierarchy: Balzac does not proclaim castration as the truth behind the readerly's blindness in as unequivocal a way as Barthes's own unequivocality would lead one to
believe. For every time Balzac's text is about to use the word
castration, it leaves a blank instead. 'Ah, you are a woman,'
cries Sarrasine in despair; 'for even a . . .' He breaks off. 'No,'
he continues, '*he* would not be so cowardly' (p. 251). Balzac
repeatedly castrates his text of the word castration. Far from
being the unequivocal answer to the text's enigma, castration is
the way in which the enigma's answer is withheld. Castration is
what the story must, and cannot, say. But what Barthes does in
his reading is to label these textual blanks 'taboo on the word
castrato' (pp. 75, 177, 195, 210). He fills in the textual gaps with
a name. He erects castration into *the* meaning of the text, its ultimate signified. In so doing, however, he makes the idea of castra-

tion itself into a readerly fetish, the supposed answer to all the text's questions, the final revelation in the 'hermeneutic' code. Balzac indeed shows that the answer cannot be this simple not only by eliminating the word 'castration' from his text, but also by suppressing the name of its opposite. When Sarrasine first feels sexual pleasure, Balzac says that this pleasure is located in 'what we call the heart, for lack of any other word' (p. 238). Later Zambinella says 'I have no heart' (p. 247). Barthes immediately calls 'heart' a euphemism for the sexual organ, but Balzac's text, in stating that what the heart represents cannot be named, that the word is lacking, leaves the question of sexuality open, as a rhetorical problem which the simple naming of parts cannot solve. Balzac's text thus does not simply reverse the hierarchy between readerly and writerly by substituting the truth of castration for the delusion of wholeness; it deconstructs the very possibility of naming the difference.

On the basis of this confrontation between a literary and a critical text, we could perhaps conclude that while both involve a study of difference, the literary text conveys a difference from itself which it 'knows' but cannot say, while the critical text, in attempting to say the difference, reduces it to identity. But in the final analysis, Barthes's text, too, displays a strange ambivalence. For although every metaphorical dimension in Barthes's text proclaims castration as the desirable essence of the writerly – the writerly about which 'there may be nothing to say' (p. 4), just as the castrato is one 'about whom there is nothing to say' (p. 214) – the literal concept of castration is loudly disavowed by Barthes as belonging to the injustices of the readerly: 'To reduce [the text] to the unity of meaning by a deceptively univocal reading, is . . . to sketch the castrating gesture' (p. 160). By means of this split, Barthes's own text reveals that it, like Balzac's, cannot with impunity set up any unequivocal value in opposition to the value of unequivocality. Just as Balzac's text, in its demystification of idealised beauty, reveals a difference not between the readerly and the writerly, but within the very ideals of the readerly, Barthes's text, in its ambivalence toward castration, reveals that the other of the readerly cannot but be subject to its own difference from itself. Difference as such cannot ever be affirmed as an ultimate value because it is that which subverts the very foundations of any affirmation of value. Castration can neither be assumed nor denied, but only enacted in the return of unsituable difference in every text. And the difference between literature and criticism consists perhaps only in the fact that criticism is more likely to be blind to the way in which its own critical difference from itself makes it, in the final analysis, literary.

FURTHER READING

BARTHES, ROLAND, 'S/Z', trans. Richard Miller, London, Cape, 1975.
— 'Sade/Fourier/Loyola', trans. Richard Miller, London, Cape, 1977.
— 'Roland Barthes by Roland Barthes', trans. Richard Howard, London, Macmillan, 1977.
BROOKS, PETER, 'The Melodramatic Imagination: Balzac, Henry James, Melodrama and the Mode of Excess', New Haven, Yale, .1976.
DALLENBACH, LUCIEN, Du fragment au cosmos ('La Comédie humaine' et l'opération de lecture), in 'Poétique', 40, 1979, pp. 420–31.
HEATH, STEPHEN, 'Vertige du déplacement', Paris, Fayard, 1974, pp. 83–119.
— Narrative Space, in 'Screen', 17:3, Autumn 1976, pp. 68–112.
JAMESON, FREDRIC, The Ideology of the Text, in 'Salmagundi', 31/2, Fall 1975/Winter 1976, pp. 204–46.
— The Ideology of Form: Partial Systems in 'La Vielle Fille', in 'Substance', 15, 1976, pp. 29–49.
JOHNSON, BARBARA, 'Défigurations du langage poétique', Paris, Flammarion, 1979.
— Melville's Fist: The Execution of Billy Budd, in 'Studies in Romanticism', 18:4, Winter 1979, pp. 567–99.
KERMODE, FRANK, The Use of the Codes, in Seymour Chatman (ed), 'Approaches to Poetics', New York, Columbia University Press, 1973, pp. 51–79.
SOLLERS, PHILIPPE, Reading 'S/Z', in Stephen Heath, Colin MacCabe and Christopher Prendergast (eds), 'Signs of the Times: Introductory Readings in Textual Semiotics', Cambridge, Granta, 1971, pp. 37–40.

Part Three

PSYCHOANALYSIS/
LITERATURE

We approach here a certain withering of the all too academic
question of the relation between psychoanalysis and literature.
For our answer to that question of theory will be a demonstration of the way in which a transformation of psychoanalysis may
be made to help effect a certain displacement of literature as
well. The abstract problem of theory gives way to a concrete
textual analysis that is undecidably psychoanalytic or literary.
'Psychoanalysis' and 'Literature': terms to be inscribed on the
'opposite' sides of a Möbius strip (Jeffrey Mehlman).

8 TRIMETHYLAMIN:
Notes on Freud's Specimen Dream

Jeffrey Mehlman

[In -Trimethylamin-, Jeffrey Mehlman demonstrates the effects of the new psychoanalysis on the work of *reading*. Mehlman characterises the French re-reading of Freud as the reading of Freud's theoretical texts 'with attention to surprising repetitions and displacements of meaning normally brought to bear on clinical data'. This implication - that there is a 'fantasmatics of the meta-psychology' - has consequences too for literary criticism in so far as it draws attention to the way in which the literary critic will be implicated in the effects of the text which he is analysing. The distance between subject and object is eroded, there is no meta-language, no 'ground' from which the critic can read or discuss literature objectively, or, indeed, subjectively. The very polarity subject/object is subverted.

Mehlman begins by drawing attention to an important footnote, added in 1925, at the end of Chapter VI of 'The Interpretation of Dreams'. In this footnote, Freud makes it clear that the 'essence' of dreams, what is 'peculiar to dream life and characteristic of it', is the 'dream-work'. The latent content, the hidden dream thoughts, are characteristic of the psyche in any situation, and are not what differentiates dreams from any other sort of psychic activity. Only the dream-work explains the 'peculiar nature' of dreams. The dream-work is essentially a process, made up of 'characters and syntactic laws', that perform the transformation of the dream thoughts. In other words, what is peculiar to dreams is not a hidden meaning, but a peculiar movement, process, or syntax. In -Irma's Injection-, it is precisely because Irma's letter is not allowed to *tell* (or even to appear in the analysis) that the strange syntax of the dream is made possible.

Repression could be characterised as the desire to produce a fixed meaning, a stable meaning assimilable to the ego. With dreams, this would mean the reduction of the dream-work to a hidden, fixed, assimilable latent content: a pressure towards the semantic, a changing of the signifiers into signifieds, reminiscent of the methodology of structuralism itself. The force of the Lacanian reading of Freud is to show that the ego is not a totality that can assimilate unconscious processes. The term 'ego' covers a number of diverse functions - narcissism, introjection, identification, etc. - that never have been and never will be assimilated into a whole. Nevertheless the subject, as a bundle of different functions, identifies with an image of the desired totality. The repressive movement in psychic activity, including dreams, will be against the movements of the unconscious that disrupt the ego's illusion of its own totality. In texts, the repressive function of reading will be against processes or structures in a text which disrupt the plenitude of meaning. In spite of this, of course, unconscious movements will always escape. Indeed, the unconscious *is* that which always escapes. And this, as Mehlman shows, is what happens both in the dream of Irma's injection and in Freud's own interpretation.

Mehlman's essay has radical consequences for both psychoanalysis and for literature. For if the 'meaning' of the dream is in fact the repressive wish that attempts to fix the destabilising movements of the unconscious (manifested in the dream-work), then we must revise the whole of 'The Interpretation of Dreams'. This is because the 'Interpretation' is founded on the 'discovery' that the 'key' to the secret of dreams is that their meaning is the fulfilment of a wish. Instead, Mehlman's analysis requires that we see dreams in terms of 'a polemical field of interpretative forces', energised and (dis)organised by the repetition of unmastered unconscious effects. This is, in fact, compatible with Freud's own revision of his theory of dreams in 'Beyond the Pleasure Principle'. This revision obviously affects the 'vulgar' Freudian account of art as the sublimation of desire. To read any work of art in such a way is to make the same mistake as to turn the dream-work into its latent content, its hidden 'meaning', and to repress the syntactical transformations of the unconscious manifested at the level of the text. A psychoanalytical criticism should not therefore read for meaning, but for 'leaning' (anaclisis). A psychic troping, a deviation or turn, constitutes the fantasmatic.

This is, of course, much easier said than done. The implication of Mehlman's account of the collusion between Freud's analysis and the repressing wish in -Irma's Injection- is that any interpretation will be repressive, and will attempt to reduce the work of the text to a fixed, stabilised meaning assimilable to the ego. It is also possible to trace a proliferating structure, already noted in -The Critical Difference-, in which a first text will always be awarded priority over a second text by a third: here, for instance, Mehlman contrasts the undecidability of the dream with the closure of Freud's interpretation, and so Barbara Johnson, in -The Critical Difference-, finds that Balzac's 'Sarrasine' achieves a plurality which Barthes's 'S/Z' denies, and so too, in -The Frame of Reference-, she finds that Derrida reduces the play of Lacan's text. The critic's desire for mastery over a preceding text takes the curious form of revealing the way in which the preceding text masters and reduces a still earlier text. This, however, is only another way of saying that if interpretation is repression, then repression *is* interpretation - and all texts are interpretations. Or to put it yet another way, otherness perpetually escapes, but always reappears elsewhere. This structure is analysed still further in Barbara Johnson's second essay, -The Frame of Reference-.]

If one were to isolate the distinctive trait characterising a number
of recent French readings of Freud, it would perhaps be the effort
to read Freud's theoretical texts with the attention to surprising
repetitions and displacements of meaning normally brought to bear
on clinical data. The wager that the French, in their encounter
with Freud's texts, have been winning is that there is a fantasmatics of the metapsychology, and that the latter can be properly
comprehended only through an adequate analysis of the former.
In the words of J.-B. Pontalis: 'one would be hard put, in Freud's
work, to differentiate the practical writings from the theoretical
ones. "Beyond the Pleasure Principle", for instance, which is
viewed as Freud's most theoretical work, can very well be read -
here I'm extrapolating - as a kind of self-analysis with its mean-
ders, its contradictions, and even its fantastic constructs' (interview with J.-B. Pontalis in 'VH 101', No. 2 [1970] p. 77). The
erosion of the distinction between the 'theoretical' and the
'practical' - and of the metalinguistic distance it implies - is thus
crucial to the recent French perception of Freud, and it is in that
perspective that the following (re)analysis of Freud's specimen
dream in 'The Interpretation of Dreams' is offered. Our effort
will complement the orientation referred to by examining the meta-
psychology - or theory - implicit in the famous dream - or fantasy
- whose analysis constitutes the point of departure of Freud's
major work.[1]
Before plunging into the dream itself, we should do well to take
note of two frequently overlooked passages in 'The Interpretation
of Dreams'. The first is a footnote added in 1925:

> I used at one time to find it extraordinarily difficult to accustom
> readers to the distinction between the manifest content of
> dreams and the latent dream-thoughts. Again and again argu-
> ments and objections would be brought up based upon some un-
> interpreted dream in the form in which it had been retained in
> the memory, and the need to interpret it would be ignored. But
> now that analysts have at least become reconciled to replacing
> the manifest dream by the meaning revealed by its interpreta-
> tion, many of them have become guilty of falling into another
> confusion which they cling to with equal obstinacy. They seek
> to find the essence of dreams in their latent content and in so
> doing they overlook the distinction between the latent dream-
> thoughts and the dream-work. At bottom, dreams are nothing
> other than a particular form of thinking, made possible by the
> conditions of the state of sleep. It is the dream-work which
> creates that form, and it alone is the essence of dreaming - the
> explanation of its peculiar nature. (p. 545; 649-50).

There is thus a tempting misinterpretation of (the interpretation
of) dreams. It consists in unduly 'semanticising' an unconscious
which is 'essentially' syntactical, in reducing the process of
dream-work to a single moment in the overall series of transformations. Such a misreading, in binding the free flow of unconscious

'energy' (from representation to representation), would be the characteristic mode of defence of the ego (in relation to the unconscious). As such it would constitute the misinterpretation of dreams par excellence: the repression of (the concepts delineating the specificity of) the unconscious. Freud, in fact, had already written, in the chapter on dream-work, that the 'dream content seems like a transcript of the dream-thoughts into another mode of expression, whose characters and syntactic laws it is our business to discover by comparing the original and the translation' (p. 312; 381). Once more dream analysis is concerned less with discovering 'the original' than with charting the transformation performed between 'original' and 'translation', less in search of a latent content beneath the manifest than a latent organisation of the manifest. But once more the reader senses that such indications, on Freud's part, are offered in resistance against a certain pressure in the text toward the semantic, reducing dreams to the stability of a fixed meaning assimilable to the ego.

In turning to the specimen dream (of Irma's injection), we are therefore struck by the extent to which the entirety of that dream seems the expression of a central intentional core, referred to by Freud as the 'meaning' of the dream. For the dispersion of the dream-text and its analysis is nevertheless subordinated to the primary concern of exonerating Freud of any guilt for the lingering illness of his patient Irma. Whether the reason given be Irma's failure to accept the diagnostic solution offered by Freud, the organic (as opposed to psychical) origin of the illness, or the thoughtless injection of an unsuitable drug by Freud's colleague Otto, the mutually exclusive explanations fuse in the fulfilment of the common wish that Freud emerge from the dream intact, untouched by the myriad accusations which threaten his integrity.

Yet we have just examined Freud's insistence that the reduction of (the interpretation of) dreams to a semantic core constitutes an important and characteristic psychoanalytic error. For that misreading consists in assimilating the transformative processes of the unconscious to the bound, stable constructs of the ego. It is thus an error best understood in terms of the psychoanalytic category of repression: the ego's effort to blot out (the specificity of) the unconscious. Now not only does Freud reduce the Irma dream to its 'meaning', but the content of that central wish has important resonances with our previous remarks. For it might be summarised as follows: I Freud am not threatened by all that is happening in the dream and shall emerge intact from it. But if what 'is happening in the dream' is, on one level, a trial of the doctor which threatens his personal integrity, in a more psychoanalytic sense what is transpiring is the dream-work itself as it exceeds and disrupts the narcissistic (imaginary) autonomy of the ego. Thus the content of the wish - the wish as content - presented by Freud in his analysis is less a manifestation of the 'repressed' than of that which represses. It is an affirmation, in the semantic mode, of the self-sufficiency of the semantic: the 'original meaning' of the dream.

Such an interpretation is consonant with a number of important motifs in the dream. It allows us, for instance, to bring new weight to bear on the crucial manifest element: 'I was alarmed at the idea that I had missed an organic illness' (p. 141; 184). Freud's interpretation is that if Irma's pains had an organic basis, he could not be held responsible for curing them since his treatment only set out to get rid of hysterical pains. 'It occurred to me, in fact, that I was actually wishing that there had been a wrong diagnosis; for, if so, the blame for my lack of success would also have been got rid of' (p. 142; 184-5). Thus there is a complicity between the ego of the dreamer retaining a certain invulnerability or intactness and the rebiologisation of a domain (the hysterical, the psychoanalytic) whose specificity lies in its imperceptible deviation from the organic, in its virtual simulation of the biological. At this juncture, we would agree with the comments of J. Laplanche demonstrating the specificity of Freud's vocabulary to lie in a wrenching of a terminological apparatus resonant with functionalist and vitalist overtones into an entirely different register, which, for economy's sake, we might describe as 'structuralist' (Jean Laplanche, 'Vie et mort en psychanalyse' [Paris: Flammarion, 1970]; 'Life and Death in Psychoanalysis' [Baltimore, JHUP, 1976]). That subversion of the vitalistic, however, is by no means stable in Freud, and the masked return in his texts of the initial register is tantamount to the repression of his major discovery (of the fact of repression). An example may clarify matters: as opposed to the ego defined as a permanent narcissistic instance – or stasis of libido – within the general structure of the subject, Freud was increasingly inclined to view the ego as the progressively differentiated surface of a psychical 'organism', mediating between inner and outer worlds. This second (functionalist) version of the ego, which ultimately informs psychoanalytic ego psychology, constitutes the repression of the first (narcissistic) version. Or, since it is the ego itself which represses, we might say that the second is a hoax engendered by the first, that ego psychology is but the subtlest ruse of narcissism. Thus, to return to our dream, the solidarity between the two motifs of the inviolability of the ego and of the reduction of the psychoanalytic to the biological – as well as the highly semanticised mode in which these motifs figure as the truth of the dream – constitutes the principal element in the process of repression.

The intactness of the (dreamer's) ego is affirmed at the expense of another. For if Freud now seems safe from what is threatening in the dream, it is only by inflicting (if only in imagination) an organic illness on Irma: 'Nevertheless I had a sense of awkwardness at having invented such a severe illness for Irma simply in order to clear myself' (p. 147: 190). Such is the clearest manifestation of the characteristic aggressiveness of the narcissism informing the repressive instance in the dream, and in its interpretation.[2] A second version of such narcissism, whereby the ego's wholeness is celebrated by obliterating another, concerns the manifest element: 'I reproached Irma for not having accepted

my solution; I said: "if you still get pains, it's your own fault" '
(p. 141; 183). The therapeutic model presupposed here, entail-
ing an omniscient physician and ignorant patient (or hysteric),
is parodied later in the dream when we find Freud staring down
Irma's throat in front of a window, apparently in the vain hope
that she will cough back the truth of his diagnosis to him. 'She
[actually a surrogate for Irma] would then have opened her mouth
properly and have told me more than Irma' (p. 143; 186). If the
patient fails to accept the absoluteness of the doctor's interpretation, the doctor is once more exonerated of any guilt. Thus to
the (repressive) series of plenitude of meaning, intactness of
ego, and reduction of the psychoanalytic to the organic, we may
add the therapeutic model of patient as servile means for the
physician narcissistically to affirm his mastery.

In the course of the dream analysis, Freud himself offers a critique of the error entailed by the therapeutic model in the dream:
'It was my view at that time (though I have since recognised it as
a wrong one) that my task was fulfilled when I had informed a
patient of the hidden meaning of his symptoms: I considered that
I was not responsible for whether he accepted the solution or not
– though this was what success depended on' (p. 141; 184). What
was overlooked or not yet discussed at the time of the dream was
the phenomenon Freud would later thematise as transference
[Übertragung]: the process of transferring on to the psychoanalyst feelings which originally applied and still unconsciously
apply to an infantile object. For that process eventually came to
be recognised as the very medium of therapy, and its interpretation as 'the most powerful of therapeutic instruments'. It is plainly
a phenomenon which is incompatible with the model (of knowledge-
able analyst informing ignorant analysand of the truth of his case)
featured in the dream.

Yet in 'The Interpretation of Dreams', the concept of transference has not yet been elaborated in its specifically therapeutic
sense, and the term occurs with a related but different meaning.
Thus, in Chapter VII, Freud writes:

> We learn from the [psychology of the neuroses] that an uncon-
> scious idea is as such quite incapable of entering the precon-
> scious and that it can only exercise any effect there by estab-
> lishing a connection with an idea which already belongs to the
> preconscious, by transferring its intensity on to it and by get-
> ting itself 'covered' by it. Here we have the fact of the 'trans-
> ference', which provides an explanation of so many striking
> phenomena in the mental life of neurotics (p. 601; 716).

Thus the related meaning of transference is that of displacement
of affect from representation to representation or the sheer fact
of unconscious distortion of the psychical text. But this observation brings us back into the orbit of Freud's comment that the
dream-work (condensation, displacement, etc.) and not the latent
thought, constitutes the 'essence' of the dream. For in terms of

the specimen dream and its analysis, 'overlooking the transference' would mean (a) attempting to cure Irma's hysteria by turning her into a receptacle of Freud's wisdom; (b) subordinating an analysis of the dream-work to a climatic revelation of the latent content as the essence of the dream. And both the mastery of (a) and the semantic plenitude triumphant in (b) are complicitous with the narcissism of the repressing instance in the dream (and its) analysis.

And yet if Freud, in the analysis of his specimen dream, tends to overlook the transference (in both senses of the term), by no means does the transference overlook Freud. It remains for us to clarify that proposition, to delineate the mode of insistence of the repressed – as opposed to the repressing – wish in the Irma dream as it exceeds everything in the analysis which tends to consolidate the narcissistic defences of the ego.

A discussion of what is repressed in (or by) the dream (and its analysis) should lead – in terms of the overall logic of 'The Interpretation of Dreams' – to the general area of sexuality. And in fact there is, in the associations to the almost hallucinatory appearance of the chemical formula for trimethylamin in the dream, a passage explicitly concerned with sexuality:

> What was it, then, to which my attention was to be directed in this way by trimethylamin? It was to a conversation with another friend who had for many years been familiar with all my writings during the period of their gestation, just as I had been with his. He had at that time confided some ideas to me on the subject of the chemistry of the sexual processes, and had mentioned among other things that he believed that one of the products of sexual metabolism was trimethylamin. Thus this substance led me to sexuality, the factor to which I attributed the greatest importance in the origin of the nervous disorders which it was my aim to cure [p. 149; 193].

Thus the 'origin' of Irma's illness, a 'thoughtless' injection from a dirty syringe of an inappropriate solution by Freud's friend Otto, is linked with speculations on sexuality. Yet oddly enough, if trimethylamin figures in the dream as virtual cause of Irma's disease, it functions in the analysis in a different though equally crucial way.

> I began to guess why the formula for trimethylamin had been so prominent in the dream. So many important subjects converged upon that one word. Trimethylamin was an allusion not only to the immensely powerful factor of sexuality, but also to a person whose agreement I recalled with satisfaction whenever I felt isolated in my opinions. Surely this friend who played so large a part in my life must appear again elsewhere in these trains of thought. Yes. For he had a special knowledge of the consequences of affections of the nose and its accessory cavities; and he had drawn scientific attention to some very remarkable con-

nections between the turbinal bones and the female organs of
sex (Cf. the three curly structures in Irma's throat) (p. 150;
194).

In brief, the formula for the chemical - spaced out in heavy type
- serves as a point of maximum intersection of the various associative paths along which affect is displaced. In Chapter VII, it will
figure as the example par excellence of what Freud calls a nodal
point, a hidden centre in the dream, which is itself manifest, but
whose odd centrality or structuring function remains latent. It
will be noted that in coming to terms with the dream element
trimethylamin, Freud has shifted his focus back to the dream-
work, which, in the passages quoted at the beginning of this
essay, constituted - in opposition to the latent dream-thought -
the 'essence' of dreams. But it is important to distinguish between
the (imagined) bio-chemical substrate trimethylamin and its role
in Irma's illness on the one hand and the structuring function of
the written formula for that chemical in the dream (analysis) on
the other. The first participates in a (pseudo-) biological register,
which is the very medium Freud will be obliged to think against
in formulating the concepts of his science. The second, the
written formula of the chemical, is a simulacrum of the first, available to the strange syntactical transformations of 'primary process'
thinking. We are tempted to suggest that the crux of psychoanalysis lies in the deviation between the chemical and its formula
as they function in the dream, between Otto's thoughtless injection and the complex mode of thoughtnessness injected into the
dream and its analysis through the nodality of trimethylamin.

Along with the introduction of sexuality, the structuring function of the chemical formula, and the (re)emergence of the dream-
work as constitutive of the 'essence' of dreams, there enters
simultaneously on the scene of the dream analysis Freud's friend,
the theorist of 'sexual metabolism,' Wilhelm Fliess. Which is to
say that precisely at the point when transference - in the sense
attributed to the term in 'The Interpretation': as the fact of unconscious displacement itself - emerges as central to the analysis,
we encounter the figure who served as the focus of Freud's transference - in the later sense - in his self-analysis. This is not the
forum in which to discuss the strange content of Fliess's biological
fantasia (concerning the menstrual-like cycle of all human beings,
the identity of structure between nose and genital organs, the
physiological bi-sexuality of all humans). We are inclined to agree
with O. Mannoni that Fliess's 'science' resembles nothing so much
as an elaborately thematised and poorly resolved castration complex (O. Mannoni, - L'Analyse originelle, - in 'Clefs pour l'imaginaire ou L'Autre Scène' [Paris: Seuil, 1966], p. 121). Nor shall
we discuss at any length Freud's strangely impassioned relation
to that 'science' (and its practitioner). For on a number of occasions Freud identified so thoroughly with Fliess's theoretical
positions that the friendship between the two was threatened by
accusations of plagiarism. The crucial point for us is to observe

that the discovery of psychoanalysis was inseparable from the disruption of that identification, the deviation from Fliess's 'science', the dismantling of his fantasia and, consequently, the elaboration of the analytic concept of 'castration'.

One of Freud's more provocative formulations of that event (or process) occurs in a letter of 6 October 1910 in which he responds to Ferenczi's complaint that he has been insufficiently forthcoming in their correspondence: 'You've noticed that I no longer have any need of revealing my personality completely. . . . Ever since the Fliess affair that need have been eliminated. A homosexual cathexis has been partially withdrawn and used for the aggrandisement of my ego. I have succeeded at the very point at which a paranoiac fails' (Mannoni, p. 118). Thus the discvoery of psychoanalysis – and, concomitantly, of the interpretation of dreams – was, at some level, tantamount to an avoidance of paranoia. But in the specimen dream we have come across a perfect instance of paranoia: in the scene in which we find Freud feeling simultaneously 'divine' and 'persecuted' because his patient refuses to speak back to him the correctness of his solution. That scene, it will be recalled, constituted one version of the repressing wish. In the dream analysis, the move beyond such repression was toward a delineation of the nodal function of the (manifest) formula for trimethylamin. Perhaps then the avoidance of paranoia (or the discovery of psychoanalysis) has to be achieved afresh in every act of interpretation. And (a more or less respectable form of) paranoia would be the risk courted by every unduly semanticised interpretation.[3] Paranoia is defined by Laplanche and Pontalis as a 'chronic psychosis characterised by a more or less well systematised delirium (dominated by a tendency to interpret, an absence of intellectual weakening and which does not generally evolve toward any deterioration)' (J. Laplanche and J.-B. Pontalis, 'Vocabulaire de la psychanalyse' [Paris: P.U.F. 1967], p. 299; 'The Language of Psycho-Analysis', [London, Hogarth, 1973], p. 296). One need not after all be a blind opponent of psychoanalysis to sense how close that statement comes to defining – or parodying – much of psychoanalytic theory.

In our discussion of trimethylamin, we located the specifically psychoanalytic dimension in the infinitesimal difference between the substance (as 'origin' of Irma's illness) and the written formula (as 'node' of Freud's dream). Such a deviation of the biological into the fantasmatic occupies an important (though insufficiently perceived) place in Freud's metapsychology, and bears the name 'Anlehnung' (anaclisis, étayage). For in the 'Three Contributions to the Theory of Sex', the sexual drive initially 'leans on' the biological function and separates from it when the real object (e.g., mother's milk) is replaced by a fantasied object (breast) and the desire to repeat hallucinatorily the (marginal) pleasure of an exchange generated by contact of lips on breast (cf. French Freud, 'Yale French Studies', 48 [1972], p. 179). Just so does the formula for trimethylamin in the dream 'lean on' the substance in order to achieve its independence as a node structuring, in Lacan's formula, 'a signifying flux, the mystery of which consists in the fact that the subject does not even know where to pretend to be its organiser' ('Ecrits', p. 623), Ultimately the wish interpreted by Freud is, through repression, to be free of the threat to the integrity of one's ego posed by that 'flux'.

In opposing in the dream (and its) analysis a repressed and a repressing wish, epitomised perhaps by the 'dark spaced type' of a formula and the vocal confirmation of his mastery which Freud attempts in vain to elicit from Irma, we have attempted to constitute Freud's text as a polemical field of interpretative forces. On the one hand, an erosion of semantic plenitude entailed by the 'Anlehnung' of the formula on the substance. But on the other, the reconstitution of such narcissistic plenitude within the dream as repressive of the bizarre syntax of the unconscious: Freud 'leaning on' Irma – in the Mafioso sense, this time – making her cough up (his) truth. The question posed by the history of psychoanalysis, from its inception, has been which way, between those two interpretations of 'leaning on', psychoanalytic interpretation will lean.

NOTES

1   The text of the dream:

> A large hall – numerous guests, whom we were receiving. –
> Among them was Irma. I at once took her on one side, as
> though to answer her letter and to reproach her for not
> having accepted my 'solution' yet. I said to her: 'If you
> still get pains, it's really only your fault.' She replied: 'If
> you only knew what pains I've got now in my throat and
> stomach and abdomen – it's choking me'. – I was alarmed
> and looked at her. She looked pale and puffy. I thought to
> myself that after all I must be missing some organic trouble.
> I took her to the window and looked down her throat, and
> she showed signs of recalcitrance, like women with artificial
> dentures. I thought to myself that there was really no need
> for her to do that. – She then opened her mouth properly
> and on the right I found a big white patch; at another place
> I saw extensive whitish grey scabs upon some remarkable
> curly structures which were evidently modelled on the tur-
> binal bones of the nose. – I at once called in Dr M. and he
> repeated the examination and confirmed it . . . Dr M.
> looked quite different from usual; he was very pale, he
> walked with a limp and his chin was clean-shaven . . . My
> friend Otto was now standing beside her as well, and my
> friend Leopold was percussing her through her bodice and
> saying: 'She has a dull area low down on the left.' He also
> indicated that a portion of the skin on the left shoulder was
> infiltrated. (I noticed this, just as he did, in spite of her
> dress.) . . . M. said: 'There's no doubt it's an infection,

but no matter; dysentery will supervene and the toxin will
be eliminated.' . . . We were directly aware, too, of the
origin of the infection. Not long before, when she was
feeling unwell, my friend Otto had given her an injection
of a preparation of propyl, propyls . . . proprionic acid
. . . trimethylamin (and I saw before me the formula for
this printed in heavy type). . . . Injections of that sort
ought not to be made so thoughtlessly. . . . And probably
the syringe had not been clean.

Page references in the text are to the convenient Avon [New
York, 1965] paperbound reprint of James Strachey's translation of 'The Interpretation of Dreams' in Volumes IV and V of
the Standard Edition, followed by page references
to the Pelican Freud library, vol. 4 [Harmondsworth, 1976].

2   Cf. Lacan: 'Aggressiveness is the tendency correlative with
a mode of identification that we term narcissistic and which
determines the formal structure of man's ego and of the register of entities characteristic of his world' ('Ecrits', Paris:
Seuil, 1966).

3   To this extent one appreciates Vladimir Nabokov's rejection
of psychoanalytic readings of his works as acts of aggression:
efforts to litter his texts with the contents of 'the garbage can
of a Viennese tenement'. Such is his position in a devastating
rejoinder to W.W. Rowe's study of 'Nabokov's Deceptive World'
entitled – Rowe's Symbols – (reprinted in 'Strong Opinions',
New York, McGraw-Hill, 1973). But the sterility of the para-
noid tug-of-war in which he engages his critic is betrayed
by the values informing his effort: the ultimate inviolability
of his precious 'bloom' to interpretation. In brief, Nabokov
would counter an abuse of psychoanalysis with a wholesale
rejection of psychoanalysis which seems a specular reflection
of the abuse.

FURTHER READING

BERSANI, LEO, 'Baudelaire and Freud', Berkeley, University of
California Press, 1977.
CHASE, CYNTHIA, Oedipal Textuality: Reading Freud's Reading
of 'Oedipus', in 'Diacritics', 9:1, Spring 1979, pp. 54-68.
LACAN, JACQUES, (analysis of the Dream of the Burning Child)
in 'The Four Fundamental Concepts of Psycho-Analysis', trans.
Alan Sheridan, London, Hogarth Press, 1977, pp. 34-5.
LACOUE-LABARTHE, PHILIPPE, Theatrum Analyticum, in 'Glyph',
2, 1977, pp. 122-43.
LAPLANCHE, JEAN and LECLAIRE, SERGE, The Unconscious:
A Psychoanalytic Study, in 'Yale French Studies', 48, 1972,
pp. 118-78.
LAPLANCHE, JEAN and PONTALIS, J.-B., Fantasy and the Origins
of Sexuality, in 'The International Journal of Psycho-Analysis'

49:1, 1968, pp. 1-18.

LAPLANCHE, JEAN, 'Life and Death in Psychoanalysis', trans. Jeffrey Mehlman, Baltimore, Johns Hopkins University Press, 1976.

MEHLMAN, JEFFREY, 'A Structural Study of Autobiography: Proust, Leiris, Sartre, Lévi-Strauss', Ithaca, Cornell University Press, 1974.

— How to Read Freud on Jokes: The Critic as Schadchen, in 'New Literary History', 6:3, Spring 1975, pp. 439-61.

— La Boétie's Montaigne, in 'The Oxford Literary Review', 4:1, 1979, pp. 45-61.

ROSE, JACQUELINE, 'Dora' - Fragment of an Analysis, in 'm/f', 2, 1978, pp. 5-21.

SPIVAK, G.C., The Letter as Cutting Edge, in 'Yale French Studies', 55/56, 1978, pp. 208-26.

WEBER, SAMUEL, The Divaricator: Remarks on Freud's 'Witz', in 'Glyph', 1, 1977, pp. 1-27.

9 DISREMEMBERING DEDALUS:
'A Portrait of the Artist as a Young Man'

Maud Ellmann

[One of the most productive areas for post-structuralist criticism
has been the work of Germ's Choice, just as Shame's Voice, with
his meaning-as-play, played-out-meanings, and punning dissem-
inations, could be said to have had a hand in producing post-
structuralism itself. Whereas for orthodox critics, 'Finnegans
Wake' is often seen simply as the aberration of a great man, for
post-structuralist critics the 'Wake' is *the* literary par excellence.
If it has demanded this special place, it has also had the effect of
demanding a re-reading of Joyce's other works - backwards, as
it were, from the 'Wake'. Reading backwards: the structure, in
fact, of autobiography.
   Anglo-American criticism has largely been engaged in the attempt
to recuperate Joyce - so that Bloom in 'Ulysses' becomes the 'real-
est' everyman of all, while, paradoxically, he is surrounded by
ever more erudite systems and texts of allusion, reference and
influence. Criticism of 'A Portrait' has largely been preoccupied
with the 'problem' of aesthetic distance in the novel, as if 'A
Portrait' were about the tension between sympathy and judgment,
as in the conventional reading of Browning's dramatic monologues.
Yet what such approaches do not take into account is the materiality of writing in the novels: at all points, Joyce's texts resist
their appropriation back into the discourse of realism, of representation, because of the oddness and opacity of their language.
What is perhaps most remarkable, in view of the challenge which
Joyce's novels present, has been the tenacity with which they
have been read as windows on to the world or into the mind.
   In -Disremembering Dedalus-, Maud Ellmann shows how in 'A
Portrait' language does not seek to express, represent, reconstitute or describe 'experience' or 'reality', but constructs it. In
particular, she examines the accomplice to the fiction of transparent language, the subject, here the subject of (auto) biography.
If the novel is a portrait, a representation, at all, it is because
it shows the becoming of the subject in writing (bio-graphy).
Rather than portraying the well-rounded 'character', it shows
the fading of the subject as serial. 'A Portrait' presents a Stephen
Dedalus who is disremembering, not developing but devolving, not
achieving an identity but dissolving into a nameless scar. A full
and self-present consciousness, 'His Majesty the Ego' as Freud
put it, gives way to the self-mutilation of the subject in and as
metaphor. The description of the subject in the following essay
emerges from Lacan's reformulation of the theory of castration
through a reading of Freud's theory of anality. But Lacan's own

formulation need not, and should not, be conceived as a 'theory' so much as an interpretation of the Freudian text, a redisposition of the text's own terms. Maud Ellmann's essay does not, therefore, justify itself via Lacan, but adapts such procedures to Joyce. The movements of fragmentation, dispersal, exchange and substitution, should be compared with the (re)cycles of litter and letters, literature and the letter, in 'Finnegans Wake':

Shem was a sham and a low sham and his lowness creeped out first via foodstuffs. . . . For this was a stinksome inkenstink, quite puzzonal to the wrottel. Smatterafact, Angles aftanon browsing there thought not Edam reeked more rare. My wud! The warped floor of the lair and soundconducting walls thereof, to say nothing of the uprights and imposts, were persianly literatured with burst loveletters, telltale stories, stickyback snaps, alphybettyformed verbiage, ahems and ahahs, imeffible tries at speech unasyllabled, you owe mes, eyoldhyms, fluefoul smut, fallen lucifers, counterfeit franks, best intentions, curried notes, upset latten tintacks, painful digests, once current puns, quoshed quotatoes, messes of mottage, unquestionable issue papers, seedy ejaculations, to which, if one has the stomach to add the breakages, upheavals, distortions, inversions of all this chambermaid music one stands, given a grain of goodwill, a fair chance of actually seeing the whirling dervish, Tumult, son of Thunder, self exiled in upon his ego, a nightlong a shaking betwixtween white or reddr hawrors, noondayterrorised to skin and bone by an ineluctable phantom (may the Shaper have mercery on him!)writing the mystery of himsel in furniture (pp. 170, 183-4, omissions not noted).

In the 'Wake', the dispersal of 'character' reaches the stage where the central 'character', HCE, is merely a series of letters, litter-attired across the text in a constant metamorphosis - an acronym who transforms himself into anything to hand.]

A stranger once came up to Joyce in a café and cried, 'Let me kiss the hand that wrote Ulysses!' Joyce promptly replied, 'It's done a lot of other things too.' In 'A Portrait of the Artist as a Young Man', a thought occurs to Stephen which seems, curiously, to anticipate this joke without - for the thinker - being jokey:

If ever his soul, re-entering her dwelling shyly after the frenzy of his body's lust had spent itself, was turned towards her whose emblem is the morning star, *bright and musical, telling of heaven and infusing peace*, it was when her names were murmured softly by lips whereon there still lingered foul and shameful words, the savour itself of a lewd kiss.[1]

What appals Stephen - as it amuses Joyce - is the way lust and language may converge in a single bodily member. The hand, in the one case, and the lips, in the other, are stained by their intimacy. These organs are puns in bad taste. They betray, between the text and sexuality, an intercourse more cunning than a rhyme.

How, then, can these members remember? Among the things the hand that wrote 'Ulysses' did was to write 'A Portrait of the Artist'. In fact, it wrote three portraits of him: a first draft, whose rejection gave rise to 'Stephen Hero' and to what we regard, teleologically, as the final text. As for this last version, the indefinite article of its title suggests that it, too, may represent yet another Wordsworthian preparation to write. It is a portrait, not 'The Portrait'. At first, a repetition of the author's life, Joyce's autobiography seems henceforth destined to repeat itself. What can it be about self-portraiture, for Joyce as for Wordsworth, that makes them so reluctant to conclude?

To account, in the case of 'The Prelude', for the growth of a poet's mind, Wordsworth must read his own life backwards. Through memory, he must retrieve the seeds from which – organically speaking – the poem and the mind that wrote it grew. If memory is constructed in the present, the past, as such, can never be recovered. So we behold, in autobiography, a paradoxical procedure by which memory writes the past to discover how the past wrote and determined memory. In this sense, the autobiographer decomposes the present that the past composed: unwrites the hand that writes. Remembering becomes dismembering: or more precisely, 'disremembering' – to borrow Davin's Irishism from 'A Portrait' (p. 181). It is to forget oneself – in the most indiscreet ways.

If 'A Portrait' borrows from 'The Prelude' any model of the poet's mind, it is not the metaphor of growth. Rather it is Wordsworth's notion of 'spot of time' that fascinates the text. 'Islands in the unnavigable depth of our departed time': the spot of time, which Wordsworth seems to use to mean a space, or place, or interlude, includes, among a plethora of definitions, the idea of a blemish, stain, or scar. And indeed, it is a scar which hollows out the 'spot' in the Gibbet-Mast episode of Wordsworth's autobiography: the scar that remains of an identity.[2] This scar is the name of a murderer. Neither the name, nor the hand that carved it, is disclosed: all that the passage intimates is the act of cutting it and its indelibility. Naming is maiming. 'To this hour,' the text insists, the letters, 'carved by some unknown hand', are 'all still fresh and visible'. 'A Portrait', too, as I shall try to show, conceives identity as a scar without an author, without an origin, and at last, without even a name. And this identity is a wound that constantly re-opens, so that its letters may remain 'all fresh and visible'.

It is important, however, to stress that 'A Portrait' is not 'about' a scar. To say that the text is 'about' something reinstitutes the polarity of content and form which Joyce's writing constantly stretches and transgresses. Daedalus's labyrinth lurks in 'A Portrait's imagery as if to halt us in our hermeneutics. For the secret of a labyrinth is only the way out, whereas I, for one, am looking for a way in. The scar is not a secret, but a principle of structure: a punctuation. Because it is a living scar, it constantly resurges and reiterates itself. And the signification of the text is lodged in the very blanks and repetitions that mark and mask its cicatrix. For the scar belongs not only to the subject but to the text itself, which both suffers and enacts the mutilation by which identity reconstitutes itself. Purloined letters, the lacunae of the narrative – its scars – are only hidden in that they are too blatant to be seen. Rather than the secret of 'A Portrait', the scar insinuates itself as a secretion: a word which describes at once the operations of hoarding, fission, and emission which undo the fixity of identity and hyphenate autobiography.

In this essay I shall pursue the notion of identity as process: in fact, as a series of processes, which 'A Portrait' joins in a 'brisure'. 'Brisure', which I borrow from Derrida, encompasses the ambiguities of 'cleaving' in the sense of splitting, and 'cleaving' in the sense of joining or embracing. So in translation let's enflesh brisure by calling it a cleavage.

One process that proceeds from the cleavage of identity consists of scarrification. This has two sides, which could be described as nomination and punctuation. In the act of nomination, word is stained with flesh and flesh with word, for the name, like the name of Wordsworth's 'murderer', emerges in this text as a cicatrix. Once named and maimed, the subject, rather than a plenitude, erupts henceforth as punctuation, as a gap or wound that rips the fabric of the text at irregular intervals.

```
Punctuation )                    (repeats
           )      SCAR           (
           )                     (
Nomination )                    (secretes
```

Both aspects of scarrification make themselves felt in the fourth section of Chapter 2 (pp. 86-96), the trip to Cork, which I shall take as a point of departure.

But we only know the scar by its secretion: by that which issues from and enters into it. What proceeds from scarrification is circulation: and 'A Portrait' sets in motion a complex circulation of sexual and textual economies. The diagram will suggest, inevitably, a schematic rigidity: but if we keep in mind that each overlaps and overleaps the others, to abstract them in this way may help us to discern their furious rhythm.

Circulation occurs in three forms, each of which involves the linguistic and corporeal equivalents that I have listed, respectively, under WORD and FLESH. Each also corresponds to the strategies of disremembering that constitute the subject of autobiography.

SEXUAL/TEXTUAL ECONOMIES

	ECONOMY	FLESH	WORD
MARKET PLACE	1 Flows	dismembering emission	synecdoche
	2 Influence	remembering incorporation	metaphor or tautology
LITERATURE	3 'Detaining' Hoarding	retention chastity	lacunae and the 'literal'

The first is an economy of flows, whereby the subject purges or evacuates himself, and issues forth in all kinds of secretions.

> His sins trickled from his lips, one by one, tricked in shameful drops from his soul, festering and oozing like a sore, a squalid stream of vice. The last sins oozed forth, sluggish, filthy (p. 144).

Semen, blood, urine, breath, money, saliva, speech and excrement provide the currencies for this economy. Menstruation also figures among these flows, for the text at this level (though not at others) is as indifferent to gender as to the formal separation of excrement and sexuality. Not to mention vomit, which is a perpetual danger in this text - not only for Stephen but for his reader. Rhetorically, the economy of flows corresponds to the trope of synecdoche - the part for the whole - for through these flows, any notion of totality disintegrates, and the subject is dispersed into the fragments and the waste that stand for him.
  What passes out of Stephen must, however, first pass into him. So, working in tandem with the rhythm of his flows is an economy of influence. Food, particularly the bread and wine of the Eucharist, figures in this economy, but on the whole it is Stephen's nose, rather than his mouth, that opens him to influence.
  The odours that so besiege our hero's nose are more frequently noxious than sweet. In fact, they are the odours of mortality: of dead flesh, and, as I shall show, dead speech. The worst stench of all is that of writing - dead speech stored in literature - which passes into Stephen through his nose and passes through his mouth as speech again. So, 'influence' retains its literary implications: Stephen inhales the literary tradition and re-members it in his secretions.
  This transaction with the past resembles the Eucharist which changes spirit into wine, until at last - as Mulligan mischievously adds - the wine becomes water again. It compares also to the other conversions which enthrall the text: of money into goods, lust into language, peristalsis into metre, or the gross earth into art. And vice versa. Trans-substantiation and digestion meet as the loci of metaphor. But Stephen's own transactions with influence tend to conclude, as we shall see, not in metaphor, but in repetition and tautology.

'Literature' is the name that Stephen gives to the third economy, the economy of hoarding. This baptism occurs in the context of a conversation with the English dean:

- One difficulty, said Stephen, in aesthetic discussion is to know whether words are being used according to the literary tradition or according to the tradition of the marketplace. I remember a sentence of Newman's in which he says of the Blessed Virgin that she was detained in the full company of the saints. The use of the word in the marketplace is quite different. *I hope I am not detaining you.*
- Not in the least, said the dean politely.
- No, no, said Stephen, smiling, I mean . . .
- Yes, yes: I see, said the dean quickly, I quite catch the point: detain (p. 188).

In this conversation, the word 'detain' itself becomes 'literature' when it elicits no response. 'Detain', of course, is not unlike 'retain' except, importantly, that its implications are less absolute. 'Literature' consists of words and flesh detained, held back, withdrawn from a time from circulation. In opposition to the marketplace of flow and influence, literature detains language as the miser hoards his money and the petulant infant withholds what Lacan calls his 'gift of shit'. Nor is it by accident that it is Mary, in this passage, who is detained: for her chastity also represents a form of hoarding. Speech in storage, 'literature' functions as hiatus, blocking the exchange of word for flesh and flesh for words. Literature - to borrow a word from 'Dubliners' - is the paralysis of language.

Stephen's proclaimed aesthetic of 'silence, exile, and cunning' seems, like 'scrupulous meanness', to bespeak the linguistic avarice of 'literature'. His 'Portrait' too practises a politics of 'detaining', hoarding words in the transcendentalised retentions of epiphany. These occulted episodes erupt as blank spots in the narrative. In their very literality they refuse to flow, to undergo the exchange and transformation of synecdoche or metaphor.

But withdrawing words from circulation can only bring about a temporary pause, before the text embezzles them in new transactions. In the passage I shall presently discuss, the word 'Foetus', paralysed as 'literature', surreptitiously, and with explosive implications, reinfiltrates the text's economies. But before we embark on these semantics, let's survey the text's whole economic policy.

A capitalist economy operates by withdrawing funds from circulation in order, paradoxically, for money and commodities to circulate at all. All these economies depend upon the hoarding of the bank vault and the interest racket. Thus, in 'A Portrait', words and flesh take the place of money and commodities, and 'literature' or hoarding mischievously completes the cycle of a capitalist economy in miniature.

I now turn to the further section of Chapter 2 (pp. 86-96), which will provide a paradigm for the procedures of disremembering. Nomination, punctuation, and all the sexual and textual economies work their commerce here. What is more, the section represents an autobiography within an autobiography: for it describes Simon Dedalus's sentimental journey to his origins in Cork, and his struggle to remember his fugitive history. His nostalgia reaches its climax in the search for his own initials, carved as indelibly as the name of Wordsworth's 'murderer' in the dark stained wood of a school desk.

But another scar precedes these initials, and in a sense preempts them: the word 'Foetus', which I alluded to before, whose carved letters move Stephen to a horror as extreme as it is unexplained.

While the father's rehearsals of his past, and his excavation of his name, seem to represent a repossession of identity, the brute material motive of the journey belies his sentiment. For he returns to his origins only to sell them away. He is to auction his belongings, and to dispossess himself and his resentful son. Remembering reverts to disremembering.

Duplicity, indeed, begins with the opening sentence of the section.

> Stephen was once again seated beside his father in the corner of a railway carriage at Kingsbridge (p. 86).

'Once again' is a curious sleight of hand: Stephen has never shared a railway carriage with his father in the text before. This is a first time masquerading as a repetition. It recalls the first sentence of the whole autobiography: 'Once upon a time and a very good time it was', where the first time turns out not to be the beginning of Stephen's story, but of a story told to Stephen by his father. The trip to Cork is also an episode in which Stephen's story grafts itself upon his father's story, and they compete for autobiographies. We begin to suspect some relation between the father and false starts; and to suspect, perhaps, the very notion of beginning.

But some form of recollection is taking place here, which prevents the 'once again' from startling us. In the second half of the paragraph, the reader undergoes a repetition:

> He saw the darkening lands slipping away past him, the silent telegraph poles passing his window swiftly every four seconds, the little glimmering stations, manned by a few silent sentries, flung by the mail behind her and twinkling for a moment in the darkness like fiery grains thrust backwards by a runner (p. 87).

This passage does not repeat a real event, but a dream that Stephen had at Clongowes:

> The train was full of fellows: a long long chocolate train with cream facings. The guards went to and fro opening, closing,

locking, unlocking the doors. They were men in dark blue and silver; they had silvery whistles and their keys made a quick music: click, click: click, click.

And the train raced on over the flat lands and past the Hill of Allen. The telegraph poles were passing, passing. The train went on and on. It knew (p. 20).

Just as the beginning of Stephen's story is another story, so here the real train evolves out of the dream. This order makes a fiction of experience.

What the reader undergoes, through the repetition of the dream-sequence, is the constitution of his own memory. The logic of repetition works backward in this text: the second episode reverts upon the first, and modifies its structure and its sense. In other words, it takes the second episode to activate the scar left by the first. This, perhaps, is why the text cannot begin. By the same strategy of repetition, text and reader are deprived of their originality. Like the autobiographer himself, we as readers are forced to read backwards: we, too, are disremembering.

We recall that the autobiographer must unwrite the present in order to write the past. These two passages capture the moment when remembering reverses into disremembering: when the present 'passes' into memory and the past 'presents' itself as desire. They enact the very process of 'passing', a word invested in 'A Portrait' with multiple reverberations, and which repeats itself insistently in these two homecomings:

The telegraph poles were passing, passing (p. 20).

He saw the darkening lands slipping away past him, the silent telegraph poles passing his window swiftly every four seconds (p. 87).

The two journeys themselves do not precisely represent events, but passages between events: interstices between the present and the past. They have no content: none, that is, but the passing and the missing of a content: the landscape that slips past, and the stations and the sentries flung behind. This train not only passes by content but passes it out, evacuates and disremembers it. All that remains is a wake: the trail of fiery flakes thrust backwards as by a runner.

Another wake occurs a little further on: the wake of Stephen's words, which falls into the rhythm of the train's evacuation:

At Maryborough he fell asleep. When he awoke the train had passed out of Mallow and his father was stretched asleep on the other seat. The cold light of the dawn lay over the country, over the unpeopled fields and the closed cottages. The terror of sleep fascinated his mind as he watched the silent country or heard from time to time his father's deep breath or sudden sleepy movement. The neighbourhood of unseen sleepers filled

him with strange dread as though they could harm him; and he
prayed that the day might come quickly. His prayer, addressed
neither to God nor saint, began with a shiver, as the chilly
morning breeze crept through the chink of the carriage door to
his feet, and ended in a trail of foolish words which he made to
fit the insistent rhythm of the train; and silently, at intervals
of four seconds, the telegraph poles held the galloping notes
of the music between punctual bars. This furious music allayed
his dread and, leaning against the windowledge, he let his eyelids close again (p. 87).

Twice Stephen falls asleep, and twice he wakes; but while he
wakes, his father, instead, dozes with the neighbourhood of
unseen sleepers. Merging with the intermittency of the telegraph
poles, this alternation makes consciousness the music of its inter-
ruptions: the rhythm of its own repeated exile. It suggests, also,
that Stephen's being will involve the eclipse of his father's, and
that his consciousness achieves itself by means of the annihilation
of his father and the world. And while the punctual bars of the
telegraph poles puncture and punctuate, rupture and redistri-
bute, the galloping music of the train, a trail of foolish words
gushes from Stephen's lips to complete the cycle of evacuation.
These words, too, have no content: none, at least, that the
text conceded to circulate. They only mark the fading of consciousness and the gaps between the poles.
    What's left, then, of the subject after all this 'passing', all this
evacuation? In the course of disremembering, a different kind of
subject emerges from the text: different, and radically opposed
to the tradition of the human subject and to the orthodox conception of the subject matter of a text. The subject erupts as punctuation. As the silence woven into music, the absence woven into
vision: as the pulsation of the unconscious. Like Philippe in a
dream that Laplanche and Leclaire have analysed, the subject here
dissolves from a positive substance into a scar in the shape of a
comma.[3] We behold the repetition of a Mallarméan genesis, where
'les blancs' - the whites, the scars of punctuation - hollow out
a universe of space and time.
    This punctuation establishes itself even prior to the dream at
Clongowes, in a series of what we might call ontological experiments:

He leaned his elbows on the table and shut and opened the flaps
of his ears. Then he heard the noise of the refectory every
time he opened the flaps of his ears. It made a roar like a train
at night. And when he closed the flaps the roar was shut off
like a train going into a tunnel. That night at Dalkey the train
had roared like that and then, when it went into the tunnel,
the roar stopped. He closed his eyes and the train went on,
roaring and then stopping; roaring again, stopping. It was
nice to hear it roar and stop and then roar out of the tunnel
again and then stop (p. 13).

Is Stephen shutting the world out of himself, or himself out of the world? This game reverts upon the player. While he seems to be mastering the world, controlling its presence and its absence, the child is establishing his own intermittency, his own punctuation. This fiction uncreates the fabricator.

The punctuation of the earflap game gradually accrues to itself a number of semantic oppositions which invest it with a form of representability.

> First came the vacation and then the next term and then vacation again and then again another term and then again the vacation. It was like a train going in and out of tunnels and what was like the noise of boys eating in the refectory when you opened and closed the flaps of the ears. Term, vacation; tunnel, out; noise, stop. How far away it was! (p. 17).

Each time the scar recurs, it amalgamates another binarism. Now its punctuation leans upon the oppositions of in and out, home and school, vacation and term, and the train that enters and emerges from the tunnel, with its sudden roar. These alternatives articulate the scar, and constitute a bank of representatives to be embezzled by the dream.

Later in the book, the sermon seems to parody this process of accretion, when the priest gathers compound interest on the words 'ever never':

> A holy saint (one of our own fathers I believe it was) was once vouchsafed a vision of hell. It seemed to him that he stood in the midst of a great hall, dark and silent save for the ticking of a great clock. The ticking went on unceasingly; and it seemed to this saint that the sound of the ticking was the ceaseless repetition of the words: ever, never; ever, never. Ever to be in hell, never to be in heaven; ever to be shut off from the presence of God, never to enjoy the beatific vision; ever to be eaten with flames, gnawed by vermin, goaded with burning spikes, never to be free from those pains; ever to have the conscience upbraid one, the memory enrage, the mind filled with darkness and despair, never to escape; ever to curse and revile the foul demons who gloat fiendishly over the misery of their dupes, never to behold the shining raiment of the blessed spirits (pp. 132-3).

Et cetera. This is the rhythm of exile from the sight of God; the music of mortality. Reading backwards - as the text demands - we can see that the former alternations also involve an ostracism: the punctuation and its representatives all bespeak Stephen's exile from home, and his desire to return to origins. Confounding the journey home with the ticking of eternity, this rhythm links the end to the beginning, staining with mortality the search for origins. And we too, reading backwards in pursuit of a first time - a return to origins - we, too, are caught in its furious music.

As punctuation, the subject is never fully present, but is al-

ways either coming into, or dying out of, being. 'Coming' and
'dying': both are orgasmic: and the rhythm of exile also resembles a 'frottage'. The furious music of the train passes through
Stephen to die in an 'ejaculation'. Most of Stephen's verses 'come'
in this way. He vacillates between two states described habitually
as 'unrest' and 'weariness' (pp. 64, 75, 77, 103), broken by
ejaculations. This brings us to the first of the textual economies:
the economy of flows.

Like the landscape that passes by Stephen on the train, passing
out of him in foolish words, verses, throughout the book, associate themselves consistently with the circuitous itinerary of the
verb 'to pass':

> Such moments passed and the wasting fires of lust sprang up
> again. The verses passed from his lips and the inarticulate
> cries and the unspoken brutal words rushed forth from his
> brain to force a passage (p. 99).

Lust, for the hand that wrote 'Ulysses', passes incessantly
through language, staining flesh with words and words with
flesh. The two can scarcely be distinguished. No more can they
detach themselves from any other form of passing or evacuation.
The streams and floods which pass from Stephen's lips could be
urethral, or menstrual, as well as seminal: breath, blood, vomit
and saliva also issue from this orifice in the form of speech:

> He stretched forth his arms in the street to hold fast the frail
> swooning form that eluded him and incited him: and the cry
> that he had strangled for so long in his throat issued from his
> lips. It broke from him like a wail of despair from a hell of
> sufferers and died in a wail of furious entreaty, a cry for an
> iniquitous abandonment, a cry which was but the echo of an
> obscene scrawl which he had read on the oozing wall of a
> urinal (p. 100).

This cry is in the strictest sense a dirty word. It is a matter of
indifference to the metaphor whether it 'passes' or it 'comes' -
from Stephen's lips. A movement - orgasmic, bowel, or urethral -
releases it to die into a wail: to ooze into an echo of a scar on the
wall of a urinal. The subject's body is a mint which issues him in
wakes, trails, fragments and secretions. 'Issue', a word the text
relishes as much as 'passing', may be applied to publication,
currency, or generation: and all the flows which 'issue' from the
subject constitute the means by which he duplicates, or publishes,
or coins himself. These secretions - verbal or corporeal - invisibly
depart, and enter henceforth into circulation.

Everything that 'passes' through Stephen's consciousness
'issues' forth emptied or dismembered. In one of his attempts at
poetry:

> It seemed as if he would fail again but, by dint of brooding on

the incident, he thought himself into confidence. During this
process all those elements which he deemed common or insignificant fell out of the scene. There remained no trace of the tram
itself nor of the tram-men nor of the horses: nor did he and
she appear vividly. The verses told only of the night and the
balmy breeze and of the maiden lustre of the moon. Some unde-
fined sorrow was hidden in the hearts of the protagonists as
they stood in silence beneath the leafless trees. . . . After
this the letters L.D.S. were written at the foot of the page
(pp. 70-1).

Only the initials at the end of this verse receive direct quotation,
as Stephen, earlier, had halted, blocked, at the initials of its
dedication (p. 70). Apart from these detained letters ('literature')
the passage offers a paralyptical account of the content of the
verses: or rather, of the voiding of their content. Also without
content are the letters of a different kind – epistles – which
emerge as frequently from Stephen's failures in verse:

He saw himself sitting at his table in Bray the morning after
the discussion at the Christmas dinnertable, trying to write a
poem about Parnell on the back of one of his father's second
moiety notices. But his brain had then refused to grapple with
the theme and, desisting, he had covered the page with the
names and addresses of certain of his classmates (p. 70).

These are letters that are never sent.
    Both forms of reduction to the letter occur in the following
passage:

He could scarcely interpret the letters of the signboards of
the shops. By his monstrous way of life he seemed to have put
himself beyond the limits of reality. . . . He could scarcely
recognise as his his own thoughts, and repeated slowly to himself:
– I am Stephen Dedalus. I am walking beside my father whose
name is Simon Dedalus. We are in Cork, in Ireland. Cork is a
city. Our room is in the Victoria Hotel (p. 92).

As well as the words he writes, the words Stephen reads are
constantly disintegrating into a debris of letters. And he responds by composing a letter to himself: his name and his address,
without a message. This is the art of disremembering.
    An art of living. Just as the word is shattered into letters, so
the flesh decomposes into an inventory of its members and secretions. Other people Stephen apprehends as voices, faces, eyes,
hands, clothes, glances, or footsteps. The woman he desires, for
instance, he perceives as breath, a glance, and the tapping of
shoes:

Her glance travelled to his corner, flattering, taunting, search-

ing, exciting his heart . . . sprays of her fresh warm breath
flew gaily above her cowled head and her shoes tapped blithely
on the glassy road (p. 69).

The text, however, demolishes the flesh fastidiously. Here it reduces the woman's body specifically to its exchange values. Not
just any parts are itemised, but the parts that issue forth in
circulation. The face, the gaze, the footstep and the voice represent the currency through which the subject enters the economies
of flow and influence.

But the text does not halt at mere dismemberment. The face, the
gaze, the footstep and the voice degenerate into images and echoes
of themselves. This is how, for instance, its rhetoric mutilates the
priest at Clongowes:

> Stephen smiled again in answer to the smile he could not see on
> the priest's shadowed face, its image or spectre only passing
> rapidly across his mind as the low discreet accent fell upon his
> ear (p. 155).

These are smiles of the order of the Cheshire cat. In this reverse
apotheosis, the priest dematerialises, leaving in his wake a trace
in Stephen's consciousness: an image or a spectre of an accent
and a smile.

There seems to be no agency apart from consciousness that
could assume responsibility for the priest's explosion. Yet
Stephen's consciousness appears to be the victim of the fall-out
too. His own gestures are not precisely self-determined actions,
but mimetically return the images projected from the priest.
Blinded by the shadows - which also are projections of the inter-
locutors - Stephen answers, rather than broaches, the first smile,
whose image passes of its own accord across his mind, while the
disembodied accent falls upon his passive ear. Both parties to
this dialogue reflect, refract, and echo one another: each is the
other's mirror, and the subject but the speculation of the object,
in a triple sense. Dismembering reverts upon the disrememberer.

It is through an ambush of synecdoche that Emma Clery and
the priest disintegrate into their exchange values. But it is also
by means of this dismemberment that either gains admission to
Stephen's consciousness as an 'image'. So that synecdoche represents a kind of rhetorical chewing which prepares experience for
ingustation. This second process takes us into the domain of
metaphor; or in fleshly terms, into the economy of influence. Flow
and influence constantly converge, however, in that Stephen's
overflows, spontaneous as they may be, are always derived from
a previous source. Many of his verses are only paraphrased: but
those few that the text vouchsafes directly tend to be quotations.
Even the word 'weariness' which terminates his feelings of 'unrest' is recycled from Shelley and Ben Jonson (pp. 96, 103, 176).
Or else 'the soft speeches of Claude Melnotte' rise to his lips to
'ease his unrest' (p. 99). Even Stephen's dirty word is the echo

of the graffitto in the urinal, where the wake of language –
writing – is stained by urine, the wake of the flesh. Every word
that 'passes' out of Stephen originates in 'literature': from
whence its stench conducts it to his nose, and issues henceforth
from his lips. While the dirty word reeks of excrement, the
legends in shop windows which confront him later stink of
mortality,

> diffusing in the air around him a tenuous and deadly exhalation
> and he found himself glancing from one casual word to another
> on his right or left in stolid wonder that they had been so
> silently emptied of instantaneous sense until every mean shop
> legend bound his mind like the words of a spell and his soul
> shrivelled up, sighing with age as he walked on in a lane
> among heaps of dead language. His own consciousness of
> language was ebbing from his brain and trickling into the very
> words themselves which set to band and disband themselves in
> wayward rhythms:
>
> > The ivy whines upon the wall,
> > And whines and twines upon the wall,
> > The yellow ivy on the wall,
> > Ivy, ivy up the wall.
>
> Did anyone ever hear such drivel? Lord Almighty! Who ever
> heard of ivy whining on a wall? (pp. 178-9).

This is the smell of dead language. It is the smell of words which
have been heaped up in mean shop legends: withdrawn from circulation and hoarded in writing. These words, like flesh, disintegrate in Stephen's consciousness into meaningless concatenations.
He cannot help but absorb their deadly exhalations and pass
them out again – in 'drivel'.

This passage, then, unfolds the interactions of all three economies: the 'flow' of drivel: the 'influence' of mortal odours; and
the dead language, the 'literature' which occasions these deferred effects. To complete the disremembering of Dedalus, we have
only now to see how the letters of his name – his founding 'literature' – also constitute, with their deferred effects, a cicatrix.

So, by this commodious vicus of recirculation, we return to
Cork. Stephen, now, is trying to track down the initials that
stand for his father's name – and also, incidentally, his own:

> They passed into the anatomy theatre where Mr Dedalus, the
> porter aiding him, searched the desks for his initials. Stephen
> remained in the background, depressed more than ever by the
> darkness and silence of the theatre and by the air it wore of
> jaded and formal study. On the desk he read the word 'Foetus'
> cut several times in the dark stained wood. The sudden legend
> startled his blood: he seemed to feel the absent students of the
> college about him and to shrink from their company. A vision of

their life, which his father's words had been powerless to
evoke, sprang up before him out of the word cut in the desk.
A broad-shouldered student with a moustache was cutting in
the letters with a jack-knife, seriously. Other students stood
or sat near him laughing at his handiwork. One jogged his
elbow. The big student turned on him, frowning. He was dressed in loose grey clothes and had tan boots.
  Stephen's name was called. He hurried down the steps of the
theatre so as to be as far away from the vision as he could be
and, peering closely at his father's initials, hid his flushed
face (pp. 89-90).

Concerned as this passage is with spotting, it also functions as a
blank spot in the narrative. It remains, like the legend of the
desk, unalterably literal: no trope can induce it into circulation.
Neither Stephen, nor the reader, nor the text, can incorporate
the word 'Foetus' which erupts so inexplicably.

What the passage emphasises most about these letters is the act
of cutting them. Like a scar, and like the dead letters in shop
windows, this literature administers deferred effects. Clearly, it
is not just a word that we are dealing with, but a wound: an old
wound, indeed, that Stephen activates in reading it. He responds
with an hallucination: he feels himself surrounded by the absent
students who once scarred the desk with this uncanny legend.
This word, unlike the father's memories, can resurrect the dead.

By two strategies, then, this word usurps the father's place:
it emerges where the father's name should be; and it summons up
a vision of the dead which his father's words - thinks Stephen -
had been 'powerless to evoke'. But the initials that the word preempts are also the initials of Stephen Dedalus.

That the initials of the name of the father should present themselves as a scar is thinkable within a psychoanalytic frame of
reference. In 'Moses and Monotheism', Freud connects the scar
of circumcision to the patronym; and Lacan uses the term 'Name
of the Father' as a synonym for the Law of Castration. For the
psychoanalytic critic, it is almost wearisome to find that SD has
been made into a wound. But why, in this account of things,
should another word achieve priority, and an earlier scar fore-
stall the laceration of the name? And why is this word 'Foetus'?

Why, if not because this first scar is a navel, to which the
Foetus is, of course, attached? Attached, not to the father's
name, but to the mother's namelessness? Why the horror, if not
because the phallus has surrendered to the omphalos?

In another autobiography, 'The Interpretation of Dreams',
Freud's heuristics direct him to the navel as ineluctably as those
of his Irish namesake:

There is often a passage in even the most thoroughly interpreted dream which has to be left obscure; this is because we
become aware during the work of interpretation that at that
point there is a tangle of dream-thoughts which cannot be un-

ravelled and which moreover adds nothing to our knowledge of
the content of the dream. This is the dream's navel, the spot
where it reaches down into the unknown. The dream-thoughts
to which we are led by interpretation cannot from the nature
of things have any definite endings; they are bound to branch
out in every direction into the intricate network of our world
of thought. It is at some point where this meshwork is particularly close that the dream-wish grows up, like a mushroom
out of its mycelium.[4]

According to this description, the navel represents at once the
origin and essence of the dream - its wish - and yet contributes
'nothing' to its content. At once a knot and a lacuna, where
meaning, in its very density, dissolves, the navel is the seam of
the dream. Strangely, this absence occurs where sense is most
concentrated, in the closest tangle of the dream thoughts. If, as
Freud suggests, the navel constitutes the dream's origin, it is,
moreover, an incongruous metaphor for him to use. For even
anatomically, the navel is the point at which the foetus was once
fastened parasitically upon its mother: where, indeed, the body
has no definite ending, nor beginning, but branches out in every
direction into the intricate network of its amniotic world. The
navel marks the spot at which identity dissolves.

    In -The Oxen of the Sun- in 'Ulysses', Stephen repudiates the
notion that our first parents' bellies lacked a blemish. Similarly,
in Michelangelo's 'Creation' in the Sistine Chapel, Adam's navel,
in mute blasphemy, foreswears the fatherhood of God. The umbili-
cus, that Stephen calls the 'strandentwining cable of all flesh',
belies the firstness of the father, and the originality of His
creation. For rather than an origin, this blemish is the footnote
of the flesh.

    To award this footnote the status of an origin offers as a model
of artistic evolution only the alternatives of foetal theft or natal
fragmentation. 'Finnegans Wake' and 'A Portrait' are both, in their
different ways, omphalocentric. 'The last word in stollentelling',
the 'Wake' adopts the first alternative of foetal theft, and circum-
navigates the navel. It restores to the currencies of word and
flesh a seamless amniotic fluency. Narrative itself becomes umbili-
form. If, in 'A Portrait', to remember is to dismember, in the
'Wake', memory is mammary.

    'A Portrait', on the other hand, incessantly short-circuits. In
its repeated births, its repeated exiles, it compulsively returns
to the moment of the fracture and the scar. After the phallus,
then, and Derrida's corrective technics of the hymen, I proffer
the navel as the prototype of Dedalus's scars.[5] A prototype, but
not an origin: for already we have seen, in the knotting and
entanglement of Freud's own metaphor, that the navel necessarily
resists the very structures of priority, centrality, originality.
Omphalocentrism is that movement which deflects, supplants,
transverses and attenuates the notion of a first, or a last, instance.
In 'A Portrait', the word 'Foetus' does not 'mean' navel, but rather

carves the spot where word and flesh meet in a single scar. These scars, or letters, or 'scarletters' - to contract Hawthorne's pertinent title - are littered through the 'Wake', and weave also through 'Ulysses' like an umbilical cord. 'Gaze in your omphalos', Stephen counsels to himself in -Proteus-: and his 'Portrait' is a contemplation of the navel, with all its narcissistic implications. As onanistic as the 'Wake' is incestuous, the rhythms of 'A Portrait' are not those of fluid interchange, but the rhythms of 'ejaculation' in the loneliness of exile, those of a hundred wet and navelled dreams.

NOTES

1   James Joyce, 'A Portrait of the Artist as a Young Man', New York, Viking Press, 1964, p. 105. Further references will be by page numbers in the text.
2   ['The Prelude' (1805), XI, 278-315].
3   [Jean Laplanche and Serge Leclaire, The Unconscious: A Psychoanalytic Study, in 'Yale French Studies', 48, 1972, pp. 118-78.]
4   [S. Freud, 'The Interpretation of Dreams', Pelican Freud Library, 4, pp. 671-2.]
5   [For 'the technics of the hymen' see La Double séance, in Jacques Derrida's 'La Dissémination', Paris, Seuil, 1972, pp. 199-317.]

FURTHER READING

CIXOUS, HÉLÈNE (ed), 'Poétique', special issue on 'Finnegans Wake', 26, 1976.
ELLMANN, MAUD, Floating the Pound: The Circulation of the Subject in 'The Cantos', in 'The Oxford Literary Review', 3:3, 1979, pp. 16-27.
FREUD, SIGMUND, Character and Anal Erotism (1908b), in 'The Standard Edition of the Complete Psychological Works', 24 vols, London, Hogarth Press, 1953-74, IX, pp. 167-76.
— On Transformations of Instinct as Exemplified in Anal Erotism (1917c), 'Standard Edition', XVII, pp. 125-34.
HEATH, STEPHEN, Trames de lecture (à propos de la dernière section de 'Finnegans Wake'), in 'Tel Quel', 54, Summer 1973, pp. 4-15.
LACAN, JACQUES, The Direction of the Treatment and the Principles of its Power, in 'Ecrits: A Selection', trans. Alan Sheridan, London, Tavistock, 1977, pp. 226-280.
— Of the Gaze as Objet Petit a, in 'The Four Fundamental Concepts of Psycho-Analysis', trans. Alan Sheridan, London, Hogarth Press, 1977, pp. 67-119.
LEVINE, JENNIFER, Rejoycings in 'Tel Quel', in 'James Joyce Quarterly', 16:1/2, Fall 1978/Winter 1979, pp. 17-26 (contains

useful bibliography of 'Tel Quel' material).
— Originality and Repetition in 'Finnegans Wake' and 'Ulysses',
   in 'PMLA', 94:1, January 1979, pp. 106-20.
NORRIS, MARGOT, 'The Decentered Universe of Finnegans Wake:
   A Structuralist Analysis', Baltimore, Johns Hopkins University
   Press, 1977.
SHARPE, ELLA, An Examination of Metaphor: Psycho-Physical
   Problems Revealed in Language, in Robert Fliess (ed.), 'The
   Psychoanalytic Reader', London, Hogarth Press, 1950.
SOLLERS, PHILIPPE, Joyce and Co., trans. Stephen Heath, in
   'Tel Quel', 64, Winter 1975, pp. 3-13.

10 AN ART THAT WILL NOT ABANDON THE SELF TO LANGUAGE:
Bloom, Tennyson and the Blind World of the Wish

Ann Wordsworth

[Eliot's -Tradition and the Individual Talent- (1919) problematised
the question of the relations between poems, and between poets
and poems; but though the conservative elements of that essay
have long been assimilated, the radical elements have been ignored.
The work of Harold Bloom, however, has made it no longer possible to discuss poetic influence in terms of the reductive element
of source-hunting, or in terms of the young poet's integration
within a tradition which he subsequently transforms through the
full-flowering of his 'original' genius. Bloom's work, starting
with 'The Anxiety of Influence' (1973), has had the effect of
showing that the relations between poems are not something we
can assume in any simple, undialectical way. In the context of
Bloom's stress on the process of 'misprision', or (mis)interpreta-
tion, even Kristeva's and Barthes's account of 'intertextuality'
as a discursive space of infinite, anonymous networks, begins to
seem too innocent a description of intra-poetic relations.

Bloom's work, however, is more than a theory of influence, in
so far as he sees influence anxiety as constitutive of poetry itself. Bloom proposes a radical method of reading freed from the
normal protocols of logic and representation. For Bloom there is
a profound, if unconscious, interaction between psyche and
text, or psychic defences and tropes, and poetry is read 'anti-
thetically' not as a representation that refers to an object world,
but metaphorically as the work of an Oedipal struggle between
the belated newcomer poet (ego) and the seemingly unassailable
voice of his ('idealised and frequently composite') precursor (id).
The stakes in this struggle are those of poetic identity, 'voice',
and the triumph of poetic immortality over time and death. The
poet's voice or identity is achieved through tropological differentiation rather than from any new beginning, or any individual
'experience'. The struggle, 'at once intra-poetic and interpoetic',
is evidenced at the level of the very processes of the text, by
tropes of limitation and substitution that revise and negate the
figuration of the precursor poem. Meaning, or 'the anxiety that
is the poem', is seen not in terms of a referential content but as
the relationship between poems, as the dialectical series of tropes
by which the belated poet works against the linguistic presence
of the precursor. In 'Poetry and Repression' (1976), the formal
and temporal model of the 'revisionary ratios', or system of tropes
and defences that structure the struggle in a similar way to Anna
Freud's description of the defensive mechanisms between ego and
id, gives way to a greater emphasis on the repetition of repression

rather than Oedipal anxiety per se as the necessary determinant
of all 'strong' poetry; allusion to another poem occurs in what
the later poem *does not say*. This produces a characteristic
triadic structure of tropological substitution which has the effect
of overdetermining language and underdetermining meaning. This
'dearth of meaning' is, in Bloom's terms, the strong poetic imagination, which is not privileged as some transcendental category of
poetic experience, but defined rather in Hobbes's phrase as
'decaying sense'.

Bloom's psychopoetics does not offer itself as a simple model.
For the creative slippages, that destabilise an always improvised
metalanguage with each new act of 'misprision', emphasise that
the 'map of misreading', or revisionary ratios, is never quite
simply a rhetorical, psychoanalytical, or kaballistic model which
can be appropriated as a theory of criticism. Bloom's description
of the power of poets is equally applicable to his own work: 'A
power of evasion may be the belated strong poet's most crucial
gift, a psychic and linguistic cunning that energises what most
of us have over-idealised as the imagination' ('The Breaking of
Form', p. 20).

Bloom conducts a critical struggle on two fronts; first with
orthodox criticism, whose greatest current strength is its en-
trenched position of institutional power. Beyond this, and more
specifically, the attack is on the father and instigator of those
institutional critical traditions, Matthew Arnold. The second
struggle is with deconstruction. Since an important review of
'The Anxiety of Influence' by Paul de Man in 'Comparative
Literature', Bloom has conducted a formidable intellectual quarrel
with what he calls deconstruction's 'thoroughgoing linguistic
nihilism'. In the review, de Man contrasts Bloom's own earlier
description of the poetic imagination as an autonomous power that
goes beyond nature with 'The Anxiety of Influence's 'naturalistic
language of desire, possession and power.' In this way, de Man
argues, Bloom's later theory actually constitutes a relapse into
the very realm of the natural that the earlier theory of imagination
had freed itself from. Bloom's theory of influence is, he claims,
'a step backward':

> From a relationship between words and things, or words and
> words, we return to a relationship between subjects. Hence the
> agonistic language of anxiety, power, rivalry, and bad faith . . .
> the argument is stated in Oedipal terms and the story of influ-
> ence told in the naturalistic language of desire. . . . But no
> theory of poetry is possible without a truly epistemological
> moment when the literary text is considered from the perspec-
> tive of its truth or falsehood rather than from a love-hate point
> of view.

De Man's alternative is thus his own claim that 'we are governed
by linguistic rather than by natural or psychological models'. He
suggests the necessity of a translation of Bloom's subject-centred

theory of influence into 'a taxonomy of recurrent patterns of
error in the act of reading'. The misprisions that Bloom detects
would thus become deconstruction's 'interplay of various modes
of error that constitute a literary text'. But Bloom has resisted
this translation.
  In the following essay, Ann Wordsworth focuses on Bloom's
quarrel with these two (antithetical) modes of criticism. First,
she analyses the problems involved in Bloom's subsequent reply
to de Man: his assertion of the need to restitute 'other-than-
verbal needs and desires' in poetry, his refusal of the privileging
of epistemology, and his claim for the significance of genealogy –
including deconstruction's own. In the second part of the essay,
Ann Wordsworth examines the terms of the quarrel with (post)
Arnoldian criticism, and demonstrates through an analysis of
Tennyson's 'In Memoriam' the limitations of orthodox critical
accounts when compared to the powerful and strange poem that
emerges from an antithetical reading.]

I

To describe Harold Bloom's work as his defence of poetry gets in
both its polemical energy and the importance of Freud. Since
1970, when the book on Yeats was published, Bloom has worked
to clarify and extend an interpretative method to use against both
orthodox critical assumptions and deconstruction – each of which
he sees as having failed to recognise what in his eyes is the constitutive and irreducible energy of poetry: the relationship between the necessarily belated poem and its generative source, a
mind impelled, consciously and unconsciously, to write over and
beyond the always already written works of the precursor poet.
  Bloom's rejection of other critical positions is uncompromising.
Primary (orthodox) criticism he shows as obliged to depend either
on paraphrase or on the importing of evaluative and background
commentaries from other fields – a choice between tautology and
irrelevance. The unresourcefulness of such criticism would make
it an insignificant threat if it weren't academically favoured;
deconstruction, however, is rather more formidable. Bloom
acknowledges it as 'the most advanced form of a purely rhetorical
criticism now available to us'.[1] Here, his resistance is set against
a powerful account of writing which allows no constitutive place
to the creative will. As Derrida puts it, 'there is no constituting
subjectivity. The very concept of constitution itself must be deconstructed.' And in 'Of Grammatology', 'the person writing is
inscribed in a determined textual system.'[2] Inscription within an
indifferent text removes all the effects of what Bloom calls 'the
blind world of the wish' (W.S., p. 387). Instead of the exchanges
of memory, desire, and Oedipal violence – the constituents of the
anxiety of influence – writing enacts processes without origin and
with no founding either in referentiality or in psychic necessities.
The most scrupulous deconstructive critic, Paul de Man, in his

recent work on Rousseau and Shelley, makes this last exclusion
clear: 'the possibility now arises that the entire construction of
drives, substitutions, repressions, and representations is the
aberrant, metaphorical correlative of the absolute randomness of
language, prior to any figuration or meaning' (A.R., p. 299).
For Bloom the limitation of deconstruction is precisely its insistence that poetry is 'a conceptual rhetoric, *and nothing more*'
(W.S., p. 386). Against 'the serene linguistic nihilism' of Derrida
and Paul de Man (a far greater threat to humanist concerns than
the inadequacies of primary criticism), Bloom sets up his claim
for poetry as 'an art that will not abandon the self to language'
(D.C., p. 37), a claim for a psycho-poetics. It's now easy to recognise the strategic force of Bloom's antithetical criticism. Although
the six ratios that map out poems in Bloom's system are outwardly
movements of rhetoric, they are supported and produced by the
belated poet's sixfold work of defence against the precursor.
Figures of rhetoric and the moves of psychic defence articulate
in the image-scape of the poem, and are contexted by the precursor poem whose presence generates the creative process, specifically, three defensive moves of limitation alternating with three
defensive moves of representation. Poetic meaning is made entirely
by this play of psycho-creative and intra-poetic relations; Bloom's
aim is to show the creative logic each poem enacts as it alternately
restrains and asserts the challenge of belatedness which organises
meaning.

As tropes of contraction or limitation, irony withdraws meaning
through a dialectical interplay of presence and absence (clinamen); metonymy reduces meaning through an emptying-out that
is a kind of reification (kenosis); metaphor curtails meaning
through the endless perspectivising of dualism, of inside-out
dichotomies (askesis). As tropes of restitution or representation,
synecdoche enlarges from part to whole (tessera); hyperbole
heightens (daemonization); metalepsis overcomes temporality by
a substitution of an earliness for a lateness (apophrades) (M.M.,
p. 95).

These processes embody the poem and provide all its energy,
content, and expression. Against primary criticism which relates
poems to experience or to philosophical and aesthetic rumination,
Bloom insists 'all interpretation depends upon the antithetical
relation between meanings, and not on the supposed relation be-
ween a text and its meaning' (M.M., p. 76); against deconstruction, he insists 'as the sixfold, composite trope outlined above,
influence remains subject-centred, a person-to-person relationship, not to be reduced to the problematic of language' (M.M.,
p. 77).
    The relation of influence, the complex organisation of creative
energy that links poem to belated poem is for Bloom the guarantee
of poetic meaning. The claim of deconstructive criticism that
poetry consists of 'the poem's own subversion of its own closure'

(W.S., p. 386) strikes at the very heart of Bloom's celebration
of the pleasure and satisfaction that poetry provides: its proof
of the boldly resourceful energies of narcissism.

A mind that can turn to its own figurations and constitute an
ego by love of those figurations, is a Whitmanian, transcen-
dentalising mind of summer. Such a mind is also that of Freudian Man, since Freud defines narcissism as being the self's
love of the ego, a love that by such cathexis veritably *constitutes* the ego (D.C., pp. 26-7).

To master the threat of deconstruction, Bloom makes a careful
critique and expansion of de Man's work on rhetoric - work which
in its radical and complex redefinitions of poetic thinking has
much in common with Bloom's own. Both critics envisage textuality
as a three-part movement; de Man draws his description from a
development of Nietzsche's theory of rhetoric.

Nietzsche's final insight may well concern rhetoric itself, the
discovery that what is called 'rhetoric' is precisely the gap that
becomes apparent in the pedagogical and philosophical history
of the term. Considered as persuasion, rhetoric is performative,
but when considered as a system of tropes, it deconstructs its
own performance. Rhetoric is a *text* in that it allows for two
incompatible, mutually self-destructive points of view and therefore puts an insurmountable obstacle in the way of any reading
or understanding. The aporia between performative and constative language is merely a version of the aporia between trope
and persuasion that both generates and paralyses rhetoric and
thus gives it the appearance of a history (A.R., p. 131).

This aporia has the same destabilising effects as Derrida's 'gross
spelling mistake', the inaudible *a* of differance; that is, it mimes
the movement of deconstruction which in each text produces the
play of enactment and cancellation which constitutes rhetoricity -
and (Bloom's point) nothing more.[3] To avoid a direct entanglement
with the most radical effect of Derrida's theory of writing - the
decentring of consciousness by a 'preverbal lithography' that
writes in the effects of psyche and consciousness alike - Bloom
turns to the rhetorical theory of the Kabbalah. This sidesteps
Derrida's attack on logocentrism by shifting interpretative processes from reliance on the classical logos (word) whose root is
from gathering and putting in order, to the Hebrew dahvar (word)
whose root meaning is the drawing forward of a repressed thing.
Kabbalah - texts of interpretation of 'a central text that perpetually
possesses authority, priority, and strength' (M.M., p. 4) -
provides Bloom with a model for the processes of strong poetry -
writing formulated by 'its *stance towards the precursor text*, its
revisionary genius and mastery of the perverse necessities of
misprision' (M.M., p. 4). The effect of this move is to reinvest
the trope as a figure of will (or of failed will), and therefore to

reinstate psychic triumph and desire as part of the act of writing. Instead of being an undecidable play of rhetoricity, texts embody 'instances of *the will to utter within a tradition of uttering*' (W.S., p. 393). The relation of the Kabbalah to Talmudic tradition is that of a misreading that reopens reading – a diachronic move across texts that defies the stasis of deconstruction. Misprision, the productive power of thought, and therefore of writing and of reading, can thus be seen in two ways: either, 'the process by which the meanings of intentionality trope down to the mere significances of language' (W.S., p. 394) (Bloom's characterisation of deconstruction), or 'conversely the process by which the significations of language can be transformed or troped upward into the meaningful world of our Will-to-power over time and its henchman, language' (W.S., p. 394-5) (characterisation of antithetical criticism).

So there *is* a troper, a poet who tropes, but Bloom's belated poet, for whom misprision is the only generative and saving power against the paralysis of his own belatedness, is a far cry from the historically and biographically placed poet of orthodox criticism. The expansion of Paul de Man's three-part movement (trope, persuasion, aporia) involves the complex interventions of creative energy which are given a part basis in Freudian materialism. In his most recent work Bloom has clarified his position against deconstruction and historical criticism by expanding his account of the creative will, but this movement is not simply a resourceful drawing together of rhetorical theory and Freud. To escape the circularity of the rhetorical description ('every notion of the will that we have is itself a trope, even when it tropes against the will, by asserting that the will is a linguistic fiction' (W.S., p. 396), Bloom needs a further position. His argument therefore moves from the play of tropes to the topological, to the places of invention which in classical theory invested writing with traditional means of elaboration. Interestingly, he links the disappearance of classical rhetoric in the seventeenth century with the rise of associationism: psychological theories accounting for the formation of ideas take over from the classical places of invention. This connection is another twist of belatedness; for Bloom, the topos is not only a place of memory, it is also irradiated by memory. 'A topos . . . is not so much a commonplace or a memory place as more nearly *the place of a voice,* the place from which the voice of the dead breaks through' (W.S., p. 399). Classical instructions for writing and associative linking of ideas are each secretly fraught with anteriority: each implicates the writer by forcing him to circumvent the crisis of his own late-coming. This insight alters the nature of the aporia that Paul de Man identifies. Instead of indifferently marking the disequilibriums of trope and persuasion, the gap makes for implicit movements across or under stages of writing. 'The movement from topos to topos, the crossing, is always a crisis because it is a kind of judgment or criticism between images of voice and between the different kinds of figurative thinking that opposed topics generate' (W.S., p. 399).

By linking the imagistic and tropological patterns of Romantic and post-Romantic poetry to associationist psychology and to its earlier form in classical rhetoric, Bloom justifies the organising principle of his critical theory, the recurrent pattern of the re-visionary ratios. The Freudian theory of psychic defences then becomes a further corroboration of a constitutive movement which generates literary space by repressing and negating the paralys-ing burden of belatedness.

Bloom's criticism stems from the refusal to abandon poetry either to orthodox ethics and aesthetics or to the impersonal pro-cesses of deconstruction. Rather, the strong poet masters his belatedness by all the means at his disposal, limited as they inevitably must be; he is caught up in an unconscious and trans-poetic process and the tactics to hand are psychic, rhetorical and imagistic revisions, a play of ratios and crossings. Although Bloom divides poetry up between strong poets constituted through the struggles against influence and weak poets who evade it, criticism is not so much for him an evaluative act as an act of deciding - 'what it tries to decide is meaning'. This is not of course a return to a form and content debate: if belatedness is the necessary condition of poetry, then interpretation will have to take into account a rather stranger fusion of form and content than is customary. In Bloom's words, 'the language of British and American poetry, from at least Wordsworth to the present, is overdetermined in its patternings and so necessarily is under-determined in its meanings' (W.S., p. 377). That is, the demands of the poetic condition are such that the cognitive workings of the poem are patterned as defensive moves of rhetoricity and image, a word-consciousness so intense that the semantic content is less important than the meaning generated by the tropic patterns in themselves. This insistence of Bloom's is the ground of his dis-agreement with biographical critics for whom the poem's content is the uneasy mix of life and art: for Bloom the mix is always and only of precursor and belated poet - hence, overdetermined pat-ternings, underdetermined meanings.

The processes which Bloom most wishes to clarify are what he now calls relations of ethos, logos and pathos, classical terms used in preference to the earlier kabbalistic triad - limitation, substitution, representation - though functioning in a similar way. Logos, the relation of substitution, is the generative movement by which poems are able to direct and mobilise linguistic process; this identification enables Bloom to reject the deconstructive account of poetry as 'conceptual rhetoric and nothing more'. He moves out by way of Paul de Man's definition of rhetoric as text, his exit being through the ambiguous status of rhetoric as persuasion. 'Rhetoric, considered as a system of tropes, yields much more readily to analysis than does rhetoric considered as persuasion, for per-suasion in poetry, takes us into a realm that also includes the lie' (W.S., p. 386). The necessity of the lie and all the human invest-ment it involves gives Bloom the conceptual space for the return of the poet. Poems are made to lie: against themselves, against

other poems, against time and against death. Poems therefore inhabit 'the blind world of the wish', not the indifferent space of
language only. For Bloom, the trope is animated by the will, 'a
cut or gap made in or into the anteriority of language, itself an
anteriority in which "language" acts as a figurative substitution
for time' (W.S., p. 393). Figure and place interact significantly
because the place of meaning is the place of a voice, the place at
which the voice of the dead breaks through. This interaction is
marked in poems by three crossings which in Bloom's reworkings
direct the otherwise indecidable aporia between language as trope
and language as persuasion. Each stages a creative crisis: the
crossing of election marks fear of losing poetic strength, the
crossing of solipsism marks the fear of rejecting love for self
love, the crossing of identification marks the confrontation with
death. At each of these moments the rhetorical logic of the poem
becomes disjunctive, breaking the smooth unifying flow which is
assumed to be the work of a good style and signalling the need
for processes of reading that can recognise these crises. In the
rhetorical scheme, the crossings take place between irony and
synecdoche, between metonymy and hyperbole and between metaphor and metalepsis; the structures of defence are equally involved. The description is an abstract one because the constitutive
processes of poetry are a rhetorical and defensive patterning;
the orthodox pressure to follow poems semantically as narrative
or evocative exercises is precisely what Bloom resists. Instead
of reading through experience, gauging a poem by its fidelities
of description, the critic must find meaning in rhetorical patterns
which are humanly invested in psycho-creative not biographical
ways and which work to condense and displace precursor poems
by revisions whose deepest but still discoverable processes are
latent. Antithetical readings require therefore a recognition of
movements of thought enacting rhetorical energies whose relation
is to past poems and also, because of the psychic nature of the
bond, to desire and death.

II

It's easier to see the conceptual effects of Freudian theory in
Bloom's work if a comparison is made between antithetical criticism and the use of psycho-biography in primary criticism. According to Bloom, the constitutive motive for writing poetry is the
new poet's desire for the never-to-be-given fullness, presence
and earliness of his own poetry - which is like the narcissistic
ego's desire for a lost object. A psycho-poetics - a work of reading which links image, trope and psychic defence - organises
poems as ratios of limitation and representation structured further
by disjunctions which act as hidden placements of energy and
new moves of meaning. The principle of the reading throughout
is the relation of poet to poet and therefore the recognition of
each new poet's ferocious expense of defensive energy to prevent

his work being blocked by the past. Linguistic play is never
pinned to the poet's lived experience but always to his struggle
with earlier figurations. Thus Tennyson's -Ulysses- ends metaleptically in Tennyson's temporal victory over Milton: the belated
poet triumphs over the precursor in words that overreach Satan's
cry for courage, 'never to submit or yield'; whereas in primary
criticism, taking Christopher Ricks's study of Tennyson as
example, the poem is taken to end on a dying fall, its language
dimmed by yearning and a morbid reluctance to use the future
tense.[4]

> . . . that which we are, we are;
> One equal temper of heroic hearts,
> Made weak by time and fate, but strong in will
> To strive, to seek, to find, and not to yield.

To see why two critical accounts reach such different conclusions
involves working out the different explanatory structures used.
In contrast to antithetical criticism, the centre of Ricks's interpretation is the psychologising of the poem so that it matches
Tennyson's experiences. Ulysses' injustice to his son Telemachus
is the displacement of Tennyson's own relation to his father, 'a
recalcitrance deep in the material itself' (Tennyson, p. 127),
which is not merely mimed in the story but even more revealingly
by the very writing: the misjudgments of tone and the syntactical
awkwardness of relevant parts of the verse. It's characteristic
of the different approaches that Hallam's death is hardly referred
to by Bloom, but is taken by Ricks as the probable cause of the
equivocal nature of the poem, undermining all Ulysses' 'staunch-
ness' and insinuating 'a deeper wan hope'. Tennyson said: 'There
is more about myself in -Ulysses-, which was written under the
sense of loss and that all had gone by, but that still life must be
fought out to the end. It was more written with the feeling of his
loss upon me than many poems in "In Memoriam".' Surely then the
biographical critic must be right, and Bloom wrong in seemingly
excluding grief and the dead presence from the poem? We may not
like it, but the Freudian theory of mourning is very different
from the humanist description. Of course one would expect Tennyson's grief to mark poems written soon after Hallam's death with
despondent and equivocal feelings - but this reaction too may
be part of the repressive and idealising nature of experiential
wisdom. Both Freud's essay -Mourning and Melancholia- and
Bloom's theory of influence show a harsher assessment of psychic
life than is found in the more flattering descriptions of humanism.
According to Freud, the work of mourning is to force the ego into
a testing of reality which will prove that the beloved no longer
exists and that therefore all libido must be withdrawn from the
dead and reinvested. This process is so painful that a turning
away from reality can ensue, allowing the ego to cling to its
lost object through 'hallucinatory wish psychoses'. Wordsworth,
Tennyson, Browning, Hardy - all wrote poems marking deaths of

great creative significance: how far are these poems written as works of mourning, achieving one or other of the bereaved ego's aims? In so far as Bloom finds this work in Tennyson, he absorbs it into the processes of denying belatedness (P.R., p. 168), implying perhaps that the power of death-poems is their deflection of grief into (psychotic) triumph. Hence the psycho-creative work of -Ulysses- is to assert a narcissistic triumph over time and death - to outbid Satan, despite the death by drowning that awaits Ulysses outside the poem's context, and to force a poetic immortality for Tennyson himself, just as Shelley does in -Adonais-, a poem ostensibly an elegy for Keats.

The same conceptual differences mark critical accounts of 'In Memoriam'. This poem, as T.S. Eliot quite rightly observes, is 'unorthodox in its deepest aims' ('Introduction to Poems of Tennyson', Nelson Classics, 1936); nevertheless the poem's subversions can be controlled and obscured if the unorthodoxy is represented by the critic in experiential terms: that is, as the record of Tennyson's uneasy struggle between faith and doubt. Eliot presents the poem and his reading of it in this single context, emphasising the consistency and relevance of every part of the poem to this end. There is 'only the unity and continuity of a diary, the concentrated diary of a man confessing himself'. Sincerity is the hallmark, whether faith or doubt is the final outcome, and throughout its 131 passages the poem is a transcription of the essential experiential record of the response to Hallam's death. Bloom comments dryly:

> One never ceases to be puzzled that 'In Memoriam', an outrageously personal poem of Romantic apotheosis, a poem indeed of vastly eccentric myth-making, should have been accepted as a work of consolation and moral resolution in the tradition of Christian humanism (R.T., p. 153).

In orthodox criticism, critical judgments are backed by a consensus of opinion whose assumptions are not necessarily declared. Behind the accepted (primary) description of 'In Memoriam' lie certain notions about poetry: Poems have a fully referential status: 'In Memoriam' records Tennyson's response to his friend's death; poems achieve unity: 'In Memoriam' fully transcribes 'the many moods of grief' and composes (or fails to compose) them into a coherent whole; poems discover truth: 'In Memoriam' is (or isn't) a truthful documentary of Tennyson's experience and its emotional outcome. And, obviously enough, these positions preclude others: Poems are non-referential: they are the product of psychic and linguistic processes which differ from referential language in specific and identifiable ways; hence Bloom's insistence that interpretation depends upon 'the antithetical relation between meanings and not on the supposed relation between a text and its meaning'. Poems do not express unity: a full deconstructionist reading makes it clear that there's no unified subject and no given plenitude for the poem to compose or enact. Bloom's position requires that poems

be ordered by the relation of influence which makes it clear that
this is a purely abstract psycho-linguistic bond with no ulterior
commitments. As for truth, with no referential or metaphysical
investments, poems can be left to their own logic, whether antithetical or deconstructionist.

The first set of assumptions provide the accepted reading of
'In Memoriam' - and the reasons why a number of its readers
find it unacceptably dull. If it's treated as a record of experience
then it could well seem too long, too pious, too garrulous - too
'anglais', as Verlaine unkindly said. Stress on the literal means
that the passages of argument have to be respected: reason
enough for Yeats to make 'the moral and scientific discursiveness
of "In Memoriam" ' part of the general failure of nineteenth-
century poetry to reach visionary power. The overall effect is to
lose the poem under summaries of nineteenth-century debates on
science and religion or subjective assessments of Tennyson's
sincerity. The treatment amounts to a censorship, protecting
Victorian readers from the subversive and unorthodox aspects of
the work and preventing later critics from noticing that arguments
about faith and doubt give way readily enough to an erotic and
narcissistic triumph over death and belatedness in large sections
of the poem.

Experiential readings gauge poetic tone in terms of the immediate
human subject; in antithetical criticism this relation between poem
and biography is not made. 'A poem can be *about* experience or
emotion or whatever only by initially encountering another poem'
(D.C., p. 15). Thus the writing of 'In Memoriam' presupposes a
creative ravelling of the psychic work exacted by Hallam's death,
a strong poet's drive for his own immortality and an encounter
with precursor poems like -Lycidas-, -Adonais- and -the Immortality
Ode-. Narcissism and aggressivity mark both the work of mourning
and the writing of poems: of all poetry, elegy is the most likely to
show their powerful effects, for here the poetic ego outfaces or
resists the loss of the beloved, the dread of his own extinction
and the crowding presence of earlier death poems, themselves
just as deeply implicated in these processes.

Nevertheless the context of faith and doubt is not just the
imposition of primary critics - shifting 'In Memoriam' out of its
own discursive evasions is not so simple as separating 'Wuthering
Heights' from Charlotte Brontë's repressive introduction to the
second edition. Tennyson had every reason for wanting to write
an orthodox Christian poem after his friend's death: Hallam was
a Christian with a tested faith and his influence on Tennyson had
been ethical as well as - or despite - being creatively sustaining.
'No poet in English,' Bloom writes, 'seems to me as extreme and
fortuitous as Tennyson in his sudden moments of recognition of
his own powers, bursts of radiance against a commonplace conceptual background that cannot accommodate such radiance' (R.
T., p. 154). If there is an unevenness in the poetry as radical
as suggested here, then notions of unity are more than ever
irrelevant: neither its content nor its language can be made con-

sistent. But if 'In Memoriam' can be seen as an uneasy mixture of a referential language and a rhetorically and psychically determined one, then at least it becomes easier to explain why some stanzas are ponderous and banal and others uncannily beautiful. When Tennyson is trying to versify Hallam's thoughts from his essay -On Sympathy- as a mark of love and respect, the verse is as irreproachably dull as Hallam's deductions. Stanza XLV is a paraphrase of Hallam's account of spiritual growth:

> The infant cannot separate the sensations of nourishment from the form of his nurse or mother. . . . So soon, therefore, as the infant makes the recognition . . . that is, assumes a conscious subject of those expressions, he is competent to make a second assumption, to wit, that the looks and tones in the other being which accompany his own pleasure, are accompanied at the same time by pleasure in that other. . . . A great step is thus gained in the soul's progress.[5]

In dutifully matching his verse to Hallam's speculations, Tennyson paraphrases an account of infancy remarkable only for its piety and repressiveness.

> The baby new to earth and sky,
>   What time his tender palm is prest
>   Against the circle of the breast,
> Has never thought that 'this is I:'
>
> But as he grows he gathers much,
>   And learns the use of 'I', and 'me',
>   And finds 'I am not what I see,
> And other than the things I touch.'
>
> So rounds he to a separate mind
>   From whence clear memory may begin,
>   As through the frame that binds him in
> His isolation grows defined.

Yet in stanza XCV, intricately connected with this passage, the dyadic relation of mother and child emerges in all its bliss to bring back the vision of the lost Hallam. Revisionary poetry and the refusal of the work of mourning coalesce so uncannily that it is not easy to see what happens. The poet encounters both precursor poem and unconscious desire, and as hallucinatory wish psychoses the dead returns. 'The living soul was flashed on mine.' Under the visionary 'flashed', the implicit para-rhyme 'fleshed' marks the carnality of desire and links with the censored Oedipal violence of the talismanic lines that Tennyson repeats in order to bring back vision after the repressive 'matter-moulded' demands of representability have nearly destroyed it. Glimpsed through the lines

> The white kine glimmered, and the trees
> Laid their dark arms about the field

is a condensed and displaced scene of Oedipal desire, censored
into a dyadic tenderness – a mother by candlelight embracing a
sleepy child. If this is so, Hallam's banal thoughts on infancy
are erotically transformed and used to restore the dead, and a
'timely utterance' ends the stanza by transumptively restoring
poetic priority over another's 'Recollections of Early Childhood'.
The visionary gleam returns and Tennyson's dawn transfigures
metaleptically Wordworth's 'light of common day';

> At length my trance
> Was cancelled, stricken through with doubt.

> Vague words! but ah, how hard to frame
> In matter-moulded forms of speech,
> Or even for intellect to reach
> Through memory that which I became:

> Till now the doubtful dusk revealed
> The knolls once more where, couched at ease,
> The white kine glimmered, and the trees
> Laid their dark arms about the field:

> And sucked from out the distant gloom
> A breeze began to tremble o'er
> The large leaves of the sycamore
> And fluctuate all the still perfume,

> And gathering freshlier overhead,
> Rocked the full-foliaged elms, and swung
> The heavy-folded rose, and flung
> The lilies to and fro, and said

> 'The dawn, the dawn', and died away;
> And East and West, without a breath,
> Mixt their dim lights, like life and death,
> To broaden into boundless day.

The triumph of this stanza brings Tennyson to the mythopoeic
splendours of stanza CIII, which rewrites the desolate scene at
the end of –Morte d'Arthur–

> So said he, and the barge with oar and sail
> Moved from the brink, like some full-breasted swan
> That, fluting a wild carol ere her death,
> Ruffles her pure cold plume, and takes the flood
> With swarthy webs. Long stood Sir Bedivere
> Revolving many memories, till the hull
> Looked one black dot against the verge of dawn,
> And on the mere the wailing died away.

Each detail is re-enacted and the three queens become the maidens
who at Hallam's invitation join the transfigured lovers on the boat
that sails amid eerie music into a crimson cloud. It is almost too
literal a triumph and more influence anxiety might have made it
rhetorically craftier. Perhaps the psychic impulses are too strong
and win out over the more complex and impersonal revisionary
processes; perhaps Tennyson is too often only refiguring his own
laments and the full rhetorical catachresis, which in -Mariana-
made his version of Keats's romance so strong, is reduced to self-
representation. But even when Tennyson only achieves a version
of his own earlier figuration of the death, this still reverses the
tone of the poem so radically that it is truly surprising that
Eliot could only hear the accents of doubt and despair. 'Dark
house', stanza VII, returns as stanza CXIX, 'I see/Betwixt the
black fronts long-withdrawn/A light-blue lane of early dawn . . .'
And, more strange, an image of utter negativity and disorientation used for the transience of even sorrow itself, is then richly
and ecstatically reversed and spatially reorganised as a gauge of
joy. The image that

> . . . knows no more of transient form
> In her deep self, than some dead lake

> That holds the shadow of a lark
> Hung in the shadow of a heaven (XVI)

returns in CXV:

> Now rings the woodland loud and long,
> And distance takes a lovelier hue,
> And drowned in yonder living blue
> The lark becomes a sightless song.

Even if the creative process owes more to the refusal to undergo
the work of mourning than to its adversary links with the precursor, 'In Memoriam' has its triumph - though this is to be censored
by the biologistic fairy tale of the epithalamium. But this is
perhaps the clearest proof of the quite incompatible modes of the
poem: rhetorical, uncanny, antithetical on the one hand, achieving an immortality forced from death by the narcissistic energies
of creativity and desire; and referential, narrative and idealistic
on the other, asserting a humanist optimism sealed by the pseudo-
scientific notion of Hallam's reincarnation as Cecilia's unborn son.
   Once extracted from the biographical and cultural impediments
of orthodox criticism, Tennyson's beautiful and uneasy poetry
shows the strange amalgam of psyche and text which Bloom continues to identify and explore. As the struggle against deconstruction becomes more crucial, Bloom's work develops further
and the original triadic movement opens into a more complex relation of two sets of ratios and three under-textual places of crossing. But this is still wholly consistent with his valuation of poetry

as the creative will's triumph over belatedness and death. The claim for poetry made in 1970 still stands: 'As scholars we can accept what grieves us as isolate egos, but poets do not exist to accept griefs' (Yeats, p. 5).

NOTES

1 'Wallace Stevens: The Poems of Our Climate', Ithaca, Cornell University Press, 1977, p. 386 (hereafter W.S.; other works by Bloom and de Man will be abbreviated as follows: 'The Ringers in the Tower: Studies in Romantic Tradition', Chicago, University of Chicago Press, 1971, R.T.; 'Yeats', New York, Oxford University Press, 1970, Yeats; 'A Map of Misreading', New York, Oxford University Press, 1975, M.M.; 'Poetry and Repression: Revisionism from Blake to Stevens', New Haven, Yale University Press, 1976, P.R.; Harold Bloom et al., 'Deconstruction and Criticism', London, Routledge & Kegan Paul, 1979, D.C.; Paul de Man, 'Allegories of Reading: Figural Language in Rousseau, Nietzsche, Rilke, and Proust', New Haven, Yale University Press, 1979, A.R.).
2 Jacques Derrida, 'Speech and Phenomena, And Other Essays on Husserl's Theory of Signs', trans. David B. Allison, Evanston, Northwestern University Press, 1973, p.85 fn.9; 'Of Grammatology', trans. G.C. Spivak, Baltimore, Johns Hopkins University Press, 1976, p. 160.
3 [For Derrida's 'différance', see above, p. 15.]
4 Christopher Ricks, 'Tennyson', London, Macmillan, 1972 (hereafter, Tennyson). All references to Tennyson's poetry are from 'The Poems of Tennyson', ed. Christopher Ricks, London, Longmans, 1969.
5 ['The Writings of Arthur Hallam', ed T.H. Vail Molter, New York, M.L.A., 1943, p. 134.]

FURTHER READING

BLOOM, HAROLD, 'The Anxiety of Influence: A Theory of Poetry', New York, Oxford University Press, 1973.
— 'A Map of Misreading', New York, Oxford University Press, 1975.
— 'Poetry and Repression: Revisionism from Blake to Stevens', New Haven, Yale University Press, 1976.
— 'Figures of Capable Imagination', New York, The Seabury Press, 1976.
— Freud's Concepts of Defense and the Poetic Will, in 'The Literary Freud: Mechanisms of Defense and the Poetic Will', ed Joseph H. Smith, New Haven, Yale University Press, 1980, pp. 1-28.
— For the debate with de Man, see Coda: Poetic Crossing, in 'Wallace Stevens', pp. 375-406; The Breaking of Form, in

'Deconstruction and Criticism', pp. 1-37.
HARTMAN, GEOFFREY, War in Heaven (review of 'The Anxiety of Influence'), in 'Diacritics', 3:1, Spring 1973, pp. 26-32.
De MAN, PAUL, Review of 'The Anxiety of Influence', in 'Comparative Literature', XXVI:3, Summer 1974, pp. 269-75.
— 'Allegories of Reading: Figural Language in Rousseau, Nietzsche, Rilke, and Proust', New Haven, Yale University Press, 1979.
REED, ARDEN, Abysmal Influence: Baudelaire, Coleridge, De Quincey, Piranesi, Wordsworth, in 'Glyph', 4, 1978, pp. 189-206.
WORDSWORTH, ANN, Psyche and Text: The Antithetical Criticism of Harold Bloom, in 'The Oxford Literary Review', 2:2, 1977, pp. 6-8.
— Review of 'Figures of Capable Imagination', in 'The Georgia Review', XXXI:2, 1977, pp. 528-33.
— Browning's Anxious Gaze, in 'Browning', ed Harold Bloom, Englewood Cliffs, Prentice Hall, 1979, pp. 28-38.

Part Four

RHETORIC AND DECONSTRUCTION

The 'rationality' - but perhaps that word should be abandoned for reasons that will appear at the end of this sentence - which governs a writing thus enlarged and radicalized, no longer issues from a logos.

If every sign refers to a sign, and if 'sign of a sign' signifies writing, certain conclusions . . . will become inevitable (Jacques Derrida).

11 THE FRAME OF REFERENCE
Poe, Lacan, Derrida

Barbara Johnson

[To offer a further frame or interpretation for an essay that
problematises the nature of the frame and interpretation in three
successive texts requires at the very least an acknowledgment of
the power of a repetition compulsion across texts. This repetition,
Neil Hertz suggests, may be but another name for, or figuration
of, what Harold Bloom calls 'the anxiety of influence'. In -The
Frame of Reference-, Barbara Johnson analyses the strange encounter of Poe, Lacan, and Derrida, together with the consequences of this encounter for literature, psychoanalysis and deconstruction. Lacan's -Seminar on 'The Purloined Letter'-, which
was to become the introductory essay to his 'Ecrits' (1966),
analyses the effects of repetition within Poe's story as an allegory
of the signifier in order to illustrate a re-reading of Freud's
'Beyond the Pleasure Principle' (1919). Lacan argues that 'the
repetition automatism finds its basis in what we have called the
insistence of the signifying chain' - here the 'letter' which
successively positions the subject(s) in the symbolic dimension.

At stake for Derrida is what he calls Lacan's 'restoration of the
"signifier" and of psychoanalysis in general in a new metaphysics';
in -The Purveyor of Truth-, his critique of Lacan's -Seminar-,
he focuses on the effects of the psychoanalytical 'appropriation'
of literature. By demonstrating the absence of an objective frame
of reference, or 'metalinguistic overview', Derrida challenges
Lacan's 'closure' of Poe's text which he claims results from the
drive to analytical mastery. Derrida's attack on Lacan centres
around three related points: (1) Lacan's alleged 'phallogocentrism',
his privileging of the phallus as a 'prime' or transcendental signifier,
as the truth of his system. (2) Derrida argues that Lacan's interpretation of Poe's text, with its desire for a final signified, truth
unveiled, refuses the text's status as writing, as play, signifying
drift, or 'dissemination'. Argument here centres around the
notion of the signifier as a final truth (Lacan's 'phallogocentrism',
according to Derrida) or as an uncontrollable, infinite divisibility.
(3) Derrida claims that Lacan's metalanguage, which attempts to
'close' or arrest the movement of the text, is in fact undone in
that very movement:

It is not . . . a matter of protecting the literary from the
assaults of psychoanalysis. I would even suggest the opposite
. . . certain literary texts have an 'analytic' and deconstructive
capacity greater than certain modes of psychoanalytic discourse
which *apply* to them their theoretical apparatus - a specific stage

of their theoretical apparatus - with its insights but also with
its presuppositions, at a given moment of its elaboration. Such
would be the relation between the theoretical apparatus underlying the -Seminar on 'The Purloined Letter'- . . . Poe's text,
and, no doubt, several others (Pos E II, p. 44).

Lacan neglects, according to Derrida, what Derrida calls the
'parergonal' logic of the 'frame'. The parergon, a word that
Derrida finds in Kant, is the supplement to the 'ergon' (work) -
against, beside, above and beyond it. In the visual arts, the
parergon will be the frame, or drapery, or enclosing column. The
parergon could also be a (critical) text, which 'encloses' another
text. But what it precisely is not, is a simple inside/outside
dichotomy. As Derrida puts it:

> Every analytic judgment presupposes that we can rigorously
> distinguish between the intrinsic and the extrinsic. Aesthetic
> judgment *must* concern intrinsic beauty, and not the around
> and about. It is therefore necessary to know - this is the
> fundamental presupposition, the foundation - how to define
> the intrinsic, the framed, and what to exclude as frame *and*
> beyond the frame. We are thus *already* (i.e. although we are
> *at the margins*) at the unlocatable centre of the problem. Since,
> when we ask, 'What is a frame?', Kant responds, 'It is a
> *parergon*, a composite of inside and outside, but a composite
> which is not an amalgam or half-and-half, an outside which is
> called inside the inside to constitute it as inside' (-The
> Parergon-, 'October', 9, Summer 1979, p. 26).

The 'frame' is one of the 'brisures' ('hinge-words') whose paradoxical logic deconstructive analysis explores. Framing must always
occur in both its senses - pictoral and criminal. The problem,
as Barbara Johnson notes in a longer version of the following
essay, is that 'if "comprehension" is the framing of something
whose limits are undeterminable, how can we know *what* we are
comprehending?' ('Yale French Studies', 55/56, 1977, p. 482).
   While Derrida accuses Lacan of 'framing' Poe's story, Johnson
shows that he himself inevitably 'frames' Lacan's -Seminar- also.
The problem of the frame, as Derrida says, brings us 'already
(although we are at the margins) at the *unlocatable centre* of the
problem' (my italics). Thus Johnson goes on, not to 'vindicate'
Lacan, but to show how there always remains an irreducible
otherness which can never be placed. As she says, it is not a
simple crumbling away at the edges but 'the *precise* otherness of
the abyss *to itself*' (p. 486). Hence the argument between
Derrida and Lacan over the letter and its significance (letter=
signifier=phallus) can itself not be placed or decided, because
the letter as a signifier is not a substance but a function - and
it functions as difference. The letter therefore dictates 'the
rhetorical indetermination of any theoretical discourse about it' -
in other words, the 'oscillation between unequivocal statements of

undecidability [Derrida] and ambiguous assertions of decidability [Lacan]' is precisely its effect. (p. 504). The letter, in fact, makes the reader perform, makes analysis a performative which repeats the reading of the letter, while the letter itself escapes into - insignificance.]

A literary text that both analyses and shows that it actually has neither a self nor any neutral metalanguage with which to do the analysing calls out irresistibly for analysis. And when that call is answered by two eminent thinkers whose readings emit an equally paradoxical call to analysis of their own, the resulting triptych, in the context of the question of the act of reading (literature), places its would-be reader in a vertiginously insecure position.

The three texts in question are Edgar Allan Poe's short story -The Purloined Letter-,[1] Jacques Lacan's -Seminar on 'The Purloined Letter'-,[2] and Jacques Derrida's reading of Lacan's reading of Poe, -The Purveyor of Truth- (Le Facteur de la Vérité).[3] In all three texts, it is the act of analysis that seems to occupy the centre of the discursive stage and the act of analysis of the act of analysis that in some way disrupts that centrality, subverting the very possibility of a position of analytical mastery. In the resulting asymmetrical, abysmal structure, no analysis - including this one - can intervene without transforming and repeating other elements in the sequence, which is thus not a stable sequence, but which nevertheless produces certain regular effects. It is the functioning of this regularity, and the structure of these effects, that will provide the basis for the present study.

Any attempt to do 'justice' to three such complex texts is obviously out of the question. But it is precisely the nature of such 'justice' that is the question in each of these readings of the act of analysis. The fact that the debate proliferates around a crime story - a robbery and its undoing - can hardly be an accident. Somewhere in each of these texts, the economy of justice cannot be avoided. For in spite of the absence of mastery, there is no lack of effects of power.

I shall begin by quoting at some length from Lacan's discussion of -The Purloined Letter- in order to present both the plot of Poe's story and the thrust of Lacan's analysis. Lacan summarises the story as follows:

> There are two scenes, the first of which we shall straightway designate the primal scene, and by no means inadvertently, since the second may be considered its repetition in the very sense we are considering today.
> The primal scene is thus performed, we are told, in the royal boudoir, so that we suspect that the person of the highest rank, called the 'exalted personage', who is alone there when she receives a letter, is the Queen. This feeling is confirmed by the embarrassment into which she is plunged by the entry

of the other exalted personage, of whom we have already been told prior to this account that the knowledge he might have of the letter in question would jeopardize for the lady nothing less than her honour and safety. Any doubt that he is in fact the King is promptly dissipated in the course of the scene which begins with the entry of the Minister D. . . . At that moment, in fact, the Queen can do no better than to play on the King's inattentiveness by leaving the letter on the table 'face down, address uppermost'. It does not, however, escape the Minister's lynx eye, nor does he fail to notice the Queen's distress and thus to fathom her secret. From then on everything transpires like clockwork. After dealing in his customary manner with the business of the day, the Minister draws from his pocket a letter similar in appearance to the one in his view, and, having pretended to read it, he places it next to the other. A bit more conversation to amuse the royal company, whereupon, without flinching once, he seizes the embarrassing letter, making off with it, as the Queen, on whom none of his manoeuvre has been lost, remains unable to intervene for fear of attracting the attention of her royal spouse, close at her side at that very moment.

Everything might then have transpired unseen by a hypothetical spectator of an operation in which nobody falters, and whose quotient is that the Minister has filched from the Queen her letter and that – an even more important result than the first – the Queen knows that he now has it, and by no means innocently.

A remainder that no analyst will neglect, trained as he is to retain whatever is significant, without always knowing what to do with it: the letter, abandoned by the Minister, and which the Queen's hand is now free to roll into a ball.

Second scene: in the Minister's office. It is in his hotel, and we know – from the account the Prefect of Police has given Dupin, whose specific genius for solving enigmas Poe introduces here for the second time – that the police, returning there as soon as the Minister's habitual, nightly absences allow them to, have searched the hotel and surroundings from top to bottom for the last eighteen months. In vain – although everyone can deduce from the situation that the Minister keeps the letter within reach.

Dupin calls on the Minister. The latter receives him with studied nonchalance, affecting in his conversation romantic ennui. Meanwhile Dupin, whom this pretence does not deceive, his eyes protected by green glasses, proceeds to inspect the premises. When his glance catches a rather crumpled piece of paper – apparently thrust carelessly in a division of an ugly pasteboard card-rack, hanging gaudily from the middle of the mantelpiece – he already knows that he's found what he's looking for. His conviction is reinforced by the very details which seem to contradict the description he has of the stolen letter, with the exception of the format which remains the same.

Whereupon he has but to withdraw, after 'forgetting' his
snuffbox on the table, in order to return the following day to
reclaim it – armed with a facsimile of the letter in its present
state. As an incident in the street, prepared for the proper
moment, draws the Minister to the window, Dupin in turn seizes
the opportunity to snatch the letter while substituting the
imitation, and has only to maintain the appearances of a normal
exit.

Here as well all has transpired, if not without noise, at least
without all commotion. The quotient of the operation is that the
Minister no longer has the letter, but, far from suspecting that
Dupin is the culprit who has ravished it from him, knows nothing of it. Moreover, what he is left with is far from insignificant
for what follows. We shall return to what brought Dupin to in-
scribe a message on his counterfeit letter. Whatever the case,
the Minister, when he tries to make use of it, will be able to
read these words, written so that he may recognize Dupin's
hand: '. . . Un dessein si funeste/S'il n'est digne d'Atrée est
digne de Thyeste',[4] whose source, Dupin tells us, is Crébillon's
'Atrée'.

Need we emphasize the similarity of these two sequences? Yes,
for the resemblance we have in mind is not a simple collection
of traits chosen only in order to delete their difference. And it
would not be enough to retain those ,common traits at the expense
of the others for the slightest truth to result. It is rather the
intersubjectivity in which the two actions are motivated that
we wish to bring into relief, as well as the three terms through
which it structures them.

The special status of these terms results from their corresponding simultaneously to the three logical moments through
which the decision is precipitated and the three places it assigns
to the subjects among whom it constitutes a choice.

That decision is reached in a glance's time. For the ma-
noeuvres which follow, however stealthily they prolong it, add
nothing to that glance, nor does the deferring of the deed in
the second scene break the unity of that moment.

This glance presupposes two others, which it embraces in its
vision of the breach left in their fallacious complementarity,
anticipating in it the occasion for larceny afforded by that
exposure. Thus three moments, structuring three glances,
borne by three subjects, incarnated each time by different
characters.

The first is a glance that sees nothing: the King and the
police.

The second, a glance which sees that the first sees nothing
and deludes itself as to the secrecy of what it hides: the Queen,
then the Minister.

The third sees that the first two glances leave what should
be hidden exposed to whoever would seize it: the Minister and
finally Dupin.

In order to grasp in its unity the intersubjective complex thus

described, we would willingly seek a model in the technique
legendarily attributed to the ostrich attempting to shield itself
from danger; for that technique might ultimately be qualified
as political, divided as it here is among three partners: the
second believing itself invisible because the first has its head
stuck in the ground, and all the while letting the third calmly
pluck its rear; we need only enrich its proverbial denomination
by a letter, producing 'la politique de l'autruiche',[5] for the
ostrich itself to take on forever a new meaning.

Given the intersubjective modulus of the repetitive action, it
remains to recognize in it a repetition automatism in the sense
that interests us in Freud's text (SPL, pp. 41-4).

Thus, it is neither the character of the individual subjects, nor
the contents of the letter, but the position of the letter within
the group that decides what each person will do next. It is the
fact that the letter does not function as a unit of meaning (a
signified) but as that which produces certain effects (a signifier)
that leads Lacan to read the story as an illustration of 'the truth
which may be drawn from that moment in Freud's thought under
study – namely, that it is the symbolic order which is constitutive
for the subject – by demonstrating . . . the decisive orientation
which the subject receives from the itinerary of a signifier'
(SPL, p. 40). The letter acts like a signifier precisely to the
extent that its function in the story does not require that its
meaning be revealed: 'the letter was able to produce its effects
within the story: on the actors in the tale, including the narrator,
as well as outside the story: on us, the readers, and also on its
author, without anyone's ever bothering to worry about what it
meant.'[6] 'The Purloined Letter' thus becomes for Lacan a kind of
allegory of the signifier.

Derrida's critique of Lacan's reading does not dispute the validity of the allegorical interpretation on its own terms, but questions
rather its implicit presuppositions and its modus operandi. Derrida
aims his objections at two kinds of targets: (1) what Lacan puts
into the letter, and (2) what Lacan leaves out of the text.

(1) What Lacan puts into the letter: While asserting that the
letter's meaning is lacking, Lacan, according to Derrida, makes
this lack into *the* meaning of the letter. But Derrida does not
stop there: he goes on to assert that what Lacan means by that
lack is the truth of lack-as-castration-as-truth: 'The truth of
the purloined letter is the truth itself. . . . What is veiled/ unveiled in this case is a hole, a nonbeing (non-étant); the truth of
being (l'être), as nonbeing. Truth is "woman" as veiled/unveiled
castration' (PT, pp. 60-1). Lacan himself, however, never uses
the word 'castration' in the text of the original seminar. That it
is suggested is indisputable, but Derrida, by filling in what
Lacan left blank, is repeating precisely the gesture of blank-
filling for which he is criticising Lacan.

(2) What Lacan leaves out of the text: This objection is itself
double: on the one hand, Derrida criticises Lacan for neglecting

to consider -The Purloined Letter- in connection with the other
two stories in what Derrida calls Poe's 'Dupin Trilogy'.

And on
the other hand, according to Derrida, at the very moment Lacan
is reading the story as an allegory of the signifier, he is being
blind to the disseminating power of the signifier in the text of
the allegory, in what Derrida calls the 'scene of writing'. To cut
out part of a text's frame of reference as though it did not exist
and to reduce a complex textual functioning to a single meaning
are serious blots indeed in the annals of literary criticism. Therefore it is all the more noticeable that Derrida's own reading of
Lacan's text repeats precisely the crimes of which he accuses it:
on the one hand, Derrida makes no mention of Lacan's long development on the relation between symbolic determination and random series. And on the other hand, Derrida dismisses Lacan's
'style' as a mere ornament, veiling, for a time, an unequivocal
message: 'Lacan's "style", moreover, was such that for a long
time it would hinder and delay all access to a unique content or
a single unequivocal meaning determinable beyond the writing
itself' [PT, p. 40]. The fact that Derrida repeats the very gestures he is criticising does not in itself invalidate his criticism
of their effects, but it does render problematic his statement
condemning their existence. And it also illustrates the transfer
of the repetition compulsion from the original text to the scene of
its reading.

In an attempt to read this paradoxical encounter more closely,
let us examine the way in which Derrida deduces from Lacan's
text the fact that, for Lacan, the 'letter' is a symbol of the
(mother's) phallus. Since Lacan never uses the word 'phallus' in
the seminar, this is already an interpretation on Derrida's part,
and quite an astute one at that. Lacan, as a later reader of his
own seminar, implicitly agrees with it by placing the word 'castrated' - which had not been used in the original text - in his
'Points' presentation. The disagreement between Derrida and
Lacan thus arises not over the validity of the equation 'letter=
phallus', but over its meaning.

How, then, does Derrida derive this equation from Lacan's
text? The deduction follows four basic lines of reasoning:

1 The letter 'belongs' to the Queen as a substitute for the phallus she does not have. It feminises (castrates) each of its successive holders and is eventually returned to her as its rightful
owner.

2 Poe's description of the position of the letter in the Minister's
apartment, expanded upon by the figurative dimensions of Lacan's
text, suggests an analogy between the shape of the fireplace,
from the centre of whose mantelpiece the letter is found hanging,
and that point on a woman's anatomy from which the phallus is
missing.

3 The letter, says Lacan, cannot be divided: 'But if it is first
of all on the materiality of the signifier that we have insisted,
that materiality is odd (singulière) in many ways, the first of
which is not to admit partition' (SPL, p. 53). This indivisibility,

says Derrida, is odd indeed, but becomes comprehensible if it is seen as an idealisation of the phallus, whose integrity is necessary for the edification of the entire psychoanalytical system. With the phallus safely idealised the so-called 'signifier' acquires the 'unique, living, non-mutilable integrity' of the self-present spoken word, unequivocally pinned down to and by the signified. 'Had the phallus been per(mal)chance divisible or reduced to the status of a partial object, the whole edification would have crumbled down, and this is what has to be avoided at all cost' (PT, pp. 95-6).

4 Finally, if Poe's story 'illustrates' the 'truth', as Lacan puts it, the last words of the seminar proper seem to reaffirm that truth in no uncertain terms: 'Thus it is that what the "purloined letter". . . means is that *a letter always arrives at its destination'* (SPL, p. 72, emphasis mine). Now, since it is unlikely that Lacan is talking about the efficiency of the postal service, he must, according to Derrida, be affirming the possibility of unequivocal meaning, the eventual reappropriations of the message, its total equivalence with itself. And since the 'truth' Poe's story illustrates is, in Derrida's eyes, the truth of veiled/unveiled castration and of the transcendental identity of the phallus as the lack that makes the system work, this final sentence in Lacan's seminar seems to affirm both the absolute truth of psychoanalytical theories and the absolute decipherability of the literary text. Poe's message will have been totally, unequivocally understood and explained by the psychoanalytical myth. 'The hermeneutic discovery of meaning (truth), the deciphering (that of Dupin and that of the Seminar), arrives itself at its destination' (PT, p. 66).

Thus, the law of the phallus seems to imply a reappropriating return to the place of true ownership, an indivisible identity functioning beyond the possibility of disintegration or unrecoverable loss, and a totally self-present, unequivocal meaning or truth. The problem with this type of system, counters Derrida, is that it cannot account for the possibility of sheer accident, irreversible loss, unreappropriable residues, and infinite divisibility, which are in fact necessary and inevitable in the system's very elaboration. In order for the circuit of the letter to end up confirming the law of the phallus, it must begin by transgressing it: the letter is a sign of high treason. Phallogocentrism mercilessly represses the uncontrollable multiplicity of ambiguities, the disseminating play of writing, which irreducibly transgresses any unequivocal meaning.

Not that the letter never arrives at its destination, but part of its structure is that it is always capable of not arriving there. . . . Here dissemination threatens the law of the signifier and of castration as a contract of truth. Dissemination mutilates the unity of the signifier, that is, of the phallus (PT, p. 66).

In contrast to Lacan's *Seminar*, then, Derrida's text would seem to be setting itself up as a *Disseminar*.

From the foregoing remarks, it can easily be seen that the dis-
seminal criticism of Lacan's apparent reduction of the literary
text to an unequivocal message depends for its force upon the
presupposition of unambiguousness in Lacan's text. And indeed,
the statement that a letter always reaches its destination seems
straightforward enough. But when that statement is reinserted
into its context, things become palpably less certain:

> Is that all, and shall we believe we have deciphered Dupin's
> real strategy above and beyond the imaginary tricks with which
> he was obliged to deceive us? No doubt, yes, for if 'any point
> requiring reflection', as Dupin states at the start, is 'examined
> to best purpose in the dark', we may now easily read its solu-
> tion in broad daylight. It was already implicit and easy to
> derive from the title of our tale, according to the very formula
> we have long submitted to your discretion: in which the sender,
> we tell you, receives from the receiver his own message in
> reverse form. Thus it is that what the 'purloined letter', nay,
> the 'letter in sufferance' means is that a letter always arrives
> at its destination (SPL, p. 72).

The meaning of this last sentence is problematised not so much
by its own ambiguity as by a series of reversals in the preceding
sentences. If the best examination takes places in darkness, what
does 'reading in broad daylight' imply? Could it not be taken as
an affirmation not of actual lucidity but of delusions of lucidity?
Could it not then move the 'yes, no doubt' as an answer not to
the question 'have we deciphered?' but to the question 'shall we
believe we have deciphered?' And if this is possible, does it not
empty the final affirmation of all unequivocality, leaving it to
stand with the force of an assertion, without any definite content? And if the sender receives from the receiver his own message
backwards, who is the sender here, who is the receiver, and what
is the message? I will take another look at this passage later, but
for the moment its ambiguities seem sufficient to problematise, if
not subvert, the presupposition of univocality that is the very
foundation on which Derrida has edified his interpretation.
   Surely such an oversimplification on Derrida's part does not
result from mere blindness, oversight, or error. As Paul de Man
says of Derrida's similar treatment of Rousseau, 'the pattern is
too interesting not to be deliberate'.[7] Derrida's consistent forcing
of Lacan's statements into systems and patterns from which they
are actually trying to escape must correspond to some strategic
necessity different from the attentiveness to the letter of the
text that characterises Derrida's way of reading Poe. And in fact,
the more one works with Derrida's analysis, the more convinced
one becomes that although the critique of what Derrida calls
psychoanalysis is entirely justified, it does not quite apply to
what Lacan's text is actually saying. What Derrida is in fact arguing against is therefore not Lacan's text but Lacan's power, or

rather, 'Lacan' as the apparent cause of certain effects of power in French discourse today. Whatever Lacan's text may say, it functions, according to Derrida, as if it said what he says it says. The statement that a letter always reaches its destination may be totally undecipherable, but its assertive force is taken all the more seriously as a sign that Lacan himself has everything all figured out. Such an assertion, in fact, gives him an appearance of mastery like that of the Minister in the eyes of the letterless Queen. 'The ascendancy which the Minister derives from the situation,' explains Lacan, 'is attached not to the letter but to the character it makes him into.'

Thus Derrida's seemingly 'blind' reading, whose vagaries we are following here, is not a mistake, but the positioning of what can be called the 'average reading' of Lacan's text, which is the true object of Derrida's deconstruction. Since Lacan's text is read as if it said what Derrida says it says, its actual textual functioning is irrelevant to the agonistic arena in which Derrida's analysis takes place. If Derrida's reading of Lacan's reading of Poe is thus actually the deconstruction of a reading whose status is difficult to determine, does this mean that Lacan's text is completely innocent of the misdemeanors of which it is accused? If Lacan can be shown to be opposed to the same kind of logocentric error that Derrida is opposed to, does that mean that they are both really saying the same thing? These are questions that must be left, at least for the moment, hanging.

But the structure of Derrida's transference of guilt from a certain reading of Lacan onto Lacan's text is not indifferent in itself, in the context of what, after all, started out as a relatively simple crime story. For what it amounts to is nothing less than - a frame. And if Derrida is thus framing Lacan for an interpretative malpractice of which he himself is, at least in part, the author, what can this frame teach us about the nature of the act of reading, in the context of the question of literature and psychoanalysis?

Interestingly enough, one of the major crimes for which Lacan is being framed by Derrida is precisely the psychoanalytical reading's elimination of what Derrida calls the literary text's frame. That frame here consists not only of the two stories that precede -The Purloined Letter-, but of the stratum of narration through which the stories are told, and 'beyond' it, of the text's entire functioning as 'écriture'.

It would seem that Lacan is guilty of several sins of omission: the omission of the narrator, of the non-dialogue parts of the story, and of the other stories in the trilogy. But does this criticism amount to a mere plea for the inclusion of what has been excluded? No, the problem is not simply quantitative. What has been excluded is not homogeneous to what has been included. Lacan, says Derrida, misses the specifically literary dimension of Poe's text by treating it as a 'real drama', a story like the stories a psychoanalyst hears every day from his patients. What has been left out is precisely literature itself.

Does this mean that the 'frame' is what makes a text literary?

In a recent issue of 'New Literary History' devoted to the question 'What is Literature?' and totally unrelated to the debate concerning the purloined letter, this is precisely the conclusion to which one of the contributors comes: 'Literature is language, . . . but it is language around which we have drawn a frame, a frame that indicates a decision to regard with a particular self-consciousness the resources language has always possessed.'[18]

Such a view of literature, however, implies that a text is literary because it remains inside certain definite borders: it is a many-faceted object, perhaps, but still, it is an object. That this is not quite what Derrida has in mind becomes clear from the following remarks:

> By overlooking the narrator's position, the narrator's involvement in the content of what he seems to be recounting, one omits from the scene of writing anything going beyond the two triangular scenes.
> And first of all one omits that what is in question – with no possible access route or border – is a scene of writing whose boundaries crumble off into an abyss. From the simulacrum of an overture, of a 'first word', the narrator, in narrating himself, advances a few propositions that carry the unity of the 'tale' into an endless drifting off course: a textual drifting not at all taken into account in the Seminar (PT, pp. 100-1; translation modified).

> These reminders, of which countless other examples could be given, alert us to the effects of the frame, and of the paradoxes in the parergonal logic. Our purpose is not to prove that -The Purloined Letter- functions within a frame (omitted by the Seminar, which can thus be assured of its triangular interior by an active, surreptitious limitation starting from a metalinguistic overview), but to prove that the structure of the framing effects is such that no totalization of the border is even possible. Frames are always framed: thus, by part of their content. Pieces without a whole, 'divisions' without a totality – this is what thwarts the dream of a letter without division, allergic to division (PT, p. 99; translation modified).

Here the argument seems to reverse the previous objection: Lacan has eliminated not the frame but the unframability of the literary text. But what Derrida calls 'parergonal logic' is paradoxical because both of these incompatible (but not totally contradictory) arguments are equally valid. The total inclusion of the 'frame' is both mandatory and impossible. The 'frame' thus becomes not the borderline between the inside and the outside, but precisely what subverts the applicability of the inside/outside polarity to the act of interpretation.

What enables Derrida to problematise the literary text's frame is, as we have seen, what he calls 'the scene of writing'. By this he means two things:

1 The textual signifier's resistance to being totally transformed into a signified. In spite of Lacan's attentiveness to the
path of the letter in Poe's story as an illustration of the functioning of a signifier, says Derrida, the psychoanalytical reading is
still blind to the functioning of the signifier in the narration itself. In reading -The Purloined Letter- as an allegory of the
signifier, Lacan, according to Derrida, has made the 'signifier'
into the story's truth: 'The displacement of the signifier is
analysed as a signified, as the recounted object in a short
story' (PT, p. 48). Whereas, counters Derrida, it is precisely
the textual signifier that resists being thus totalised into meaning, leaving an irreducible residue: 'The rest, the remnant,
would be -The Purloined Letter-, the text that bears this title,
and whose place, like the once more invisible large letters on the
map, is not where one was expecting to find it, in the enclosed
content of the "real drama" or in the hidden and sealed interior
of Poe's story, but in and as the open letter, the very open
letter, which fiction is' (PT, p. 64).
    2 The actual writings - the books, libraries, quotations, and
previous tales - that surround -The Purloined Letter- with a frame
of (literary) references. The story begins in 'a little back library,
or book-closet' (Poe, p. 199) where the narrator is mulling over
a previous conversation on the subject of the two previous instances of Dupin's detective work as told in Poe's two previous
tales (the first of which recounted the original meeting between
Dupin and the narrator - in a library, of course, where both
were in search of the same rare book). The story's beginning is
thus an infinitely regressing reference to previous writings. And
therefore, says Derrida, 'nothing begins. Simply a drifting or a
disorientation from which one never moves away' (PT, p. 101).
Dupin himself is in fact a walking library: books are his 'sole
luxuries', and the narrator is 'astonished' at 'the vast extent of
his reading' (Poe, p. 106). Even Dupin's last, most seemingly
personal words - the venomous lines he leaves in his substitute
letter to the Minister - are a quotation; a quotation whose transcription and proper authorship are the last things the story tells
us. 'But,' concludes Derrida, 'beyond the quotation marks that
surround the entire story, Dupin is obliged to quote this last
word in quotation marks, to recount his signature: that is what
I wrote to him and how I signed it. What is a signature within
quotation marks? Then, within these quotation marks, the seal
itself is a quotation within quotation marks. This remnant is still
literature' (PT, pp. 112-13).
    It is by means of these two extra dimensions that Derrida in-
tends to show the crumbling, abysmal, non-totalisable edges of
the story's frame. Both of these objections, however, are in themselves more problematic and double-edged than they appear. I
shall begin with the second. 'Literature,' in Derrida's demonstration, is indeed clearly the beginning, middle and end - and even
the interior - of the purloined letter. But how was this conclusion
reached? To a large extent, by listing the books, libraries, and

other writings recounted in the story. That is, by following the
theme, not the functioning, of 'writing' within 'the content of a
representation.' But if the fact that Dupin signs with a quotation,
for example, is for Derrida a sign that 'this remnant is still literature', does this not indicate that 'literature' has become not the
signifier but the signified in the story? If the play of the signifier
is really to be followed, doesn't it play beyond the range of the
seme 'writing?' And if Derrida criticises Lacan for making the
'signifier' into the story's 'signified', is Derrida not here transforming 'writing' into 'the written' in much the same way? What
Derrida calls 'the reconstruction of the scene of the signifier as a
signified' seems indeed to be 'an inevitable process' in the logic
of reading the purloined letter.

Derrida, of course, implicitly counters this objection by protesting – twice – that the textual drifting for which Lacan does
not account should not be considered 'the real subject of the
tale', but rather the 'remarkable ellipsis' of any subject. But the
question of the seemingly inevitable slipping from the signifier
to the signified still remains. And it remains not as an objection
to the logic of the frame, but as its fundamental question. For
if the 'paradoxes of parergonal logic' are such that the frame is
always being framed by part of its contents, it is precisely this
slippage between signifier and signified (which is acted out by
both Derrida and Lacan against their intentions) that best illustrates those paradoxes. If the question of the frame thus problematises the object of any interpretation by setting it at an angle
or fold with itself, then Derrida's analysis errs not in opposing
this paradoxical functioning to Lacan's allegorical reading, but in
not following the consequences of its own insight far enough.

Another major point in Derrida's critique is that psychoanalysis,
wherever it looks, is capable of finding only itself. The first
sentence of –The Purveyor of Truth– is: 'Psychoanalysis, supposing, finds itself' ('La psychanalyse à supposer, se trouve'). In
whatever it turns its attention to, psychoanalysis seems to recognise nothing but its own (Oedipal) schemes. Dupin finds the letter
because 'he knows that the letter finally *finds itself* where it must
be *found* in order to return circularly and adequately to its proper
place. This proper place, known to Dupin and to the psychoanalyst
who intermittently takes his place, is the place of castration' (PT,
p. 60; translation modified). The psychoanalyst's act, then, is
one of mere recognition of the expected, a recognition that
Derrida finds explicitly stated as such by Lacan in the words he
quotes from the Seminar:

> Just so does the purloined letter, like an immense female body,
> stretch out across the Minister's office when Dupin enters. But
> just so does he already *expect to find it* [emphasis mine – J.D.]
> and has only with his eyes veiled by green lenses, to undress
> that huge body (PT, pp. 61–2; original emphasis and brackets
> restored).

But if recognition is a form of blindness, a form of violence to the otherness of the object, it would seem that, by lying in wait between the brackets of the fireplace to catch the psychoanalyst at his own game, Derrida, too, is 'recognising' rather than reading. All the more so, since he must correct Lacan's text at another point in order to make it consistent with his critique. For when Lacan notes that the 'question of deciding whether Dupin seizes the letter above the mantelpiece as Baudelaire translates, or beneath it, as in the original text, may be abandoned without harm to the inferences of those whose profession is grilling' (SPL, p. 67), Derrida protests: 'Without harm? On the contrary, the harm would be decisive, within the Seminar itself: *on* the mantelpiece, the letter could not have been . . . "between the legs of the fireplace" ' (PT, p. 69). Derrida must thus rectify Lacan's text, eliminate its apparent contradiction, in order to criticise Lacan's enterprise as one of rectification and circular return. What Derrida is doing here, as he himself says, is recognising a certain classical conception of psychoanalysis: 'From the beginning,' writes Derrida early in his study, '*we recognise* the classical landscape of applied psychoanalysis' (PT, p. 45; emphasis mine). It would seem that the theoretical frame of reference that governs recognition is a constitutive element in the blindness of any interpretative insight. And it is precisely that frame of reference that allows the analyst to frame the author of the text he is reading for practices whose locus is simultaneously beyond the letter of the text and behind the vision of its reader. The reader is framed by his own frame, but he is not even in possession of his own guilt, since it is that guilt that prevents his vision from coinciding with itself. Just as the author of a criminal frame transfers guilt from himself to another by leaving signs that he hopes will be read as insufficiently erased traces or referents left by the other, the author of any critique is himself framed by his own frame of the other, no matter how guilty or innocent the other may be.

What is at stake here is thus the question of the relation between referentiality and interpretation. And here we find an interesting twist: while criticising Lacan's notion of the phallus as being too referential, Derrida goes on to use referential logic against it. This comes up in connection with the letter's famous 'materiality' that Derrida finds so odd.

> It would be hard to exaggerate here the scope of this proposition on the indivisibility of the letter, or rather on its identity to itself inaccessible to dismemberment, . . . as well as on the so-called materiality of the signifier (the letter) intolerant to partition. But where does this idea come from? A torn-up letter may be purely and simply destroyed, it happens (PT, pp. 86-7; translation modified).

The so-called materiality of the signifier, says Derrida, is nothing but an idealisation.

But what if the signifier were precisely what puts the polarity 'materiality/ideality' in question? Has it not become obvious that neither Lacan's description ('Tear a letter into little pieces, it remains the letter that it is') nor Derrida's description ('A torn-up letter may be purely and simply destroyed, it happens') can be read literally? Somehow, a rhetorical fold (pli) in the text is there to trip us up whichever way we turn. Especially since the expression 'it happens' (ça arrive) uses the very word on which the controversy over the letter's arrival at its destination turns.

This study of the readings of -The Purloined Letter- has thus arrived at the point where the word 'letter' no longer has any literality. But what is a letter that has no literality?

It seems that the letter can only be described as that which poses the question of its own rhetorical status. It moves rhetorically through the two long, minute studies in which it is presumed to be the literal object of analysis, without having any literality. Instead of simply being explained by those analyses, the rhetoric of the letter problematises the very rhetorical mode of analytical discourse itself.

The letter in the story - and in its readings - acts as a signifier not because its contents are lacking, but because its rhetorical function is not dependent on the identity of those contents. What Lacan means by saying that the letter cannot be divided is thus not that the phallus must remain intact, but that the phallus, the letter, and the signifier are not substances. The letter cannot be divided because it only functions as a division. It is not something with 'an identity to itself inaccessible to dismemberment' as Derrida interprets it; it is a *difference*. It is known only in its effects. The signifier is an articulation in a chain, not an identifiable unit. It cannot be known in itself because it is capable of 'sustaining itself only in a displacement' (SPL, p. 59). It is localised, but only as the nongeneralisable locus of a differential relationship. Derrida, in fact, enacts this law of the signifier in the very act of opposing it:

> Perhaps only one letter need be changed, maybe even less than a letter in the expression: 'missing from its place' ['manque à sa place']. Perhaps we need only introduce a written 'a', i.e. without accent, in order to bring out that if the lack has its place ['le manque a sa place'] in this atomistic topology of the signifier, that is, if it occupies therein a specific place of definite contours, the order would remain undisturbed (PT, pp. 44-5).

While thus criticising the hypostasis of a lack - the letter as the substance of an absence - (which is not what Lacan is saying), Derrida is *illustrating* what Lacan is saying about both the materiality and the localisability of the signifier *as the mark of difference* by operating on the letter as a material locus of differentiation: by removing the little signifier 'ˆ', an accent mark that has no meaning in itself.[9]

The letter as a signifier is thus not a thing or the absence of a thing, nor a word or the absence of a word, nor an organ or the absence of an organ, but a knot in a structure where words, things, and organs can neither be definably separated nor compatibly combined. This is why the exact representational position of the letter in the Minister's apartment both matters and does not matter. It matters to the extent that sexual anatomical difference creates an irreducible dissymmetry to be accounted for in every human subject. But it does not matter to the extent that the letter is not hidden in geometrical space, where the police are looking for it, or in anatomical space, where a literal understanding of psychoanalysis might look for it. It is located 'in' a symbolic structure, a structure that can only be perceived in its effects and whose effects are perceived as repetition. Dupin finds the letter 'in' the symbolic order not because he knows where to look, but because he knows what to repeat. Dupin's 'analysis' is the repetition of the scene that led to the necessity of analysis. It is not an interpretation or an insight, but an act. An act of untying the knot in the structure by means of the repetition of the act of tying it. The word 'analyse', in fact, etymologically means 'untie', a meaning on which Poe plays in his prefatory remarks on the nature of analysis as 'that moral activity which disentangles' (Poe, p. 102). The analyst does not intervene by giving meaning, but by effecting a dénouement.

But if the act of (psycho) analysis has no identity apart from its status as a repetition of the structure it seeks to analyse (to untie), then Derrida's remarks against psychoanalysis as being always already 'mise en abîme' in the text it studies and as being only capable of finding itself, are not objections to psychoanalysis but in fact a profound insight into its very essence. Psychoanalysis is in fact itself the primal scene it is seeking: it is the first occurrence of what has been repeating itself in the patient without ever having occurred. Psychoanalysis is not itself the interpretation of repetition; it is the repetition of a trauma of interpretation – called 'castration' or 'parental coitus' or 'the Oedipus complex' or even 'sexuality'. It is the traumatic deferred interpretation not of an event, but as an event that never took place as such. The 'primal scene' is not a scene but an interpretative infelicity whose result was to situate the interpreter in an intolerable position. And psychoanalysis is the reconstruction of that interpretative infelicity not as its interpretation, but as its first and last act. Psychoanalysis has content only in so far as it repeats the dis-content of what never took place.

In a way, I have come back to the question of the letter's destination and of the meaning of the enigmatic 'last words' of Lacan's Seminar. 'The sender,' writes Lacan, 'receives from the receiver his own message in reverse form. Thus it is that what the "purloined letter", nay, the "letter in sufferance" means is that a letter always arrives at its destination' (SPL, p. 72). What the reversibility of the direction of the letter's movement between sender and receiver has now come to stand for is precisely the fact, underlined by Derrida as if it were an objection to Lacan, that there is no position from which the letter's message can be read as an object: 'no neutralisation is possible, no general point of view' (PT, p. 106). This is also precisely the 'discovery' of psychoanalysis – that the analyst is involved (through transference) in the very 'object' of his analysis.

Everyone who has held the letter – or even beheld it – including the narrator, has ended up having the letter addressed to him as its destination. The reader is comprehended by the letter: there is no place from which he can stand back and observe it. Not that the letter's meaning is subjective rather than objective, but that the letter is precisely that which subverts the polarity subjective/objective, that which makes subjectivity into something whose position in a structure is situated by the passage through it of an object. The letter's destination is thus wherever it is read, the place it assigns to its reader as his own partiality. Its destination is not a place, decided a priori by the sender, because the receiver is the sender, and the receiver is whoever receives the letter, including nobody. When Derrida says that a letter can miss its destination and be disseminated, he reads 'destination' as a place that pre-exists the letter's movement. But if, as Lacan shows, the letter's destination is not its literal addressee, nor even whoever possesses it, but whoever is possessed by it, then the very disagreement over the meaning of 'reaching the destination' is an illustration of the non-objective nature of that 'destination'. The rhetoric of Derrida's differentiation of his own point of view from Lacan's enacts that law:

> Thanks to castration, the phallus always stays in its place in the transcendental topology we spoke of earlier. It is indivisible and indestructible there, like the letter that takes its place. And that is why the *interested* presupposition, never proved, of the letter's materiality as indivisibility was indispensable to this restricted economy, this circulation of propriety.
>
> The difference I am *interested* in here is that, a formula to be read however one wishes, the lack has no place of its own in dissemination (PT, p. 63; translation modified, emphasis mine).

The play of interest in this expression of difference is quite too interesting not to be deliberate. The opposition between the 'phallus' and 'dissemination' is not between two theoretical objects but between two interested positions. And if sender and receiver are merely the two poles of a reversible message, then Lacan's substitution of 'destin' for 'dessein' in the Crébillon quotation – a misquotation that Derrida finds revealing enough to end his analysis upon – is in fact the quotation's message. The sender (dessein) and the receiver (destın) of the violence that passes between Atreus and Thyestes are equally subject to the violence the letter is.

The sentence 'a letter always arrives at its destination' can thus either be simply pleonastic or variously paradoxical: it can mean 'the only message I can read is the one I send', 'wherever the letter is, is its destination'; 'when a letter is read, it reads the reader'; 'the repressed always returns'; 'I exist only as a reader of the other'; 'the letter has no destination'; and 'we all die'. It is not any one of these readings, but all of them and others in their very incompatibility, that repeat the letter in its way of reading the act of reading. Far from giving us the Seminar's final truth, these last words, and Derrida's readings of them, can only enact the impossibility of any ultimate analytical meta-language, the eternal oscillation between unequivocal undecid-ability and ambiguous certainty.

NOTES

An extended version of this essay can be found in 'Yale French Studies', 55/56, 1977 (special issue entitled 'Literature and Psychoanalysis'), pp. 457-505.

1 In Edgar Allan Poe, 'Great Tales and Poems of Edgar Allan Poe', New York Pocket Books, 1951, pp. 199-219, hereafter designated as Poe.

2 In Jacques Lacan, 'Ecrits', Paris, Seuil, 1966 [reissued in Seuil's 'Collection Points' (No. 5) 1969]. Quotations in English are taken, unless otherwise indicated, from the partial translation in 'Yale French Studies', no. 48, 1973 (special issue entitled 'French Freud'), pp. 38-72, hereafter designated as SPL.

3 This article was published in French in 'Poétique', 21, 1975: pp. 96-147 [reprinted in 'La Carte postale' (1980), pp. 441-524], and, somewhat reduced, in English in 'Yale French Studies', 52, 1975 (special issue entitled 'Graphesis'), pp. 31-113. Unless otherwise indicated, references are to the English version, hereafter designated as PT.

4 'So infamous a scheme/If not worthy of Atreus, is worthy of Thyestes.'

5 'La politique de l'autruiche' combines the policy of the ostrich (autruche), others (autrui), and Austria (Autriche).

6 Lacan, 'Ecrits', p. 57; translation and emphasis mine. Not translated in SPL.

7 Paul de Man, 'Blindness and Insight', New York, Oxford University Press, 1971, p. 140.

8 Stanley E. Fish, How Ordinary is Ordinary Language?, 'New Literary History' 5 (Autumn 1973): p. 52.

9 It is perhaps not by chance that the question arises here of whether or not to put the accent on the letter 'a.' The letter 'a' is perhaps the purloined letter par excellence in the writ-ings of all three authors: Lacan's 'objet *a*,' Derrida's 'différ-ance,' and Edgar Poe's middle initial, A, taken from his foster father, John Allan.

FURTHER READING

DERRIDA, JACQUES, [Writings most specifically concerned with psychoanalysis:] 'La Carte postale, de Socrate à Freud et au-delà', Paris, Aubier-Flammarion, 1980. (Parts of this have been translated as follows: Speculations – on Freud, 'The Oxford Literary Review', 3:2, 1978, pp. 78-97; Coming into One's Own, in G. Hartman (ed), 'Psychoanalysis and the Question of the Text', Baltimore, Johns Hopkins University Press, 1978, pp. 114-48; The Purveyor of Truth, 'Yale French Studies', 52, 1975, pp. 31-113.)
— Freud and the Scene of Writing, in 'Yale French Studies', 48, 1972, pp. 74-117; also in 'Writing and Difference', trans. Alan Bass, London, Routledge & Kegan Paul, 1978, pp. 196-231.
— Positions (Part II), in 'Diacritics', 3:1, Spring 1973, pp. 33-46.
— Fors; The Anglish Words of Nicolas Abraham and Maria Torok, in 'The Georgia Review', 31:1, 1977, pp. 64-116.
— Me – Psychoanalysis: An Introduction to the Translation of 'The Shell and the Kernel' by Nicolas Abraham, in 'Diacritics', 9:1, Spring 1979, pp. 4-12.
HEATH, STEPHEN, Difference, in 'Screen', 19:3, Autumn 1978, pp. 51-112.
HERTZ, NEIL, Freud and the Sandman, in 'Textual Strategies: Perspectives in Post-Structuralist Criticism', ed Josué V. Harari, Ithaca, Cornell University Press, 1979, pp. 296-321.
LACAN, JACQUES, Lituraterre, in 'Littérature', 3, 1971, pp. 3-10.
— Seminar on 'The Purloined Letter', in 'Yale French Studies', 48, 1972, pp. 39-72.
LECLAIRE, SERGE, 'Psychanalyser: Un essai sur l'ordre de l'inconscient et la pratique de la lettre', Paris, Seuil, 1968.
MEHLMAN, JEFFREY, The 'Floating Signifier'; From Lévi-Strauss to Lacan, in 'Yale French Studies', 48, 1972, pp. 10-37.
— Poe Pourri: Lacan's Purloined Letter, in 'Semiotext(e)', 1:3, 1975, pp. 51-68.
'Screen' Special issues: Psychoanalysis and the Cinema, 16:2, Summer 1975; Suture, 18:4, Winter 1977/8.
SPIVAK, GAYATRI C., Translator's Preface to Jacques Derrida's 'Of Grammatology', trans. G.C. Spivak, Baltimore, Johns Hopkins University Press, 1976, pp. lxii-lxvii.

12 THE STONE AND THE SHELL:

The Problem of Poetic Form in
Wordsworth's Dream of the Arab

J. Hillis Miller

[Derrida's immediate precursors are the phenomenologists
Heidegger and Husserl, and his own position is best defined in
terms of his critique of them. Here J. Hillis Miller, before 1970
a prominent phenomenological critic associated with the Geneva
school of Georges Poulet and now a deconstructionist, examines
the differences between the two in terms of their relation to literary criticism and their different effects on ways of reading. These
differences devolve on to the problem of the subject, and the
relation of consciousness to writing. Phenomenology gives priority
to the consciousness of the subject. Even though phenomenological
criticism does not try to get at a subject behind a work, but constructs one in and through it, it nevertheless tries to produce
the totality of a moment of pure self-consciousness. For Derrida,
however, the privileging of this moment of self-presence can only
be achieved at the expense of language and writing:

> Pure perception does not exist: we are written only as we write,
> by the agency within us which always already keeps watch over
> perception, be it internal or external. The 'subject' of writing
> does not exist if we mean by that some sovereign solitude of the
> author. The subject of writing is a *system* of relations between
> strata: [Freud's] Mystic Pad, the psyche, society, the world.
> Within that scene, on that stage, the punctual simplicity of the
> classical subject is not to be found ('Writing and Difference',
> pp. 226-7).

Consciousness does not simply 'exist' as some pure essence, cogito,
or being, but is itself constituted as process by the interplay and
interpretation of signs, signs that in themselves are merely marks
of difference. Consciousness is contingent upon writing, which
never presents, but always defers, presence.

Wordsworth would seem, at first, to be a good example of a poet
who asserts the primacy of consciousness, who assumes that speech
involves the pure presence of an undivided and originating subjectivity, and that writing, to use his own word, is merely a
dangerous 'counterspirit'. But, as Hillis Miller shows, the poetry
of 'The Prelude' does not sustain the simplicity of such a reading.
The poem begins, certainly, with claims for the pure presence of
voice, but they are revealed, significantly, as already flawed:
'My own voice cheered me, and far more / The mind's internal
echo of the imperfect sound.' A much more paradoxical and
undecidable relation between consciousness and language

emerges in the Arab Dream of Book V.
The proem and the dream are dominated by the metaphor of the
mind as writing: a book, inscription, a 'stamping'. This would
imply that consciousness is only possible through division (the
sign as difference), and that the mind cannot know itself without
the play of the signs which it interprets. The dream proper leaves
the reader only with signs, which have no necessary relation between signifier and signified, and the endless permutations of
displacements and substitutions of language which show that signifier and signified are both arbitrary in themselves, as well as
in their relation to each other. In the paradoxical metaphors that
dominate the proem, in the displacements within the dream, and
in the series of interpretations made in the process of waking/
sleeping/waking, it becomes clear that what is being enacted is
metaphor itself. The necessity to name one thing by another puts
the very process of naming into question; in Derrida's description,
'metaphor shapes and undermines the proper name. The literal
(propre) meaning does not exist; its "appearance" is a necessary
function . . . in the system of differences and metaphors' ('Of
Grammatology', p. 89). As George Eliot suggests in an absorbing
discussion of metaphor in 'The Mill on the Floss', the necessity
to name one thing by another is the ground of all epistemological
problems:

> O Aristotle! if you had had the advantage of being 'the freshest
> modern' instead of the greatest ancient, would you not have
> mingled your praise of metaphorical speech, as a sign of high
> intelligence, with a lamentation that intelligence so rarely shows
> itself in speech without metaphor - that we can so seldom de-
> clare what a thing is, except by saying it is something else?
> (Book II, Chapter 1).

For Plato, in the 'Cratylus', the name was the one element in
language which anchored word to thing, since a name has reference but no sense. But in 'The Prelude' Book V this stability is
no longer assured. The traveller whom the dreamer meets is both
an Arab and a knight, yet 'of these was neither and was both at
once'. He is, precisely, a floating signifier.]

If any man speak in an unknown tongue, let it be by two, or at
the most by three, and that by course; and let one interpret
(1 Corinthians, 14 : 27).

To investigate the problem of poetic form as one of the strands
woven into the systematic web of Wordsworth's language it will
be best to concentrate on the text in which these issues are
raised most directly. This is Book Five of 'The Prelude', and,
within that, the admirable dream of the Arab with his stone and
shell, lines 1-165. Critics from De Quincey on have recognised
the special importance and difficulty of this passage, as well as

its great power, and I cannot hope to interpret it wholly here.
To do that would in fact involve an analysis of all Wordsworth's
writings. Even so, I can hope to move some distance around the
spirals of the hermeneutical circle.

This may be done by exploring the implications of this passage
for an issue already raised in my discussion of the sonnet
-Composed upon Westminster Bridge-,[1] that is, the question of
the radical ambiguity of meaning in that poem. Why is it that the
finite elements within the enclosed space of the sonnet cannot be
resolved into a neat pattern of meaning, neither in themselves
nor in their relation to other texts by Wordsworth? This question
may be related to the problem of the origin of the meaning of
signs, a problem also implicit in the metaphors of the sonnet on
sonnets, for example, in the relation of breath, trumpet, and the
soul-animating strains played on the trumpet.[2] Does the meaning
pre-exist the signs for it, so that it is only expressed, copied, or
represented by them, or does it come into existence only in its
signs? Does Word precede words, or is it the other way around?
To this may be related the general question of the function of
written, as opposed to oral, language, of inscription as opposed
to speech.

Wordsworth has often been enlisted into the ranks of those who
see poetry as primarily oral. Such men look upon written language
as a mere copy of living speech. There are passages by Wordsworth which seem to affirm this view unequivocally, but in fact
Wordsworth's thinking on this matter is considerably more complicated than such passages would imply. If he sometimes seems
to see authentic poetry as existing only orally, in the 'spontaneous' 'pouring forth' of the poet's 'soul' 'in measured strains', on
the other hand he is a poet 'not used to make/A present joy the
matter of a song' (P, I. 46-7), and his poetry was in fact written
down.[3] The distinction between immediate experience and the
poetry which arises later on when that experience, or its accom-
panying emotion, is recollected in tranquillity implies at least
enough distance from immediate experience to allow it to be 'recorded' in a secondary present, as in fact he says of the experience of spontaneous oral poetic creation described at the opening
of 'The Prelude' (P, I. 50). This would seem to put the written
text at a double remove from the original experience which it describes. The spontaneous overflow of powerful feelings when the
original emotion is later on recollected in tranquillity is in its turn
'recorded' on the page in a representation of a representation.
The writing down of a poetic text is a making present for the
reader of what was itself the making present of an experience once
present but no longer so. On the other hand it is clear that both
in theory and in practice the recollection in tranquillity for Wordsworth brings something new into existence, something not present
in the original experience. If this is so, one may wonder whether
or not this is also the case with the act of writing down the experience as re-experienced. In fact the issue here is not the opposition of primary oral speech against secondary, derived, written

language, but the more fundamental question which lies behind
this opposition in its usual form. This is the question whether
expression in either oral or written form brings new meaning into the world or only copies a pre-existing meaning.

Wordsworth's concern for this question is indicated by his fas-
cination with all kinds of written language. This includes not only
the 'Books' which are the title and the overt subject of Book Five
of 'The Prelude', but also many other forms of inscription: epitaphs, monuments, memorial plaques, signs, and so on. One of
Wordsworth's earliest poems is called - Lines left upon a Seat in a
Yew-tree, which stands near the Lake of Esthwaite, on a desolate part of the Shore, commanding a beautiful prospect -. The
- Essay on Epitaphs - investigates the nature and function of
that kind of poetry which is inscribed on stone to mark a grave.
One section of the collected poems is called 'Epitaphs and Elegiac
Pieces'. Another is called 'Inscriptions'.[4] The latter group contains short poems with titles like the following: - Written with a
Pencil upon a Stone in the Wall of the House (an Out-house), on
the Island at Grasmere -, - Written with a Slate Pencil on a Stone,
on the Side of the Mountain of Black Comb -, - Written with a
Slate Pencil upon a Stone, the largest of a Heap lying near a
deserted Quarry, upon one of the Islands at Rydal -. These titles,
almost longer than the poems they name, are striking in the extreme circumstantiality of detail with which they identify the act
whereby the poem was given physical existence. The exact place,
the stone, the act of writing, the tool used for the inscription -
all are described with precision. This precision suggests that the
most important aspect of these particular poems may be the act of
writing, that act whereby a mute stone becomes a structure of
signs speaking a silent message to any passerby. Such poems are
by their titles so wedded to the stone on which they were written
that one wonders if they can survive being copied in the book in
which we read them today. Their 'primary' existence was not as
living speech but as marks made with a slate pencil on a stone.

An essay could be written investigating the role of stones in
Wordsworth's poetry, the rocks and stones to which Lucy is assimilated after her death in - A Slumber Did My Spirit Seal -, the
comparison of the old leechgatherer to a huge stone 'Couched on
the bald top of an eminence' in - Resolution and Independence -,
the moving line of - Michael -: 'And never lifted up a single stone',
the 'old grey stone', 'a rude mass / Of native rock' which used to
stand in the square of the village where Wordsworth grew up
(P, II, 38 ; 33-34), and many others. Charles du Bos, commenting with great insight on a passage from - The Thorn - and on
another from Book Fourteen of 'The Prelude',[5] has observed that
stones for Wordsworth are often seen as vital, alive with an
obscure organic existence which may assimilate them to trees, and
that such a living stone is Wordsworth's best symbol for his own
soul, his inmost being. Du Bos says:

The trunk of a tree, with gnarled bark, which the sap invades

and abandons in turn, and which, without that sap, would collapse if its rigid posture did not belong to the realm of stone,
and if it was not endowed with the strange majesty of a cromlech
– it is thus that I represent to myself the structure and stature
of being in Wordsworth. . . . Because this soul, a natural
phenomenon, is itself a rock in its origin; and its co-ordinates
– near or far, moving or fixed – are great natural forces –
mountain streams, clouds, stars. Its native element is the air
of the mountain.[6]

Another important aspect of Wordsworth's attitude toward stones,
however, may be defined by saying that he not only was fascinated
by stones in themselves, found them precious objects,[7] but also
was impelled, when he found on an island or on a mountain top a
stone he especially admired, to scratch or carve a poem on it.
Such inscriptions are evidence that Wordsworth, far from always
believing that poetry exists primarily as spoken language, sometimes felt that a poem only comes into existence in a satisfactory
form when it has not only been written down but inscribed permanently on the perdurable substance of a rock. The implications
of this strange strand in Wordsworth's conception of poetry are
brought most clearly into the open in the admirable dream of the
Arab in 'The Prelude'. Here the role of written language both as
an indispensable metaphor for what it seems to derive from and
as a primary or originating act becomes the overt subject of
Wordsworth's verse.

The opening lines of Book Five of 'The Prelude' establish the
theme which is to be investigated in the narrative of the dream
which follows.[8] The theme is established in terms of a metaphor of
the book, of printing or inscription, which is latent throughout
but becomes fully explicit only in the closing lines of the proem,
lines 45-9. In these lines the fragility of books as physical objects
is lamented. The human mind has a power to project itself outside
itself, a power to articulate itself in verbal or symbolic structures,
poetry or geometry. These productions of 'Bard and Sage' constitute 'adamantine holds of truth / By reason built, or passion'
(P, V. 39-40). The 'sadness' is that these rocklike grips on
truth must be embodied in an element which far from having the
indestructibility of adamant, may be destroyed by fire or flood,
namely the paper, ink, glue, cardboard, or leather of a book:

> Oh! why hath not the Mind
> Some element to stamp her image on
> In nature somewhat nearer to her own?
> Why, gifted with such powers to send abroad
> Her spirit, must it lodge in shrines so frail? (P, V. 45-9).

The system of thought leading up to these lines is peculiar, as is
so often the case with Wordsworth. Peculiar also is the relation
of the proem of forty-nine lines which opens the book and the narrative of the dream which follows it. That narrative is at once an
extension of the proem, a commentary on it, and a curious rever-

sal of its apparent premises, a rearrangement of all its elements,
literal and metaphorical, to generate unforeseen permutations of
meaning. The book, marks stamped or inscribed on frail paper
pages, appears as part of a double metaphor in which the secondary is used as the only adequate metaphorical expression of the
primary, of that from which it is derived or on which it is
modelled. This reversal is part of the Western tradition and may
be traced back to Plato as one of those structures of thought inherent in the metaphorical tissue of our languages. The relation
between the 'soul divine' as Wordsworth calls it in the 1805 text
(P, V. 16), and nature is like the relation between a human soul
and its body. Just as the human body, especially the face, with
its power of modulating breath into speech, is the 'image' of the
soul which is diffused throughout that body and animates it, so
nature is the body of the 'sovereign intellect' which lies behind
and within nature. This intellect uses nature as its means of
self-expression and as its means of communicating to man. The
personification of nature as a human body and in particular as an
expressive and speaking face runs throughout 'The Prelude' and
Wordsworth's works generally. It is present, for example, in the
sonnet written on Westminster Bridge and in the grand climactic
passage of interwoven metaphors describing the crossing of the
Simplon Pass in Book Six of 'The Prelude'. The intermingled elements of the Alpine scene 'Were all like workings of one mind,
the features/Of the same face' (P, VI. 636-7). The names of a
part of the creation, human beings, are used to describe the
working of the creator in his relation to the creation:

> Hitherto,
> In progress through this Verse, my mind hath looked
> Upon the speaking face of earth and heaven
> As her prime teacher, intercourse with man
> Established by the sovereign Intellect,
> Who through that bodily image hath diffused,
> As might appear to the eye of fleeting time,
> A deathless spirit. (P, V. 11-18).

The difference, doubtless, between the combination of spirit
and body in the human being and the combination of intellect and
physical nature in the creation is that the human mind is limited.
Its perspective is that of 'fleeting time', moreover, is mortal. The human body, moreover, is mortal. The divine Intellect, on the other hand, is 'sovereign'. It has a regal power of origination, establishment, and
government which cannot die, or which at any rate 'appears' to
be 'a deathless spirit'. The element on which it stamps itself or
which it makes use of as the medium of its speech is also indest-
ructible. If the apocalyptic fire and earthquake were to come to
burn the earth and dry up the ocean, even then both the sovereign Intellect and the earth which is its speaking face would remain. Nature would still be the living countenance and the book
of God:

Yet would the living Presence still subsist
Victorious, and composure would ensue,
And kindlings like the morning - presage sure
Of day returning and of life revived (P, V. 34-7).

Only in a line added in the 1850 version, 'As might appear to
the eye of fleeting time', is any doubt cast on the adequacy of
Wordsworth's formulation, the shade of a suspicion raised by the
apparently innocuous words 'as might appear' that the vision of
earth as a 'speaking face' expressing the thoughts of a 'sovereign
Intellect' may be an appearance projected on nature by the 'eye
of fleeting time'. This appearance may be somehow generated by
the temporal transience of the human perspective on nature. Is
the 'living Presence' within nature a pre-existing deathless spirit,
or does it only appear that way to the eye of fleeting time? Is the
Presence an illusion or phantom developed by the angle of vision
peculiar to human consciousness? That consciousness dwells within
time as its movement and as the power of seeing created by that
movement. This movement is determined by man's mortality. Could
it be that the appearance of a deathless spirit which has stamped
its image on nature, the interpretation of nature as a speaking
face, is generated by the movement of a finite consciousness within time toward death? The romantic poets, as Georges Poulet has
demonstrated in his admirable essay on - Les Romantiques anglais -,[9]
responded to an acute experience of the transitory quality of
human time by developing in one way or another a human equivalent of the divine 'totum simul'. This eouivalent was found in certain privileged moments which seemed to escape from time's re-
morseless flowing. Poulet asks:

> Is it surprising that in a period when the ruling philosophy
> made the transitory character of time appear so distinctly, the
> Romantics thought they could escape, at least provisionally,
> from the general flight of being by fixing their minds on such
> privileged moments? In the face of moments perpetually carried
> along by the flow of time, there are certain favourable moments,
> says Goethe (günstige Augenblicke), which live in themselves,
> intact, as if they were exempt from time or belonged to another
> time. What the Romantics longed for was a personal, subjective
> eternity: an eternity for their own use. Hence their need to
> make eternity descend from its empyrean, to place it on earth
> in their thoughts and in their hearts. Paradoxically, what they
> did was to incarnate eternity in time, in their personal exper-
> ience of time.[10]

An eternity incarnated within a poet's personal experience of
time, an eternity for the poet's private use, will, however, have
a different structure from that 'nunc stans' attributed to the eternity of God. The temporal experience described by Wordsworth
in the dream of the Arab is one example of an eternity paradoxically generated from the 'nunc fluens' of human time as it flows

toward its last end.

The paradox of the use of a mortal, limited, and derived combination of spirit and physical image, namely the human soul and
its body, as the metaphor for that on which it is modelled, the
relation of the immortal intellect and nature, is made even more
problematical by the introduction, at first surreptitiously, of a
second metaphor, that of the book. If nature is the bodily image
of a deathless spirit, the things that man has wrought for commerce of his nature with itself are not vocal or bodily expressions,
but precisely books, those frail shrines of man's consecrated works.
The articulation of the deathless spirit behind nature into the
signs and emblems of the speaking face of earth is like the articulation of man's spirit in the words stamped on the printed page.
The book replaces the human body as the incarnation of the otherwise undifferentiated power of the human spirit. Body and book
are the same, and vocal and written speech are seen as performing a similar differentiating function. In both cases there is the
same structure of spiritual energy, modulating instrument, and
expressive signs which is also present in Wordsworth's sonnets
on sonnets. The traditional metaphor describing the body as the
garment of the soul, rags that soul will no more need in heaven,
is here transferred to the books man writes when Wordsworth says
it causes 'tremblings of the heart' 'to think that our immortal being/
No more shall need such garments' (P, V. 22-4). Wordsworth always found it difficult to imagine any state of disembodiment, even
that of heavenly beatitude, and he here expresses the same trembling before the idea of a condition in which man would no longer
need books. If the speaking face of nature is necessary for the
'intercourse' of the sovereign intellect with man, so that the
deathless spirit behind nature would be invisible or inaudible if
it were not for its articulation in natural types and symbols, so
man must have books in order to maintain the 'commerce of [his]
nature with herself' (P, V. 19) which is a kind of internal dialogue. Wordsworth's phrasing recalls the use by Plato in the
'Philebus' of the image of the book to describe that internal dialogue which takes place for a man when there are no other men
with whom to talk.[11] The mind of man in order to communicate with
itself must separate itself from itself, project itself into the external and mediate form of books, divide its oneness into the multiplicity of signs stamped on the printed page, add to his natural
power the supplementary power of the written word. In heaven
we shall need neither book nor body, those garments of the soul,
but as long as we are children of the earth we cannot go naked.

The peculiarity of this situation merits meditation. Just as the
sovereign intellect, however regal its power, cannot communicate
directly to man, but must divide itself from itself, go outside itself into nature, and use the things of nature as supplements to
itself, mediate signs by means of which it can speak to man, so
the mind of man cannot communicate with itself, either collectively
or individually, without a rupture of its unity, simplicity, and
self-enclosed perfection. Man cannot bear God's voice directly but

must read what God has to say as he has printed it on nature, and man too, in order to speak even to himself, must divide himself from himself, project himself outside himself, exile himself into his printed image or double. If he remains unbroken he is naked, forlorn. He becomes whole or sole only when he has been rent, divided into immortal being and those strange garments woven of geometrical or poetic texts. Man's naked spirit must clothe itself in the leaves of a book. As the lover in Shakespeare's Sonnet LXIV is tormented by the thought that his beloved must die, and as he suffers that thought as if it were his own death, so the anticipation of the loss of his books is to man like a death. In this death he foresees a loss which would leave him his own survivor, alive still but absolutely denuded, separated from all power of discourse. 'Abject, depressed, forlorn, disconsolate' (P, V. 28). The fear of this stripping bare is like a foretaste of death. To ' "weep to have" what he may lose' (P, V. 26) brings death into the mind as a present reality. Nevertheless, whereas physical nature would, so the poet says, survive any catastrophe and still be available as the book of God, the lament of this proem to Wordsworth's meditation about books is not only that books are destructible but that they must inevitably come to be destroyed. When this happens man will be left bare of all those holds on truth he has so laboriously constructed for commerce of his nature with itself:

> And yet we feel - we cannot choose but feel -
> That they must perish (P, V. 21-2).

The dream of the Arab takes its place in the context of the group of metaphors established in the proem as a further displacement of what has already been displaced from the mind/body relation to the mind/book relation. In fact the dream may be described as a complex system of displacements, displacement within displacements, displacements added in chain fashion to previous displacements, displacements interwoven with other displacements. This movement of substitution or dislocation may be defined as the fundamental structuring principle of the text as well as its theme. Only by threading his way through the labyrinth of these permutations can the reader interpret correctly the extraordinary climax of the passage, the waking poet's reaffirmation of the Arab's madness, his sober daylight assertion that, in view of the coming end of the world, 'by signs in earth/Or heaven made manifest'. (P, V. 158-9), the proper thing to do, in order to protect and preserve the great books of the world, Shakespeare's or Milton's, is to bury them, as if they were coffined corpses. What can this mean?

The dream as a whole is a displacement in the sense that it is a response to the poet's waking anxiety about the fragility of books. Like all dreams it is a transformation into other terms of daylight concerns, a reworking of elements drawn from waking experience. If it demands interpretation, it is itself an interpretation of elements the reader has already encountered. In this case, however,

the relation between dream and waking is so immediate and is made
so explicit that the dream may almost be called a daydream, or at
any rate a so-called 'hypnagogic' dream, that sort of dream which
provides an immediate reworking by a man who has just fallen
asleep of what he has been perceiving and thinking, rather than
the rising up within deep sleep of buried images and memories.
The poet has been reading 'Don Quixote' in a rocky cave by the
wide sea and meditating once again on the sad destructibility of
books, in spite of the exemption from 'internal injury' of poetry
and geometric truth. Quixote, poetry, geometry, rock, cave,
shore, sea, sultry air - all these elements return in the dream,
but transformed, as the poet returns to them once again when
the dream is over, so that the sequence from waking to dream to
waking again establishes a chain of sideways substitutions in
which each scene is an interpretation of the others or is interpreted by them. Thomas De Quincey, in reminiscences written
some twenty years after he had seen the text of this dream in
manuscript form, emphasised this aspect of the sequence. 'The
form of the dream,' he said, '. . . is not arbitrary; but with
exquisite skill in the art of composition, is made to arise out of
the situation in which the poet had previously found himself, and
is faintly prefigured in the elements of that situation'.[12] If the
dream refashions the elements which have been present to the poet
just before he falls asleep, so that, for example, the end of the
world is to come by flood in the dream rather than by fire and
earthquake, as in the poet's waking reverie, his waking thoughts
at the end fashion the dream into the fancy that there might really
be such a man, 'A gentle dweller in the desert, crazed/By love
and feeling, and internal thought/Protracted among endless soli-
tudes' (P, V. 145-7). This man's quest takes the form of wishing
to preserve books from the end of the world rather than to care,
as most men would, for wife, child, or 'virgin loves' (P, V. 154).
The shift from loved one to books, parallel to Christ's injunction
to leave 'house, or parents, or brethren, or wife, or children,
for the kingdom of God's sake' (Luke, 18 : 29), though Wordsworth adds 'virgin loves', is of course another displacement,
based upon another metaphorical ratio. As most men are to their
beloveds, so the semi-Quixote of Wordsworth's waking fancy is
to books. The poet displaces the madness once more when he
takes upon himself the 'Maniac's anxiousness' and his 'errand':

> Oftentimes at least
> Me hath such strong entrancement overcome,
> When I have held a volume in my hand (P, V. 161-3).

Moreover, the dream itself is structured around a sequence of
metaphorical condensations or metonymic displacements in which
one thing stands for another which was contiguous to it or in
which one thing is two things at once.[13] The essential 'daring'
of the imagination in great poetry is defined in Wordsworth's
Preface of 1815 as the 'operations of the mind upon [absent

external] objects'.[14] These operations produce a linguistic transfer whereby one thing or group of things is given the name of another. The imagination is the power of the mind over the external world, the power of the mind to 'endow' the 'images' of things 'with properties that do not inhere in them' (p. 754), the power to create fictions. These fictions are embodied in language in the use of the name of one thing for the name of another. So Milton, describing Satan as like a far-off fleet, 'dares to represent it as hanging in the clouds' (p. 754). In his commentary on the linguistic transformations enacted in the lines from -Resolution and Independence- beginning 'As a huge stone is sometimes seen to lie', Wordsworth makes explicit the way the imagination uses language to turn one thing into another, in a sequence of mutations which has no reason to end - stone into sea-beast into old man into cloud. The imagination, in this extraordinary text, is shown to be the exercise of a sovereign power over nature. The instrument of this conferring, divesting, or transforming energy is language, or more exactly, figures of speech, linguistic transfers. The things of nature can be transformed in this way only when they have become 'images', emblems, signs:

> In these images, the conferring, the abstracting, and the modifying powers of the Imagination, immediately and mediately acting, are all brought into conjunction. The stone is endowed with something of the power of life to approximate it to the sea-beast; and the sea-beast stripped of some its vital qualities to assimilate it to the stone; which intermediate image is thus treated for the purpose of bringing the original image, that of the stone, to a nearer resemblance to the figure and condition of the aged Man; who is divested of so much of the indications of life and motion as to bring him to the point where the two objects unite and coalesce in just comparison. After what has been said, the image of the cloud need not be commented upon (p. 754).

It need not be commented upon because it will surely be another exercise of the same modifying power which has produced the other images, or which has made things into images by putting them beside themselves into the things to which they may be 'approximated' or 'assimilated'. Rarely has 'the mind in its activity, for its own gratification' (p. 754) been so blithely celebrated in its dominion over things as they are. In the dream of the Arab this dominion is affirmed not as figures of speech but as the paradoxical reality beheld by the dreamer. This is appropriate for a dream, since dreams enact as vivid appearances what poetic language performs in overt tropes. In his dream the poet sees a stone and shell which are also books and an Arab who is at the same time Don Quixote. 'I wondered not', he says, 'although I plainly saw/ The one to be a stone, the other a shell: /Nor doubted once but that they both were books' (P, V. 111-13), and of the Arab: 'He, to my fancy, had become the knight/Whose tale Cervantes tells; yet

not the knight. / But was an Arab of the desert too; /Of these
was neither, and was both at once' (P, V. 122-5). Of these was
neither and was both at once - in dream as in the language of
poetry nothing is its solid self. It is neither what it is nor the
thing whose name or whose image displaces it, but is both at
once, and so is nothing but the oscillation or interchange between
them, stone or shell for books, Arab for Quixote.

If this pattern of replacement operates not only in the relation
of the dream to what precedes and follows it but also within the
dream itself as its structuring principle, it may also be detected
in the relation of the dream to its 'sources'. It is no accident
that Wordsworth's dreamer has been reading 'Don Quixote' before
he falls asleep. His dream is in one of its aspects a commentary
on Cervantes's book. Just as Don Quixote was crazed by reading
romances, and just as his madness took the form of seeing giants
in place of windmills, an army in a herd of sheep (it was a power
of transfer engendered by reading too many fictions: Quixote
saw each thing in its metaphor), so the dream of Wordsworth's
speaker has been generated by reading and by his anxiety for the
fragility of books. He too sees things as what they are not, as he
encounters in his dream a stone and shell which are books and
an Arab who is yet Don Quixote too. Cervantes's novel, it may be
remembered, is supposed, within its own fiction, to have been
written by an Arab. It is also supposed to be reproduced from an
incomplete manuscript, its lacunae testifying to the fact that it
has survived a catastrophe, perhaps a disaster like the one which
awaits those books the Arab hurries to bury in Wordsworth's
dream. There is, moreover, an episode of book-burning in 'Don
Quixote' which demonstrates that Cervantes, like Wordsworth, was
concerned not only for the power to induce madness possessed by
books, but also for their impermanence. Multiple resonances
associate the passage in Wordsworth with the book which is
overtly mentioned as one of its generative sources.

There are, however, other 'sources' for the dream. Apparently
Wordsworth himself did not dream it, and it is not so much a real
dream as the deliberate invention of a dream sequence.[15] In the
1805 version of 'The Prelude' the dreamer is not the poet but the
'Philosophic Friend', perhaps Michel Beaupuy, to whom he says
he had expressed his anxiety about the vulnerability of books,
and, as Jane Worthington Smyser has demonstrated,[16] the dream
was probably not dreamed by the 'Friend' either, but was borrowed from one of the three famous dreams of Descartes, described
in Baillet's 'Life of Descartes' (1691). Descartes, like Wordsworth's
dreamer, also dreamed of two books, a dictionary gathering all
the sciences and a 'Corpus Poetarum', containing together all of
human knowledge and wisdom. Descartes also dreamed of a mysterious stranger with whom he discussed the books. Descartes, like
Wordsworth's dreamer, interpreted the elements in the dream while
he was dreaming it, in particular the two books. Descartes resolved when he woke up to undertake a religious pilgrimage, just
as the awakened poet in 'The Prelude' says that when he contem-

plates the signs of the approaching apocalyptic deluge he shares
'that maniac's fond anxiety' and feels that he too could 'go/Upon
like errand' (P, V. 160-1). From Descartes to the philosophic
friend to Wordsworth the dream has migrated, undergoing accre-
tions and mutations in each metempsychosis, in a chain of interpretations and reinterpretations in which Descartes's dream, like
any other dream, is not an 'origin' but is itself already interpretation, enigmatic signs for a hidden meaning which remains
always prior to its displaced expression.[17]

From all these forms of displacement it may be concluded that
the process of substitution is not only the form but also the theme
of the dream of the Arab, which is to say its theme is the book,
defining a book as the replacement of a reality which always remains at a distance from its printed image. To put this another
way, the theme of the dream is language or the sign-making power.
The essence of this power is in this text affirmed to be that naming of one thing by the name of another which puts in question
the possibility of literal naming and suggests that all names are
metaphors, moved aside from any direct correspondence to the
thing named by their reference to other names which precede and
follow them in an endless chain. A question, however, remains.
Why do just these elements enter into the transformations of the
dream: - Arab, Quixote; stone and shell; book of geometry and
book of poetry; desert and deluge?

The stone and the shell have the same relation to one another
as do the stone and geometry or the shell and poetry or geometry
and poetry. In all the relations among these four elements may be
traced the same similarity in difference forming a multiple ratio.
The configurations of these relationships, as well as featuring
throughout the passage as a whole, suggest that binary opposition
is as important a structural principle of this text as is the movement of displacement. The displacements take place as permutations of balanced opposites which are nevertheless similar in their
difference. Each pair forms a unit in which each is neither and
yet is both at once. If the shell is like a stone hollowed out, as
if it had been carved, fluted, articulated so that it may speak
with voices more than all the winds, poetry is a transformation of
the kind of reason which produces geometry. Passion, the gener-
ator of poetry, is, says Wordsworth 'highest reason in a soul
sublime' (P, V. 41). The difference between the two forms of
wisdom is indicated in the difference between the signs for them.
A stone uninscribed, uncarved, unhollowed out is just itself. It
does not refer beyond itself in any form of displacement. It is not
a sign, or it is the null sign, the sign for the absence of signs,
like a blank face or a sheet of paper on which nothing has been
written. A stone is wholly self-contained, incapable of any lateral
displacement of signification. The stone knows not time and shares
the permanence, composure, and peace of nature. Precisely this
value is ascribed to geometry, not only in the description of the
book carried by the Arab as Euclid's 'Elements', a book, said
the Arab to the dreamer, 'that held acquaintance with the stars,

And wedded soul to soul in purest bond / Of reason, undisturbed by space or time' (P, V. 103-5), but also in the passage on the consolations of geometry in Book Six of 'The Prelude' (lines 115-67). In the latter text, after remembering how John Newton was comforted when he was shipwrecked by drawing geometric diagrams on the sand with his long staff,[18] Wordsworth asserts that geometry has a mighty charm for the man who, like the poet, has 'a mind beset / With images, and haunted by herself' (P, VI. 159-60). The mind alone is as 'abject, depressed, forlorn, disconsolate' as a shipwrecked mariner. Geometry provides an escape from this by lifting the mind to recognise the universal laws of nature, above any mortal vicissitudes, and behind them the creator God whose being is expressed in the permanence of nature and who is 'to the boundaries of space and time, / Of melancholy space and doleful time, / Superior, and incapable of change, / Nor touched by welterings of passion' (P, VI. 135-8).[19]

To substitute the shell for the stone, however, or to turn the stone into a shell by carving it or hollowing it out and so making it a speaking stone, as a stone carved with an epitaph speaks, or as the poet hears 'an Ode, in passion uttered' (P, V. 96) when he puts Arab's shell to his ear, is to replace the calm of geometry for precisely that weltering of passion which Wordsworth associates with poetry. The passion of poetry arises not from any care which might be assuaged but from an ultimate anxiety about last things. This anxiety is generated by substituting for the uninscribed stone the spiral tube of the shell. The shell can articulate the uniform sound of the sea, or of 'background noise', or of the rush of blood in the listening ear, into differentiated harmony. The rocky cave in which the waking poet sits by the sea (an example of those many nooks or caves in Wordsworth's verse emblematic of subjectivity looking out on the world) reappears in the dream as the enclosed hollow of the shell. With the shell's diacritical marking or distinction, its fracturing, featuring, or dividing of the single and featureless, comes into existence man himself, that is, consciousness, temporality, signs or the power of sign-making and sign-reading, desire, the anticipation of death, poetry, and the imagination of apocalypse. All these are names for one another, and all are also names for that displacement, substitution, or stepping aside, that splitting apart or distinguishing, which marks a thing so that it ceases to be itself and becomes a sign pointing toward something absent, something always already existing, always elsewhere existing, or always not yet existing.

Geoffrey Hartman, in his commentary on the dream of the Arab, identifies as 'imagination' the waters of the deep which are the fulfilment of the prophecy of the shell.[20] This flood, in a displacement from the signs of poetry heard in the shell to the signs of nature seen by the dreamer's eye, is approaching in a glittering wall over the sand toward the Arab as he hurries to bury the two books. Hartman's definition is correct, but it would be as true to say that the coming flood is death, or that it is the movement of

human time, as that it is imagination. All three are names for
that peculiarly human dimension which is opened by the marks on
a rock or by the spiral flutings of a shell. Such markings turn
things into what they are not, that is, into signs for something
absent. If the dream is itself an example of poetry, in which everything is and is not some other thing, the dream contains its own
commentary or explication. It turns back on itself by presenting
in the shell a symbol of its own process. The radiant shell, 'of
a surpassing brightness', 'so beautiful in shape/In colour so
resplendent' (P, V. 80, 90-1), objectifies the process of the
birth of poetry. The sound the dreamer hears in the shell is
both 'a loud prophetic blast', like a single note from a trumpet,
and at the same time it is 'articulate sounds', a 'harmony', a voice
which speaks 'in an unknown tongue' the dreamer can nevertheless
'understand' (P, V. 93-5),[21] as the inscriptions apparently written
by God on nature are in no human tongue and yet may be deciphered. The sound the dreamer hears in the shell is the birth of
language from the sound of the sea or from the sound of the wind,
but it is in fact the sound of his own blood beating in his ear
which he hears. He projects this noise into the shell and hears
it as the sound of wind and wave wrought objectively into the shell
and able to be played back from its traces or records to the man
who listens. This natural sound is then interpreted in its turn as
signs, as language, as harmony, as the voice not of the wind but
of 'a god, yea many gods' (P, V. 106). It is not single but multiple, a multitudinous murmur of 'voices more than all the winds'
(P, V. 107). The originating sound from which all words derive
is not a single word but a multiplicity of possible words. This
multiplicity must be simplified or filtered out in order to produce
articulate sounds. The original voice is already double, divided
against itself. There is no originating unity or simplicity at the
source, but an initial equivocity. In the beginning was the διάκρισιϛ.
     Such multiform voices, when they have been interpreted into
'an Ode, in passion uttered' (P, V. 96), can have only one message, the imminent demolition of the world, 'Destruction to the
children of the earth/By deluge, now at hand' (P, V. 97-8). This
apocalyptic news is the fundamental theme of poetry. This is so
because, whereas the stone knows no time, or as geometry is a
godlike natural science, free of time and space, or as Lucy knows
not time when she has become a corpse 'Rolled round in earth's
diurnal course,/With rocks, and stones, and trees',[22] the shell
brings human time into existence in the signs of it. With human
time comes the awareness of death, as something 'now at hand'.
In this multiple process of interpretation a subjective sound is
interpreted as outer, and that sound is in turn interpreted as
manifold signs. These signs, which are poetry itself, poetry
speaking with the voices of the many gods who seem to lie within
and behind nature, have a paradoxical function. On the one hand
they have 'power/To exhilarate the spirit, and to soothe,/Through
every clime, the heart of human kind' (P, V. 107-9). On the other
hand this exhilaration and soothing are performed by telling man

that the end of the world is at hand. Poetry both soothes and is
apocalyptic, just as the dream as a whole is structured around
interpretative dislocations from benign to ominous, in which the
real sea before him when he was awake is transformed into the
final flood, or the book he was reading becomes a stone and a
shell and then books again, that is, physical objects inscribed
with signs bringing death and the imagination into existence. In
the sequence of the listening to the shell imagination is born out
of the differentiations making language out of inarticulate sounds,
and then the interpretation of nature generated by these signs is
projected outward on the world as an objective and pre-existing
reality. Since signs produce consciousness which produces time
which produces death, the everpresent awareness of the imminence
of death, it is no accident that the message the poet hears in the
shell is a forewarning of the end of the world.

Moreover, in this process may be seen the fact that the stamping of the image of the human mind on a book is the same operation as the stamping of that image on physical nature. If the
differentiations of the traced word or of the articulated voice
bring the human mind and its basic thoughts or powers, death,
time, and the imagination, into existence, the same operation is,
it may be, performed in the reading of nature as signs of some
sovereign intellect. The poet in seeing nature as types and
symbols, or as speaking face, treats it in the same way as he
treats the paper or stone on which he writes a poem or an epitaph.
In fact the two operations of 'stamping' are identical. The answer
to the question, 'why hath not the Mind/Some element to stamp
her image on/In nature somewhat nearer to her own?' is that
nature is man's book too, since there can be no sign without a
physical embodiment. As long as the physical world exists, however completely all the printed books have been destroyed, man
will still have rocks, sand, and winds to stamp his image on.[23]
The truly primary or originating act is the division of breath
which makes the winds into speech, or the carving of the stone
which makes its muteness into language.

In the displacement of what the poet hears in the shell to what
he sees, the coming deluge, there is a fulfilment of the verbalised
prophecy in the actual emblems of nature. This is a displacement
from language to natural signs, but the two kinds of sign are the
same. The fulfilment of the prophecy is reinforced by another
lateral dislocation of the kind so frequent in this text, the reappearance of the 'surpassing brightness' of the shell in the 'bed
of glittering light' (P, V. 80, 129) the dreamer sees as the waters
of the deluge hurry over the sand. The shell embodies the coming
apocalypse of which it is a sign not only in the sounds heard
within it but also in its external look. Both are examples of the
stamping of the mind's image on physical elements, the interpretation of the sound in the shell as a prophetic ode, or the transformation of the sea before the waking poet into the glittering wall
of water he sees in his dream. This shining wall is the emblem of
the opening out of consciousness in a moving stasis, an approach

of the 'something evermore about to be' (P, VI. 608) which constitutes, for Wordsworth, human temporality. The coming of the
waters, always approaching but never here – a static movement
of poised violence – is the gap or interruption, the distance
between one sign and another, between signs and what they signify, between now and the future, between life and death, in the
ecstasies of finite human time. The terror of a temporal predicament which one approaches by fleeing from it, and in which one
awakes from one terror to find oneself confronting the same elements still or once more in a form whose peacefulness makes them
only somehow more ominous, is admirably expressed in the final
lines of Wordsworth's dream:

> I called after him aloud:
> He heeded not; but, with his twofold charge
> Still in his grasp, before me, full in view,
> Went hurrying o'er the illimitable waste,
> With the fleet waters of a drowning world
> In chase of him; whereat I waked in terror,
> And saw the sea before me, and the book,
> In which I had been reading, at my side. (P, V. 133–40).

NOTES

1   See The Still Heart: Poetic Form in Wordsworth, 'New Literary
    History', II, 2, Winter 1971, pp. 297–310.
2   These sonnets are also discussed in The Still Heart: Poetic
    Form in Wordsworth.
3   William Wordsworth, 'The Prelude or Growth of a Poet's Mind',
    second edition, ed Ernest de Selincourt, revised by Helen
    Darbishire, Oxford, Oxford University Press, 1959, p. 5, 1,
    48, 52. Further references to 'The Prelude', unless otherwise
    indicated, will be to the 1850 text in this edition and will be
    identified by: P. followed by book and line numbers.
4   Geoffrey Hartman has in a learned and provocative essay dis-
    cussed the traditions which lie behind Wordsworth's poems in
    this mode and their significance in Wordsworth's work: Words-
    worth, Inscriptions, and Romantic Nature Poetry, in 'Beyond
    Formalism', New Haven, Yale University Press, 1970, p. 206–
    30. See also the interesting essay by Ernest Bernhardt-
    Kabisch, Wordsworth: The Monumental Poet, in 'Philological
    Quarterly' XLIV, 4, October 1965, pp. 503–18.
5   The texts in question are the following:

> It is a mass of knotted joints,
> A wretched thing forlorn.
> It stands erect, and like a stone
> With lichens is it overgrown (The Thorn, 11. 8–11).

> . . . but for thee, dear Friend!
> My soul, too reckless of mild grace, had stood
> In her original self too confident,
> Retained too long a countenance severe;
> A rock with torrents roaring, with the clouds
> Familiar, and a favourite of the stars:
> But thou didst plant its crevices with flowers,
> Hang it with shrubs that twinkle in the breeze,
> And teach the little birds to build their nests
> And warble in its chambers (P, XIV. 247-56).

6   Charles du Bos, 'Du Spirituel dans l'ordre littéraire', Paris,
    Corti, 1967, p. 144, 147 [my translation – ed.].
7   Evidence for this is given in the lines from a poem included in
    a letter to John Kenyon of 1831 ('The Letters of William and
    Dorothy Wordsworth: The Later Years, 1831-1840', II, ed
    Ernest de Selincourt, Oxford, Oxford University Press, 1939,
    p. 572):

> . . . from the builder's hand this Stone
> For some rude beauty of its own
> Was rescued by the Bard.

8   In my discussion of this episode of 'The Prelude' I have been
    aided by the opportunity to read in manuscript the interesting
    analysis of it by my colleague, C. Michael Hancher, Jr. I
    have also made use of a number of valuable suggestions made
    by students and colleagues at various universities who have
    heard me read versions of this paper.
9   'Mesure de l'instant', Paris. Plon, 1968. p. 157-75.
10 Ibid., p. 163, 164 [my translation–ed.].
11 'Philebus', 38 Eff: 'I think the soul at such a time is like a book'.
12 'The Collected Writings of Thomas De Quincey', ed David
    Masson, II, London, A. & C. Black, 1896, p. 268.
13 For a valuable discussion of the relations between metaphor
    and metonymy, see Gérard Genette, Métonymie chez Proust,
    ou la naissance du Récit, in 'Poétique', 2, 1970, pp. 156-73.
14 William Wordsworth, 'Poetical Works', ed Thomas Hutchinson
    and Ernest de Selincourt, Oxford Standard Authors, London,
    Oxford University Press, 1966, p. 753. Further citations
    from the Preface of 1815 will be followed by page numbers
    from this edition.
15 Freud has discussed the special problems involved in analy-
    sing such a fictional dream in Delusion and Dream in Jensen's
    'Gradiva', in 'Delusion and Dream and Other Essays', trans.
    Harry Zohn, Boston, Beacon Press, 1968, pp. 25-121. [Stand-
    ard Edition, vol. 9, pp. 1-93.]
16 Wordsworth's Dream of Poetry and Science; 'The Prelude', V,
    'Publications of the Modern Language Association', LXXI, 1,
    March 1956, pp. 269-75.
17 For modern discussions of Descartes's dream see Georges

Poulet, Le Songe de Descartes, 'Etudes sur le temps humain', Paris, Plon, 1953, pp. 16–47; and Jacques Maritain, 'Le Songe de Descartes', Paris, 1932. Behind Descartes's dream, of course, lies the Biblical, medieval, and Renaissance topos of the two books, the book of nature and the book of revealed Scripture. If the Bible is the word of God revealed in a written text, the heavens too declare the glory of God, just as, in a secular displacement of the traditional topos, all human wisdom, for Descartes or for Wordsworth's dreamer, is divided into geometry or the sciences, on the one hand, the codified knowledge of the spaces of the creation, and, on the other hand, poetry, human wisdom as incarnated in the written word. See E.R. Curtius's magisterial discussion of the topos of the book, Das Buch als Symbol, in 'Europaische Literatur und Lateinisches Mittelalter', Bern, A. Francke, 1948, p. 304–51.

18 This is another place in Wordsworth, among so many others, in which attention is called to the act of writing or inscription, in this case not on stone or on paper, but on those tiny, pulverized stones, the sands which in the dream passage form the environment of the 'Arab phantom's' solitude and of his crazy quest. For John Newton see R.D. Havens, 'The Mind of a Poet', Baltimore, Johns Hopkins Press, 1941, p. 412–3.

19 Another passage on geometrical diagrams in Book Thirteen of 'The Prelude' indicates the associations Wordsworth habitually makes between geometry and the measurement or representation of the fixed patterns of the starry heavens. This is the passage about the Druid markings on Salisbury Plain. If these markings involve stones (which is not wholly clear), another connection between stones and geometry is established, that is, the use of stones as elementary marking or measuring devices, as the stones of Stonehenge, are arranged in relation to the summer solstice. 'The Plain', says Wordsworth, 'Was figured o'er with circles, lines, or mounds, / That yet survive, a work, as some divine, / Shaped by the Druids, so to represent / Their knowledge of the heavens, and image forth / The constellations' (P, XIII. 337–42). I owe thanks to Mr Gene W. Ruoff for calling my attention to the relevance of this text to my theme.

20 See Geoffrey H. Hartman, 'Wordsworth's Poetry 1787–1814', New Haven and London, Yale University Press, 1971, pp. 228–31.

21 Behind this text lies St Paul's meditation on language and on speaking in tongues, glossolalia, in 1 Corinthians, 14. Among the key terms in Paul's discourse are 'prophecy', 'unknown tongue', 'interpretation', and 'understanding'. Even the trumpet appears in the passage.

Now, brethren, if I come unto you speaking with tongues, what shall I profit you, except I shall speak to you either by revelation, or by knowledge, or by prophesying, or by

doctrine? And even things without life giving sound, whether
pipe or harp, except they give a distinction in the sounds,
how shall it be known what is piped or harped? For if the
trumpet give an uncertain sound, who shall prepare himself to the battle? So likewise ye, except ye utter by the
tongue words easy to be understood, how shall it be known
what is spoken? For ye shall speak into the air. There are,
it may be, so many kinds of voices in the world, and none
of them is without signification (1 Corinthians, 14:6-10).

22 A Slumber Did My Spirit Seal, ll. 7-8.
23 An important passage in Book One of 'The Excursion' combines
again in a characteristically problematical way the motifs of
the printed book, the book of nature, the book of Scripture,
the lineaments of a speaking face, and the projection into
nature of the presence of an immortal mind, or the interpretation of nature as the abiding place of such a mind. Describing
the childhood of the Wanderer, that extraordinary potential
poet, Wordsworth says that the Wanderer was taught by his
pious parents 'a reverence for God's word' (1. 115). The
Bible, books of 'the life and death of martyrs' in the times of
the Scottish Covenant, and 'a straggling volume, torn and incomplete', a romance illustrated with coarse woodcuts, made
up all his store of books (ll. 170 ff.). He had, however,
'small need of books' (1. 163), not only because oral traditional tales abounded in his remote mountain area, but also
because nature was a book to him. In one passage, a text
offering in its sequence of or . . . or . . . or a series of contradictory possibilities for the source of the feeling that
nature is the residence of a living mind, the Wanderer is
shown tracing the lineaments of that mind in the rocks of wild
caves:

> - in the after-day
> Of boyhood, many an hour in caves forlorn,
> And 'mid the hollow depths of naked crags
> He sate, and even in their fixed lineaments,
> Or from the power of a peculiar eye,
> Or by creative feeling overborne,
> Or by predominance of thought oppressed,
> Even in their fixed and steady lineaments
> He traced an ebbing and a flowing mind,
> Expression every varying! (ll. 153-62).

Though this passage will not commit itself definitely, the
doubt is not whether the source of the experience is subjective, but whether it comes from the senses, from feeling, or
from thought. Some lines further on, in a passage which
brings all these motifs together, the boy herdsman reads in
nature the same message he had encountered already in the
Bible. The book of Scripture and the book of nature are in-

scribed with the same promise, and nature is seen as if it were a written text. I find the phrase in this passage about the 'volume that displays / The mystery' fundamentally ambiguous. The 'volume' may be the Bible, and this would be supported by the lines in The Ruined Cottage (that is, the earlier version of Book One of 'The Excursion') which assert that the Wanderer, as a child, 'had learned to read / His bible in a school that stood alone' ('The Poetical Works of William Wordsworth', ed E. de Selincourt and Helen Darbishire, V, Oxford, Oxford University Press, 1949, p. 380, ll. 55-6). On the other hand the book of Scripture may already be in this phrase the vehicle of a metaphor describing that nature which the Wanderer already knows deeply as a book. As is so often the case with such texts in Wordsworth, only the interpreter's tact can decide between meanings which remain formally undecidable. If the second reading is taken, then the passage says that all nature is a volume which the Wanderer can read as a written promise of immortality, but in the mountains this promise is also deeply felt. The ambiguity of the term immortality is suggested not only by the complexity of the uses of the word in other contexts in Wordsworth, but also by the final lines of the quotation in which the boy's spirit is once more described as shaping the universe he sees:

A Herdsman on the lonely mountain-tops,
Such intercourse was his, and in this sort
Was his existence oftentimes *possessed.*
O then how beautiful, how bright, appeared
The written promise! Early had he learned
To reverence the volume that displays
The mystery, the life which cannot die;
But in the mountains did he *feel* his faith.
All things, responsive to the writing, there
Breathed immortality, revolving life,
And greatness still revolving; infinite:
There littleness was not; the least of things
Seemed infinite; and there his spirit shaped
Her prospects, nor did he believe, - he *saw* (ll. 219-32).

FURTHER READING

BAHTI, TIMOTHY, Figures of Interpretation, The Interpretation of Figures: A Reading of Wordsworth's 'Dream of the Arab', in 'Studies in Romanticism', 18:4, Winter 1979, pp. 601-27.
BROWN, HOMER, Creations and Destroyings: Keats's Protestant Hymn, the 'Ode to Psyche', in 'Diacritics', 6:4, Winter 1976, pp. 48-56.
CHASE, CYNTHIA, The Accidents of Disfiguration: Limits to Literal and Rhetorical Reading in Book V of 'The Prelude', in

'Studies in Romanticism', 18:4, Winter 1979, pp. 547-65.
DE MAN, PAUL, The Literary Self as Origin: The Work of Georges
Poulet, in 'Blindness and Insight: Essays in the Rhetoric of
Contemporary Criticism', New York, Oxford University Press,
1971, pp. 79-101.
MILLER, J. HILLIS, 'The Linguistic Moment', Princeton, Princeton
University Press, 1981.
— 'Fiction and Repetition' [forthcoming].
— 'Ariadne's Thread' [forthcoming].
— The Literary Criticism of Georges Poulet, in 'Modern Language
Notes', 78:5, December 1963, pp. 471-88.
— Geneva or Paris? The Recent Work of Georges Poulet, in 'The
University of Toronto Quarterly', 39:3, April 1970, pp. 212-28.
— Tradition and Difference (review of M.H. Abrams's 'Natural
Supernaturalism'), in 'Diacritics', 2:4, Winter 1972, pp. 6-13.
(See also the subsequent debate entitled The Limits of Pluralism,
in 'Critical Inquiry', 3:3, Spring 1977, especially Abrams's
reply, The Deconstructive Angel, pp. 425-38, and Miller's
counter-reply, The Critic as Host, pp. 439-47; an extended
version of this last essay is to be found in Harold Bloom et al.,
'Deconstruction and Criticism', London, Routledge & Kegan
Paul, 1979, pp. 217-53.)
— Stevens's Rock and Criticism as Cure, in 'The Georgia Review',
30:1 and 30:2, 1976, pp. 5-31, 330-48.
RIDDEL, JOSEPH N., A Miller's Tale (critique of Hillis Miller's
work, in reply to Miller's review of Riddel's 'The Inverted Bell',
Deconstructing the Deconstructors, in 'Diacritics', 5:2, Summer
1975, pp. 24-31), in 'Diacritics', 5:3, Fall 1975, pp. 56-65.

13 ACTION AND IDENTITY IN NIETZSCHE

Paul de Man

[In a foreword to Carol Jacobs's 'The Dissimulating Harmony'
(1978), Paul de Man distinguishes between methods of reading
which simplify, omit difficulties, and, in effect, paraphrase, and
'genuinely analytical reading', or deconstruction, which follows an
argument. Deconstruction 'has the sequential coherence we associate with a demonstration or a particularly compelling narrative.
But what is being argued (or compellingly told) is precisely the
loss of an illusory coherence.' The question is whether meaning
should be integral to understanding at all costs, or whether it
should 'be allowed to disintegrate under the negative elements in
a text, however marginal or apparently trivial, that can only be
silenced by suppression.' According to de Man, a rigorous analytical reading will demonstrate 'the necessary occurrence of this
disruption. . . . Reading becomes a parable (Gleichnis), an
allegory of reading as the literal designation of its undoing.'
  This disruption of meaning 'occurs when the literal or figural
status of the text's central event (its understanding) has to be,
and cannot be, decided.' A straightforward example of this is
given from 'the sub-culture of the mass media':

> Asked by his wife whether he wants to have his shoes laced
> over or laced under, Archie Bunker answers with a question:
> 'What's the difference?' (-Semiology and Rhetoric-, 'Allegories
> of Reading', p. 9).

Here, it is pointed out, 'the same grammatical pattern engenders
two meanings which are mutually exclusive: the literal meaning
asks for the concept (difference) whose existence is denied by
the figurative meaning.' It is not a question of a literal meaning
on the one hand, and a figurative meaning on the other, but a
genuine moment of blindness, an 'aporia' or figure of doubt, when
it is impossible to know which of the two mutually self-destructive
meanings should be understood. This suspension of logic and
reference is, de Man suggests, a kind of 'differance'.
  De Man is particularly interested in the 'epistemological consequences of this kind of rhetorical seduction'. In his reading of
Nietzsche, he focuses on a number of 'epistemologically destructive
texts', particularly the notes on rhetoric from the winter semester
1872-3. De Man suggests that Nietzsche's critique of metaphysics
(that is, of the concepts of causality, the subject, identity, and
truth) produces the same argument of deconstruction, for 'the
key to this critique of metaphysics . . . is the rhetorical mode of

the trope'. As Nietzsche puts it,

> It is not difficult to demonstrate that what is called 'rhetorical',
> as the devices of a conscious art, is present as a device of un-
> conscious art in language and its development. . . . No such
> thing as an unrhetorical, 'natural' language exists that could
> be used as a point of reference: language is itself the result of
> purely rhetorical tricks and devices. . . . Language is rhetoric,
> for it only intends to convey a *doxa* (opinion), not an *episteme*
> (truth). . . . Tropes are not something that can be added or
> subtracted from language at will; they are its truest nature.
> There is no such thing as a proper meaning that can be commun-
> icated only in certain particular cases (Quoted in 'Allegories of
> Reading', pp. 105-6).

Nietzsche thus here argues that language is rhetorical, and not
referential or representational. The trope is the only epistemological instrument we have. No wonder, then, the insistent urgency
of Harold Bloom's question, 'What is a trope?'
-Action and Identity in Nietzsche- develops the consequences of
this conclusion even further in a reading of two fragments from
'The Will to Power' (516 and 477). In spite of its difficulty, the
conceptual rigour of de Man's argument allows it to be exceptionally clear, and it is only necessary to bear in mind one definition
from language-philosophy. This is the distinction made by J.L.
Austin between performative and constative utterances. Austin
suggested that although philosophy and logic tended to assume
that it was possible to judge all statements as true or false (a
'constative' is the sort of statement for which this is possible),
there are a number of utterances about which this cannot be said.
He was referring to utterances that instead of describing something are in fact the performance of an act. 'I declare war', for
instance, is not a statement about the declaration of war, it is
the act of declaration of war; similarly, 'I promise that I will see
him' is not a statement about a future event, but the making of a
promise. In de Man's reading, Nietzsche's insight in these passages
from 'The Will to Power' is that statements can be both performative and constative at the same time. Nietzsche's critique of
metaphysics is thus structured in terms of an aporia between performative and constative language identical to the aporia de Man
finds between literal and figural language. This possibility, as
the essay shows, subverts both the law of non-contradiction and
the logic of identity which, since Aristotle, have provided the
basis for the epistemology of all Western philosophy. As de Man
suggests, it is clear that with Archie Bunker's question we are
playing for very considerable stakes.
   The location of the aporia, or the text's own gap of self-doubt,
might seem in danger of becoming a system, and deconstruction
a single, restricted method of reading. De Man encounters this
problem in an essay in 'Deconstruction and Criticism', entitled
-Shelley Disfigured-. He concludes, through a powerful reading

of Shelley's 'The Triumph of Life', that this is not a problem for
rigorous readers because the arbitrary nature of language itself
prevents any reification:

'The Triumph of Life' warns us that nothing, whether deed,
word, thought or text, ever happens in relation, positive or
negative, to anything that precedes, follows or exists elsewhere,
but only as a random event whose power, like the power of
death, is due to the randomness of its occurrence (p. 69).]

The question of the relationship between philosophical and literary
discourse is linked, in Nietzsche, to his critique of the main concepts underlying Western metaphysics: the concept of the one
(hen), the good (agathon) and the true (aletheia).[1] This critique
is not conducted in the tone and by means of the arguments
usually associated with classical critical philosophy. It is often
carried out by means of such pragmatic and demagogical value-
oppositions as weakness and strength, disease and health, herd
and the 'happy few', terms so arbitrarily valorised that it becomes
difficult to take them seriously. But since it is commonly admitted
that value-seductions are tolerated (and even admired) in so-
called 'literary' texts in a manner that would not pass muster in
'philosophical' writings, the value of these values is itself linked
to the possibility of distinguishing philosophical from literary
texts. This is also the crudely empirical level on which one first
encounters the specific difficulty of Nietzsche's works: the patent
literariness of texts that keep making claims usually associated
with philosophy rather than with literature. Nietzsche's work
raises the perennial question of the distinction between philosophy
and literature by way of a deconstruction of the value of values.
    The most fundamental 'value' of all, the principle of non-contra-
diction, ground of the identity principle, is the target of a posthumous passage dating from the Fall of 1887:

We are unable to affirm and to deny one and the same thing: this
is a subjective empirical law, not the expression of any 'necessity'
but only of an inability.
    If, according to Aristotle, the *law of contradiction* is the most
certain of all principles, if it is the ultimate ground upon which
every demonstrative proof rests, if the principle of every axiom
lies in it; then one should consider all the more rigorously what
presuppositions [Voraussetzungen] already lie at the bottom of
it. Either it asserts something about actual entities, as if one
already knew this from some other source; namely that opposite
attributes *cannot* be ascribed to them [können]. Or the proposition means: opposite attributes *should* not be ascribed to it
[sollen]. In that case, logic would be an imperative, *not* to know
the true [erkennen] but to posit [setzen] and arrange a world
that *should be true for us.*
    In short, the question remains open: are the axioms of logic

adequate to reality or are they a means and measure for us to *create* the real, the concept of 'reality', for ourselves? . . . To affirm the former one would, as already stated, have to have a previous knowledge of entities; which is certainly not the case. The proposition therefore contains no *criterion of truth*, but an imperative concerning that which *should* count as true.

Supposing [gesetzt] there were no self-identical A, such as is presupposed [vorausgesetzt] by every proposition of logic (and of mathematics), and the A were already mere *appearance*, then logic would have a merely *apparent* world as its pre-condition [Voraussetzung]. In fact, we believe in this proposition under the influence of ceaseless experience which seems continuously to *confirm* it. The 'thing' – that is the real substratum of A; *our belief in things* is the precondition [Voraussetzung] of our belief in logic. The A of logic is, like the atom, a reconstruction [Nachkonstruktion] of the 'thing' . . . Since we do not grasp this, but make a logic a criterion of true being, we are on the way to positing [setzen] as realities all those hypostases: substance, attribute, object, subject, action, etc.; that is, to conceiving a metaphysical world, that is a 'true world' (– *this, however, is the apparent world once more* . . .).

The very first acts of thought, affirmation and denial, holding true and not holding true, are, in as much as they presuppose [voraussetzen] not only the habit of holding things true and holding them not true, but the *right* to do so, already dominated by the belief that *there is such a thing as knowledge for us and that judgments really can reach the truth*: – in short, logic does not doubt its ability to assert something about the true-in-itself (namely that it *can* not have opposite attributes).

Here *reigns* the coarse sensualistic preconception that sensations teach us *truths* about things – that I cannot say at the same time of one and the same thing that it is *hard* and that it is *soft*. (The instinctive proof 'I cannot have two opposite sensations at the same time' – *quite coarse* and *false*.)

The conceptual ban on contradictions proceeds from the belief that we *can* form concepts, that the concept not only designates [bezeichnen] the essence of a thing but *comprehends* it [fassen]. . . . In fact, *logic* (like geometry and arithmetic) applies only to *fictitious truths* [fingierte Wahrheiten] *that we have created. Logic is the attempt to understand the actual world by means of a scheme of being posited* [gesetzt] *by ourselves, more correctly: to make it easier to formalize and to compute* [berechnen].[2]

In this text, the polarities are no longer such spatial properties as inside and outside, or categories such as cause and effect, or experiences such as pleasure and pain, all of which figure prominently in the many sections in which consciousness or selfhood are the targets of Nietzsche's critique. We are dealing with the more elusive oppositions between possibility and necessity, 'können' and 'sollen', and especially between knowing and positing, 'erkennen' and 'setzen'. To know (erkennen) is a transitive function that assumes the prior existence of an entity to be known and that predicates the ability of knowing by ways of properties. It does not itself predicate these attributes but receives them, so to speak, from the entity itself by merely allowing it to be what it is. To the extent that it is verbal it is properly denominative and constative. It depends on a built-in continuity within the system that unites the entity to its attributes, the grammar that links the adjective to the noun by predication. The specifically verbal intervention stems from the predication, but since the predicate is non-positional with regard to the properties, it cannot be called a speech act. We could call it a speech fact or a fact that *can* be spoken and, consequently, known without necessarily introducing deviations. Such a fact can, on the one hand, be spoken (können) without changing the order of things but it does not, on the other hand, have to be spoken (sollen) since the order of things does not depend on its predicative power for its existence. Knowledge (Erkenntnis) depends on this non-coercive possibility and in fact enunciates it by way of the principle of the self identity of entities, 'the self-identical A.'

On the other hand, language can also predicate entities: in this Nietzsche text, this is called 'setzen' (to posit), the key-verb around which the logic of the passage twists its snakelike way. It designates genuine *acts* of speech, the question being whether the identity-principle is an obligatory speech act or a fact merely susceptible of being spoken. Classical epistemology, Nietzsche asserts, has maintained the latter at least since Aristotle: 'according to Aristotle, the law of contradiction is the most certain of all principles . . . , the ultimate ground upon which every demonstrative proof rests'; it is the ground of all knowledge and can only be so by being a priori given and not 'put up', 'gesetzt'. The deconstruction sets out to show that this is not necessarily the case. The convincing power of the identity principle is due to an analogical, metaphorical substitution of the sensation of things for the knowledge of entities. A contingent property of entities (the fact that, as a 'thing', they can be accessible to the senses) is, as Nietzsche's early treatise on rhetoric puts it, 'torn away from its support[13] and falsely identified with the entity as a whole. Like Rousseau, Nietzsche assimilates the delusive 'abstraction' of the 'coarse sensualist preconception' with the possibility of conceptualisation: the contingent, metonymic link of the sensation (Empfindung) becomes the necessary, metaphorical link of the concept: 'The conceptual ban on contradiction proceeds from the belief. . . that the concept not only designates the essence of a thing but comprehends it.' The semiological moment (bezeichnen), which can simply be described as the metonymic deconstruction from necessity into contingency, is clearly apparent in this sentence. It asserts that, for Nietzsche as for Rousseau, conceptualisation is primarily a verbal process, a trope based on the substitution of a semiotic for a substantial mode of reference, of signification (bezeichnen) for possession (fassen). This is, however, only one among a variety of deconstructive gestures and it is chosen for strategic and historical rather than for intrinsic reasons.

For the text goes well beyond the assertion that the claim to know is just an unwarranted totalisation of the claim to perceive and to feel. Elsewhere, Nietzsche will devote considerable energy to questioning the epistemological authority of perception and of eudaemonic patterns of experience. But here he has other objectives. The unwarranted substitution of knowledge for mere sensation becomes paradigmatic for a wide set of aberrations all linked to the positional power of language in general, and allowing for the radical possibility that all being, as the ground for entities, may be linguistically 'gesetzt', a correlative of speech acts. The text asserts this without equivocation: 'To affirm [that logical axioms are adequate to reality] one would . . . have to have a previous knowledge of entities: which is certainly not the case' [my italics]. It has, in truth, not been shown explicitly that we have no a priori knowledge of the being of entities. What has and will be shown, within the confines of this particular fragment, is the possibility of unwarranted substitutions leading to ontological claims based on misinterpreted systems of relationship (such as, for example, substituting identity for signification). The possibility of arousing such a suspicion suffices to put into question a postulate of logical adequacy which might well be based on a similar aberration. And since this aberration is not necessarily intentional but grounded in the structure of rhetorical tropes, it cannot be equated with a consciousness, nor proven to be right or wrong. It cannot be refuted, but we can be made aware of the rhetorical substratum and of a subsequent possibility of error that escapes our control. We cannot say that we know 'das Seiende' nor can it be said that we do not know it. What can be said is that we do not know whether or not we know it, because the knowledge we once thought we possessed has been shown to be open to suspicion; our ontological confidence has forever been shaken.

Nietzsche seems to go further than this and concludes: '[The law of contradiction] therefore [my italics] contains no criterion of truth, but an imperative concerning that which should count as true.' The conclusion seems irrevocable. As is stated, in the form of a thesis at the beginning of the passage, the inability to contradict, to state at the same time that A is and is not A, is not a necessity but an inadequacy, 'ein Nicht-vermögen'. Something one has failed to do can become feasible again only in the mode of compulsion; the performative correlate of 'I cannot' is 'I (or you) must'. The language of identity and of logic asserts itself in the imperative mode and thus recognises its own activity as the posting of entities. Logic consists of positional speech acts. As such, it acquires a temporal dimension for it posits as future what one is unable to do in the present: all 'setzen' is 'voraussetzen', positional language is necessarily hypothetical.[4] But this hypothetical 'voraussetzen' is in error, for it presents a pre-positional statement as if it were established, present knowledge. This belief can

be deconstructed by showing that the truths of a logic based on
non-contradiction are 'fictitious truths'. But in so doing the temporal order has also been reversed: it now turns out that the
future-projected, prospective assertion was in fact determined by
earlier assumptions, that the future truth was in fact past error.
All 'voraussetzen' is 'Nachkonstruktion' (as when it is said that
the A of logic is 'eine Nachkonstruktion des Dinges'). The deconstruction of the metaphor of knowledge into the metonymy of
sensation is a surface manifestation of a more inclusive deconstruction that reveals a metaleptic reversal of the categories of
anteriority and posteriority, of 'before' and 'after'. The 'truth'
of identity, which was to become established in the future that
follows its formulation turns out to have always already existed
as the past of its aberrant 'position'.

Does this mean that we can now rest secure (though hardly
safe) in the knowledge that the principle of contradiction is aberrant and that, consequently, all language is a speech act that
has to be performed in an imperative mode? Can we consequently
free ourselves once and forever from the constraints of identity
by asserting and denying the same proposition at the same time?
Is language an act, a 'sollen' or a 'tun', and now that we know
that there is no longer such an illusion as that of knowledge but
only feigned truths, can we replace knowledge by performance?
The text seems to assert this without question: it acts by denying
the oneness and the sameness of things. But in so doing it does
not do what it claims to be entitled to do. The text does not simultaneously affirm and deny identity but it denies affirmation.[5] This
is not the same as to assert and to deny identity at the same time.
The text deconstructs the authority of the principle of contradiction by showing that this principle is an act, but when it acts out
this act, it fails to perform the deed to which the text owed its
status as act.

The inconsistency can be retraced by observing the play of the
same verb-root 'setzen' in the following sentence: 'Supposing
[gesetzt] there were no self-identical A, such as is presupposed
[vorausgesetzt] by every proposition of logic (and of mathematics),
and the A were already mere *appearance*, then logic would have a
merely *apparent* world as its pre-condition [Voraussetzung].' The
deconstruction of logical and mathematical truth is based on the
fact that it is not rooted knowledge but that it depends on a prior
act of assumption (Voraussetzen). This prior act is itself the target and the outcome of the deconstruction. But the conclusion
that would seem to follow from this, namely that the principle of
contradiction is to be discarded, is again formulated in a positional
mode: 'Gesetzt, es gäbe ein solches Sich-selbst-identisches A gar
nicht.' This terminology is eminently correct, for we saw that the
negative proposition (there is no such thing as an A that is equal
to A) has not been established as knowledge (proven) but merely
as a possibility, a suspicion – and any hypothetical knowledge is
positional. Yet all 'setzen' has been discredited as unable to control the epistemological rigour of its own rhetoric, and this dis-

credit now extends to the denial of the principle of identity as
well. The burden of proof shifts incessantly back and forth between incompatible propositions such as A = A, A better be equal
to A or else . . ., or A cannot be equal to A, etc. This complication
is characteristic for all deconstructive discourse: the deconstruction states the fallacy of reference in a necessarily referential
mode. There is no escape from this, for the text also establishes
that deconstruction is not something we can decide to do or
not to do at will. It is co-extensive with any use of language,
and this use is compulsive or, as Nietzsche formulates it, imperative. Moreover, the reversal from denial to assertion implicit in
deconstructive discourse never reaches the symmetrical counterpart of what it denies. In the sentence under discussion, for
example, the assertion that language is an act (the symmetrical
counterpart of the negative assertion that it is not a knowledge
based on the principle of identity) cannot be taken as final: the
term 'gesetzt' functions as a marker which undermines the authority
of such a conclusion. But it does not follow that, if it cannot
be said of language that it is an act, that it has to be a knowledge.
The negative thrust of the deconstruction remains unimpaired;
after Nietzsche (and, indeed, after any 'text'), we can no
longer hope ever 'to know' in peace. Neither can we expect
'to do' anything, least of all to expurge 'to know' and 'to do', as
well as their latent opposition, from our vocabulary.

Lest we be inclined to read this text as an irreversible passage
from a constative conception of language to a performative one,
there are several other statements from the same general period
in which the possibility of 'doing' is as manifestly being deconstructed as the identity principle, the ground of knowledge, is
being put in question here. This is not obviously the case: in
many texts that are more clearly destined for publication than the
posthumous fragments, the valorisation consistently seems to
privilege active forms of language over passive or merely reactive
ones; the 'Genealogy of Morals' is, of course, a clear case in
point. Active and passive (or reactive) modes are co-ordinated
with values of high and low or, more provocatively, with those of
master and slave, aristocracy and populace, distinction and vul-
garity. The passages from the 'Genealogy' on 'ressentiment' are
well known: 'ressentiment' is the state of mind of 'such creatures
that are denied the true reaction, that of deeds'. 'In order to
exist, slave morality always first needs a hostile external world;
it needs, physiologically speaking, external stimuli in order to
act at all - its action is fundamentally reaction. The reverse is the
case with the noble mode of valuation.'[6] And a little further in the
same work, in connection with a discussion of causality that anticipates many similar arguments in the posthumous fragments, the
hypostasis of action as the horizon of all being seems to be unques-
tionably affirmed: 'there is no "being" behind doing, effecting,
becoming; the "doer" is merely a fiction added to the deed - the
deed is everything' ('es gibt kein "Sein" hinter dem Tun, Wirken,
Werden; "der Tater" ist zum Tun bloss hinzugedichtet - das Tun

ist alles').[7] The use of the term 'hinzugedichtet' (added by poetic
invention), as well as the context, indicate that action here is
conceived in close connection with linguistic acts of writing, reading and interpretation, and not within a polarity that opposes
language, as speech or as writing, to action.

Of course, one cannot expect the same strategy with regard to
valorisation in a book like the 'Genealogy' explicitly designated as
a pamphlet and destined to condemn and to convince, as in the
more speculative treatises that Nietzsche's later book (or books)
were, among other things, destined to be. On a specific question
(such as the ontological authority of acts) the speculative statements should be given at least equal consideration next to the
emphatic, persuasive ones. One therefore has to confront a slogan
such as 'Tun ist alles' with a passage like the following:

> The 'Spirit', *something that thinks* . . . here we *first* imagine
> an act that does not exist, 'thinking', and *second* we imagine as
> substratum of this act a subject in which every act of thought
> and nothing else originates: this means that *the deed as well as
> the doer are fictions (sowohl das Tun, als der Täter sind
> fingiert).*[8]

The parallel that concerns us is the symmetry between this fictitious doing (fingiertes Tun) and the fictitious truths (fingierte
Wahrheiten) that appear in the previously discussed passage on
the principle of identity: 'Logic (like geometry and arithmetic)
applies only to fictitious truths':[9] here, in section 516, truth is
opposed to action as fiction is opposed to reality. In the later
passage (section 477), this conception of action as a 'reality'
opposed to the illusion of knowledge is, in its turn, undermined.
Performative language is not less ambivalent in its referential
function than the language of constatation.

It could be objected that, in the passage now under discussion
(section 477), it is not the reality of action in general that is
being put in question but specifically the act of thinking and,
furthermore, that the linkage between the act and the performing
subject (the principle of intentionality) is being deconstructed
rather than action as such. But Nietzsche is not concerned with
the distinction between speech (or thought) acts and, on the other
hand, acts that would not be verbal. He is interested in the distinction between speech acts and other verbal functions that would
not be performative (such as knowing). Non-verbal acts, if such
a thing were to be conceivable, are of no concern to him, since
no act can ever be separated from the attempt at understanding,
from the interpretation, that necessarily accompanies and falsifies
it. The fictional truths, which are shown to be acts, are always
oriented towards an attempt 'to *understand* [my italics] the actual
world . . . to make it easier to formalise and to compute (berechen-
bar machen)' and, in the later passage, thought is also described
as 'an artificial adjustment for the purpose of *understanding*'
[my italics] ('eine künstliche Zurechtmachung zum Zweck der

Verständlichung') [1296, II. 8-9]. Even in the 'Genealogy' the pure act that is said to be all there is, is conceived as verbal: its paradigm is denomination and the deconstruction of its genesis is best carried out by means of etymology.

As for the intentional link between act and subject, it has been the target of a considerable number of late texts, not to mention several earlier versions that go back at least as far as the 'Birth of Tragedy'. In the posthumous texts, it is often carried out as a rhetorical deconstruction of the metalepsis of cause and effect; the well-known passage on the phenomenalism of consciousness is a good case in point.[10] This moment in the deconstructive process is undoubtedly still present in the fragment with which we are concerned: it is, after all, entitled 'On psychology and epistemology'[11] and, in it, Nietzsche denounces the acceptance of an 'unmediated and causal link between ideas' as 'the crudest and clumsiest observation'.[12] There is nothing new about such utterances; what gives the passage a special significance is that the fiction of a 'subject-substratum' for the act is explicitly called secondary as compared to the prior fiction of the act itself (*'first* we imagine an act that does not exist . . . and *second* we imagine a subject-substratum for this act'). The aberrant authority of the subject is taken for granted; the new attack is upon the more fundamental notion of 'act'. Hence also the apparent contradiction between this text and the one of the phenomenalism of consciousness alluded to earlier (Section 479). Whereas the notions of an 'inner' space or time seem to be more or less definitively reduced to the status of a deception in the latter fragment, section 477 begins by asserting: 'I maintain the phenomenalism of the *inner* world, too.' But the immediate continuation of the sentence ('. . . everything of which we become conscious is arranged, simplified, schematised, interpreted through and through . . . and is perhaps purely imaginary')[13] makes clear that phenomenality is now no longer used as an authoritative term that has to be deconstructed, but as the name of a metaphysical concept considered to be aberrant. Section 477 takes for granted the deconstruction of the phenomenalism of consciousness and of the subject carried out in section 479 and it moves on to the more advanced target of 'denken' as act. If Nietzche's notes were to be re-ordered as a logical progression (in itself a nightmarish and absurd assignment), fragment 477 in the old classification would have to come after fragment 479.

The deconstruction of thought as act also has a different rhetorical structure from that of consciousness: it is not based on metalepsis but on synecdoche:

> 'Thinking,' as epistemologists conceive of it (ansetzen), simply does not occur: it is a quite arbitrary fiction, arrived at by singling out one element from the process and eliminating all the rest, an artificial arrangement for the purpose of intelligibility.[14]

Whereas the subject results from an unwarranted reversal of
cause and effect, the illusion of thought as action is the result
of an equally illegitimate totalisation from part to whole.
The rhetorical structure of the figures concern us less here
than the outcome of their analysis: the text on the principle of
identity established the universality of the linguistic model as
speech act, albeit by voiding it of epistemological authority and
by demonstrating its inability to perform this very act. But the
later text, in its turn, voids even this dubious assurance, for it
puts in question not only that language can act rightly but that
it can be said to act at all. The first passage (section 516) on
identity showed that constative language is in fact performative,
but the second passage (section 477) asserts that the possibility
for language to perform is just as fictional as the possibility for
language to assert. Since the analysis has been carried out on
passages representative of Nietzsche's deconstructive procedure
at its most advanced stage, it would follow that, in Nietzsche,
the critique of metaphysics can be described as the deconstruction
of the illusion that the language of truth (epistémè) could be replaced by a language of persuasion (doxa). What seems to lead to
an established priority of 'setzen'over 'erkennen', of language as
action over language as truth, never quite reaches its mark. It
under- or overshoots it and, in so doing, it reveals that the target which one long since assumed to have been eliminated has
merely been displaced. The epistémè has hardly been restored
intact to its former glory, but it has not been definitively eliminated
either. The differentiation between performative and constative
language (which Nietzsche anticipates) is undecidable; the deconstruction leading from the one model to the other is irreversible
but it always remains suspended, regardless of how often it is
repeated.
    This conclusion takes us back to the Course on Rhetoric, which
precedes the posthumous fragments by fifteen years. The course
starts out from a pragmatic distinction between rhetoric as a
system of tropes and rhetoric as having to do with the skills of
persuasion (Beredsamkeit). Nietzsche contemptuously dismisses
the popular meaning of rhetoric as eloquence and concentrates
instead on the complex and philosophically challenging epistemology
of the tropes. The distinction is not actually accounted for but
taken over empirically from the history of rhetoric. Privileging
figure over persuasion is a typically post-romantic gesture and
Nietzsche's dependence on his predecessors in the German romantic tradition, from Friedrich Schlegel on down, has been well
documented.[15] The question, however, is eternally recurrent and
coincides with the term 'rhetoric' itself. Within the pedagogical
model of the trivium, the place of rhetoric, as well as its dignity,
has always been ambivalent: on the one hand, in Plato for example
and again at crucial moments in the history of philosophy (Nietzsche
being one of them), rhetoric becomes the ground for the furthest-
reaching dialectical speculations conceivable to the mind; on the
other hand, as it appears in text-books that have undergone little

change from Quintillian to the present, it is the humble and not-
quite-respectable handmaiden of the fraudulent grammar used in
oratory; Nietzsche himself begins his course by pointing out this
discrepancy and documenting it with examples taken from Plato
and elsewhere.[16] Between the two functions, the distance is so
wide as to be nearly unbridgeable. Yet the two modes manage to
exist side by side where one would least expect it. Nietzsche's
philosophical contempt for oratory finds impressive confirmation
in the rigour of his epistemology, yet, as any reader of 'The
Birth of Tragedy', 'The Genealogy of Morals', or that irrepress-
ible orator Zarathustra knows, there is hardly a trick of the
oratorical trade which he is not willing to exploit to the full. In a
sense, Nietzsche has earned a right to this inconsistency by the
considerable labour of deconstruction that makes up the bulk of
his more analytical writings. For this deconstruction seems to end
in a reassertion of the active, performative function of language
and it rehabilitates persuasion as the final outcome of the deconstruction of figural speech. This would allow for the reassuring
conviction that it is legitimate to do just about anything with
words, as long as we know that a rigorous mind, fully aware of
the misleading power of tropes, pulls the strings. But if it turns
out that this same mind does not even know whether it is doing or
not doing something, then there are considerable grounds for
suspicion that it does not know *what* it is doing. Nietzsche's final
insight may well concern rhetoric itself, the discovery that what
is called 'rhetoric' is precisely the gap that becomes apparent in
the pedagogical and philosophical history of the term. Considered
as persuasion, rhetoric is performative but when considered as a
system of tropes, it deconstructs its own performance. Rhetoric
is a *text* in that it allows for two incompatible, mutually self-
destructive points of view and therefore puts an insurmountable
obstacle in the way of any reading or understanding. The aporia
between performative and constative language is merely a version
of the aporia between trope and persuasion that both generates
and paralyses rhetoric and thus gives it the appearance of a
history.

If the critique of metaphysics is structured as an aporia between
performative and constative language, this is the same as saying
that it is structured as rhetoric. And since, if one wants to con-
serve the term 'literature', one should not hesitate to assimilate
it with rhetoric, then it would follow that the deconstruction of
metaphysics, or 'philosophy', is an impossibility to the precise
extent that it is 'literary'. This by no means resolves the problem
of the relationship between literature and philosophy in Nietzsche,
but it at least establishes a somewhat more reliable point of reference from which to ask the question.

NOTES

1 Eugen Fink, 'Nietzsches Philosophie', Stuttgart, 1960.
2 Friedrich Nietzsche, 'Werke Kritische Gesamtausgabe' (KGW),
   ed by Giorgio Colli and Mazzino Montinari, Berlin, de Gruyter,
   1970, VIII, 2, 9 [97], p. 53. In earlier editions, the passage
   appears as section 516 of 'Der Wille zur Macht' (for instance,
   Musarion edition, XIX, pp. 28-9). I quote in English from
   Friedrich Nietzsche, 'The Will to Power', translated by
   Walter Kaufmann and R.J. Hollingdale, New York, Random
   House, 1967, pp. 279-80, with some slight modifications for
   the sake of terminological consistency. All italics are Nietzsche's. The syntactical form of the German terms has been
   altered to avoid lengthy quotation. See also note 9.
3 Friedrich Nietzsche, 'Gesammelte Werke', Munich, Musarion,
   1922, V, p. 319.
4 'Man sollte erwägen was (der Satz vom Widerspruch) im
   Grunde schon an Behauptungen *Voraussetzt'*, KGW 9 [97],
   ll 9-10.
5 Perhaps more clearly, in German: 'Der Text bejaht und verneint nicht ein und dasselbe sondern er verneint das Bejahen.'
6 Musarion, XV, p. 295; quoted in English from Nietzsche, 'On
   the Genealogy of Morals', edited and translated by Walter
   Kaufmann, New York, Random House, 1967, First essay, section 10, pp. 36-7.
7 Op. cit., First essay, section 13, p. 45; Musarion, XV, p.
   305.
8 KGW, VIII 2, 11 [113], p. 296, ll. 9-17. Previously published
   as section 477 of 'Der Wille zur Macht' (Musarion, XIX, p. 8),
   'The Will to Power', p. 263.
9 The earlier Nietzsche editions (including the Schlechta edition in 3 volumes) all print 'fingierte Wesenheiten' (fictitious
   entities) but the Colli and Montinari critical edition gives
   'fingierte Wahrheiten' (fictitious truths). The authoritative
   version is more germane to our argument.
10 Section 479 of 'Der Wille zur Macht', Musarion, XIX, p. 10;
    'The Will to Power', pp. 265-6.
11 This heading only appears in the new Colli and Montinari
    critical edition, VIII, 2, 11 [113], p. 295.
12 KGW, p. 295, ll. 26-30; 'The Will to Power', p. 264.
13 KGW, p. 295, ll. 15-22; 'The Will to Power', pp. 263-4.
14 KGW, p. 296, ll. 4-8; 'The Will to Power', p. 264.
15 See, for instance, Philippe Lacoue-Labarthe, Le détour in
    'Poétique', 5, 1971, pp. 53-76.
16 Musarion, V, p. 298.

FURTHER READING

BLOOM, HAROLD, Coda: Poetic Crossing, in 'Wallace Stevens: The Poems of Our Climate', Ithaca, Cornell University Press, 1977, pp. 375-406.
DE MAN, PAUL, 'Blindness and Insight: Essays in the Rhetoric of Contemporary Criticism', New York, Oxford University Press, 1971.
— 'Allegories of Reading: Figural Language in Rousseau, Nietzsche, Rilke and Proust', New Haven, Yale University Press, 1979.
— The Rhetoric of Temporality, in Charles S. Singleton (ed), 'Interpretation: Theory and Practice', Baltimore, Johns Hopkins University Press, 1969, pp. 173-209.
— The Epistemology of Metaphor, in 'Critical Inquiry', 5:1, Autumn, 1978, pp. 13-30.
— Autobiography as De-facement, in 'Modern Language Notes', 94, 1979, pp. 919-30.
— Shelley Disfigured, in Harold Bloom et al., 'Deconstruction and Criticism', London, Routledge & Kegan Paul, 1979, pp. 39-73.
DERRIDA, JACQUES, 'Spurs: Nietzsche's Styles', trans. Barbara Harlow, Chicago, Chicago University Press, 1979.
— White Mythology: Metaphor in the Text of Philosophy, in 'New Literary History', 6:1, 1974, pp. 5-74.
— The Retrait of Metaphor, in 'Enclitic', 2:2, Fall 1978, pp. 5-33.
FELMAN, SHOSHANA, 'Le Scandale du corps parlant: Don Juan avec Austin ou la séduction en deux langues', Paris, Seuil, 1980.
GASCHÉ, RODOPHE, Deconstruction as Criticism, in 'Gylph', 6, 1979, pp. 177-215.
JACOBS, CAROL, 'The Dissimulating Harmony: The Image of Interpretation in Nietzsche, Rilke, Artaud, and Benjamin', Baltimore, Johns Hopkins University Press, 1978.
LYOTARD, JEAN-FRANÇOIS, 'Discours, Figure', Paris, Klincksieck, 1971.
NIETZSCHE, FRIEDRICH, On Truth and Lies in an Extra-Moral Sense, in 'Philosophy and Truth: Selections from Nietzsche's Notebooks of the Early 1870s', trans. and ed Daniel Breazeale, New Jersey, Humanities Press, 1979, pp. 79-97.
— How the 'Real World' at last Became a Myth: History of an Error, in 'Twilight of the Idols', trans. R.J. Hollingdale, Harmondsworth, Penguin, 1968, pp. 40-1.
PAUTRAT, BERNARD, 'Versions du soleil; Figures et système de Nietzsche', Paris, Seuil, 1971.
RICOEUR, PAUL, 'The Rule of Metaphor: Multi-Disciplinary Studies in the Creation of Meaning in Language', trans. Robert Czerny, London, Routledge & Kegan Paul, 1978.

14 GERALDINE

Richard A. Rand

[But is not a mark, wherever it is produced, the possibility of
writing? (Jacques Derrida)

-Geraldine- provides a powerful illustration of the way in which
deconstructionist criticism can open up a text. Coleridge's poem
-Christabel- has always baffled its readers, but it is also true
that it has always been read in the same way - in terms of its
thematic and semantic content. It has remained as unreadable and
uninterpretable as its own elusive character Geraldine, or more
accurately, as Richard Rand points out, as the mysterious mark
on her body, which is where Rand locates a reading-effect which
operates not only on Geraldine's 'readers' within the poem, but
continues to operate upon readers of the poem: 'a common trait
of all these aftershocks is their failure, their incapacity, to uncover the mark itself, to comprehend it, and so to arrest the unlimited repetition of its shock.'
Rather than see Geraldine's mark for what it is - literally, a
mark - criticism tends to see it as a sign for something else, tends
to interpret it, to try and find its meaning. The signifier is always effaced, and read only as a signified. This, however, is
exactly what is done by all the characters within the poem, so
criticism only follows and produces more of the movements of the
same rhetorical discourse. If criticism reflects and continues the
poem outside its own limits, within the poem we find that events
mime the rhetorical condition of the text itself: in Rand's analysis,
the relation of the mark to the story is the same relation as that
of a signifier to a signified, of a sign to its meaning(s) - neither
exactly coincides with the other, nor does the second dissolve
the first. This produces a strange 'mise-en-abîme' effect, involving
the doubling relation of the sign to what it signifies - 'it is both
itself, yet must dissemble as something else - such as a story, or
a tropological system.' To see the mark or sign for itself is to
find the non-semantic element - the 'anacoluthon' - which disrupts
meaning, interpretation, readability, and all forms of semantic
plenitude. In -Christabel- the mark does not communicate with
the story of which it is the sign, and thereby provides a kind of
'allegory of reading'. As Rand puts it, 'the forms of reading that
concentrate on the tale never attain the recognition of the mark' -
they merely sense the contamination of the story by writing, by
its stain and sin. 'What is intolerable and fascinating', suggests
Derrida, 'is indeed the intimacy intertwining image and thing,
graphie and phonè . . . a dangerous promiscuity and a nefarious

complicity between the reflection and the reflected which lets itself be seduced narcissistically' ('Of Grammatology', p. 36).

-Geraldine- in effect is also a deconstructionist analysis of
neo-classical and Romantic theories of rhetoric and signification
Whereas in 'Of Grammatology' Derrida focuses on Saussure's
theory of the sign, Rand analyses eighteenth-century conventions of tropes and theories of the sign in the context of the
tropology of Romantic poetry. It is because that way of reading,
and the same implicit assumptions, still dominate criticism today
that criticism has got no nearer the mark than Sir Leoline or Bard
Bracy. The values attached to the sign assume its transparency
and its effacement before the self-presence of its meaning; Rand
points to the residual element that undoes this serene conceit of
'proper' meaning – the materiality of the sign itself. To see the
mark is simply to see the mark – a signifier, *of* and *as* difference.

Sign, seal, mark, signature: in the final section Rand argues
that to find the mark we must turn away from 'the tropes, from
the logic and premise of the sign, and the hope that resides in
those premises, of making the "seal" present, punctual, meaningful, sensible.' To turn away from the sign is to turn away from
the usual way of reading, which goes *straight* for the signified.
Paradoxically, this means that reading normally also enfolds the
signifier within the veils of its own interpretative discourse, and
never breaks the silence of the seal. To break the seal poses a
drastic step for tropology, for it opens up 'a new and potentially
limitless chain of discourse'. The graphemes which Rand locates
scattered across texts 'overflow any discursive boundaries of
any kind' and, in the words of Paul de Man, open up 'vertiginous
possibilities of referential aberration'. Each reading that Rand
provides he proceeds to undo – to produce a new slide; again and
again he transgresses the folds of the last reading, dropping the
reader into an abyss in a final fugitive footnote.]

'The reason of my not finishing -Christabel- is not that I don't
know how to do it – for I have, as I always had, the whole plan
entire from beginning to end in my mind; but I fear I could not
carry on with equal success the execution of the idea, an
extremely subtle and difficult one' (S.T. Coleridge, 'Table Talk',
6, July 1833).

I

Leaving her father's hall at midnight, by a 'gate that was ironed
within and without',[1] and kneeling in prayer in a forest, beneath
a huge oak tree, the lady Christabel hears a low sound of moaning. She springs to her feet, listens again, then steals around
the tree for a look at the other side:

> There she sees a damsel bright
> Drest in a silken robe of white,
> That shadowy in the moonlight shone:
> The neck that made that white robe wan,
> Her stately neck, and arms were bare;
> Her blue-veined feet unsandal'd were,
> And wildly glittered here and there
> The gems entangled in her hair (58-65).

What follows is a taking in: Christabel questions this remarkable figure ('and who art thou?' 70), and takes in the answer ('My sire is of a noble line, / And my name is Geraldine' 79-80); takes in as well the tale of forcible kidnapping; and takes in, finally, the person of Geraldine herself, into the safety of her father's hall. Once there, however, she does not take in some absolutely suspicious signs, such as Geraldine's too brief seizure of pain at the threshold (129ff.), her refusal to join in prayer (141ff.), the 'angry moan' of the mastiff (145ff.), or the strange flaring of the brand (156ff.). Is it Christabel's turn to be taken in by Geraldine? Ignoring these signs, and others like them, she draws closer to her guest, close to the point of lying at her side, naked, and in bed.

There it is that a shock occurs, shocking first of all to Geraldine ('Ah! what a stricken look was hers!' 256): Christabel, reclining on her elbow and watching Geraldine, takes in something she was never meant to see, the sight of Geraldine's horrible 'bosom and half her side' (252). In her closeness, Christabel suffers an irreversible moment of *accuracy*, confirmed by Geraldine's defiant embrace:

> Yet Geraldine nor speaks nor stirs;
> Ah! what a stricken look was hers!
> Deep from within she seems half-way
> To lift some weight with sick assay,
> And eyes the maid and seeks delay;
> Then suddenly, as one defied,
> Collects herself in scorn and pride,
> And lay down by the Maiden's side! -
> And in her arms the maid she took,
>   Ah wel-a-day! (225-64).

What is the import of this embrace? If the shock of accuracy does not prevent the women from drawing closer still, does it not change, at least, the character of that closeness? Geraldine continues with a speech that is often read as a malediction but also serves as a statement of fact:

> And with low voice and doleful look
> These words did say:
> 'In the touch of this bosom there worketh a spell,
> Which is lord of thy utterance, Christabel!

Thou knowest to-night, and wilt know to-morrow,
This mark of my shame, this seal of my sorrow;
   But vainly thou warrest,
   For this is alone in
Thy power to declare,
   That in the dim forest
Thou heard'st a low moaning,
And found'st a bright lady, surpassingly fair;
And didst bring her home with thee in love and in charity,
To shield her and shelter her from the damp air' (265-78).

A strange turn: Christabel, taking in Geraldine, draws so close
that she sees the 'mark', a sight that is like a dream, vivid and
unforgettable, but not to be put into words, 'a sight to dream of,
not to tell!' (253). The mark is thus a 'seal' in two senses of that
word – a hallmark or signature, but one that also 'seals' up, or
encrypts, the fact of its own existence, of its meaning (if it has
one) and its history (which is never revealed). And this seal, by
sight and by touch, also seals up Christabel, and so becomes her
seal and signature as well. Christabel, who cannot forget the
mark, nor openly and articulately 'declare' it, must live henceforth
as Geraldine lives, bearing, even as she dissembles, the sealing
up of the seal, concealing the mark of her difference, saying one
thing and meaning, knowing and being something else.
   The consequences of this moment are spelled out in Part II, but
before we pursue them, we ought to remark that Coleridge is treating something of interest to readers of poetry. For Geraldine, who
dissembles, is a kind of poem, and the story of Christabel is the
story of one of her readers. In writing the poem, Coleridge tells
about the process of reading, the process, indeed, of reading the
poem known as -Christabel-. The poem exhibits a number of
mirroring tendencies, or specular properties: it begins, for
example, with a prosodic and phonemic symphony of bell tones,
cock crows and owl hoots, interspersed with the regular responses
of the mastiff - 'sixteen short howls, not over loud' (12) - which
happen to mime the loose octosyllabic couplet of the poem.
Christabel's bed chamber, also like a poem, is a place of intellectual delights, figured and sensuous, but not to be grasped by
the light of nature alone:

The moon shines dim in the open air,
And not a moonbeam enters here.
But they without its light can see
The chamber carved so curiously,
Carved with figures strange and sweet,
All made out of the carver's brain,
For a lady's chamber meet:
The lamp with twofold silver chain
Is fastened to an angel's feet (175-83).

Taking, then, the poem named -Christabel- as a meditation on itself, with the figure named 'Geraldine' as its own interior mirror-image; and taking the figure named 'Christabel' as one of her readers, perhaps a naive one, or perhaps an exemplary one, whose openness to Geraldine is a kind of willing suspension of disbelief; we begin to feel that the poem extends a particular question to the reader: what is the 'seal' or 'mark' of the poem called -Christabel-, and if we should happen to see it, would we, like the lady Christabel, also lack the 'power to declare' it, and therefore carry it, cryptically, within?

It remains to *see* the mark, a situation anticipated in the second part of the poem. There, we encounter two readings of Geraldine that miss the mark completely: Sir Leoline's and Bard Bracy's.

Unlike his daughter, Sir Leoline does not simply take in Geraldine's story, but puts it to the test as he hears it. He verifies it in terms of an earlier story, the story of his own life. Posing his own life as the known truth, he hears the tale of Geraldine as a more or less credible figure, or trope, of that truth. The trope is complex in structure. It is first of all a metonymy:

> But when he heard the lady's tale,
> And when she told her father's name,
> Why waxed Sir Leoline so pale,
> Murmuring o'er the name again,
> Lord Roland de Vaux of Tryermaine? (403-7).

For Sir Leoline, the name of his erstwhile friend Lord Roland is a memory-trace or 'scar' (421), and 'neither heat, nor frost, nor thunder,/ Shall wholly do away, I ween, / The marks of that which once hath been' (424-6). Sir Leoline thus verifies the story of Geraldine by association or metonymy, by the connection of one name to another. He then goes on to read by analogy, or metaphor, comparing two faces:

> Sir Leoline, a moment's space,
> Stood gazing on the damsel's face:
> And the youthful Lord of Tryermaine
> Came back upon his heart again (427-30).

Validating the tale in this manner, Sir Leoline accepts it without further challenge. In other words, having refused to take in Geraldine's tale as Christabel did, with no questions asked, he does take it in with a very slight degree of rhetorical circumspection. He never suspects that her tale differs from her condition as a figure differs from its meaning; and he never suspects that his own true thoughts are cast in the form of figures, that they are the figures furnished by Geraldine herself, Geraldine being the first to utter the name of Lord Roland de Vaux of Tryermaine.

Unlike his master Sir Leoline, the servant Bard Bracy also misses the mark, but with the highest degree of rhetorical understanding. His reading is oblique: he never says anything to, or about, Geraldine, at least explicitly, but speaks only to his master,

in the context of his master's commands. His reading comes in the
midst of a speech about clearing 'yon wood from thing unblest'
(529), where its pertinence to Geraldine is bound to be lost on
the master. Also, the reading itself is offered up in the form of
a 'dream' or 'vision', an allegory in the medieval style: the Bard,
a paragon of rhetorical lucidity, does not present his reading as
a truth, but as a fiction or veiled hypothesis, which may, or may
not, be true:

> '. . . in my sleep I saw that dove,
> That gentle bird, whom thou dost love,
> And call'st by thy own daughter's name -
> Sir Leoline! I saw the same
> Fluttering, and uttering fearful moan,
> Among the green herbs in the forest alone.
> Which when I saw and when I heard,
> I wonder'd what might ail the bird;
> For nothing near it could I see,
> Save the grass and green herbs underneath the old tree.
>
> 'And in my dream methought I went
> To search out what might there be found;
> And what the sweet bird's trouble meant,
> That thus lay fluttering on the ground.
> I went and peered, and could descry
> No cause for her distressful cry;
> But yet for her dear lady's sake
> I stooped, methought, the dove to take,
> When lo! I saw a bright green snake
> Coiled around its wings and neck.
> Green as the herbs on which it couched,
> Close by the dove's its head it crouched;
> And with the dove it heaves and stirs,
> Swelling its neck as she swelled hers!' (531-54).

This 'dream' interprets Geraldine's tale at a second remove, as
a reading of Sir Leoline's (assenting) interpretation. First, the
Bard adopts the terms or themes of his master. In his own comments on Geraldine's tale, Sir Leoline employs the terms of serpent and dove: he says that Geraldine's kidnappers have 'reptile
souls' (442), and is also quoted as calling Christabel a 'dove'
(532-3), a term that he later applies to Geraldine (569). Along
with his master's terms, the Bard also adopts his instruments of
reasoning, the tropes of metonymy and metaphor: he says that
the serpent menaces the dove with its nearness or contiguity
(metonymy of place), and with the powers of mimicry (metaphor)
that make it almost invisible: 'Green as the herbs on which it
couched, / Close by the dove's its head it crouched' (551-2). But
the Bard does not merely adopt the terms and reasoning, the
concepts and values, of his master: he also subjects them to a
systematic reversal; thus, the 'dove' known as 'Geraldine' is re-

cast in the role of the 'snake', and the verifying instruments of
metonymy and metaphor are shown to be the vehicles of falsehood.
Reversed and reinscribed in a new story, Geraldine's tale has
been, in the strict sense of the word, 'deconstructed'.[2]

It goes without saying that the force of this deconstruction
would be lost on Sir Leoline: a firm believer in the truth, he would
not be tempted to connect the fiction of the dream to the real
circumstances of the actual moment. And if he made the connection
he could not accept the judgments implied in the dream, for it
would annul the authority of his truth and so put an end to his
standing as a master. And such an end would finish off the Bard
as a servant; for the Bard depends on his master: he must hear
what the master says before he can follow up with his own critical
reply. Each supplies what the other lacks - a language on the one
hand, and an insight on the other. Taken together, they round
off the limits of a certain discourse, a discourse of assertions and
counter-assertions, of 'truths' and 'falsehoods', furnished in the
first place by the text itself, by Geraldine, whose tale holds forth
the invitation to make sense of her person, of arriving at her
truth, be it a truth that lies in the veracity of her assertions, or
in their falsehood.

But does this understanding, Sir Leoline's or Bard Bracy's,
come to any real and sufficient account of Geraldine? Certainly
her story is open to interpretation, and indeed it inevitably sets
that process in motion, with its drama of an innocent maiden in
distress, and its telling reference to Lord Roland de Vaux of
Tryermaine. And the readings of master and Bard are not without a certain real interest: Christabel, for instance, pays careful attention to them both, and her responses inevitably influence
our own reactions to them. On the one hand, she finds her father's
reading almost effaced by the memory of the mark:

> And now the tears were on his face,
> And fondly in his arms he took
> Fair Geraldine, who met the embrace,
> Prolonging it with joyous look.
> Which when she viewed, a vision fell
> Upon the soul of Christabel,
> The vision of fear, the touch and pain!
> She shrunk and shuddered, and saw again . . . (447-54).

Bard Bracy's reading, on the other hand, has an actual impact
or influence on the text it reads, on the figure of Geraldine herself, which it transforms, briefly, into one of a snake:

> A snake's small eye blinks dull and shy;
> And the lady's eyes they shrunk in her head,
> Each shrunk up to a serpent's eye,
> And with somewhat of malice, and more of dread,
> At Christabel she looked askance! - (583-7).

This impact extends to Christabel, who, being gifted with a sympathetic imagination, mimes ('with a hissing sound' 591), the image of Geraldine thus transformed, an event that the poem goes on to relate in the following way:

> The maid, alas! her thoughts are gone,
> She nothing sees - no sight but one!
> The maid, devoid of guile and sin,
> I know not how, in fearful wise,
> So deeply had she drunken in
> That look, those shrunken serpent eyes,
> That all her features were resigned
> To this sole image in her mind:
> And passively did imitate
> That look of dull and treacherous hate!
> And thus she stood, in dizzy trance,
> Still picturing that look askance
> With forced unconscious sympathy (597-609).

Certainly, then, the Bard's reading, unlike the master's, has a powerful impact on Geraldine and Christabel alike; and yet the image of the snake does not last: 'the trance was o'er' (613), to be followed by the enduring and horrible memory of the mark, a memory to which the image of the snake does not finally adhere:

> And when the trance was o'er, the maid
> Paused awhile, and inly prayed:
> Then falling at the Baron's feet,
> 'By my mother's soul do I entreat
> That thou this woman send away!'
> She said: and more she could not say:
> For what she knew she could not tell,
> O'er-mastered by the mighty spell (613-20).

The effacement of the vision of the snake by the memory of the mark is a signal moment in the poem: for, up to a point, Geraldine can be read as a being of truth or falsehood, as a 'dove', or as a 'snake' acting as a 'dove'. We could say, for example, that the tale she tells, like the dress she wears, is a veil of fiction that covers the truth of her mark. But what, in the end, is the truth of her mark? Does the mark give the lie to the tale? Yes, in the narrow sense that the tale does not include the mark, but differs from it; no, in the sense that the mark, being unintelligible, has nothing to add of significance to the tale. Which is to say that the tale, true or false, does not communicate with the mark but only coincides with it, and that the forms of reading that concentrate on the tale never attain the recognition of the mark. Christabel, who accepts the tale without challenge, and who saw the mark as a consequence, finds that the other readings do not engage her as the mark does. For the tale is joined to the mark not as a false-hood to the truth it conceals, but rather as the juxtaposition or superimposition of one text, containing truth and falsehood alike, and another text, or palimpsest, that says nothing, tells no truth or falsehood, and falls under no one's control. This palimpsest controls everyone instead, including the poet or poem called Geraldine, who, though she can use her body to certain effect, and can make it tell a story, cannot make the body tell the only story that really matters, which is the story of the mark and how it got there.

-Christabel- is thus a poem that breaks off at the moment of least communication, with Christabel caught in her spell, Sir Leoline enraged at her strange behaviour, and Bard Bracy sent off on an errand he wants to avoid. Clearly this scene of non-communication, dramatically rendered as an interaction between various characters, also mimes the condition of Geraldine, who is made up of these different and incompatible strata, one level communicating with Sir Leoline and the Bard, and another level, that of the 'mark', communicating with Christabel in her trance-like moments of recollection. And recalling that Geraldine is a kind of poem, we can see that the non-communication of the end of -Christabel-, which mimes the condition of Geraldine, reflects the rhetorical condition of the text itself: the poem tells a story that does not communicate with its own mark or seal.[3]

Must we give up the quest for the seal?

Three issues remain unexplored. Taken together, they suggest a programme.

First is the matter of closeness: we have not drawn close enough to Coleridge for his mark to surprise us. In textual terms, we haven't sufficiently taken in the system of his tropes and their deconstruction. The better part of this essay must attempt to do so.

Second, in reading the tropes we must bear in mind what they do not reveal, namely the mark. They cover up the mark. But this covering up is not a resource of the tropes themselves: if it were, they could also disclose the mark. Rather, the covering up belongs to the power of the mark itself, which can always efface itself by taking the form of something else, of something other than a mark, for example of a story, or of a tropological system.

Third, this effacement and divulgence of the mark is a kind of alternation, or winking movement: Christabel hears the story and recalls the mark, in alternation. The two movements never take place at the same time. In this respect, the relation of the mark to story is like the relation of a sign to its meaning, each to be focused on in turn, but not together. Geraldine, that is, is structured in certain respects like a sign, and it is not an accident that Coleridge ends his poem with a meditation on the sign-structure:

> A little child, a limber elf,
> Singing, dancing to itself,
> A fairy thing with red round cheeks,
> That always finds, and never seeks,
> Makes such a vision to the sight

As fills a father's eyes with light;
And pleasures flow in so thick and fast
Upon his heart, that he at last
Must needs express his love's excess
With words of unmeant bitterness (656-65).

This enigma stands in relation to the poem as a sign stands in relation to its meaning. It means the poem, but in a way that we cannot rationally analyse. And the meaning of this meaning is . . . a sign: a father who wishes to express a certain kind of thought ('love's excess'), does so by means of certain shocking words, words of 'unmeant bitterness'. It is the bitterness of the words that is 'unmeant', their bitterness being used to signify 'love' instead of 'bitterness'. If we take the bitter words to mean what they seem to mean, then we miss their intended meaning. If we read the words as a trope - as a metaphor, in which the bitterness of the words resembles the bitterness of the feeling - then we inevitably miss the import of the words, and we also miss, therefore, the bizarre coincidence of the words with their meaning, a coincidence which is not organised like a metaphor.

Trope, sign, and seal, then: a sequence of places to turn to. If not in the form of a progress, at least in the form of a juxtaposition.

II   TROPOLOGY

Merely to find the tropology in the poems of Coleridge is not an easy thing to do. For the tropes pertain in some way to the hidden, elusive, or occulted dimensions of language that make up its rhetoric. It is not surprising that readers disagree on the definitions of the tropes - on the meaning, say, of the word 'metaphor'; or, if faced with a figure in a given text, on the class of trope that it might be said to belong to. It is not unusual, in the literature surrounding a romantic text, for one reader to see nothing of the figural about it, while another sees the entire text as a figure that figures forth its own tropology. Moreover, the tropes 'exist', if that is the word, not as facts of language but as arguments or positions taken by the text. They 'exist' as arguments in support of their own existence, and, as arguments, they are open to dispute or rebuttal, counter-arguments to be posed, indeed, by the very text that argues their existence in the first place. To 'find' the tropes is thus to argue, convincingly, that the text in question poses an argument, and that there lies hidden, in the poetry of Coleridge, for example, an 'art of rhetoric' that argues, in a certain way, that language works in a certain way, this argument having an impact on the organisation of the poetry itself.

The better to argue the existence of such an argument - to give our own argument the force of an incontestable fact - we turn first of all to a poem composed by Coleridge in 1797, at the time of

-Christabel-. A brief and somewhat whimsical exercise, it is also rich in the explication of tropological issues. Next, we turn to a brief résumé of the issues themselves, as they were taken up in the rhetorical literature of the eighteenth century. We then proceed to a second poem by Coleridge, in which the tropology is certainly hidden, but also dominates the topics in which it so tactfully takes place.

A

ON THE CHRISTENING OF A FRIEND'S CHILD

This day among the faithful plac'd
   And fed with fontal manna,
O with maternal title grac'd,
   Dear Anna's dearest Anna!

While others wish thee wise and fair,
   A maid of spotless fame,
I'll breathe this more compendious prayer -
   May'st thou deserve thy name!

Thy mother's name, a potent spell,
   That bids the Virtues hie
From mystic grove and living cell,
   Confess'd to Fancy's eye;

Meek Quietness without offence;
   Content in homespun kirtle;
True Love; and True Love's Innocence,
   White Blossom of the Myrtle!

Associates of thy name, sweet Child!
   These Virtues may'st thou win;
With face as eloquently mild
   To say, they lodge within.

So, when her tale of days all flown,
   Thy mother shall be miss'd here;
When Heaven at length shall claim its own
   And Angels snatch their Sister;

Some hoary-headed friend, perchance,
   May gaze with stifled breath;
And oft, in momentary trance,
   Forget the waste of death.

Even thus a lovely rose I've view'd,
   In summer-swelling pride;
Nor mark'd the bud, that green and rude
   Peep'd at the rose's side.

It chanc'd I pass'd again that way
  In Autumn's latest hour,
And wond'ring saw the selfsame spray
  Rich with the selfsame flower.

Ah fond deceit! the rude green bud
  Alike in shape, place, name,
Had bloom'd where bloom'd its parent stud,
  Another and the same![4]

The apparent subject of this poem, the occasion designated in
the title, is a christening that gives rise to a train of decorous
moral sentiments. Figures of rhetoric are not obviously at issue
here. There is a figure of some kind to be found in the last three
stanzas (the conceit about the rosebud), but it looks like an
ornamental afterthought, or exemplum, and not a thematic issue
in its own right.

Approaching the poem through its cast of characters, we find
'Anna', a full-grown woman who is also a mother, and who possesses the qualities listed in the fourth stanza ('Quietness', 'Content',
'Love', and 'Innocence'); an infant girl of indeterminate age, also
called 'Anna', who happens to be the mother's daughter and the
subject of the baptism, and who possesses none of her mother's
moral qualities, being, at her young age, a kind of tabula rasa;
and two admiring men who are the poet himself, acting as a kind
of reader looking on at mother and daughter, and an imaginary
'hoary-headed friend', who will perform a similar office in the
distant future.

It is the argument of the poem that the name 'Anna', which
seems semantically neutral, actually has a specific meaning or
group of meanings. Its meanings, in fact, are 'quietness', 'content', 'love' and 'innocence', which, in stanza five, are called the
'associates of the name'. Such is the 'potent spell' of the name
'Anna' that it 'bids the Virtues hie' (stanza three). When we hear
the name, we think of the virtues also, and thus the name functions as the sign of the virtues in question.

This sign, in fact, has a specific and complex structure, two of
whose features call for comment:

1 The name 'Anna' did not function as a sign before its association with the mother. Rather, it was formed by the linking up of
two unrelated elements: the virtues of 'quietness', 'content', 'love'
and 'innocence', and the meaningless vocable 'Anna' (we can imagine the problems that might arise from the names 'Jocasta' or
'Electra'). Such a forging fulfils the traditional concept of a 'conventional', as opposed to a 'natural', sign, because the link between sign and meaning does not arise from some quality inherent
in the meaning, as it would, say, if the name in question were
'Innocentia' or 'Tranquillity'. The logic of the poem arises from
the fact that the link posed between the sign 'Anna' and its meaning is a thing of happenstance.

2 There is, however, a crucial feature of this sign that modi-

fies its conventional character. Though 'Anna' is not a natural
sign, the meaning is at least present to the name if not in the
name: the virtues are there, along with the name 'Anna', in
person. Anyone who doubts that the word 'Anna' means 'Quietness' can test it in the person herself. The person is thus a site,
or place, where a name coincides with certain qualities, and com-
pels us to associate the two.

For Coleridge, then (at least in this poem), a sign, at its origin, is at once conventional - it lacks a natural bond - but also
in some sense not entirely so: its meaning may be arbitrary, but
it is also verifiably present. The presence of the meaning makes
the word come into existence as a sign.

What happens, however, when the meaning of the word becomes
absent? This development, which may be said to make up the
history of the word, is explored in the situation of the little girl.
Strictly speaking, she should not have a name, for she has no
qualities, no virtues. At best, she might be called 'baby'. The
name 'Anna' is really a wrong name, referring to something it
should not refer to - a person without the associated virtues.
While the name still has a meaning - such is its 'potent spell' -
its meaning is no longer present in person: in the words of the
poem, the virtues 'hie' around the little girl, but they do not
'lodge within' (stanza five). The name, by comparison to its
original usage, is now an untrue or deficient sign, at best the
sign of another and truer sign. Elsewhere, Coleridge uses a
special term for this kind of sign - 'cipher'[5] - another term being
the more technical one of 'homonym': the name 'Anna' designates
both a person in whom the virtues are present, and one in whom
they are absent. The history of the name, as sketched out in this
poem, is the history of what the linguists call a 'homonymic clash',
to be resolved, most frequently, by the phasing out of one meaning in favour of another.[6] Coleridge suggests, indeed, that this
particular clash can be amended, or annulled, if only the daughter
will bring her name into the presence of its original meaning:

> Associates of thy name, sweet Child!
> These virtues may'st thou win;
> With face as eloquently mild
> To say, they lodge within.

This done, the daughter will have answered the poet's prayer
of deserving her mother's name (stanza two), and so resolve the
clash of the two meanings. Or will she? The poet has his doubts,
and letting his prayer, as it were, come true, proceeds to study
the consequences:

> So, when her tale of days all flown,
> Thy mother shall be miss'd here;
> When Heaven at length shall claim its own
> And Angels snatch their Sister;

> Some hoary-headed friend, perchance,
> May gaze with stifled breath;
> And oft, in momentary trance,
> Forget the waste of death.

It is this 'forgetting' that gives rise to the conceit in the last three stanzas:

> Even thus a lovely rose I've view'd
> In summer-swelling pride;
> Nor mark'd the bud, that green and rude
> Peep'd at the rose's side.

> It chanc'd I pass'd again that way
> In Autumn's latest hour,
> And wond'ring saw the selfsame spray
> Rich with the selfsame flower.

> Ah fond deceit! the rude green bud
> Alike in shape, place, name,
> Had bloom'd where bloom'd its parent stud,
> Another and the same!

Something has happened that was not prayed for. Little Anna, making the absent meaning present to the name, and making herself into the 'selfsame flower' as her mother, activates a 'fond deceit', obscuring the essential difference between herself and her mother in a show of sameness, a mendacious identity. It turns out that the presence of the meaning to the name is no guarantee of truth: name and meaning alike have to be present to the first instance of their association, that 'instance' being conceived, in the terms of the poem, as the working-out of a single person's lifetime. Every true name, according to this theory, is a proper name, and every subsequent usage of that name is therefore improper, a kind of expropriation. Little Anna, indeed, should never have been named 'Anna' in the first place; to give her this name was to consign her to a life of falsehood.[7]

The stage of this little drama is not primarily ethical or even epistemological, much as the poem's effects may lead us to think so. Its main stage is the more 'compendious' one (stanza two) of the art of using language, of rhetoric. The 'rose' of the closing conceit is not the only flower in this poem; little Anna herself is a flower – a flower of rhetoric, and, in fact, more than one kind of rhetorical flower. She starts off her life as a metonymy which, according to Pierre Fontanier, is a 'trope of correspondence which consists in the designation of one object by the name of another object which functions, like itself, as a completely separate entity, but to which, more or less, it owes its existence'.[8] In our poem, mother and daughter function as completely separate beings (separate lives), with the one taking her name from the other, to whom she more or less owes her existence. But when she goes on to acquire her mother's virtues as well, she ceases to be a metonymy and becomes, instead, a metaphor, a trope which consists, says Fontanier, 'in presenting one idea under the sign of another, and more striking, or better known, idea, the link between them being one of a certain conformity or analogy'.[9] In the language of the closing stanza - itself a metaphor for the metaphor known as little Anna - the daughter resembles the mother as the bud resembles the bloom, 'alike in shape, place, name', a fine instance of Aristotle's metaphor by proportional analogy. This trope, according to the poem, bears a far heavier charge of deception than the metonymy it displaces: for the metonymy was only a deficient sign, causing us to wish for a meaning where it was absent; but the metaphor causes us to forget that two meanings - two proper meanings - are indeed different from one another. Metaphor, here described as the basis for the formation of common, as opposed to proper, names, puts us in a 'trance', and makes us yield to a 'fond deceit'.

And yet, in the terms of the poem, metaphor is not the most deceptive possible trope: that distinction belongs to the mother, who is herself a flower of rhetoric. The validity of her name, the original and proper form of the sign 'Anna' meaning 'quietness', 'content', 'love' and 'innocence', depends on the premise that the name 'Anna' is truly neutral in a semantic sense, which is to say, meaningless. There is, however, no such a thing, linguistically speaking, as a really meaningless vocable. If a sound belongs to a language, then it also belongs to its lexicon. Every sound can be thought of as a sign of some kind, whose meanings may be forgotten, concealed or effaced. The name 'Anna' has had the meaning of 'grace' - in the Hebrew from which it comes, and in the Christian tradition that inherits it. In this poem, the mother is said to make us forget the previous meaning of her name by bringing that name into association with a new meaning. And 'into association' means - into a metonymic connection. The mother is a metonymy, but of a kind that is far more violent, more deceitful and entrancing than any metonymy, or metaphor, embodied by her daughter. For Coleridge, the most powerful trope of all is the metonymy that lies at the heart of the so-called 'proper meaning'. The sign structure, which for Coleridge constitutes the meaning of the word, is itself a trope, a metonymy. Its meaning is 'proper' only by improper force: it is finally neither original nor proper, but always already improper, as much a trope as its subsequent extensions and figurations. In this poem, the figure of the daughter re-figures the *figure* of the mother, herself the misconstruction of an earlier misconstruction.

Before leaving this poem, we sum up three of its points:

1   Every instance of the word 'Anna' is a sign.

2   Each instance of the sign 'Anna' varies, in its structure, from other instances of the same sign. Those different structures have different names - the names of the tropes of classical rhetoric. (According to Coleridge, the original sign structure, the proper meaning, is itself a trope, a 'variation' among others.)

3   It follows from the first two points that the tropes not only share a common theme (the sign structure), they also signify that theme, in the sense that any variation signifies the theme from which it varies. A trope represents not only its meaning, and its particular mode of meaning that meaning, but also its condition as a sign among other signs. Reading the tropes is an exercise in semiology, and that semiology is a topic of the tropes, inevitably overlooked if we assume that signs, in representing their meanings, need not at the same time also represent themselves.

Such, then, as figured forth in this apparently slight and occasional lyric, are the elements of the tropological system in Coleridge's poetry, the tropes deployed as instances and variations of the sign. How does such a system arise, and how does it attain a high degree of generality? Coleridge himself had very little to say about the origins of the system; indeed, those origins hardly called for discussion, since they made up the commonplaces of critical discourse at the time. To situate Coleridge's system in a context, we therefore provide a brief summary of those commonplaces, under the headings of 'sign', 'synonym', 'homonym', and hidden sign', closing with a comment about the position of the tropes in the Romantic treatment of the human subject.

B

Sign   In his 'Essay on Human Understanding', Locke provides a formulation of the concept of the sign that has been decisive for Anglo-Saxon rhetorical thinking:

> *Words* . . . came to be made use of by men as the signs of their ideas; not by any natural connection that there is between particular articulate sounds and certain ideas, for then there would be but one language amongst all men; but by a voluntary imposition, whereby such a word is made arbitrarily the mark of such an idea. The use, then, of words, is to be sensible marks of ideas; and the ideas they stand for are their proper and immediate signification.[10]

Locke condenses, in this definition, a group of premises originating in classical antiquity, two of which are pertinent to Coleridge: first, that sounds and ideas are joined by means of a 'voluntary imposition', and not by any 'natural connection'; and second, that a word is, or ought to be, the 'proper and immediate', or univocal, sign of a meaning.

The metaphysical premises of this concept are by now well known: meanings are thought to exist independently of their signs, prior to their representation in language. They have an existence, a presence - in fact a self-presence - preceding the language that identifies and represents them in words. It is therefore the office of the word (signans) to make its meaning (signatum) present in discourse, clearly and distinctly; when the word fulfils this office, it becomes transparent, and effaces itself before the presence of its meaning.[11]

But the theory of the sign, if thought through to its limits, also undermines or annuls the metaphysics that it supposedly upholds. In the first place, if a sign, as Locke says, is 'articulate', it can only be so as an element in a system of articulations or differing values. Signs are not self-present or self-referring; they refer to other signs in a field of signs. And what is true for a sign is also true for the meaning. A meaning is 'clear and distinct' because it also occupies a position in a system of differentiated articulations. Just as the word 'camel' takes its meaning from the context of other words in the English language, so too the creature takes its meaning from the context of the other animals from which it differs. And those 'differences', in meaning as in sign, are always potentially infinite: a given language will insist on those differences or not according to its needs. If there are forty words for 'camel' in Arabic, it is because the difference between 'camels' is so important there as to warrant a wide range of linguistic signs.

Contrary, then, to the metaphysics of presence underlying the theory of the sign, a meaning is not present in itself, but belongs to a system of differences just as the sign is said to do. In the apt words of Jacques Derrida, 'every meaning is already in the position of a sign'.[12] And when this sign (called a 'meaning') is represented by another sign (called a 'word') it is not so much 'made present' when referred to as it is translated. In translation, a language deploys its own signs according to the laws of its own system; and, while these signs can be made to refer to the signs of another language, the bodies of the signs thus referred to do not cross from their own system to the other. Nor is the 'translated' or 'translating' sign a univocal one: just as, between languages, a sign in one language can be used to translate various signs in another, so too, within a language, a word can 'translate' a wide range of meanings, and a single meaning can find a wide range of words for its rendition. For the system of articulations that makes one word (or meaning) differ from another also enables a single word (or meaning) to differ in itself, by referring to a wide range of meanings (or words).

Neo-classical theories of language could be said to recognise that words do not behave as 'proper and immediate' and 'unequivocal' signs. They seem to acknowledge that a given word can refer to many meanings, and many meanings to a given word, and that the choice of words is an intricate passage between the two, a translation that is never really self-effacing. But they recognise this fact by wishfully asserting its opposite, by pretending that words are, or ought to be, signs as Locke describes them. It is only in the process of allowing for certain 'exceptions' that the theories begin to account for the facts of language. For example, it is recognised that a word may have more than one meaning, in which case the word is called a 'homonym'; or a meaning may have more than one word, in which case it is called a

'synonym'. It is in the tension caused by these 'exceptions' to
the theory of the sign that the facts of language make themselves
felt.

Synonym Neo-classical writers treat the synonym as a pseudo-
problem that will disappear if approached with the right degree of
rigour. Arguing retrospectively, from the standpoint of the sign,
they hold that synonyms cannot exist because they are a logical
impossibility. For if every sign has a single meaning, how can a
given meaning have more than one sign? In the words of Cesar
Chesneau du Marsais, 'the principal reason that there are no perfect synonyms, is that, if there were perfect synonyms, there
would be two languages within a single language'.[13]
   It remains an empirical fact that there are indeed synonyms,
whose synonymy can only be challenged on empirical grounds,
one instance at a time. The instrument for this challenge is the
dictionary of synonyms, of which the most ambitious was initiated
by the Abbé de Girard: his 'Dictionnaire des Synonymes', first
published in 1719, was frequently reissued and expanded over
the next hundred years, with new entries added by such distinguished contributors as d'Alembert and Beauzée. The following
entries give some sense of the futility of this enterprise, and of
the ingenuity it inspired:

   To abhor, to detest: To abhor, imports, simply, strong dis-
   like; to detest, imports also strong disapprobation. One abhors
   being in debt; he detests treachery.

   To remark; to observe: We remark, in the way of attention, in
   order to remember; we observe, in the way of examination, in
   order to judge. A traveller remarks the most striking object he
   sees; a general observes all the motions of his enemy.[14]

The synonym, of course does not disappear before such a
challenge; it simply returns in other entries, to haunt the dictionary. Of these, the most crucial, the most haunting, is the
synonym that is caught up within the logic of the sign structure
itself, the synonym of 'sign' and 'meaning', and of its synonymous
pairs, such as 'form' and 'content', or 'model' and 'copy'. That
these terms are reversible - each can be taken as signans or
signatum, depending on the position that one accords them - and
are therefore synonymous, is repeatedly and unintentionally demonstrated by the contradictions of the dictionary: thus, in one
place a 'copy' is defined as a 'model' (entry 274), while in another
an 'original' is also defined as a 'model' (entry 1168).[15] But the
fact of such synonymy - which also, in this instance, makes a
homonym of the word 'model' - is never recognised as such; if it
were, the tissue of premises at work in the (metaphysical) concept of the sign would come unravelled, and the impossible weaving of a double fabric would begin: there would be 'two languages
within a single language'.

Homonym   Where the synonym is considered not to be real, and
the problems it poses for the sign structure not openly enter-
tained, the situation of the homonym receives a different treatment, for no one can deny that it really exists. We can always
pretend that the word 'abhor' has a different meaning from the
word 'detest'; we cannot so easily deny that the word 'bat' looks
and sounds like the word 'bat'.

   Students of language, from the time of Locke to the present
day, have tended to deal with the homonym first of all by deploring it: one could assemble a thick dossier of invectives against
homonyms over the last three centuries, from Dryden and Addison, who denounce them as the most obnoxious instance of 'false
wit', to Robert Bridges, who describes them as a 'nuisance', and
to Stephen Ullmann, who treats them, in his 'Principles of Semantics', as 'invalids' giving rise to 'pathological conflicts'.[16] But
deploring the homonym does not remove it from the language, and
so another strategy is called for, allowing for the existence of the
homonym even as it annuls its disruptive force.

   This strategy, which consists of bringing the homonym under
the orderly dominion of the sign itself, was first developed sys-
tematically by Du Marsais, who transformed one of the branches
of classical rhetoric - elocutio, or the study of figures - into a
tool for the analysis of homonyms. For Du Marsais, a homonym
should be studied as a rhetorical figure, as he indicates by the
title of his seminal study, called 'On the Tropes', or 'On the
Different Ways a Given Word Can Be Meant in a Given Language'.[17]

   The key to this approach is the proper-meaning hypothesis,
which presupposes that a word will have a central or 'proper'
meaning from which its other meanings are said to derive or
deviate. This 'proper meaning' is usually identified either as the
earliest meaning of the word, or as the meaning of widest currency, or, especially in the work of such British writers as Lord
Kames, George Campbell and Hugh Blair, as the most concrete
meaning. Often the most concrete meaning is taken to be the
earliest, and a genetic link is then posited between it and the
other, more abstract (and supposedly derivative) meanings. That
link is a 'figural' one. Blair puts it the following way:

> The causes to which I ascribed the origins of Figures, concur
> in producing this effect at the *beginnings* of society. Language
> is then most barren; the stock of proper names, which have
> been invented for things, is small; and, at the same time, imag-
> ination exerts great influence over the conceptions of men, and
> their method of uttering them; so that, both from necessity and
> from choice, their Speech will, at that period, abound in Tropes
> [my emphasis].[18]

He then goes on to rationalise the homonym:

> No language is so copious, as to have a separate word for every
> separate idea. Men naturally sought to abridge this labour of

multiplying words *in infinitum*; and, in order to lay less burden on their memories, made one word, which they had already appropriated to a certain idea or object, stand also for some other idea or object; between which and the primary one, they found or fancied, some relation.[19]

That 'found or fancied' relation is tropological. A good example can be found in the word 'sense'; it is a scandal, from the standpoint of the concept of the sign structure, that a word that means 'meaning' would also mean 'somatic reception'. Rather than tolerate this divided and 'senseless' conjunction, we can, following Blair, bring reason to it by designating one of its meanings – the more concrete meaning of 'somatic reception' – as the 'proper meaning', and then 'relate' it to the more abstract meaning of 'meaning' by way of the tropes: a meaning may be 'like' a sensation (metaphor); it may be an extended or generalised sensation (synecdoche); or it may be 'associated' with a sensation (metonymy). The possible relations between meanings are as numerous as the tropes – of which Du Marsais, for example, provides a list of nineteen – and as various as the meanings themselves.

Hidden Signs   The tropological approach to the homonym has repercussions for the discussion of the sign structure itself. It modifies the discourse of the sign, but in a manner consistent with its underlying metaphysical telos of transparency, of the effacement of the sign before its (univocal) meaning. This modification can be traced in three steps:

1   We recall that the homonymic clash disturbs the illusion of the sign's transparency, by directing our attention away from the meaning(s) and back to the offending sign. But in looking for the links between one meaning and another, we direct our attention away from the sign and back to the meanings. In so doing, we appear to restore the transparency of the sign, for we no longer think of the homonym as a clash of signs, but rather as an ambiguity of meanings.

2   What, however, is the structure of this (tropological) relationship between meanings? Is it not itself the structure of the sign? To say that the relationship between two different meanings is itself meaningful is to make those meanings signify each other, and thus to install the structure of the sign within the chain of meanings. The relationship of tenor to vehicle in a trope is the relation of a sign to its meaning.

3   There is, however, an important difference between a trope and a sign as conceived by Locke: for where the link between a sign and its meaning is held, as in Locke's analysis, to be purely conventional, the link between tenor and vehicle is always a motivated one: motivated by analogy, in metaphor; by correspondence, in metonymy; and by connection, in synecdoche. On the other hand, not all tropes are equally motivated: in metonymy, the trope of correspondence, the conventional structure of the sign is kept almost intact, while in metaphor, the trope of resem-

blance in which the identity of tenor and vehicle can be confused,
the structure may be motivated to the point of unity between
sign and meaning.

As one might expect, this difference in the degree of motivation
becomes the basis for a powerful and persisting value judgment.
Jakobson and others have pointed out that British and American
critics consistently and massively valorise the trope of metaphor.[20]
The motive for doing so, indeed, is the same as the motive for
valorising the conventional structure of the sign: it is to efface
the structure of the sign before the presence of a single meaning,
an effacement which can take the form either of a confusion of
sign and meaning (as in metaphor) or of a transparency of sign
before meaning (as in the univocally clear and distinct sign).

Thematic Versions: The Human Subject   Though the concepts of
sign and trope are mainly explicated in neo-classical semantic
theory, they also operate as guiding concepts in such different
fields as theology, epistemology, or psychology, from which they
are then woven back into the thematic fabric of Romantic poetry.
Psychology provides a well-studied instance of this: drawing on
Locke and the neo-classical psychologists, for whom ideas are
the signs of things, and the relation of subject to object therefore one of sign to meaning, Coleridge and Wordsworth, in adopt-
ing the human subject as their principal theme, consistently
render its relations by means of a tropological model. The following
passage from 'The Prelude' is a celebrated instance of this so-
called 'Romantic image':

> I felt the sentiment of Being spread
> O'er all that moves, and all that seemeth still,
> O'er all that, lost beyond the reach of thought
> And human knowledge, to the human eye
> Invisible, yet liveth to the heart,
> O'er all that leaps, and runs, and shouts and sings
> Or beats the gladsome air, o'er all that glides
> Beneath the wave, yea, in the wave itself
> And mighty depth of waters. Wonder not
> If such my transports were; for in all things
> I saw one life, and felt that it was joy.[21]

This passage is structured as a metaphorical conceit, whose
tenor and vehicle, the poet and the world of nature, engage in a
reciprocal exchange or double transfer: where natural beings
take on human attributes ('all that leaps, and runs, and shouts,
and sings'), the poet responds from a natural, or pre-reflexive,
region of his sensibility ('I felt the sentiment of Being spread /
O'er all that, lost beyond the reach of human thought / And
human knowledge . . . yet liveth to the heart').[22] As a metaphor,
moreover, this passage exhibits just that high level of motivation
that effaces the boundaries between terms: the border between
poet and nature seems to disappear, because they are said to

share a common space, and because the properties in transfer, such as 'life', 'feeling', 'song', and 'movement', are said to originate on both sides and to cross over freely, so that the transfer is taken as the 'circulation' of properties within a single entity ('one life'). The passage is nonetheless a metaphor, with a distinct tenor and vehicle: the poet has his own 'heart', and things 'live to' his heart without displacing it from its centre; nature also has a heart of its own, a place 'beyond the reach of thought / And human knowledge, to the human eye / Invisible.'

Romantic poets coin innumerable tropes of this kind: they pose the world as consisting of single things (man, natural entities, God) standing in relation to one another, those relations being conceived in the form of tropes. This position extends to the themes of theology and ethics as well as of psychology, and, like the discourse of the sign which it restates, it invests its themes with the values of univocity, transparency and presence, values which commonly appear as a judgment in favour of one tropological relation over another.

C

Deconstruction   -Frost at Midnight- dramatises the elements of Coleridge's tropology on the stage of the human subject, and along the lines of the logic outlined above. This drama stems, linguistically, from the different ways of reading the homonym at play in the word 'stranger'. A footnote, appended to the text in two editions published during the poet's lifetime, and referring to a line in the first paragraph - 'Only that film, which fluttered on the grate' (15) - reads as follows:

> *Only that film.* In all parts of the kingdom these films are called *strangers* and supposed to portend the arrival of some absent friend.[23]

The word 'stranger', according to the note, not only means, in the etymological sense of the French 'étranger', a person in a distant place, but also 'film on a grate'. This homonym has been motivated by means of a tropological link with the secondary meaning made into the sign or 'portent' of the primary meaning. The link between them is one of metonymy, of the connection of two independent entities by nearness in time, of antecedent and consequent.[24] The argument of the poem, developed in three separate moments - the nocturnal 'musings' of the first paragraph, the recollections of the second paragraph, and the predictive assertions of the third and fourth paragraphs - builds on the semantic material set forth in the fugitive footnote. The second paragraph analyses, generalises, and dramatises the metonymic motivation in terms of a state of mind:

> But O! how oft,
> How oft, at school, with most believing mind,

Presageful, have I gazed upon the bars,
To watch that fluttering *stranger*! and as oft
With unclosed lids, already had I dreamt
Of my sweet birth-place, and the old church-tower,
Whose bells, the poor man's only music, rang
From morn to evening, all the hot Fair-day,
So sweetly, that they stirred and haunted me
With a wild pleasure, falling on mine ear
Most like articulate sounds of things to come!
So gazed I, till the soothing things, I dreamt,
Lulled me to sleep, and sleep prolonged my dreams!
And so I brooded all the following morn,
Awed by the stern preceptor's face, mine eye
Fixed with mock study on my swimming book:
Save if the door half opened, and I snatched
A hasty glance, and still my heart leaped up,
For still I hoped to see the *stranger's* face,
Townsman, or aunt, or sister more beloved,
My play-mate when we both were clothed alike! (23-43).

As a schoolboy with a 'most believing mind' (24) Coleridge read
all relations in terms of metonymy: he not only accepted the link
between 'strangers', he also awaited a stranger to whom he was
connected by metonymy, either of place ('townsman' 42), of
family ('aunt' 42), or of place, family and dress – the 'sister
more beloved, / My play-mate when we both were clothed alike!'
(42-3) – the clothes of the children duplicating the very kind of
coincidence to be found in a homonym. In keeping with this portrait, Coleridge also relates a dominant daydream of the time, the
recollection of an earlier 'portent', the sound of the bells on the
'hot Fair-day' (30), that 'stirred and haunted me / With a wild
pleasure, falling on mine ear / Most like articulate sounds of things
to come' (31-3). The bell-tones were not themselves the 'things
to come', but only associated with them metonymically.

As indicated by the phrase 'most believing mind' (an earlier
version reads 'most believing superstitious wish')[25] this mind is
a deluded one, exposed repeatedly to error and disappointment.
And to this portrait Coleridge opposes, in the first paragraph,
the portrait of a mind which he calls 'self-watching' and 'subtilis-
ing', awake when others sleep (4) and given to 'abstruser musings' (6). This sceptical mind, like the 'most believing mind',
also construes such things as the homonym 'stranger' in terms
of a trope:

. . . the thin blue flame
Lies on my low-burnt fire, and quivers not;
Only that film, which fluttered on the grate,
Still flutters there, the sole unquiet thing.
Methinks, its motion in this hush of nature
Gives it dim sympathies with me who live,
Making it a companionable form,

> Whose puny flaps and freaks the idling Spirit
> By its own moods interprets, everywhere
> Echo or mirror seeking of itself,
> And makes a toy of Thought (13-23).

Here the 'stranger' on the grate is taken not as a metonymy portending an arrival, but as an analogy duplicating a person: the 'stranger' is now linked to a 'stranger' as the vehicle to the tenor of a metaphor, and Coleridge calls the mind that can pose such a link 'subtle' and 'self-watching', error-free. In the third paragraph, the governing trope of this mind is generalised to the status of a language, the language of God himself, one that the infant son will learn to speak, as opposed to the language of metonymy:

> My babe so beautiful! it thrills my heart
> With tender gladness, thus to look at thee,
> And think that thou shalt learn far other lore,
> And in far other scenes! For I was reared
> In the great city, pent 'mid cloisters dim,
> And saw nought lovely but the sky and stars.
> But *thou*, my babe! shalt wander like a breeze
> By lakes and sandy shores, beneath the crags
> Of ancient mountain, and beneath the clouds,
> Which image in their bulk both lakes and shores
> And mountain crags: so shalt thou see and hear
> The lovely shapes and sounds intelligible
> Of that eternal language, which thy God
> Utters, who from eternity doth teach
> Himself in all, and all things in himself (48-62).

Like the metaphor of the 'stranger' in the first paragraph, the elements of God's 'eternal language' are metaphors: the clouds 'image in their bulk both lakes and shores / And mountain crags.' And thus the superiority of metaphor to metonymy, argued in epistemological terms, harmonises with the poem's related themes of psychology and theology, sharing a common metaphysical ground in the concept of a presence transcending language.

So runs, at least, the argument of the poem. But this argument only turns on the sign structure, favouring one version of the sign over others. And since the sign structure is itself just a fiction of the language as it ought to work, and not a description of the language as it is, should we not expect of a poem that celebrates the virtues of 'subtlety' and 'self-watching' that it also acknowledge, somewhere, the realities to which the concept of the sign is opposed? May it not, for example, demote its claims for one trope by somehow reinstating the other, as being just as 'truthful' or valid? Or, since homonymy makes no sense, should we not expect of a rigorous poem that it will also recognise, some-how, that it makes no sense to make sense of a homonym, by means of one trope rather than another? Our suspicions are encouraged

in the first paragraph of the poem, where the metaphor of the
stranger is called a 'toy of Thought' (23): to coin a trope is a
form of play, of make-believe, of 'fantastic playfulness'.[26] Its
claims for truth are not scientific, but a playful mimesis of
science.

How, then, does -Frost at Midnight- undo its own arguments
for the trope of metaphor? Where does Bard Bracy challenge Sir
Leoline in this text? Shall we find him lurking on the level of the
argument, in the form of a logical contradiction? On what basis,
for example, does Coleridge make the confident predictions of
the last two paragraphs? Are they, like the predictions of the
second paragraph, founded on a false portent? If so, the poem
would certainly stand accused of posing an argument elsewhere
shown to be false.

In fact the poem is too well reasoned to be undone at the level
of argument: the predictions of the last two paragraphs are not
based on a 'false' portent but, in the terms of this poem, on a
'true' one, a portent grounded in metaphor. The passage from
present to future – that is, from the poet's 'present' to the babe's
'future' – is effected on the basis of analogy: the metaphor of the
stranger in the first paragraph is like the images that make up
the 'eternal' language in the third, it being the difference between them that the first is a single particular, and the second a
general law. Nor is the link between father and son merely contiguous or metonymic, as one might be led to expect by the line
'Dear Babe, that sleepest cradled *by my side*' (44, emphasis
added). By analogy with his father, and with all other human
beings, the babe will, indeed, learn a language. The argument
of the poem is thus a syllogism, in which the movement from present to future, and from particular to general, is grounded in a
universal experience: all people learn language, the Babe is a
person, therefore the Babe will learn language. It is, logically
speaking, an unshakeably sound argument.

The deconstruction of the argument does not take the form of a
logical contradiction, but the form, instead, of the supplemental
use of the (supposedly) castigated metonymy in the organisation
of the text. In a surreptitious return, the trope of metonymy puts
the trope of metaphor in place: thus, while metaphor is argued as
error-free, metonymy is shown to be more powerful, because it
distributes the metaphor according to the laws of contiguity and
association. It is the son, for example, and not the father, who
will acquire the language of God, the 'eternal language which
thy God / Utters' (not 'our God', or 'my God'); for the acquisi-
tion of language may be universal, and the language of God may
be 'eternal', but the 'eternal language' is not a universal one. It
is associated (by metonymy) with the countryside, as a rural
dialect unknown in 'the great city'; and if the father can speak
it on this occasion, he does so in the context of a lifetime's association with another language.

Metonymy returns in a second way, one touching the language
of God himself. If we examine the metaphor of the 'stranger', we

find that metonymy performs an invisible (or silent) but decisive
role in its epistemological success. If the metaphor of the stranger
does not delude us, then it differs from the 'rose' in the -Christen-
ing- poem. How? Not only because the tenor of the metaphor
'stranger' differs from the vehicle in every material respect,
whereas the tenor and vehicle of the metaphor 'rose' were both
'roses'; but also because the tenor and vehicle of the metaphor
'stranger' are associated with one another in space, like an
object and its reflection in a 'mirror' (22). And Coleridge repeats
this gesture in the third paragraph, defining the figure as metaphor, but deploying it as a metonymy:

> But *thou*, my babe! shalt wander like a breeze
> By lakes and sandy shores, beneath the crags
> Of ancient mountain, and beneath the clouds,
> Which image in their bulk both lakes and shores
> And mountain crags (54-8).

Certainly the clouds 'image' the forms of nature in their 'bulk',
but the two are also connected by virtue of their correspondent
spacing: the forms are 'beneath' the clouds just as the 'stranger'
on the grate is in the room with the 'stranger' watching it. It is
the 'spacing', and not the duplication, that makes these shapes
'intelligible' (59). More precisely, it is the spacing that makes
the duplication possible in the first place: a metaphor is always
and already metonymic, an affair of 'duplicity' like the homonym
from which it stems.

Thus the poem deconstructs the hierarchy of values that it
claims to uphold: it aligns those values with one trope in the
chain of its argument, but then it reverses that judgment and
reinscribes it in a second chain, the chain of the poem's topography.

Bard Bracy, after all, does not *take issue* with his master.

III

> The proteiform graph itself is a polyhedron of scripture
> ('Finnegans Wake', 107.08).

Is it accidental that the tropes, and the readings that arise from
them, should so thoroughly miss the mark? What would happen,
for instance, if Geraldine disrobed before the court, before the
judges or readers known as Baron and Bard? Could such a thing
actually take place?

It seems unthinkable that Geraldine should disrobe if the court
is to remain a court: the Baron is a Baron, and the Bard is his
Bard, only if the rules that govern, and bring the court into
existence, are strictly observed. The conventions of the court -
as a place of judgment as well as of manners - requires that
everyone wear clothes. Those conventions *are* the court, and

this fact is the source of Christabel's distress at the close of
Part II. She has seen something that interferes with the reality
of courtly decorum, and her conduct suffers as a result. The
logic of courtly behaviour is no longer real, having been displaced
by the shocking perception of the mark. Who doubts that the
same would happen to Baron and Bard if they too were to see
the seal? Geraldine's clothing belongs to the court, pertains to
the scene of the tropes, to their construction and their deconstruction. Her garments *are* the tropes, and to take them off
would be to finish off the scene, the court, the Baron and the
Bard.

The tropes, however, though a necessity of the court, are
only Geraldine's cover-up, and it follows that their shape, their
placement, their texture and their appeal are all to be counted
among the effects of the seal. The seal shapes the text – the
text known as Geraldine, and also the text, the sequence of
readings, known as -Christabel-. The force of the mark determines the text through a series of after-shocks, in the silence
and dissembling of Geraldine, in the astonishment of Christabel,
in the errancy of Baron and Bard, and in the ruminations of
readers thereafter. And the common trait of all these after-
shocks is their failure, their incapacity, to uncover the mark itself, to comprehend it and so to arrest the unlimited repetition
of its shock. The mark indeed *makes* sense, but it never makes
sense – of itself.

Where do we turn?

Away from the tropes, from the logic and the premise of the
sign, and from the hope that resides in those premises, of making the 'seal' present, punctual, meaningful, sensible.

Let us pause at the turn-off, at the divergence of the road
without a sign.

To turn away from the sign is to turn away from the usual
mission of reading, which is to make sense, to locate the text's
meaning, its truths, falsehoods, arguments, system of values,
stance and gestures – all the topics, in sum, that appear in the
pages above. Essential as they are to the text, and therefore
pertinent as they no doubt somehow are to the 'seal', those topics
and procedures do not prepare a passage to the 'seal', do not
disclose it, but hide it instead in a decent mass of fine folding
cloth. This cloth is the fabric of rhetorical discourse, the fabric
of the New Critics, with their infinitely patient attention to
ambiguity, structure and paradox; of the structuralists, with
their refined applications of semiology and rhetoric; and the
fabric, as well, of authors like Geoffrey Hartman and Harold
Bloom, who aim to go beyond the formalism of their precursors.
Great as the differences are between these critical tendencies,
they all have it in common that they cover the seal with their
meaningful folds, folds that go by the names of 'metaphor',
'metonymy', 'synecdoche', 'metalepsis', 'allegory', 'irony',
'litotes', 'hyperbole', 'tessera', 'clinamen', 'kenosis', 'daemoni-
sation', 'askesis', 'apophrades', 'limitation', 'substitution',

'representation', 'reaction-formation', 'reversal', 'undoing',
'repression', 'sublimation', 'introjection', 'pathos', 'ethos', 'misprision', 'misreading', 'poetic crossing', 'aporia', 'akedah',
'after-image', 'blending' and 'omphalos'. To recite this chain of
coinings - and no reading seems possible that does not tarry in
their conceptual space - is to indicate just how drastic a step
the seal of Geraldine seems to pose, drastic, among other reasons,
because Coleridge himself is a chief source of our habits of reading, of our logic, of our tropology.

Since, then, a turn from the tropes is a turn from the claims
of logic, of reason, and of truthfulness, the remarks that follow
cannot claim to tell the truth, to break the riddle of the seal, to
represent the seal. They can only speculate on certain possible
apparitions of the seal, in hopes of breaking the silence that invests it. To break a silence is precisely not to solve a riddle:
solving a riddle furnishes us with the last word; but breaking a
silence, by process of speculation, is merely to open up, as
riddles are known to do, a new and potentially limitless chain of
discourse.

Here, then, are a few speculative comments on the mark, fur-
nishing notes for other speculations yet to come.

We turn, as we must, to the person of Geraldine herself, to
the body that stays when the clothes fall away. We observe three
things: first, the mark belongs to the body, not as something
applied, like a tattoo, but as a part of the body itself: 'Behold!
her bosom and half her side - / A sight to dream of, not to tell!'
(252-3). Second, the seal of the body, or the body of the seal,
outlasts, as the body does, the circumstances of its own formation, and furthermore outlasts, as the body does not, the
material fact of its own bodily existence - in the infinite chain of
repercussions that it sets up among its readers and the readers
of its readers. Third, as Geraldine herself indicates when she
calls the seal the 'mark of my sorrow', this material mark that
lasts is personal to her; or rather, for such is the force of the
mark, Geraldine is personal to this mark, belongs to it as no
other person does.

These three features - materiality, perdurability, and uniqueness - are the essence of any 'seal' that is a signature, and they
serve to explain why a signature is also the kind of seal that
hides or encrypts.[27] For a signature encrypts, or 'seals', the
story of its own formation, its uniqueness and pastness: no one
can tell how or why a signature comes to be as it is, just as no
one doubts, when seeing one, that it is invested with a history,
the history of the person who carries it. Indeed, it furnishes
that person with whatever history he has; and this, it seems, is
where we find the chief interest of Geraldine's horrible 'bosom
and half her side' - in its condition as a signature. Our interest
does not primarily lie in its ugliness, because its ugliness is not
essential to it. It would still be a signature, and a fascinating
one, if it were beautiful, as Coleridge makes clear in his descriptions of another, lesser-known seal:

As when a mother doth explore
  The rose-mark on her long-lost child,
  I met, I loved you, maiden mild!
As whom I long had loved before.[28]

Geraldine's scar is thus a signature. But what is the signature,
the scar, of the poem known as -Christabel-? It is not the signature at the bottom of the page that we refer to, but the signature
as it lies concealed in the body of the text, carried by the text
as an invisible or unacknowledged but powerful force, material,
individual, and persisting.

Because speculations must really take off at this point, we
take a step backwards and sideways to another text called -A
Tombless Epitaph-, which itself traces a speculative movement
backwards and sideways along a path:

For not a hidden path, that to the shades
Of the beloved Parnassian forest leads,
Lurked undiscovered by him; not a rill
There issues from the fount of Hippocrene,
But he had traced it upward to its source,
Through open glade, dark glen, and secret dell,
Knew the gay wild flowers on its banks, and culled
Its med'cinable herbs. Yea, oft alone,
Piercing the long-neglected holy cave,
The haunt obscure of old Philosophy,
He bade with lifted torch its starry walls
Sparkle, as erst they sparkled to the flame
Of odorous lamps tended by Saint and Sage.[29]

This path leads beyond the 'gay wild flowers', which we con-
strue - and we hope that the reading is not an abusive one - as
a figure for the figures themselves, the tropes, the 'flowers' of
rhetoric. The tropes are found in the Parnassian forest, by the
light of day. The poet, turning away from the daylight of the
tropes, enters a subterranean space, a 'long-neglected holy cave',
a place of darkness, where, by the light of his torch, he sees
the 'starry walls' of the cavern. Those stars are visible where the
flowers are not, and vice versa; which is to say, in keeping
with the trend of our own speculation, that the stars are situated
like a signature. They are a metaphor for the signature.

Could they not also be a signature in their own right?

There are at least two poems by Coleridge that close with starlit
settings, the -Dejection Ode- and -To William Wordsworth-. The
starlit settings act, in their respective contexts, as signatures
in the sense of affirmations, endorsing a movement articulated
by the poem. We quote the second of these passages, because
there the poet seems to countersign, or endorse, the signature
of the great poem that he was listening to:

In silence listening, like a devout child,

My soul lay passive, by thy various strain
Driven as in surges now beneath the stars,
With momentary stars of my own birth,
Fair constellated foam, still darting off
Into the darkness.[30]

Here the image of the constellation is certainly situated like a signature, but we are not yet prepared to insist that it literally is one, if only because it is an image, and because this image occurs so rarely in Coleridge's poetry, whereas a signature should occur repeatedly.

What we seek is something more frequent and more material, more literal, a literal sense of the figure 'star', a sense that is lost, perhaps, in the word 'star' itself.

Coleridge once again points the way in an epigram that was not published in his lifetime, and which does not find a place in the anthologies:

The stars that wont to start, as on a chace,
Mid twinkling insult on Heaven's darken'd face,
Like a conven'd conspiracy of spies
Wink at each other with confiding eyes!
Turn from the portent – all is blank on high,
No constellations alphabet the sky:
The heavens one large Black Letter only shew,
And as a child beneath its master's blow
Shrills out at once its task and its affright –
The groaning world now learns to read aright,
And with its Voice of Voices cries out, O![31]

This epigram condenses, in epitome, issues elaborated throughout this paper: it shows a night sky, sown with stars, in the process of being covered over with a storm cloud. The 'groaning world' that 'reads' this scene sees one text, the 'constellations', cancelled out by a second 'Black Letter' text, a text of academic ideology and coercion embodied in the letter 'O' – the vocalic phoneme that mimics a cloud in its shape and the wind in its sound, and expresses as well a meaning, the terror imposed by the 'master' and rendered back by a submissive readership. To this 'right reading' of the sky – a reading, be it pointed out, that issues forth from the sky itself, as one of its levels or stratifications – the epigram opposes the text of the stars, which is nothing other than the alphabet itself: 'no constellations alphabet the sky'. It is the silent and graphic inscription itself that the storm-cloud hides, the multiform and meaningless winking of the stars. The letters of the alphabet – excepting the letter 'O' (and perhaps the letter 'I') – have nothing whatever to tell us: they do not say, and do not have, a meaning. They are not signifiers, and they certainly cannot be called 'arbitrary'; as non-significant writing, the letters of the alphabet are readily confounded with stars, with natural forms. Lacking significance,

they only play, 'starting, as on a chace': they are the stuff of
language before the drive for meaning sets in.

How, then, does an 'alphabetical' constellation appear as a
signature, in the literal sense of an arrangement of graphemes
adhering to a single individual? When is a constellation not just
a metaphor, but a real signature of Samuel Taylor Coleridge?

How does he sign his name?

As he does, for example, in the -Epitaph- that closes his
works:

> Stop, Christian passer-by! - Stop, child of God,
> And read with gentle breast. Beneath this sod
> A poet lies, or that which once seem'd he.
> O, lift one thought in prayer for S.T.C.;
> That he who many a year with toil of breath
> Found death in life, may here find life in death!
> Mercy for praise - to be forgiven for fame
> He ask'd, and hoped, through Christ. Do thou the
>   same![32]

Let us suppose, then, that 'S.T.C.' is one of the poet's signatures, the seal in its most graphic or alphabetical form. Where
does he fix his seal? Where do we find it, and how do we know
that it is his?

We take a step backward.

The issues opened up by the notion of the signature, of the
presence or absence of the signature, seem to us enormously
complex in that they ramify with the classical problems of literary
criticism, the themes, for example, of intention (did the poet mean
what he seems to say? Did he mean to sign this poem, and in this
or that fashion?); of sincerity and authenticity, that is, of the
presence or absence of the poem in the text (did he really express
himself in this text? Is the signature really his own, or is it a
forgery?); of context (does this text have a purpose or function
that exceeds its explicit theme? Does this signature pertain to a
contract, of whose terms and parties we are unaware?); and of
the notion of text itself, of the 'bord du texte', as Derrida
phrases it (what is the inside or the outside of the text? If the
signature does not fall outside, but belongs to the body of the
text, has the notion 'inner/outer' been put into jeopardy?). But
the most fundamental question posed by a signature is the question of its eligibility, which ramifies with the classical issues of
visibility and legibility: a signature may be 'visible' but not
legible (because deformed), and therefore not eligible as a signature. There are different degress of legibility, and, in the
remaining paragraphs of this paper, we propose to touch upon a
few of the differences in those degrees. It is a topic which defies
rigour; nor have we re-read the works of Coleridge in the vain
hope of mastering the effects of the seal. It is enough to open
up a thorough-way.

One clue lies in a footnote to the closing couplet of Coleridge's epitaph, 'Mercy for praise, to be forgiven for fame / He ask'd, and hoped, through Christ. Do thou the same!' To clear up the syntax he appends a note in the manuscript, and signs the note: 'N.B. "for" in the sense of "instead of". ἔστη, κεῖται, ἀναστησει- stetit: restat: resurget. ΕΣΤΗΣΕ [133] The signature passes through at least four transformations: first, 'S.T.C.' has been transliterated into the Greek letters sigma, tau, and sigma-eta; second, the Greek letters have been translated, by homophony, into the third person singular of the past tense, ἔστησε ; this, in turn, into its Latin equivalent, stetit; the Latin form, in its turn, into a Christological chain describing the resurrection ('he hath stood; he rests; he arises'), which brings us back to the co-incidence, in the name of Christ, of the letters S, T, and C, an association which is advanced, thematically, by the closing line of the epitaph, 'he asked, and hoped, through Christ'.

This irruption of the signature is not an isolated event: for example, the Greek word ἔστησε occurs as a signature repeatedly throughout the manuscripts of Coleridge's poetry, beginning at least in the year 1800.[34] Coleridge includes it, and insists on the value (as a signature) of its meaning, in the autobiographical poem entitled −A Character−:

> Thus, his own whim his only bribe,
> Our Bard pursued his old A.B.C.
> Contented if he could subscribe
> In fullest sense his name ἔστησε ;
> ('Tis Punic Greek for 'he hath stood!')
> Whate'er the men, the cause was good;
> And therefore with a right good will,
> Poor fool, he fights their battles still.[35]

Where Coleridge *stands*, he may be said to sign:

> I sate, my being blended in one thought
> (Thought was it? or aspiration? or resolve?)
> Absorbed, yet hanging still upon the sound −
> And when I rose, I found myself in prayer.[36]

But the chief feature of the seal, the one that the footnote to the −Epitaph− reveals, is its ability not only to overflow the boundaries of grapheme and lexeme, as it does in the figure 'he hath stood'; but its ability to overflow any discursive boundary of any kind. It can be arranged and distributed in any sequence and across any chain of signifiers, as, for example, in the word 'Christ', or in the word 'Christian', or, for that matter − a matter of some interest to this paper − in the word 'Christabel'. In −A Tombless Epitaph−, Coleridge rearranges his initials and seals them up in the pseudonym 'Idoloclastes Satyrane'.[37]

The letters of the alphabet 'start', as Coleridge says, 'as on a chace'. They occur, not as sequences, but as groups, as constellations. As, for example, in the word 'constellation', or in the word 'inscription', instances in which the graphism of the word encrypts, or seals, the seal to which it refers. 'Secret', another word connoting the seal, the sealing-up of the seal, encrypts the signature of the poet within. And since the letters really do play a game of hide and seek, what is to prevent us from noticing the seal in those thematically prominent words – prominent for Coleridge – that begin with 'st'? For example, the word 'star', or 'stop', or 'stood' (graphic as well as lexical), or 'stranger'.[38] Consider the effects of signature at play in the first line of –Frost at Midnight– ('The frost performs its secret ministry'), or the effects of signature in the closing lines of that poem, as they gravitate around the image of the 'silent icicles'. Consider, finally, the play of the signature in the –Inscription for a Fountain on a Heath–, presenting a 'locus amoenus' that may well be the scene of the signature itself, a 'spring' in an hour of 'Twilight' and 'Coolness', where can be found, soundlessly and forever dancing, a 'tiny cone of sand':

> This Sycamore, oft musical with bees, –
> Such tents the Patriarchs loved! O long unharmed
> May all its agéd boughs o'er-canopy
> The small round basin, which this jutting stone
> Keeps pure from falling leaves! Long may the Spring,
> Quietly as a sleeping infant's breath,
> Send up cold waters to the traveller
> With soft and even pulse! Nor ever cease
> Yon tiny cone of sand its soundless dance,
> Which at the bottom, like a Fairy's Page,
> As merry and no taller, dances still,
> Nor wrinkles the smooth surface of the Fount.
> Here Twilight is and Coolness: here is moss,
> A soft seat, and a deep and ample shade.
> Thou may'st toil far and find no second tree.
> Drink, Pilgrim, here; Here rest! and if thy heart
> Be innocent, here too shalt thou refresh
> Thy spirit, listening to some gentle sound,
> Or passing gale or hum of murmuring bees![39]

Here the traveller does indeed stop, his eye reposing on the tiny cone of sand. He lapses into silence, attending to the metrical pulse of the waters and to the quiet circulation of liquids and sibilants in the surrounding air. This silence is not a curse, not an imposition, but a kind of blessing, a pause in the daily round of one's business.

(After the rest, one returns to business, to the preparation, analysis, scrutiny, and conflict that attends the drawing up, and the signing, of a contract. For example, in the poetry of Wordsworth, whose signature attempts to compact with its own inscription.)

NOTES

1   Christabel, 1. 127, in 'Coleridge: Poetical Works', ed. E.H.
    Coleridge (Oxford, 1967), p. 220. All quotations of the
    poetry of Coleridge are taken from this edition, and are
    cited by line in the text of the article.
2   As defined, for example, by Jacques Derrida in 'Positions',
    Paris, 1972, pp. 56-8.
3   The 'seal' functions, in this poem, like the 'anacoluthon'
    described by Paul de Man in his essay on Rousseau entitled
    The Purloined Ribbon ('Glyph', I, 1977, pp. 28-49): [re-
    printed in 'Allegories of Reading', pp. 278-301]. The tropes
    of a text do not represent the anacoluthon (an effect of
    what de Man calls the non-referential, performing grammar
    of the text), but instead are disrupted by it.
4   Coleridge, PW, pp. 176-7.
5   In Lines Written in the Album at Elbingerode, in the Harz
    Forest, PW, pp. 315-16, 1. 19.
6   As described by Stephen Ullmann in his 'Principles of Seman-
    tics', London, 1967, pp. 144-52.
7   The first paragraph of The Nightingale (PW, pp. 264-7) re-
    peats this position in terms of the conventional association
    of the nightingale's song with melancholy: '. . . some night-
    wandering man. . . . First named these notes a melancholy
    strain, / And many a poet echoes the conceit' (16, 22-3).
    The poem then proceeds, by reciting a real experience of
    the poet's, to 'associate' the nightingale's song with 'joy'
    (109).
8   Pierre Fontanier, 'Les Figures du discours', Paris, 1968,
    p. 79 (my translation).
9   Ibid., p. 99.
10 John Locke, 'An Essay Concerning Human Understanding',
    ed Maurice Cranston, London, 1965, p. 231. Gerard Genette,
    in his 'Mimologiques', Paris, 1976, provides a magisterial
    reading of this passage, situating it in the context of Euro-
    pean poetics from the eighteenth century to the present day.
    See, in particular, pp. 59-70.
11 The logic and metaphysics of the sign have received their most
    thorough analysis in the work of Jacques Derrida. See espec-
    ially, in 'De la grammatologie', Paris, 1967, the chapter on
    Linguistique et Grammatologie, pp. 42-108. ['Of Gramma-
    tology', trans. G. C. Spivak, Baltimore, 1976, pp. 27-73].
12 Ibid., p. 108 [p. 73].
13 'Des Tropes' in 'Oeuvres', 7 vols, Paris, 1797, vol. 3, p. 260
    (my translation).
14 These examples were drawn from the dictionary by Hugh
    Blair and translated in his chapter on Precision in Style, in
    'Lectures on Rhetoric and Belles Lettres', Philadelphia, 1784,
    pp. 86-7. There has always been, of course, a massive soli-
    darity between the notion of a good English style, the logic
    of the sign, and a certain view of political economy. This

solidarity is nicely expressed in the following passage,
written by Blair's Edinburgh colleague George Campbell:

> Nothing, then, surely, can serve more to corrupt [the
> language], than to overturn the barriers use hath erected,
> by confounding words as synonymous, to which distinct
> significations have been assigned. This conduct is as bad
> policy with regard to style, as it would be with regard to
> land, to convert a great part of the property into a com-
> mon. On the contrary, as it conduceth to the advancement
> of agriculture, and to the increase of the annual produce
> of a country, to divide the commons, and turn them into
> property, a similar conduct, in the appropriation of words,
> renders a language more useful and expressive ('The Art
> of Rhetoric', Boston, 1823, p. 243).

15   Abbé de Girard et al., 'Dictionnaire des Synonymes', Paris,
1826.
16   Dryden attacks the homonym in 'MacFlecknoe', and Addison
echoes the attack in his essays on 'false wit' ('Spectator',
58-63, and especially 61, which is entirely given over to a
diatribe against 'punning'). Ullmann's phrase comes from a
sentence which reads: 'a word associated with a homonymic
invalid is substituted for the latter to avert a pathological
conflict' (op. cit., p. 149).
By way of indicating the pressures of economic and political ideology that lie concealed in all discussion of semiology
and rhetoric, we quote at length from Robert Bridges, a
paragraph that is remarkable for its phonocentrism, its phallo-
centrism, and also its ethnocentrism:

> An objector who should plead that homophones are not a
> nuisance might allege the longevity of the Chinese language,
> composed, I believe, chiefly of homophones distinguished
> from each other by an accentuation which must be delicate,
> difficult and precarious. I remember that Max Muller in-
> stanced a fictitious sentence 'ba bà bâ bá', 'which (he wrote)
> is said to mean if properly accented *the three ladies gave a
> box on the ear to the favourite of the princess.*' This sug-
> gests that the bleating of sheep may have a richer signi-
> ficance than we are accustomed to suppose; and it may
> perhaps illustrate the origin as well as the decay of human
> speech ('On English Homophones', London, 1919, p. 19).

17   'Des Tropes, ou des diférens sens dans lesquels on peut
prendre un même mot dans une même langue.'
18   Blair, op. cit., p. 123.
19   Ibid., p. 121.
20   Roman Jakobson, 'Essais de linguistique générale', Paris, 1963,
pp. 61-7. The point is developed by Gérard Genette in his article Rhétorique Restreinte, in 'Figures III', Paris, 1972, pp. 21-40.

21 William Wordsworth, 'The Prelude', ed E. de Selincourt,
    London, 1959, Bk. II, 420-30 (1805 version).
22 Paul de Man, in his introduction to Rilke, 'Oeuvres', Paris,
    1972, calls this kind of double transfer a 'chiasmus' (v. II,
    pp. 22-31) ['Allegories of Reading', pp. 37-46].
23 Coleridge, PW, p. 240.
24 Du Marsais (op. cit., pp. 84-9), calls this figure a 'metalep-
    sis', and classifies it as a sub-species of metonymy.
25 PW, p. 241.
26 Ibid., p. 240.
27 The pages that follow derive from, or mime, the astonishing
    work of Jacques Derrida on the topic of the signature, not-
    ably in the essay Signéponge ('Digraphe', 8, 1976, pp. 17-
    39).
28 Recollections of Love, 16-19, in PW, p. 410.
29 A Tombless Epitaph, 21-33, in PW, pp. 413-14.
30 To William Wordsworth, 95-100, in PW, pp. 403-8.
31 Coeli Enarrant, in PW, p. 486.
32 Epitaph, in PW, pp. 491-2.
33 Ibid.
34 PW, p. 345.
35 A Character, 69-76, in PW, pp. 451-3.
36 To William Wordsworth, 109-12.
37 A Tombless Epitaph, 1.
38 Coleridge repeatedly refers to himself as a 'stranger': thus,
    'I have roam'd through life / Still most a stranger, most with
    naked heart / At mine own home and birth-place' (To the
    Rev. George Coleridge, 40-2, in PW, pp. 173-5); so, too,
    'Oft to my eager soul I whisper blame, / A Stranger bid it
    feel the Stranger's shame' (To Two Sisters, 30-1, in PW,
    pp. 410-12). See also the poem entitled To Matilda Betham
    from a Stranger (PW, pp. 374-6). The force of this signature
    lies in its conjunction with the homonym 'stranger', communi-
    cating with the theme of the double, and the emotion of
    'strangeness' which the double is said, by Freud in his essay
    on The Uncanny, to inspire. That it arises, according to
    Freud, from a fear of castration; that the poem Frost at
    Midnight presents a scene between father and son, in which
    the father meditates on a future in which he imagines his son
    contemplating a 'silent icicle', image of the phallus and a
    version - in its graphemes - of the paternal signature; that
    poem, icicle and son are thus implicated in a limitless repli-
    cation of the detached paternal phallus, where the effects of
    framing (mise-en-abîme) cannot be arrested, dominated, or
    put into place; all are issues whose interlacing we propose to
    untie elsewhere.
39 PW, pp. 381-2.

FURTHER READING

CHARLES, MICHEL, 'Rhétorique de la lecture', Paris, Seuil, 1977.
DALLENBACH, LUCIEN, 'Le Récit speculaire: Essai sur la mise en abîme', Paris, Seuil, 1977.
DERRIDA, JACQUES, Signéponge, in 'Francis Ponge', Colloque de Cerisy, Paris, Union Générale d'Editions, 1977, pp. 115-44.
— Signéponge [part two], in 'Digraphe', 8, April 1976, pp. 17-39.
— Signature Event Context, in 'Glyph', 1, 1977, pp. 172-97.
— Scribble (writing-power), in 'Yale French Studies', 58, 1979, pp. 117-47.
GASCHE, RODOLPHE, The Scene of Writing: A Deferred Outset, in 'Glyph', 1, 1977, pp. 150-71.
GENETTE, GÉRARD, 'Figures, I - III', Paris, Seuil, 1966, 1969, 1972.
— 'Mimologiques', Paris, Seuil, 1976.
— 'Narrative Discourse, An Essay in Method', trans. Jane E. Lewin, Ithaca, Cornell University Press, 1979 (translation of the Proust essay in 'Figures III').
— Valéry and the Poetics of Language, in 'Textual Strategies: Perspectives in Post-Structuralist Criticism', ed Josué V. Harari, Ithaca, Cornell University Press, 1979, pp. 359-73.
HERTZ, NEIL, Recognising Casaubon, in 'Glyph', 6, 1979, pp. 24-41.
HUXLEY, FRANCIS, 'The Raven and the Writing Desk', London, Thames & Hudson, 1976.
MEHLMAN, JEFFREY, Orphée Scripteur: Blanchot, Rilke, Derrida, in 'Structuralist Review', 1:1, Spring 1978, pp. 42-75.
'Semiotext(e)', The Two Saussures, 1:2, 1974.
— Saussure's Anagrams, 2:1, 1975.
SHERRY, PEGGY MEYER, The 'Predicament' of the Autograph: 'William Blake', in 'Glyph', 4, 1978, pp. 130-55.
STAROBINSKI, JEAN, 'Words Upon Words: The Anagrams of Ferdinand de Saussure', trans. Olivia Emmet, New Haven, Yale University Press, 1979. (Original French version reviewed by Sylvère Lotringer, The Game of the Name, in 'Diacritics', 3:2, Summer 1973, pp. 2-9).

INDEX

An asterisk after a page number denotes definition or major discussion.